THE NEW EMPIRE

An Interpretation of American Expansion

1860-1898

THE NEW EMPIRE

An Interpretation of American Expansion

1860-1898

By WALTER LAFEBER

Cornell University

Cornell Paperbacks

CORNELL UNIVERSITY PRESS

ITHACA, NEW YORK

CORNELL UNIVERSITY PRESS

The original clothbound edition, an
Albert J. Beveridge Award winner, was
published for the American Historical
Society.

First published 1963
Second printing 1965
First printing, Cornell Paperbacks, 1967

Library of Congress Catalog Card Number: 63-20868

PRINTED IN THE UNITED STATES OF AMERICA

BY VALLEY OFFSET, INC.

BOUND BY VAIL-BALLOU PRESS, INC.

FOR
My Mother and Father

Preface

THIS monograph attempts to examine the crucial incubation period of the American overseas empire by relating the development of that empire to the effects of the industrial revolution on United States foreign policy. I have employed this approach because the industrial transformation that occurred during the last half of the nineteenth century marked the beginning of modern America. This momentous transformation has never been adequately linked with the maturation of the United States into a world power, an event almost equal in significance to the industrial revolution. These, then, are the themes of the work: that those historians who label this era as the Age of the Robber Barons or as the time when "Industry Comes of Age" are correct, and that foreign policy formulators were not immune to the dominant characteristic of their time.

These themes suggest two conclusions implicit in this work. First, the United States did not set out on an expansionist path in the late 1890's in a sudden, spur-of-the-moment fashion. The overseas empire that Americans controlled in 1900 was not a break in their history, but a natural culmination. Second, Americans neither acquired this empire during a temporary absence of mind nor had the empire forced upon them. I have discovered very little passivity in the systematic, expansive ideas of Seward, Evarts, Frelinghuysen, Harrison, Blaine, Cleveland, Gresham, Olney, and McKinley and the views of the American business community in the 1890's.

In developing an interpretation of this period, I have discovered that it is difficult to use accurately the terms imperialism, colonialism, and expansion. I have not used the first term, since the connotations given to it in the Cold War make it almost meaningless. I have used the term colonialism when I mean a policy which attempted to obtain both formal political and economic control of a given area and which especially aimed to use this area as a source of direct economic benefits (that is, returns on capital investment or markets for surplus goods). I have used the term expansion in discussing American attempts to find trade and investment opportunities in areas where the United States did not want to exert formal political control. I have also used this term in characterizing the United States policy toward Hawaii and the Philippines, since I believe that American policy makers and businessmen did not want these islands primarily in order to obtain direct economic returns. Rather, the United States annexed these areas in order to develop interests in Asia and, in the case of Hawaii, to safeguard the commercial passageway which Americans hoped to build in Central America.

This study does not pretend to be a thorough examination of all aspects of American foreign policy during the last half of the nineteenth century. I have emphasized the economic forces which resulted in commercial and landed expansion, because these appear to be the most important causes and results in the nation's diplomatic history of that period. Little material is included on fisheries, seals, and immigration, for example, unless these problems bear directly on American commercial and landed expansion. The first chapter is a long introductory section, written mostly from secondary sources, which attempts to show that the climactic decade of the 1890's can be properly understood only when placed in the context of the last half of the century.

Chapter VIII, which discusses the outbreak of the Spanish-American War, is not an analysis of day-to-day events, but rather an attempt to stress the operative economic forces and to point out the interaction of events in Asia, Cuba, and the American business community.

Finally, I must add that I have been profoundly impressed with the statesmen of these decades. I find it very difficult to label them idealists (if this means visionaries cut off from the realities of their society), or isolationists (as this term is used in its derogatory sense), or spineless victims of rabid mass public opinion. I found both the policy makers and the businessmen of this era to be responsible, conscientious men who accepted the economic and social realities of their day, understood domestic and foreign problems, debated issues vigorously, and especially were unafraid to strike out on new and uncharted paths in order to create what they sincerely hoped would be a better nation and a better world. All this, however, is not to deny that the decisions of these men resulted in many unfortunate consequences for their twentieth-century descendants.

WALTER LaFEBER

Cornell University
May 1963

Contents

THE NEW EMPIRE

An Interpretation of American Expansion

1860-1898

I

Years of Preparation, 1860-1889

MODERN American diplomatic history began in the 1850's and 1860's. By then the continental empire of which Madison, Jefferson, and John Quincy Adams had dreamed spanned North America from sea to sea. Cords of rails and water, common economic and social interests, and a federal political system tied the empire together. Edmund Burke had stated the principle: "An empire is the aggregate of many states under one common head, whether this head be a monarch or a presiding republic."

But by the time William Seward became Lincoln's Secretary of State in 1861, a new empire had started to take form. Two important features distinguished it from the old. First, with the completion of the continental conquest Americans moved with increasing authority into such extracontinental areas as Hawaii, Latin America, Asia, and Africa. Second, the form of expansion changed. Instead of searching for farming, mineral, or grazing lands, Americans sought foreign markets for agricultural staples or industrial goods. In the late 1840's American export figures began their rapid climb to the dizzying heights of the twentieth century. Between 1850 and 1873, despite an almost nonexistent export trade during the Civil War, exports averaged $274,000,000 annually; the yearly average during the 1838–1849 period had been only $116,000,000.[1]

As these figures indicate, the United States was not isolated from the rest of the world in the years 1850–1873. When examined in economic and ideological terms, the familiar story of American isolation becomes a myth. It is true, however, that from the end of the Napoleonic Wars until the 1890's the vast Atlantic sheltered America from many European problems. Many problems, but not all, for even before the 1890's the United States became involved in such episodes as the international slave trade, Latin-American revolutions, numerous incidents in Asia with the major powers of the world, and even colonial questions in Africa and Madagascar.

External factors, such as England's command of the seas and the balance of power in Europe, might have given the United States the luxury of almost total isolation; but internal developments, as interpreted by American policy makers, led the United States to become increasingly involved in world affairs. The economic revolution, new scientific and ideological concepts, and the policy makers' views of these changes had begun to accelerate this involvement before the Civil War.

This development is sometimes overlooked, since economic and ideological expansion are often considered apart from political entanglements. American history, of course, belies such a separation, for the United States annexed a continental empire by undermining, economically and ideologically, British, French, Spanish, Mexican, and Indian control and then taking final possession with money, bullets, or both. Similarly, one rule may be suggested which particularly helps in understanding the course of American foreign policy in the nineteenth century: the United States could not obtain either continental or overseas economic benefits without paying a political and often a military price.

[1] C. J. Bullock, J. H. Williams, and R. S. Tuckner, "The Balance of Trade of the United States," *Review of Economics and Statistics*, I (July, 1919), 215–266, especially 216–221.

Economic expansion and political involvement became so inter-linked that by 1900 a reinvigorated Monroe Doctrine, participation in an increasing number of international conferences, and a magnificent battleship fleet necessarily made explicit America's world-wide political commitments.

This initial chapter briefly discusses the economic, social, and political transformations of the 1865–1889 period—a metamorphosis which must be comprehended in order to understand American foreign policy during these years—and the more important policy makers who tried to meet the challenges of these transformations. First, however, it is useful to describe the historical backdrop of the new empire.

The Roots of the New Empire

Long before the 1860's Americans had been involved in the affairs of Canada, Latin America, Hawaii, and Asia. In its first moments of independence, the United States had struck quickly and unsuccessfully in an effort to bring into the new nation the territory north and east of the Great Lakes. The Americans failed no less miserably in their second try during the War of 1812. But two strikes were not out, and time and again in the first half of the nineteenth century Americans tried more subtle measures for adding Canada to the Union. The carrot of trade replaced the stick of war when in 1854 the United States and Canada entered into a reciprocity treaty which many Americans hoped would tie the northern nation to them with unbreakable economic bonds. When the treaty tended instead to strengthen Canadian autonomy, a disgusted American Senate allowed the agreement to terminate in 1866.

The United States did not attempt to annex Latin America as it did Canada, but there was no lack of interest in the southern continent. Jefferson had declared that North America would be the nest from which the entire Western Hemisphere would be peopled. Henry Clay later admonished the United States to put itself at the head of the entire hemisphere through a "Good

Neighborhood" policy. Increasing interest in Latin-American markets as replacements for those lost with the closing of the Napoleonic Wars in Europe provided adequate material reasons. In a negative sense, the Monroe Doctrine, as formulated by President James Monroe and Secretary of State John Quincy Adams, had tried to exclude European powers from affairs in this hemisphere. Viewed positively, the Doctrine staked out the hemisphere as an area for future American economic opportunities and *de facto* political control.[2] In the mid-1890's an American Secretary of State would announce the positive aspects of the Doctrine in blunt terms. The annexation of Texas in 1845, which had formerly been a part of Mexico, the war with Mexico in 1846–1848, which resulted in the enlargement of the United States by one-fifth, and the numerous filibustering expeditions into Central America in the 1850's only partially indicated American interest in lands south of the border.

Also to the south lay Cuba, an island which Jefferson had considered annexing as early as 1808 and which John Quincy Adams delayed taking only because he believed that the "laws of political . . . gravitation" demanded that Cuba, like "an apple, severed by the tempest from its native tree," would "gravitate only towards the North American Union." By the 1850's Cuba had refused to fall in spite of increased American interest, so three distinguished United States envoys to Europe decided to shake the tree. Failing to persuade Spain to sell the island, they issued the Ostend Manifesto, which proclaimed the right of the United States to take the island if Spain would not sell it. Washington, however, quickly disavowed the Manifesto. Such expansionist projects failed in the 1850's, not because they were unpopular, but because too many of them were advocated by men who spoke with the drawl of southern slaveholders. Even

[2] For an excellent summary of the American empire in the nineteenth century with specific reference to a positive Monroe Doctrine, see Richard W. Van Alstyne, *The Rising American Empire* (New York, 1960), 1–194.

such northern expansionists as Seward refused to cooperate in attempts to extend the slavocracy.

American attention had also turned to the Pacific. Trading and whaling vessels from Massachusetts had early stamped the Hawaiian Islands as outposts of United States trade. New England missionaries established colonies during the 1820's. Soon American interests grew from within as well as from without. In the 1840's the United States began sending notices to England and France (the mailing list would later include Germany and Japan) that it would not tolerate European control of the islands. By the decade before the Civil War, the American Secretary of State, William L. Marcy, tried to negotiate a treaty of annexation with Hawaii, was outsmarted by the antiannexationist bloc in Honolulu, and retreated with the warning that future annexation by the United States was "inevitable." More than forty years later William McKinley would say, while successfully annexing the islands, that his action was "the inevitable consequence" of "three-quarters of a century" of American expansion into the Pacific.

By the time of the Civil War, the Monroe Doctrine had been implicitly extended as far as Hawaii, but important American interests were developing still farther west. (Textbooks call the Orient the Far East, but this hinders the understanding of American expansion, for the United States has more often considered this area as the Far West.) The "Empress of China" had sailed out of New York City in 1784 to make the first important contact. The United States signed its first commercial treaty with China in 1844. Ten years later Commodore Matthew C. Perry opened Japan. By the time Seward assumed his duties as Secretary of State, the United States had been caught in the web of Asian power politics. The State Department had to maintain trade privileges and safeguard traders and missionaries either by cooperating with the European powers or by developing a go-it-alone policy. Americans debated only the means, not the fact of involvement.

The Industrial Revolution

United States interest in these extracontinental areas intensified after 1850 with the completion of the continental empire and the maturation of the American industrial economy. Between 1850 and 1900 this industrial complex rapidly developed into one of the two greatest economic forces in the world. During the same half century the United States battled with other industrial nations for control of the Latin-American, Asian, and African markets. It was not accidental that Americans built their new empire at the same time their industrial complex matured.

As recent studies have indicated, the industrial economy rolled into high gear after recovering from the 1837 panic. To use Professor Walt W. Rostow's apt phrase, the economy reached its "take-off" stage between 1843 and 1857, that is, long before the cannons of Charleston bombarded Fort Sumter. The Civil War actually retarded the rate of economic growth, but the industrial economy then accelerated again after 1866. Value added to manufactured goods (in terms of constant dollars of purchasing power) rose 157 per cent from 1839 to 1849, 76 per cent from 1849 to 1859, but only 25 per cent during the next ten years. During the 1870's, however, the figures show 82 per cent added for the decade after 1869 and 112 per cent for that after 1879.[3]

This does not mean that the Civil War was unimportant as a cause of this burgeoning industrial sector. It was important, but in a political and social sense. Charles Beard caught an important aspect of the conflict when he noted that it marked the shift of political power from planters to the industrialists and financiers. The legislation passed by the northern- and eastern-dominated war Congresses included a measure for stronger central banking,

---

[3] Thomas C. Cochran, "Did the Civil War Retard Industrialization?" *Mississippi Valley Historical Review*, XLVIII (September, 1961), 197–210; see also Douglass North, *The Economic Growth of the United States, 1790–1860* (Englewood Cliffs, N.J., 1961).

high tariffs for budding (and blossomed) industries, the Homestead Act to develop interior markets and provide new opportunities for speculative capital, the giving of millions of acres and generous loans to build rail links between the industries in the East and Midwest and the growing markets of the West, and a contract labor law which allowed employers to import cheap foreign labor. During the Civil War, then, industrialists received political help of no small value, but the fact remains that the manufacturers simply used these benefits to build a superstructure (though it was towering) on a solid foundation which had been constructed before the war.[4]

These two facts—that by 1860 the industrial economy was already moving ahead rapidly and that the Civil War marked the transference of power from planters to industrialists and financiers—do much to explain the dynamics of the new empire. The roots of this empire date back at least to the 1843–1860 period, which climaxed in the taking off of the economy, for during this era eastern industrial interests, working through such men as Daniel Webster and William Marcy, began showing interest in the vast China market and in such areas as California and Hawaii to serve as stepping-stones to that market. William Seward, rising to a lofty position in American politics during the 1850's, developed an expansive philosophy within the context of this industrialism which he attempted to realize during the next decade. Policy makers in the post-1870's completed what these men had begun, but the later empire builders succeeded because the Civil War had given them the political power to carry out their plans. The control of policy making by the industrialists and financiers was a prerequisite to the creation of a new commercial empire in such noncontiguous areas as China and South America.[5]

[4] Charles A. and Mary R. Beard, *The Rise of American Civilization* (New York, 1927), II, 199; Cochran, "Did the Civil War Retard Industrialization?" 197–200.

[5] See especially Van Alstyne, *Rising American Empire*, for an excellent discussion on the 1840's. Seward is discussed below in this chapter.

The United States thus developed into a great industrial power, but it paid a high price for the privilege. As efficient machines produced more and more industrial and agricultural goods, consumption could not maintain the pace. The resulting deflation needed only the impetus derived from a few failures of large banks or Wall Street firms to push the economy into a full-scale depression. In the twenty-five years after 1873, half were years of depression: 1873–1878, 1882–1885, and 1893–1897. As each panic struck, Americans became convinced that the new one was worse than the last. Although they believed the 1893–1897 crisis to be most destructive, and although it did have the greatest impact on the formulation of foreign policy, economists have demonstrated that the depression of the 1870's was actually the worst. If the 1873 general price index is figured as 100, then the index took a precipitous drop to 77 in the next few years. In the 1880's it again fell from 87 to 76 and from 78 in 1890 to 71 in 1894 and 1896. The break in the early eighties was especially sharp. Agricultural prices fell when good European crops combined with still greater American wheat production in 1881 and 1882. Industrial prices followed suit. Between 1880 and 1884 business failures tripled in number to almost 12,000 annually. The economy would not stand upright again until after 1897. Carroll D. Wright, first United States Commissioner of Labor, reported in 1888: "The day of large profits is probably past. . . . The market price of products will continue low." [6]

In some respects, however, the mushrooming industrial economy fed upon these depressions. In discussing the 1873 panic Andrew Carnegie later acknowledged: "So many of my friends needed money, that they begged me to repay them. I did so and bought out five or six of them. That was what gave me my lead-

[6] Edward C. Kirkland, *Industry Comes of Age: Business, Labor, and Public Policy, 1860–1897* (New York, 1961), 6–8; David M. Pletcher, *The Awkward Years: American Foreign Relations under Garfield and Arthur* (Columbia, Mo., 1963). Professor Pletcher was kind enough to allow me to read his manuscript before the book was published. All references will be to that manuscript.

ing interest in this steel business." After buying the Homestead plant during the 1883 economic downturn, Carnegie could justifiably comment, "I've enjoyed this flurry after all." [7] Out of this expanded and productive plant would come vast amounts of steel, much of which sought foreign markets in the 1890's because of insufficient demand at home. It was truly twenty years of boom hidden in twenty years of crisis.

This industrial power also began to affect the historic flow of international finance capital. Foreign investments continued to expand in the United States until they reached the mountainous figure of $3,300,000,000 in 1899, but this tells only part of the story. During these years more and more money moved from the United States to Europe. As capital accumulated from the profits of the American industrial revolution, much of it went back into new machinery and plants in the United States, but some flowed into Latin America, Canada, Asia, and Europe, and other dollars went to London and Paris to buy back American stocks at panic prices. This trend was especially noticeable during the slump in the 1890's. In other words, the United States began measuring itself for Britain's shoes: exporting more than importing, and making up the difference by buying back American securities, purchasing foreign stocks and bonds, and building American-owned transportation systems and industries abroad.[8]

The importance of this industrial power was just becoming apparent by the time of the Civil War, but agricultural surpluses had played a key role in the nation's foreign relations ever since Maryland and Virginia planters had tried to find markets outside the British Empire for the rich tobacco harvests in the seventeenth century. By 1870 the American economy depended so much upon foreign markets for the agricultural surplus that the economy's ups and downs for the next thirty years can be traced

[7] Thomas C. Cochran and William Miller, *The Age of Enterprise* (New York, 1942), 145; Burton J. Hendrick, *The Life of Andrew Carnegie* (Garden City, N.Y., 1932), I, 268.

[8] Kirkland, *Industry Comes of Age,* 304–305.

in large measure to the success or failure of marketing each year's wheat and cotton crops. No matter how many markets could be found, more always seemed to be needed. With the opening of vast new lands after 1865 and under the impact of farm mechanization, the production of wheat and cotton soared beyond all previous figures. In 1870 the United States produced 4,300,000 bales of cotton; by 1882 it counted 6,900,000 bales, and in 1891 it grew 9,000,000 bales. Prices meanwhile dropped from 18 cents per pound in 1871 to 10 cents in 1880 and to a little over 7 cents in 1891. Wheat figures tell the same story. From 1873 to 1882 wheat production jumped from 368,000,000 to 555,000,000 bushels, while exports soared from 40,000,000 to 150,000,000 bushels. But prices slumped from $1.52 per bushel in 1866 to 77 cents in 1878, moved back up to $1.19 in 1881, and then sunk to 68 cents in 1887 and 54 cents in 1893. Between 1869 and 1900 the home market bought between 75 per cent and 85 per cent of the total value of farm products, but the most important items of cotton, tobacco, and wheat depended much more on foreign markets. Cotton exports, for example, fluctuated between 66 per cent and 82 per cent of the total crop, and tobacco exports accounted for 41 per cent to 79 per cent of total production.[9] If foreign markets meant good instead of mediocre or poor profits for some industrialists, adequate markets abroad meant the difference between being solvent or bankrupt to many farmers.

Westward the Course of Empire—and Discontent

Historians have long fixed the 1865–1877 period as the era of Reconstruction. For some chroniclers, such as those concerned

---

[9] Fred Shannon, *The Farmer's Last Frontier* . . . (New York, Toronto, 1945), 355, 415, tables in appendix (for the spectacular results of farm mechanization see *ibid.*, 140–147); Morton Rothstein, "America in the International Rivalry for the British Wheat Market, 1860–1914," *Mississippi Valley Historical Review*, XLVII (December, 1960), 401–418, especially 402.

with the history of the South, this demarcation has certain values. But for historians of American diplomacy this emphasis on the South can entice them to take their eyes off events during these years which had more importance in the making of foreign policy. Certainly the energy and time devoted to waving the bloody shirt in the 1870's did divert some attention from external affairs; and no doubt the beginnings of industrialism in the South deserve attention since many southern industrialists soon joined their compatriots in the North in the search for foreign markets. All this can be granted and the point can still be emphasized that, as far as the internal dynamics of American foreign policy are concerned, the most important events occurred outside the South.[10]

When coupled with the maturing of the economy, especially in the industrial segment, America's western history provides valuable insights into the formulation of foreign policy after Seward. This is so for several reasons. First, the American West supposedly held the great open frontier of opportunities for both individual farmers seeking land and for eastern and midwestern industrialists searching for markets and raw materials. When in the 1880's many Americans feared that this frontier was closing, they reacted in the classic manner of searching farther west for new frontiers, though primarily of a commercial, not landed, nature. This swept them into the Pacific and Asiatic area and hence into one of the maelstroms of world power politics. Second, when the belief spread that the internal frontier had quit expanding and had begun to stagnate, the newly restored Union faced an intensified internal threat. This came from bankrupt farmers, unemployed laborers and miners, and bitter social critics including some of the foremost novelists of the day. Foreign policy formulators and many businessmen viewed expanding

[10] For a good discussion of the South's industrial development, see Paul H. Buck, *The Road to Reunion, 1865–1900* (New York, 1959), 182–195. A most valuable source for this development is Adolph Ochs' Chattanooga *Tradesman* in the late 1880's and 1890's.

diplomatic interests as one way to ameliorate the causes of this discontent.

At the beginning of the Reconstruction period Americans saw the area west of the Mississippi as a vast land of limitless opportunities which, they believed, would be open for many years. Horace Greeley's New York *Tribune* in April, 1865, gloried in the fact that "our country has already an ample area for the next century at least." The Chicago *Tribune* boasted at the same time, "We have already more territory than we can people in fifty years." Pioneer farmers earlier had shied from moving into the treeless Great Plains area, but they now received assurance from no less a person than the director of the Geological and Geographical Survey of the Territories that although the area just east of the Rockies might resemble a desert, this could be corrected through settlement, plowing, and the planting of trees.[11]

Farmers, cattlemen, and speculators took such statements at face value. Americans settled more land during the thirty years after 1870 than they had during the entire three hundred years before. Four new trunk railways formed an iron link with the Pacific; the booming cattle industry and bonanza wheat farms sprouted new fortunes. These gigantic granaries structured themselves for agricultural production as corporations had organized for industrial production, a significant fact for a supposedly raw frontier. Linus P. Brockett reported in *Our Western Empire* (1881) that this area was "destined to be the garden of the world." [12]

If farmers thought of this as a new frontier, so did persons in the East who had their own or European money to invest. Money

[11] Donald Marquand Dozer, "Anti-Expansionism during the Johnson Administration," *Pacific Historical Review*, XII (September, 1943), 255–256; Henry Nash Smith, *Virgin Land: The American West as Symbol and Myth* (New York, 1959), 209.

[12] Ray Allen Billington, *Westward Expansion* . . . (New York, 1949), 703; Smith, *Virgin Land*, 214–216.

poured into the West. To cite but one example, twelve million dollars settled in the Wyoming cattle industry in the single year of 1883. Brockett had no doubt that this was the "grandest empire this world has ever seen." [13]

By the 1880's, however, the weeds of discontent began to clutter this garden of the world. Supposedly limitless frontiers started to snap shut on every side. A resurgence of good European wheat crops after 1881 forced agricultural prices downward until the cost of raising wheat amounted to one-third more than its selling price. Not accidentally, the two most important agrarian revolts, those of the Grangers and the Populists, derived much strength from areas where crops of wheat and cotton depended on the world market. A horrible winter in 1885–1886 and the 1886–1887 freeze nearly ruined the range cattle industry. Between 1888 and 1892 half the population of western Kansas filtered out to search for new opportunities. At the same time the death rattle of the railroad frontier could be heard.[14]

By 1886 railroad construction had virtually halted. In 1875 half the iron produced in the United States had found its market in the American railroad system, and by 1880, 200,000 men had earned their living working on railroad construction. In the mid-1880's many of these workers had to search for other jobs. Iron industrialists were forced to find new markets at the same time their blast furnaces were increasing output from an annual average of forty-five tons in 1860 to four hundred tons in 1905. Brockett had feared that the great wealth of the West would lure settlers away from education and other "civilizing influences" and turn them into followers of any man on a horse. When the men on horseback appeared in the persons of General James B. Weaver of the Populist Party and William Jennings Bryan in

---

[13] Billington, *Westward Expansion*, 731–732; Shannon, *Farmer's Last Frontier*, 154–161; Smith, *Virgin Land*, 214–216.

[14] Billington, *Westward Expansion*, 732; Samuel Hays, *Response to Industrialism, 1885–1914* (Chicago, 1957), 8–10.

1896, westerners flocked to them because of poverty and panic, not wealth.[15]

One of the most acute observers of this or any other period of American history had warned of such dangers. Henry Adams, writing in 1870, noted that a "loose and separately responsible division of government" suited the expanding United States of 1800. But, he said, with the nature of the Union rapidly changing, "all indications now point to the conclusion that this system is outgrown." True, statistics penned on paper could demonstrate that hourly wages for wage earners in all industries almost doubled in the thirty years after 1860, although they declined somewhat in the 1890's. Real wages rose in an even more spectacular fashion according to the statisticians.[16]

But statisticians could not reconcile such figures with the organization of the first American Socialist party in the decade after the Civil War or with the violent railroad strikes of 1877. During the chaotic summer of 1877 many agreed with Jay Gould, who thought he saw the beginnings of "a great social revolution." United States Judge Walter Quintin Gresham, who remembered the nightmarish times of 1877 when he formulated foreign policy for Grover Cleveland in 1893–1895, wrote a friend immediately after the strike: "Our revolutionary fathers . . . went too far with their notions of popular government. Democracy is now the enemy of law & order." [17]

By 1879 the United States was emerging from the fearful period which had followed the 1873 panic, but the scars remained. Many Americans who had unquestioningly accepted the results of the Civil War as insurance for an indefinite period of American greatness were now shaken, never to regain their

[15] There is a good discussion of Brockett in *Literary History of the United States*, edited by R. E. Spiller *et al.* (New York, 1948), 792.

[16] Henry Adams, "The Session," *North American Review*, CXI (July, 1870), 60–62; Kirkland, *Industry Comes of Age*, 402.

[17] Robert V. Bruce, *1877: Year of Violence* (Indianapolis, 1959), 310–311, 26, 317; John Higham, *Strangers in the Land* . . . (New Brunswick, N.J., 1955), 31–32.

full confidence. In the mid-1880's disasters in the West combined with the 1884 panic to produce another series of strikes. This time the violence climaxed in the Chicago Haymarket Riot of 1886.[18]

Some Americans reacted to this strife by publishing candid novels and outspoken social criticism questioning the fundamentals of a system which could produce such suffering and turmoil. Of some sixty novels written before the end of the century which dealt with the American businessman, at least fifty of these were critical of business activities and values. Literature especially reacted to the panics and riots of the mid-1880's and 1890's; of sixty-eight utopian novels published in the half century after 1865, thirty-five appeared in the seven-year period between 1888 and 1895. Their literature, like their foreign policies, indicated the grave concern with which Americans observed how industrial maturity paradoxically helped to cause class and sectional disruptions.[19]

Hamlin Garland, Edward Bellamy, William Dean Howells, Mark Twain, Frank Norris, and E. W. Howe were among leading critics and novelists who prescribed solutions for these social problems. Howells displayed a rather watery socialism (not the less sincere because it was largely water) in his *A Hazard of New Fortunes* (1890). Immediately following the Haymarket Riot, and while Howells was changing his political viewpoint, Bellamy published *Looking Backward,* Garland wrote many of his bitter stories incorporated later in *Main-Travelled Roads,* and Twain's *A Connecticut Yankee in King Arthur's Court* appeared. Benjamin Orange Flower's *Arena,* a journal publishing the more respectable radical literature of the day, began its push toward a 70,000 subscriber list.

As these men searched for the causes of the social upheavals, they frequently commented on the frontier. One of the most

[18] Higham, *Strangers in the Land,* 53.
[19] Merle Curti, *The Growth of American Thought* (2nd ed.; New York, 1951), 523; Hays, *Response to Industrialism,* 41.

fascinating changes in American literature occurred when these and other novelists began externalizing the evil which Hawthorne and Melville had internalized. Many naturalists and realists emphasized a sordid environment, not "bad humours," to explain man's evil works. Howells neatly summarized this view of external evil in the preface to *Main-Travelled Roads* when he remarked about Garland's characters, "They felt that something is wrong, and they know that the wrong is not theirs." Mark Twain publicly stated his disillusionment with the once glorious West in his *Pudd'nhead Wilson* published in 1894, one year after Turner's frontier thesis and the economic panic. It is interesting to note that Twain became a bitter anti-imperialist in 1898; he had little faith that the American system could operate a new frontier in the far Pacific if it had trouble with the one on this continent.[20]

The violence of the labor and agrarian protests in the 1870's and 1880's, combined with the warnings from some of America's foremost authors that a beneficent frontier could no longer be taken for granted, shocked many Americans into the realization that, as Goldwin Smith phrased it during the chaos of 1877, "the youth of the American Republic is over; maturity, with its burdens, its difficulties, and its anxieties, has come." A restless society could not wait for a Darwinian fate to solve its problems. The New York *Times*, New York *Graphic*, and Minneapolis *Tribune* agreed with *Harper's:* "It is the business of the State, that is, of the people, to prevent disorder of the kind that we saw in the summer, by removing the discontent which is its cause." [21] American businessmen and policy makers in increasing numbers viewed expanding foreign markets as a principal means of removing the causes of this discontent.

[20] Richard Chase, *The American Novel and Its Tradition* (Garden City, New York, 1957), 199; Hamlin Garland, *Main-Travelled Roads. . . . With an Introduction by W. D. Howells . . .* (Chicago, 1894), 4; Smith, *Virgin Land*, 285–287; Mark Twain, *Pudd'nhead Wilson and Those Extraordinary Twins* (Hartford, Conn., 1903).

[21] Bruce, *1877*, 312, 314.

The Reaction of American Business

Andrew Carnegie's Gospel of Wealth offered one remedy for the increasing unrest. Carnegie and his followers moved from the assumption of individual freedom in the economic sphere to the belief that the resulting wealth would benefit the entire community. But as strikes followed depressions, it became evident that the Gospel of Wealth was inadequate on either quantitative or qualitative grounds, for the community did not benefit and unite; instead, it became more sectionalized and belligerent. Wealth, distributed through paternalistic methods, somehow exacerbated, not ameliorated, the nation's troubles. Other potions administered by the government, as Civil Service reform and the Interstate Commerce Commission, moved in the right direction but could not immediately correct the imbalance in the new industrial America. By the mid-1880's, John Hay, a former member of the State Department and a man who had little use for radical remedies, could nevertheless cry out: "This is a government of the people, by the people, and for the people no longer. It is a government of corporations, by corporations, and for corporations, [*sic*] How is this?" [22]

Given the increasing industrial mechanization, however, these corporations were virtually powerless in one area: their attempts to slow down production by choice instead of by bankruptcy. New machinery in huge, integrated industries cost so much that the owners early concluded that they would have to keep their plants running continually in order to pay off vastly increased overhead. Andrew Carnegie put this idea in tablet form in his so-called "Carnegie's Law of Surplus" when he said that it cost less to keep the machines running, even when no market was in sight, than it did to shut down the factories. [23]

The American internal market consumed much of this out-

[22] Ralph Henry Gabriel, *The Course of American Democratic Thought* (2nd ed.; New York, 1956), 168–169; Bruce, *1877*, 320.
[23] Kirkland, *Industry Comes of Age*, 172–173, also 8–11.

put as it exploded with a 97 per cent population increase between 1870 and 1900. Home consumers bought nine-tenths of America's production. By 1898, however, the other tenth amounted to more than one billion dollars; the important iron, steel, textile, and agricultural machinery industries accounted for much of this. In 1860 American imports totaled $353,616,000, while $316,242,000 worth of goods left as exports. By 1897 these figures shot up to $764,730,000 and $1,032,008,000, respectively. By the 1870's the staggering rise in exports changed the historically unfavorable balance of American trade to a favorable balance which would last at least through the first half of the twentieth century. From 1874 to 1898 exports exceeded imports every year except 1875, 1888, and 1893. By 1893 American trade exceeded that of every country in the world except England. Farm products, of course, especially in the key tobacco, cotton, and wheat areas, had long depended heavily on international markets for their prosperity.[24]

The United States needed export markets, not only for its surplus goods, but also to pay the large interest charges which went from America into the pocketbooks of European investors. Interest rates dropped during the 1874–1895 period from 6 per cent to about 4 per cent, but for the twenty-one year period interest charges averaged about $85,000,000 a year for a total of $1,870,000,000. New foreign investments reached $1,000,000,000 during the period. The United States therefore sent out about $870,000,000 overall or an annual average of $39,500,000 in interest on foreign investments. This interest provided the chief item of "invisible" indebtedness for which the growing American exports had to pay.[25]

[24] *Ibid.*, 278–279; see also Bullock, Williams, Tuckner, "Balance of Trade of the United States," 223–227; Ralph Dewar Bald, Jr., "The Development of Expansionist Sentiment in the United States 1885–1895, as Reflected in Periodical Literature" (unpublished Ph.D. dissertation, University of Pittsburgh, 1953), 51, 147–148.
[25] Bullock, Williams, Tuckner, "Balance of Trade of the United States," 226.

Other than its mushrooming exports, several notable characteristics marked America's foreign trade during the post-1860 period. In the 1850's over 70 per cent of American trade traveled in ships flying the Stars and Stripes, but by 1897 only 15 per cent of the imports and 8.1 per cent of the exports traveled under that flag. Ship destruction during the Civil War, American reluctance to recognize the usefulness of the steamship, increased investment in industrial rather than mercantile enterprises, and government legislation making it almost impossible to put cheaper foreign vessels under American registration, all these factors explain the decline of the United States merchant marine. The last reason was of special importance. Economist David Ames Wells grumbled, "There are three things, the importation of which is theoretically impossible, *viz.*, counterfeit money, indecent publications, and ships." [26] An 1894 survey by *Bradstreet's* revealed, however, that Americans still had their share of the world's merchant marine, even though the ships were not sailing under United States registration. The journal estimated that "Americans own and operate under foreign flags a steam tonnage equal to or greater than one-half the steam tonnage registered under the American flag." [27]

Another characteristic of this expanding trade was that with each panic and depression the American business community displayed a reintensified interest in foreign markets. The most far-reaching, concerted, and important movement outward during this period came after the panic of 1893; this will be examined in detail in Chapter IV. Foreign observers, constantly on the lookout for American threats to their own world trade, noted as early as the depression of the 1870's, however, that United States "interest in [foreign] trade has now become general." [28] But just

[26] Kirkland, *Industry Comes of Age*, 296–301.
[27] *Bradstreet's Weekly: A Business Digest*, April 28, 1894, 260—cited hereafter as *Bradstreet's*.
[28] Otto zu Stolberg-Wernigerode, *Germany and the United States during the Era of Bismarck* (Reading, Pa., 1937), 137.

as the 1884–1886 turmoil marked the real beginnings of nativism
in modern America, so also did this crisis initiate the energetic
and widespread American interest in foreign markets which continued into the twentieth century. In January, 1885, *Banker's
Magazine* noted that, since the depression of 1883 had piled up
surplus goods inside the country, foreign markets were now of
"pressing importance." *Outlook* declared the following year that
the federal government should take the responsibility "to provide" markets for the country's industry; the periodical prophesied that this idea would be the "dominant theory" of Washington policy makers within five years, especially in the formulation
of Latin-American policy. (With the advent of James G. Blaine
in 1889, this prophecy was fulfilled.) The Board of Trade and
Transportation in New York called special conventions to find
new ways of expanding overseas commerce; in 1884–1885 this
board suggested that delegates from all seacoast cities meet to
ponder this problem. The *Age of Steel*, spokesman for one of
the nation's most powerful industrial segments, wrote in January, 1885, that since the internal frontier was rapidly disappearing, the glut of industrial products "should be relieved and prevented in the future by increased foreign trade." Two months
later this publication explained the implications of this request
for the American State Department. It quoted "one of the largest
manufacturers of steam goods in the United States" as saying
that industrialists and merchants needed most of all "an intelligent and spirited foreign policy," in which the government
would "see to it" that these men had enough foreign markets,
even if the State Department had to use force to obtain the markets.[29]

But at least one business periodical proved discriminating in

[29] The quotations are given in Bald, "Expansionist Sentiment," 121,
128, 266–267, 291; and Milton Plesur, "Looking Outward: American Attitudes towards Foreign Affairs in the Years from Hayes to Harrison"
(unpublished Ph.D. dissertation, University of Rochester, 1954), 210.

the type of markets it desired. The *Commercial and Financial Chronicle* wrote in April, 1882, that the United States had survived the crises of the 1870's because of agricultural exports. This the journal interpreted as a sign of weakness. Good European crops, such as those of 1882, could undermine the entire American economy if the nation depended exclusively on agricultural exports. Industrial exports provided a much firmer foundation. A consensus on this point was still ten years off, but in the 1880's export tables began to indicate a quiet and crucial turn to industrial goods. In 1880 agricultural products reached a peak of 84.3 per cent of all exports. In 1897 and 1898 cotton exports hit an all-time high of seven million bales, but the percentage of agricultural goods in the over-all export trade nevertheless dwindled to 79.1 per cent. Five years later it had sunk to 66.8 per cent.[30]

Some acute observers saw the meaning of this slow turn to industrial exports. The Boston *Sunday Herald* as early as 1881 termed South America "the great market for our surplus manufactures . . . [which] lies at our door neglected." The New York State Chamber of Commerce cried that England infringed on American rights by dominating the South American trade and demanded the correction of such an unnatural development. The *American Protectionist* pointed out another market for United States industrial goods when it predicted that "China and Japan would soon offer us one of the largest outlets that we may ever be able to secure for our products of all kinds." By the end of the 1880's wheatgrowers and millers, tired of being over-dependent on a weak British market, began requesting governmental help in finding Latin-American outlets. One result would be the reciprocity agreements of the 1890's. In order to win the cherished Latin-American markets, however, United States textile manufacturers first had to displace British merchants who sold perhaps thirteen times the number of yards of cotton goods in

[30] Kirkland, *Industry Comes of Age*, 280–286.

the area as did the Americans. British exports of iron and steel products swamped those from American factories perhaps one hundred to one.[31]

A group led by David Ames Wells thought it had the answer to the question of how to end Great Britain's domination of international trade. A Connecticut Republican who had been commissioner of revenue after the Civil War, Wells's annual reports of 1866–1868 provided statistical and theoretical ammunition for the onslaughts of the low-tariff people. He noted that lower tariffs meant cheaper raw materials. These, along with increasing mechanization, would soon enable American industrialists to undersell England anywhere in the world. Wells was joined by economists such as Francis A. Walker (a president of the American Economic Association), publicists such as E. L. Godkin and James Russell Lowell, and importers such as Isidor and Oscar Straus, as well as many western farmers who wanted to buy cheaper British goods.[32]

Perhaps the best formulation of the free trade argument before 1893 came from Cleveland's Secretary of Treasury Daniel Manning. In his *Annual Report* of 1886 Manning used two arguments which Cleveland did not emphasize in his tariff message the following year, but which the President did use while in the White House during the 1893–1897 crisis. Manning first argued that with expanded production low wages need not result from a low tariff. Second, he believed not only that American industry could now withstand foreign competition in the home market, but that with free raw materials it could expand and successfully compete all over the world. When Cleveland marched into the tariff fight in 1887 (without Manning's two main arguments in hand), he found many industrialists staunchly opposed to any

[31] Pletcher, "Awkward Years," 3–7; Plesur, "Looking Outward," 28; Rothstein, "America in the International Rivalry," 406–407.

[32] Allan Nevins, *Grover Cleveland: A Study in Courage* (New York, 1933), 281–282; Plesur, "Looking Outward," 197–198.

free trade ideas; but he also found himself tramping alongside coastal iron manufacturers, machine tool firms, munitions and rifle makers, and especially woolen textile producers.[33]

Industries interested in foreign markets particularly wanted the aid of federal agents abroad. During the 1870's and 1880's antiexpansionists and self-styled watchdogs of the Treasury attacked American legations in overseas capitals as needless luxuries. But very few if any extended their attack to the consular service, which provided valuable aid to industrialists who sought foreign markets. Civil Service reformers especially attempted to modernize this service by discharging the political hacks and replacing them with men who knew foreign languages, international law, and commercial regulations.[34]

One important American company which moved into the world market during the 1880's deserves a small section to itself.[35] Between 1882 and 1891 foreign sales of American lubricants quadrupled. By the later date the Standard Oil Company (William Rockefeller's Standard Oil of New York controlled most of the foreign operations), accounted for 90 per cent of American kerosene exports and held over 70 per cent of the world market. William Herbert Libby, Standard Oil's cutting edge for overseas expansion, could point out that only cotton topped petroleum products in the percentage of total national production shipped overseas. Libby placed special emphasis on the oriental trade. Standard Oil's own marketing organizations began to replace the usual methods of selling overseas through independent foreign merchants and agents. Such new organizations appeared shortly after 1888 in England, Germany, Holland, Belgium, Italy, Canada, and the Far East. Libby could proudly conclude that

[33] Daniel Manning, *Annual Report of the Secretary of the Treasury, 1886* (Washington, 1887), lx, lxi; Nevins, *Cleveland*, 387–388, 293, 411.
[34] Plesur, "Looking Outward," 26–29, ch. ii.
[35] An excellent discussion of Standard Oil's foreign enterprises may be found in Ralph W. and Muriel E. Hidy, *Pioneering in Big Business, 1882–1911* (New York, 1955), 122–154.

petroleum had "forced its way into more nooks and corners of civilized and uncivilized countries than any other product in history emanating from a single source." [36]

This interest in foreign markets was not new to American history. Observing the industrial upsurge between 1843 and 1857, *Hunt's Merchant Magazine* had outlined the salient points of the new empire in 1851. It encouraged overseas economic expansion, since "the accumulations of industry furnish us with a constantly augmenting capital that must seek for new channels of employment." The journal also pointed to the enemy (Great Britain) and one of the main battlegrounds ("the whole Oriental trade"). These beliefs only increased in intensity and popularity after 1865. The *Commercial and Financial Chronicle* tersely formulated the central issue in 1885: "the time is near at hand" when the vast American "surplus must be employed in extending American interests in other countries—or not at all." [37]

Seward

In the unfolding drama of the new empire William Henry Seward appears as the prince of players. Grant, Hamilton Fish, William M. Evarts, James G. Blaine, Frederick T. Frelinghuysen, and Thomas F. Bayard assume secondary roles. Although Seward left the stage in the first act of the drama, only a few of the other players could improve on his techniques, and none could approach his vision of American empire.

Henry Adams described Seward near the end of his career as "a slouching, slender figure; a head like a wise macaw; a beaked nose; shaggy eyebrows; unorderly hair and clothes; hoarse voice; offhand manner; free talk, and perpetual cigar." Seward nevertheless attracted an urbane, educated person like young Adams, for the Secretary of State, like Adams, was an intellectual in

[36] See H. M. Flagler to Senator Wilkinson Call of Florida, July 23, 1888, Thomas F. Bayard papers, Library of Congress, Washington, D.C.
[37] Curti, *Growth of American Thought,* 663; *Commercial and Financial Chronicle,* July 18, 1885, 62–63.

nearly every sense of the word. He won Phi Beta Kappa honors at Union College while still in his teens and for a short time taught school. His son later noted that Seward regularly read Chaucer, Spenser, Ben Jonson, Ariosto, Macaulay, Carlyle, Burke, Lieber, and Prescott's histories "as fast as they came out." He also knew the Latin classics, but his favorite, appropriately enough, was the theorist of the British Empire, Francis Bacon. Seward also learned from John Quincy Adams. It was not coincidental that Seward's ideas of American empire so resembled those of Adams; after Adams' death, Seward eulogized, "I have lost a patron, a guide, a counsellor, and a friend—one whom I loved scarcely less than the dearest relations, and venerated above all that was mortal among men." [38]

He also understood more mundane things—such as the value of political parties for his own advancement. When once asked how to fight slavery he answered: "Organization! Organization! Nothing but organization." This served as the motto for most of his political operations. He was tabbed by many political observers as the Republican nominee for the White House in 1860. But paradoxically, he was cut off from the strongest segments of the Republican party during the 1865–1869 period, the years when he most actively worked for the advancement of the new empire.[39]

Seward deserves to be remembered as the greatest Secretary of State in American history after his beloved Adams. This is so partially because of his astute diplomacy, which kept European powers out of the Civil War, but also because his vision of empire dominated American policy for the next century. He based this vision, as would be expected of an intellectual, on "a political law—and when I say political law, I mean a higher law, a law of Providence—that empire has, for the last three thousand

[38] Henry Adams, *The Education of Henry Adams: An Autobiography* (Boston and New York, 1930), 104; Frederic Bancroft, *The Life of William H. Seward* (New York, 1900), I, 4–6, 153, 184–185, 200–201; William Henry Seward, *Autobiography* (New York, 1877–1891), II, 203–204.

[39] Bancroft, *Seward*, I, 390, 64, 386–398.

years . . . made its way constantly westward, and that it must
continue to move on westward until the tides of the renewed
and of the decaying civilizations of the world meet on the shores
of the Pacific Ocean." In the same speech he noted, "Empire
moves far more rapidly in modern than it did in ancient times."
In this single pronouncement, noting the historic movement of
empire westward across America and into the Pacific and Asia,
Seward anticipated many (especially Brooks Adams) who would
ring the changes on this theme in the 1890's; he emphasized that
this imperial movement traveled at a much faster speed during an
industrial age than it did in ancient times; and he reiterated the
theme of imperial manifest destiny ordained by Providence for
the American people.[40]

Seward spent much of his life attempting to prepare the United
States for its proper role in this westward flight of empire. It was
his misfortune that he tried to unify and strengthen the nation
for this role at the very time slavery made his task impossible.
After the Civil War he renewed his quest. He always envisioned
an empire which would not be acquired haphazardly, but would
develop along carefully worked out lines. The best word to describe his concept of empire, perhaps, is integrated. The empire
would begin with a strong, consolidated base of power on the
American continent and move into the way stations of the Pacific as it approached the final goal of Asia. Each area would have
its own functions to perform and become an integrated part of
the whole empire.

Seward prophesied that the battle for world power would occur in Asia, since "commerce has brought the ancient continents
near to us." But the victor in this battle would be the nation
operating from the strongest economic and power base. Therefore he advised in 1853:

Open up a highway through your country from New York to San
Francisco. Put your domain under cultivation, and your ten thou-

[40] William Henry Seward, *The Works of William H. Seward*, edited
by George E. Baker (Boston, 1853–1883), IV, 319.

sand wheels of manufacture in motion. Multiply your ships, and send them forth to the East. The nation that draws most materials and provisions from the earth, and fabricates the most, and sells the most of productions and fabrics to foreign nations, must be, and will be, the great power of the earth.[41]

Seward offered concrete suggestions to realize this base of power. First, he advised the passing of a high tariff to protect small industries and attract foreign laborers. Once Europe was drained of her cheap labor, the ocean could be "reduced to a ferry" for American products. High tariffs would also allow effective planning and allocation of resources by the federal government and give the government money for internal improvements (an idea from John Quincy Adams' repertoire). Second, Seward wanted to offer the public lands quickly and at low prices. This would not only attract cheap labor, but would also provide adequate agricultural products; "commercial supremacy demands just such an agricultural basis" as American lands, when inhabited, could supply. Third, he hoped to obtain cheap labor, especially by enticing Asian workers. He accomplished this with the 1868 treaty between the United States and China, which gave Chinese laborers almost unrestricted entry into the country. Finally, he would tie the continent together with canals and one or more transcontinental railroads. Money was no object: "It is necessary; and since it is necessary, there is the end of the argument." Seward summed up these views with a favorite story of the barbarian looking at King Croesus' great hoard of gold and then remarking: "It is all very well; but whoever comes upon you with better iron than you have, will be master of all this gold." Seward would add: "We shall find it so in the end." [42]

Latin America and Canada would inevitably become a part

[41] *Ibid.*, III, 618, 109, 616.
[42] *Ibid.*, I, 163; III, 657; Bancroft, *Seward*, II, 46–57; Frederick H. Stutz, "William Henry Seward, Expansionist" (unpublished Master's thesis, Cornell University, 1937), 53.

of this continental base. Seward declared that he wanted no American colonies in Latin America, but this did not mean he found no interest in the area. He feared that establishing colonies would result in either a standing army in the United States or anarchy in the colonies. Instead, he wanted to hold islands in the Caribbean which would serve as strategic bases to protect an Isthmian route to the Pacific and also prevent European powers from dabbling in the area of the North American coastline. But Central America would come into the Union eventually when "the ever-increasing expansion of the American people westward and southward" began. Soon Mexico would "be opening herself as cheerfully to American immigration as Montana and Idaho are now." Then Mexico would not be a colony, but a state, fulfilling Seward's prophecy that Mexico City was an excellent site for the future capital of the American empire. Canada would also eventually be a part of the continental base. In an 1860 speech Seward noted that "an ingenious, enterprising, and ambitious people" are building Canada, "and I am able to say, 'It is very well, you are building excellent states to be hereafter admitted into the American Union.' " [43]

In the same speech he made a similar comment about Alaska. Seward realized this particular dream when he negotiated its purchase in 1867. The United States bought "Seward's Icebox" for several good reasons, including traditional American friendship for Russia, the hope that the deal would sandwich British Columbia between American territory and make inevitable its annexation, and the belief that Alaskan resources would more than pay the $7,200,000 price tag. But given Seward's view of empire, perhaps his son, a distinguished diplomat in his own right, later offered the best reason: "To the United States, it would give a foothold for commercial and naval operations accessible

[43] Frederic Bancroft, "Seward's Ideas of Territorial Expansion," *North American Review*, CLXVII (July, 1898), 83; J. Fred Rippy, *The United States and Mexico* (rev. ed.; New York, 1931), 276–278; Bancroft, *Seward*, II, 429; Seward, *Works*, III, 605–618; Stutz, "Seward," 11.

from the Pacific States." Nathaniel P. Banks, Chairman of the House Foreign Affairs Committee in 1867 and a strong supporter of Seward's imperial ideas, called the Aleutians the "drawbridge between America and Asia." [44]

Seward approached the Asian market cautiously and methodically. Alaska protected one flank. An American-controlled canal would provide a southern corridor. In the center would be California and Hawaii. California, Seward exulted:

California that comes from the clime where the west dies away into the rising east; California, that bounds at once the empire and the continent; California, the youthful queen of the Pacific. . . . The world contains no seat of empire so magnificent as this. . . . The nation thus situated . . . must command the empire of the seas, which alone is real empire.

Hawaii offered the next step west. Here Seward promoted the American representative to Minister Resident in 1863 and four years later tried to prepare the islands for the hug of annexation by pulling Hawaii into a reciprocity treaty. The Senate was too busy with Reconstruction to deal with Seward's proposal, but he nevertheless told the American Minister in September, 1867, that annexation was still "deemed desirable by this government." He was immediately successful in placing the Stars and Stripes above the Midway islands in 1867. These islands, 1,200 miles west of Hawaii, became an important outpost for America's Pacific interests.[45]

[44] Thomas A. Bailey, "Why the United States Purchased Alaska," *Pacific Historical Review*, III (March, 1934), 39–49; Frederick W. Seward, *Reminiscences* . . . (New York and London, 1916), 359–360; Fred Harvey Harrington, *Fighting Politician; Major-General N. P. Banks* (Philadelphia, 1948), 182–185.

[45] Stutz, "Seward," 12; William Adams Russ, Jr., *The Hawaiian Revolution, 1893–94* (Selinsgrove, Pa., 1959), 9; Donald Marquand Dozer, "Anti-Imperialism in the United States, 1865–1895: Opposition to Annexation of Overseas Territories" (unpublished Ph.D. dissertation, Harvard University, 1936), 28—cited hereafter as Dozer, "Anti-Imperialism." Stutz, "Seward," 85–86, gives a good account of Seward's attempt to obtain exclusive American rights to an Isthmian canal area.

And beyond lay the bottomless markets of Asia, "the prize" for which Europe and the United States contended, "the chief theatre of events in the world's great hereafter." Here lay the crucial area if the United States hoped to control "the commerce of the world, which is the empire of the world." Here too the United States moving westward would meet another great nation moving eastward. "Russia and the United States," the new Secretary of State wrote to the American Minister to Russia in May, 1861, "may remain good friends until, each having made a circuit of half the globe in opposite directions, they shall meet and greet each other in the region where civilization first began." [46] Seward had few illusions about the implications of his expansionist policy.

America's success in Asia depended upon the success of its open-door policy, which advocated equal commercial rights for all nations and no territorial aggrandizement by any. Seward cooperated with European powers in order to protect this American policy. The open-door concept was nothing new, dating back to the most-favored-nation clauses in the first American-Chinese treaty in 1844. What was new was Seward's vigorous moves to protect the policy. He could deal gently with China; the Burlingame Treaty of 1868 provided for the preservation of American rights of travel and residence in China as well as freer entry into the United States for Chinese laborers. But the Secretary of State was tough with Japan. When that nation proved reluctant to correct what Seward considered to be infringements upon American rights, he ordered naval units to participate in a show of strength that climaxed with the powers dictating to Japan from a British gunboat. He was equally vigorous in Korea. At one point he proposed to the French that they cooperate with the United States to force open the Hermit Kingdom to outside interests. When the French refused this offer, Seward sent his

[46] Seward, *Works*, III, 618; V, 246; Stutz, "Seward," 26; Charles Vevier, "The Collins Overland Line and American Continentalism," *Pacific Historical Review*, XXVIII (August, 1959), 237–252.

nephew, George F. Seward, to sign a trade treaty with Korea, but this attempt also failed.[47] Fifteen years later, however, Korea grudgingly opened its doors to American traders and missionaries.

Henry Adams summed it up: "The policy of Mr. Seward was based upon this fixed idea [of expansion], which, under his active direction, assumed a development that even went somewhat too far and too fast for the public." Seward's Caribbean plans, especially the purchase of the Danish West Indies and Santo Domingo, came to nothing. Nor did he bring Hawaii into the American orbit when he wanted. But he did outline in some detail his ideas of an integrated empire with a great continental base which would produce vast quantities of goods for hundreds of millions of consumers in Asia. He did see the completion of the transcontinental railroad, industries supported by tariffs and internal improvements, and the acquisition of Alaska and Midway as way stations to the Asian market. He accomplished much of his work, moreover, despite the Civil War and a strong antiexpansionist feeling in the late 1860's.[48]

The antiexpansionists effectively used several arguments to thwart Seward's ambitions. As noted earlier, they claimed that the United States suffered from a land glut already; no more land could properly be developed. If the Union acquired more territory, it might be Latin-American, and this would aggravate the race problem. Others argued that the United States should avoid a colonial policy, especially at a time when England was trying to dispose of her own unprofitable outlying areas. Finally,

[47] Tyler Dennett, "Seward's Far Eastern Policy," *American Historical Review*, XXVIII (October, 1922), 45–62; Knight Biggerstaff, "The Official Chinese Attitude toward the Burlingame Mission," *American Historical Review*, XLI (July, 1936), 682–702; Stutz, "Seward," 31–35.

[48] Adams, "The Session," 54; Bancroft, *Seward*, II, 479–491. Also Dozer, "Anti-Expansionism during the Johnson Administration," 253–275. For mention of Seward as the "chief link" between expansion before and after the Civil War, see Julius Pratt, "The Ideology of American Expansion," in *Essays in Honor of William E. Dodd* . . . , edited by Avery Craven (Chicago, 1935), 346.

some antiexpansionists urged financial retrenchment in order to start American industries and farms booming again rather than paying fancy price tags for noncontiguous territory.[49] The most notable characteristic of these arguments is not that they were effective in the late 1860's, but that they melted away in large measure after the 1870's, as the frontier closed, an open-door commercial policy eliminated colonial problems, and American factories and farms boomed so successfully that the resulting glut of goods threatened to inundate the economy. With these changes, Seward's successors were able to complete much of what he had been unable to finish.

Grant and Fish

Upon Seward's departure from office in 1869, the control of American foreign policy fell into the highly ambitious hands of Ulysses S. Grant. At several junctures during his two terms, however, Grant's avidity was restrained by his capable Secretary of State, Hamilton Fish. A conservative New Yorker who had little use for many of the President's reckless schemes of expansion, Fish nevertheless wholeheartedly cooperated with Grant in stretching American interests into certain areas of Latin America and the Pacific, the most promising hothouses for the growth of the new empire. Characterizing this administration as one of the worst in American history is no doubt correct, but such an easy interpretation loses sight of Grant and Fish as important links in the chain of economic expansion running from Seward to Theodore Roosevelt and beyond.

The last period of intense American interest in annexing Canada occurred immediately after the Civil War. The Grant administration did not debate the desirability of annexing Canada; most Americans wanted it. When Horace Greeley declared that "our country has already an ample area for the next century at least," he quickly added that Canada, however, "would always be a welcome addition." Senator Justin Morrill, the finest example

[49] Dozer, "Anti-Imperialism," ch. i.

of the few who wanted no foreign entanglements of any kind, had nevertheless doted on Canadian annexation ever since he had owned a country store at Derby Line on the northern border in 1838. Morrill fought bitterly against reciprocity agreements not only because he wanted a pure high tariff, but also because he believed that reciprocity could not result in the annexation of Canada. "Marriage," Morrill warned, "seldom follows seduction."[50]

United States interest in Canada differed in two ways from American involvements elsewhere during this period. On the one hand, almost all those Americans who professed no interest in other areas did show great interest in Canada. This interest emanated from the hope of eliminating troublesome disputes over boundaries and fisheries, dislike of Great Britain, appeals to the Irish vote, and a sincere desire to fill out the American continental empire. On the other hand, the success of such ambitions would result in a vast new area of land coming under American control. This would occur at a time when the nature of American expansion was changing because many policy makers and publicists believed the United States either had an adequate undeveloped frontier or already had too great an expanse to govern well. The widespread desire for the addition of Canada's immense domain provided an exception to the general trend of a nonpolitical, nonlanded type of expansion.

Although almost everyone wanted Canada, differences arose over means. Some demanded the northern neighbor as payment for damages caused by the "Alabama," a British-built Confederate ship which had preyed with much success on the Union's fleet and merchant marine. President Grant and a few of his more

[50] *Ibid.*, 1–3; Albert K. Weinberg, *Manifest Destiny* . . . (Baltimore, 1935), ch. viii; W. B. Parker, *Life . . . of Justin S. Morrill* (Boston, 1904), 255–256, 320–321; Harrington, *Banks*, 177–181; Allan Nevins, *Hamilton Fish: The Inner History of the Grant Administration* (New York, 1936), 150; Joe Patterson Smith, "The Republican Expansionists of the Early Reconstruction Era" (unpublished Ph.D. dissertation, University of Chicago, 1930), 117–124.

belligerent supporters in Congress, such as Zachariah Chandler and Ben Butler, advocated settling the "Alabama" claims and other squabbles with the British by marching the American army across the border and solving the problem with force. Fish assumed a more moderate position. Assured by the British Minister in Washington that England would not keep Canada if Canadians wanted annexation, Fish hoped to smooth the way with goodwill and happy negotiations. To rephrase Morrill's metaphor, Fish believed that peaceful wooing would end in a happy marriage.[51]

Such a marriage, either voluntary or shotgun, was not in store. In 1871 the Treaty of Washington resolved the outstanding issues between the United States, Great Britain, and Canada. With the onset of the 1873 panic in the United States, Canadian sentiment for political or commercial union dwindled. Late in the decade, however, the sentiment reappeared when Canada sank into the worst quarter century of her economic history. Again, however, Americans could not agree on the means of annexation. Most Americans wanted to suck Canada into their economic orbit through the workings of reciprocity, confident that this would result in political union. Eastern business interests in the United States especially favored this approach. But when Canadian representatives visited Washington in 1887 to discuss reciprocity, American Secretary of State Thomas F. Bayard politely told them that he could discuss nothing but the fisheries problem. He himself preferred annexation, but the impending election, protectionist sentiment, and loud protests from western agrarians who feared the influx of cheap Canadian wheat forced Bayard to evade the subject of closer commercial ties.[52]

Better success attended Grant's and Fish's expansionist efforts when they swam with the westward current of empire into the

---

[51] Nevins, *Fish*, 216–220.

[52] *Ibid.*, 395; Donald F. Warner, *The Idea of Continental Union . . .* (Lexington, Ky., 1960), 100–127; Rutherford Birchard Hayes, *Diary and Letters . . .* , edited by Charles Richard Williams (Columbus, Ohio, 1924), III, 554; John Bartlet Brebner, *North Atlantic Triangle . . .* (New York, 1945), 221–224.

Pacific. From this administration dates the formal beginnings of the new empire in the central and southern Pacific. As American expansionists moved in the direction of the traditional frontier, Hawaii served as the first stopping-off place beyond the continent. Seward had attempted to sign a reciprocity treaty with the islands, but his plans had fallen before the political animosities of Reconstruction. When Fish finally concluded such a pact in 1875, the motives were obvious. Growing British influence and the 1873 panic had jeopardized American interests. Fish also observed that the United States would soon "require a resting spot in the midocean, between the Pacific coast and the vast domains of Asia." Both Fish and Congress said nothing about direct commercial benefits, because none existed. The treaty benefited Hawaiian producers and American refiners, particularly refiners on the west coast, while keeping sugar prices high for consumers. The proponents stressed instead the British threat and pictured Hawaii as "the key to Oriental commerce," the "Thermopylae of the Pacific." The pact considerably restricted Hawaiian foreign policy, for Fish required that government to promise that it would never dispose in any way any part of its territory to foreign powers.[53]

As early as the 1870's the United States was demonstrating so much interest in the Pacific that Great Britain welcomed Germany into the area as a counterbalance to the acquisitive Americans. Besides Hawaii, the British could point to events in Samoa as good reason for their apprehension. Private American interests on Samoa, including California land speculators, a New York shipbuilder, and the owners of a new steamship line between San Francisco and Australia, steadily attempted to draw State Department attention to the islands. In 1872 Commander Richard W. Meade concluded a pact with the native chiefs which gave the United States the use of the fine harbor of Pago Pago. In

---

[53] Sylvester K. Stevens, *American Expansion in Hawaii, 1842–1898* (Harrisburg, 1955) 95–107, 108–140; Dozer, "Anti-Imperialism," 10–31, ch. iii.

return Meade offered American good offices in case of trouble between the chiefs and other governments. Fish and Grant approved this treaty, and Evarts finally pushed it through the Senate in 1878.[54]

The establishment of these Pacific beachheads claimed only a small part of the administration's time, most of which was spent, in the realm of foreign affairs, in expanding American interests into Latin America. Here, unlike the neighbor to the north, no vast landed expanse which might be hooked on to the newly restored Union was involved. Instead, the United States launched a four-pronged attack bearing all the characteristics of the new empire: attempted control of certain Caribbean islands, important for their strategic locations and raw materials; investment, notably in the new southwestern frontier of Mexico and Central America, by American capitalists; trade expansion, especially along lines which anticipated the blueprints offered later by James G. Blaine and Frederick T. Frelinghuysen; and American control of an Isthmian canal. By 1904 the attack launched during the previous half century had won the field.

In the 1870's, however, an enemy, strong and entrenched, occupied the approaches to this prize. Behind British bankrolls glowered the greatest navy in the world. Germany also had become a factor in the area. Grant and Fish began their attack by attempting to eliminate the political power that traveled with foreign investments. In 1869 and 1870 Grant became the first American President to proclaim in unqualified terms the non-transfer principle—"that hereafter no territory on this continent shall be regarded as subject to transfer to a European power." Fish soon had an opportunity to use the newly enforced Monroe Doctrine. When a revolution erupted in Venezuela, the Secretary

[54] George Herbert Ryden, *The Foreign Policy of the United States in Relation to Samoa* (New Haven, 1933), 44–74, 173–206; Seward, *Reminiscences*, 438–439; Pletcher, "Awkward Years," 114; see also W. D. McIntyre, "Anglo-American Rivalry in the Pacific: The British Annexation of the Fiji Islands in 1874," *Pacific Historical Review*, XXIX (November, 1960), 361–380.

of State informed Germany that she could intervene alone to protect her interests, but the United States would not countenance concerted intervention. In 1875 the Secretary of State offered American good offices to stop the use of Dutch force against Venezuela.[55]

As such State Department action attempted to undermine European political influence in Latin America, Americans looked increasingly to the positive benefits which might be derived from such policies. Fish touched on this subject in a long communication to the Senate in July, 1870. He assumed that the United States ought to have "the proportionate share" of the Latin-American trade to which it was entitled by "geographical contiguity and political friendship." He then mentioned an active Monroe Doctrine and Grant's nontransfer principle as means to acquire this trade.[56]

The Caribbean had long been considered in fancy, though not in fact, as belonging to the United States. Immediately after the Civil War, Americans set out to obtain clear title. Their first major opportunity arose in 1868 when the Cubans rebelled against a corrupt Spanish administration. The United States became involved in this fray because of geographical proximity, property interests, and its desire to assist any revolution which would eliminate a European power from this hemisphere. Many Americans worked through the well-financed New York Junta which spent a million dollars in its first year to whip up prorebel sentiment.

Fish sympathized with the revolutionaries and attempted to arrange a settlement whereby American and European capitalists would work to obtain a Spanish grant of independence while the United States would guarantee Cuban payment of

[55] *A Compilation of the Messages and Papers of the Presidents, 1789–1897*, edited by James D. Richardson (Washington, 1900), VII, 32, 61–62, 129. See the thorough discussion in Dexter Perkins, *The Monroe Doctrine, 1867–1907* (Baltimore, 1937), especially 22–26, 111–112.

[56] For Fish's important paper, see *Messages and Papers of the Presidents*, VIII, 70–78.

$100,000,000. Spain refused to listen. Although Fish wanted Cuban independence, he did not want to obtain it through a Spanish-American war. He feared that such intervention would lead to annexation. This he deprecated on racial grounds and because of his belief that American institutions might not function properly on that chaotic island. Opposed by an ambitious President and a belligerent Congress, Fish narrowly averted intervention by threats of resignation and shrewd political tactics.[57]

The end of the revolution in 1878 did not terminate American interest in Cuban affairs. The revolution destroyed many Spanish and Cuban planters by forcing them to sell their remaining holdings to pay debts. By 1895 Edwin Atkins Company of Boston had become the largest single American sugar investor in Cuba by acquiring the Soledad plantation in this manner. The war also taught many property owners that American citizenship shielded them from both Spanish troops and rebels. After the revolt ended, many foreigners became United States citizens as insurance against the inevitable outbreak of another rebellion. American capital also entered the island in large quantities when the expansion of European beet sugar production drove down sugar prices and bankrupted inefficient growers, who happily sold out cheaply to American buyers. No mystery surrounded these advancing United States interests. An article in the *North American Review* in 1888 bragged that this "species of ownership" gave Americans the financial fruits without political responsibilities.[58] But ten years later the United States began paying the price.

That Santo Domingo did not precede Cuba into the American system was no fault of Grant or certain New York adventurers. "Awestruck with the brilliant prospects" of developing Dominican riches, as one of the adventurers said, this group soon

[57] Nevins, *Fish*, 179–182, 194–200, 295–296, 354–359, 615–637.

[58] John L. Offner, "President McKinley and the Origins of the Spanish-American War" (unpublished Ph.D. dissertation, Pennsylvania State University, 1957), 12–13; Plesur, "Looking Outward," 67–69.

enjoyed the backing of such capitalists as Cyrus M. McCormick, Ben Holliday, and Spofford, Tileston & Company, the great New York banking house. Grant also had recognized the value of Samaná Bay.[59] Hamilton Fish would have accepted a protectorate, but his fear that "the incorporation of these people . . . would be but the beginning of years of conflict and anarchy" set him against the President's schemes of annexation. For other reasons many congressmen agreed with Fish's conclusion. Some feared that annexation would mean the ultimate seizure of Haiti, thus creating another explosive racial problem; hot-blooded expansionists viewed the issue as unimportant compared with Cuba and Canada; the powerful Senator Charles Sumner of Massachusetts lined up against Grant on bitter personal grounds; and some of the more righteous senators smelled, correctly, an under-the-table deal between the President and the adventurers. The results of the conflict, however, were notable. The issue gave Grant the opportunity to announce the nontransfer principle. Also, a number of senators who were repelled by other administration policies used the fight to accelerate the movement for the Liberal Republican party.[60]

Grant and Fish had made an important new addition to the Monroe Doctrine, focused attention on the Caribbean, and established the first formal United States holds on Hawaii and Samoa. Judged a failure in its domestic policies, the administration's foreign policies contributed much to the eventual success of the new empire.

Evarts

From 1877 to 1881 one of the more underrated Secretaries of State hastened the progress of this empire. Born in 1818 of a distinguished family, William M. Evarts had graduated with

[59] Nevins, *Fish*, 250–257, 263–264, ch. xii.

[60] *Ibid.*, 262, 318, 335; Dozer, "Anti-Imperialism," 43–46, 51–55, 63–66, 72–75; *Messages and Papers of the Presidents*, VII, 412; Earle Dudley Ross, *The Liberal Republican Movement* (New York, 1919), 9–10.

honors in one of the most famous classes in Yale's history. With his vast capacity for work, a quick mind, legendary wit (it was Evarts who told a puzzled British Minister that Washington had thrown a dollar across the Rappahannock because a dollar went farther in those days), and large store of legal knowledge, he dominated the American bar for the last third of his life. He learned from William Seward as well as from law books. The two men became close friends after a besieged Andrew Johnson named Evarts as Attorney General near the close of Johnson's administration. The new cabinet member worked closely with Seward in attempts to interest New York financiers in an Isthmian canal project.[61]

Carrying the heavy burden of national responsibility when the great railroad strike of 1877 erupted, Evarts apparently appreciated Seward's goal of commercial empire. At a New York City Chamber of Commerce affair at Delmonico's in 1877, almost half the Hayes cabinet, including the President and his Secretary of State, elaborated on the virtues of expanding trade. Evarts emphasized that "the vast resources of our country need an outlet." "It is for us," he proclaimed, "to enter into the harvest-field and reap it." At another time Evarts reiterated this dynamic of the new empire:

The question which now preemptorily challenges all thinking minds is how to create a foreign demand for those manufactures which are left after supplying our home demands. . . . This question appeals equally to the selfishness and patriotism of all our citizens, but to the laborer it appeals with tenfold force, for without work he cannot live, and unless we can extend the markets for our manufacturers he cannot expect steady work, and unless our manufac-

---

[61] The best accounts are Chester Leonard Barrows, *William M. Evarts, Lawyer, Diplomat, Statesman* (Chapel Hill, 1941); Brainerd Dyer, *Public Career of William M. Evarts* (Berkeley, 1933); and Frederick C. Hicks, "William Maxwell Evarts," *Dictionary of American Biography*, edited by Allen Johnson and Dumas Malone (New York, 1931), VI, 215-218.

turers can undersell foreign manufacturers, we cannot enlarge our foreign market.[62]

In his first *Report upon the Commercial Relations of the United States*, Evarts left no doubt that "the fostering, the developing, and the directing of our commerce by the government should be laid down as a necessity of the first importance." The Secretary of State worked for enlarged trading rights in the Far East, Samoa, and Madagascar and also advocated a Canadian-American *Zollverein*. He made his most lasting contribution to trade expansion when he secured a congressional appropriation which allowed the State Department to issue monthly consular reports. The first report appeared in October, 1880. Evarts explained why these reports were issued: "This step was taken in response to the wishes of the leading commercial communities of the United States as expressed through the chambers of commerce." A reticent manifest destiny thus received another push.[63]

Although viewing England as a commercial competitor, Evarts differed from many commercial expansionists in his belief that the United States could befriend England. He wanted the United States, England, and France to "keep the peace of the world until other nations gradually get ready to join us in due course of natural development." Evarts, reflecting the hopes of most American businessmen, thought that commercial empire could be acquired without war. Enlarged foreign markets to ameliorate labor discontent, governmental support of businessmen seeking these markets, and an Anglo-French-American alliance to maintain peace and stability so that these international commercial

[62] Barrows, *Evarts*, 167, 375–378; Kirkland, *Industry Comes of Age*, 291–292.

[63] Barrows, *Evarts*, 375–378; Dyer, *Evarts*, 234–235, 237; Plesur, "Looking Outward," 195; "Private Letters from the British Embassy in Washington to the Foreign Secretary Lord Granville, 1880–1885," edited with an introduction by Paul Knaplund and Carolyn M. Clewes, *Annual Report of the American Historical Association . . . 1941* (Washington, 1942), I, 100.

interests would be secure and would prosper—the pieces fell cleanly into place.[64]

Evarts did not follow such a cooperative course in Latin America, however. Picking up the thread of Fish's policy to contest increasing European political power in that area, Evarts issued strong protests against alleged British encroachment upon Guatemalan soil. When the War of the Pacific broke out between Chile and Peru, he refused to join European attempts to mediate the conflict.[65]

The State Department's Latin-American policy was beginning to operate from an economic fulcrum of great power. During Evarts' term this power became particularly noticeable in Mexico. After Porfirio Díaz won a revolutionary struggle in 1876, Mexico rapidly developed into an American investment frontier. Grant led into that country a group of railroad investors including such prominent capitalists as Collis P. Huntington, Grenville M. Dodge, and Russell Sage. Jay Gould, E. H. Harriman, and the Pennsylvania Railroad system also sought concessions. Within three years Americans had obtained from the Mexican government subsidies of $32,000,000 and concessions providing for the construction of five railways amounting to 2,500 miles. As the railroad frontier closed in the United States, a new one dawned to the south.[66]

Trade with all of Latin America amounted to only 3.74 per cent of American exports in 1885, but this figure is misleading on two counts. First, American trade was predominant in some countries. In terms of total exports and imports the United States controlled 64.5 per cent of Guatemala's, 41.6 per cent of Vene-

[64] Barrows, *Evarts*, 402; Dyer, *Evarts*, 234–235.

[65] Dyer, *Evarts*, 225.

[66] For the best discussion of this new railroad frontier see David M. Pletcher, *Rails, Mines, and Progress; Seven American Promoters in Mexico, 1867–1911* (Ithaca, New York, 1958); also James Morton Callahan, *American Foreign Policy in Mexican Relations* (New York, 1932), 475–506; Barrows, *Evarts*, 351–362; Rippy, *United States and Mexico*, 308–312.

zuela's, 39.4 per cent of Mexico's, 36.6 per cent of Colombia's, and 26.8 per cent of Brazil's. Second, exporters and importers valued these areas for their potentialities. As the United States industrialized, some Americans viewed an unindustrialized Latin America as the prime market for surplus manufactured goods. Although much more attention would be given these markets in the 1890's than in the previous decade, articles emphasizing their importance appeared in the earlier period, especially in the *North American Review, American Wool and Cotton Reporter, Engineering Magazine, Age of Steel,* and *Dixie,* one of the South's most important industrial journals.[67]

Evarts knew that the worth and effectiveness of this commercial and financial movement southward could be gravely threatened the moment a non-American power opened an Isthmian canal. The State Department feared that this moment was near at hand when in 1878 Ferdinand de Lesseps, the famed creator of the Suez Canal, began formulating concrete plans for construction of a passageway on Colombia's Panamanian Isthmus. The diary of President Rutherford B. Hayes reveals his great anxiety over Lesseps' activities. The President hurried warships to the Pacific coast area between Panama and the proposed location of the Nicaraguan canal. Evarts then attempted to use these levers to pressure Colombia to interpret an 1846 treaty negotiated by the Polk administration with that country to mean that the United States must have "potential control" over any canal. Colombia indignantly refused to concur in this interpretation. Fortunately for the United States, the Lesseps project soon became mired in the fever and damp jungles of Panama.[68]

Evarts' concern for markets reached out beyond Latin America. Like Seward, Evarts coveted the many consumers in Asia. But he differed from his predecessor in the means he employed to obtain this prize. The open-door policy, working through the

[67] Pletcher, "Awkward Years," 158; Bald, "Expansionist Sentiment," 132–133.
[68] Hayes, *Diary and Letters,* III, 583–589; Barrows, *Evarts,* 363–371.

most-favored-nation clauses, guided American policy after Seward, as it had since the 1844 treaty. This approach theoretically allowed American goods to enter Asian markets on the same basis as goods from the stronger European powers. But it also placed the State Department squarely against any European attempts to infringe upon Chinese or Japanese territorial integrity; such moves could ultimately lead to the exclusion of American trade from the absorbed areas. Since the United States had little military power in the Far East apart from a few gunboats, it had to protect this fragile policy in one of two ways. It could either cooperate with the other nations to manipulate the balance of power so no one country could overwhelm the others, or it could work for a strengthening of either China or Japan (or both) in the hope that a stronger Asia would defend itself against territorial aggrandizement, but also keep its markets open to all on equal terms.

Seward exemplified the cooperative policy, and Hamilton Fish continued this approach, though in a less vigorous manner. But in the mid-1870's the American policy took a more unilateral position. The new approach was consistent with the expansionist tendencies which the United States exhibited in Latin America and the eastern Pacific at the same time. As noted by John Russell Young, American Minister to China, 1882–1885, the new tactic freed the United States from a cooperative policy which necessarily revolved around the power of Great Britain. Many ambitious Americans did not want to cater to British wishes, especially when these wishes were often contrary to American interests. The State Department also hoped that by granting China and especially Japan certain privileges which the powers had refused, Asians would be happy to recompense Americans with trade privileges and other rights not enjoyed by Europeans. Evarts began to turn away from the cooperative policy when he concluded separate treaties with Japan in 1878 and China in 1880. The Chinese treaty primarily attempted to control the immigration of Chinese laborers into the United States, but the

American negotiators also received additional extraterritorial privileges and a change in the discriminatory duties levied on American goods.

More important was the 1878 Convention in which the United States granted Japan a large measure of tariff autonomy. The anguished words which soon appeared in the British and French press verified the belief that this treaty undermined the cooperative policy which the powers had followed toward Japan since 1854. Evarts, however, had wisely stipulated that the terms of the pact would not take effect until the other powers also granted similar privileges to the Japanese. This effectively prevented discrimination against American goods, but it also stopped the agreement from taking effect immediately, since the Europeans were extremely reluctant to grant such tariff autonomy to the Japanese. The negotiations nevertheless signified that the United States was moving toward a go-it-alone, pro-Japanese policy in the hope that it would obtain some freedom of action in Asia as well as commercial privileges.[69]

This was a dangerous gamble. It could produce an overweening Japan while estranging the United States from its traditional allies. Many wondered whether the stakes were worth the gamble. The fabled Asian market, ever promised since the 1780's, had not materialized. England dominated China and far outdistanced American exports in the Japanese trade even though the United States had first pried open the door to Japan. Between 1850 and 1890 Asia received only 5 per cent of all United States exports; at the same time the great American mercantile houses founded earlier in the century began to disappear. But as in Latin America, expansionists cherished this area for its potentialities, and many believed that this potential was beginning to be realized in the 1880's when large exports of American kerosene and cot-

---

[69] Tyler Dennett, *Americans in Eastern Asia* (New York, 1941), 512–520; Barrows, *Evarts*, 381–390; Dyer, *Evarts*, 235–236. For an analysis of the 1878 Convention, see Payson J. Treat, *Diplomatic Relations between the United States and Japan, 1853–1895* (Stanford, 1932), II, 48–55.

ton goods began to close the trade gap which the British enjoyed.

Evarts' successors, James G. Blaine and Frederick T. Frelinghuysen, did not continue the priority which the New Yorker had placed on his Asian policies. American interest in the Far Pacific would pick up again with the advent of the first Cleveland administration in 1885. Meanwhile, American policy would look southward.

Blaine and Frelinghuysen

When newly elected James Garfield chose James G. Blaine, the "Plumed Knight" from Maine, to replace Evarts in 1881, the country was slowly pulling itself out of the economic morass of the 1870's. Some observers warned that in spite of the business upturn Evarts' ideas of commercial expansion would have to be continued if the United States hoped to maintain its prosperity. John A. Kasson, one of the most able American diplomats during these years, admonished the many readers of the *North American Review* in 1881: "We are rapidly utilizing the whole of our continental territory. We must turn our eyes abroad, or they will soon look inward upon discontent." Blaine expressed a similar thought in an official instruction of 1881: "Throughout the continent, North and South, wherever a foothold is found for American enterprise, it is quickly occupied, and this spirit of adventure, which seeks its outlet in the mines of South America and the railroads of Mexico, would not be slow to avail itself of openings for assured and profitable enterprise, even in mid-ocean [Hawaii]." [70]

Blaine centered his official attention on Latin America. He later recounted that, during his brief tenure in the State Department in 1881, his policies for the Western Hemisphere had followed two principles: "first, to bring about peace . . . ; second, to cul-

[70] Edward Younger, *John A. Kasson* . . . (Iowa City, 1955), 295; *Papers Relating to the Foreign Relations of the United States* . . . [1881] (Washington, D.C., 1882), 636–639—cited hereafter as *Foreign Relations,* followed by year and page number of document.

tivate such friendly commercial relations with all American countries as would lead to a large increase in the export trade of the United States. To attain the second object the first must be accomplished." This might be interpreted as a shrewd politician rationalizing his actions after the fact were it not for the declarations of commercial manifest destiny which rang through several of Blaine's most important official messages in 1881.[71]

The Plumed Knight had served as Secretary of State only six months when Garfield's assassination brought to power Vice-President Chester A. Arthur, a member of the anti-Blaine faction of the Republican party. Dismissing Blaine, the new President named Frederick T. Frelinghuysen, a scion of a distinguished New Jersey family and a well-known corporation lawyer. Frelinghuysen had appeared briefly on the national stage as senator from 1866 to 1868 (when he worked for the impeachment of Johnson) and again from 1871 to 1877. But he made his mark on American history as Secretary of State. It is unfortunately a vague and blurry mark, for history has not yet given him his just deserts as a capable statesman. Of all those who came between Seward in 1869 and Blaine's return to office in 1889, only Evarts did as much as Frelinghuysen to prepare for and encourage the coming of the new empire.[72]

Frelinghuysen, like Blaine, devoted much of his attention to finding Latin-American markets for American goods. When the

[71] A. Curtis Wilgus, "James G. Blaine and the Pan-American Movement," *Hispanic American Historical Review*, V (November, 1922), 668. For Blaine's view of Latin America as a field for American commercial and financial expansion, see especially Blaine to C. A. Logan (Minister to Central America), May 7, 1881, *Foreign Relations, 1881*, 102–104; and Blaine to P. H. Morgan (Minister to Mexico), June 1, 1881, *ibid.*, 761–762. For another interpretation, see Russell H. Bastert, "A New Approach to the Origins of Blaine's Pan-American Policy," *Hispanic American Historical Review*, XXXIX (August, 1959), 375–412. See also Alice Felt Tyler, *The Foreign Policy of James G. Blaine* (Minneapolis, 1927), 46–47.

[72] Frelinghuysen has received adequate treatment for the first time in David Pletcher's excellent work, "The Awkward Years."

new Secretary arrived in late 1881, the British Minister in Washington accurately forecast that the Republicans would now push "the policy of sole supremacy over South America—a policy which certainly is likely to be popular among the constituencies." Frelinghuysen's approach, however, differed from that of his predecessor. Blaine had invited the Latin-American nations to meet in an inter-American conference to discuss various problems. Frelinghuysen withdrew these invitations, partly for political reasons, but also on the grounds that he did not relish the idea of submitting American hemispheric policy to a group of nations in which the United States had only one vote. American freedom of action was becoming more valuable as United States economic and naval power grew.[73]

Nor did Frelinghuysen want to discuss multilateral commercial agreements. He emphasized instead separate bilateral reciprocity treaties through which the United States could concert its power to obtain lower tariff rates for its manufacturers; in return, he would lessen the rates on imported raw materials. The Secretary of State ultimately negotiated such reciprocity treaties with Mexico, Cuba and Puerto Rico, British West Indies, Santo Domingo, El Salvador, and Colombia. He did not deal with the larger countries of Argentina, Brazil, and Chile, for here he would have to negotiate on wool, a move which would have stirred the powerful woolen lobby.[74]

Frelinghuysen, however, was aiming at bigger game than merely the markets of these countries. Each nation which finally signed a treaty controlled a crucial sector in the various approaches to the proposed Isthmian canal area. If the reciprocity treaties could work successfully, the United States would bring these nations within its economic grasp and be able to exert necessary control without assuming the political burdens of gov-

[73] "Private Letters from the British Embassy, 1880–1885," 160–161; Pletcher, "Awkward Years," 78, 256.

[74] For a good analysis of Arthur's view of the desirability of Latin-American markets, see *Messages and Papers of the Presidents*, VIII, 256–260; also James Lawrence Laughlin and H. Parker Willis, *Reciprocity* (New York, 1903), 27–29.

erning such a conglomerate assortment of people. The British
diplomat who discussed the pact for the West Indian colonies
clearly perceived this aspect of Frelinghuysen's plans. The Secretary of State, the Englishman believed, was attempting "to
attach the West India Colonies, by the creation of commercial
interests, to the United States." John Foster, the State Department's agent who negotiated several of these treaties, corrob-
orated this view. If the Spanish reciprocity treaties could be
ratified, Foster observed, "it will be annexing Cuba in the most
desirable way." [75] It should be kept in mind that such strategic reasons worked for a commercial end; any canal would be cherished
largely because it would draw millions of consumers in Asia and
western Latin America much closer to producers in the American Northeast and Southeast.

The Secretary of State enlarged upon his economic interpretation of American foreign policy in a notable letter to the Senate Foreign Relations Committee. He explained that the signing
of the reciprocity pacts negotiated with Spain for Cuba and
Puerto Rico brings "the islands into close commercial connection with the United States [and] confers upon us and upon
them all benefits which would result from annexation were that
possible." This would be "one of a series of international engagements" (including other reciprocity treaties and the Freling-
huysen-Zavala treaty providing for American control of an
Isthmian canal) "which [by] bringing the most distant parts of
our country into closer relations, opens the markets of the west
coast of South America to our trade and gives us at our doors a
customer able to absorb a large portion of those articles which
we produce in return for products which we cannot profitably
raise." This reply is especially notable since the Senate committee
had asked Frelinghuysen for the political, not economic, reasons
for the treaties.[76]

He believed that "the United States have never deemed it need-
ful to their national life to maintain impregnable fortresses along

[75] Pletcher, "Awkward Years," ch. xvi, especially 159–160.
[76] *Ibid.*, 295; also *Messages and Papers of the Presidents*, VIII, 250–251.

the world's highways of commerce," but at times Frelinghuysen could be quite inconsistent in this view. In 1883 he unsuccessfully approached the Mexican government for a coaling station at Magdalena Bay in Lower California. He also worked for an American-built and American-controlled Isthmian canal. The Clayton-Bulwer Treaty had long been a stumbling block to such a canal. In this pact Great Britain and the United States had promised each other in 1850 that neither would ever fortify or exercise exclusive control over such a passageway. As Americans developed their trade and influence in this area, however, they began to condemn this treaty as a threat to their commercial and strategic security. Blaine tried to untie this albatross from America's neck by negotiating with England changes in the agreement which would free the hands of the United States. When the Foreign Office refused Blaine's advances, Frelinghuysen tried a more direct approach.[77]

Acting as if the 1850 pact did not exist, he signed an agreement with Nicaragua which provided for a joint American-Nicaraguan canal. In return, the United States entered into a permanent entangling alliance by assuming a virtual protectorate over its new partner. When the Senate threatened to block the treaty because it conflicted with the Clayton-Bulwer agreement, Frelinghuysen pulled out the usual stops: "It opens the markets of Asia and the west coast of South America to the manufacturers of the Atlantic seaboard . . . ; it provides a new field for our coasting trade, and incidentally tends to the increase of the American steam merchant marine." The Senate gave the treaty a majority of nine, but not the necessary two-thirds. The pact finally disappeared when Grover Cleveland moved into the White House in 1885 and withdrew the treaty because it evaded American responsibilities under the 1850 pact.[78]

---

[77] Blaine to Lowell, June 24, 1881, James G. Blaine papers, Library of Congress, Washington, D.C.; Tyler, *Blaine*, 32–45.

[78] Weinberg, *Manifest Destiny*, 261; Pletcher, "Awkward Years," 123, 292–293; *Messages and Papers of the Presidents*, VIII, 256–260.

The United States did not lose interest in an Isthmian canal during the remainder of the decade. When local insurrections threatened American interests in the Panama area in 1885, the United States landed 750 sailors and marines in what one historian has described as "a wild display of force." Two American construction companies meanwhile formulated extensive plans for building the canal. The Clayton-Bulwer Treaty was still in force, but the handwriting was on the wall as clearly as at King Belshazzar's feast. When the British Foreign Office rejected Blaine's overtures in 1881, the London *Times* remarked candidly: "Blaine's position is stronger in some ways than he ventures to make it. The United States are indisputably the chief power in the New World. . . . Manifest destiny is on one side. The Clayton-Bulwer Treaty is on the other." [79]

The *Times* was correct. Great Britain and President Cleveland could stop Frelinghuysen's immediate plans, but they could not retard the onrush into Latin America of American capital and commerce, which would soon provide a solid basis for United States influence in the area. Mexico provided a prime example. What the New York *Herald* called in 1878 the "Proposed Invasion of Mexico" resulted five years later in the discovery, in the words of the Chicago *Tribune*, of an "almost virgin outlet for extension of the market of our overproducing civilization." Blaine helped relations, and neatly summarized one of the themes of the new empire, by officially informing Mexico that the United States desired no more land; it only wanted to use its labor and "large accumulation of capital, for which its own vast resources fail to give full scope," to exploit Mexico's "scarcely developed resources." Americans invested heavily in Mexican railroads, mining operations, and petroleum development. United States trade with Mexico had been $7,000,000 in 1860. It doubled to

[79] Pletcher, "Awkward Years," 28, 60–61a; Admiral D. G. Walker to Admiral S. B. Luce, Nov. 6, 1886, Area 11 file, Box 6, Naval Records Branch, United States Archives, Record Group 45 (cited hereafter, NA, RG 45). The historian quoted is John R. Spears, *The History of Our Navy* . . . (New York, 1899), V, 139–141.

$15,000,000 in 1880, doubled again to $36,000,000 in 1890, and nearly doubled again to $63,000,000 in 1900. Such economic ties nullified the defeat of the Frelinghuysen reciprocity treaty with Mexico.[80]

As American interests moved away from the Western Hemisphere, it became more difficult to make a strong case for manifest destiny. Particularly was this so when they moved eastward, against the grain of the traditional course of empire, into the African Congo in the 1880's. American interest in this area had been whetted by missionary reports of mineral wealth, the adventures of a New York *Herald* reporter, Henry M. Stanley, and by Commodore Robert W. Shufeldt, who reported after his stop at West Africa while on his round-the-world trip that the area was the "great commercial prize of the world." The New York City Chamber of Commerce and other eastern businessmen asked for governmental help in opening railroads and steamship lines. In 1884 Senator John T. Morgan of Alabama proposed an open door in the Congo for American goods. Frelinghuysen immediately sent a mission to the Congo to survey the commercial possibilities.[81]

A European power struggle broke out in the area in the late 1870's. The United States sided with King Leopold II of Belgium, who had made extensive claims, and opposed British and French interests. Thus when the European powers headed for a final settlement in the Berlin Conference of 1884–1885, the United States had already reserved a place at the negotiating table. The American delegation, led by John A. Kasson, played a major role at the meeting in the formulation of trade rights. But the Senate was reluctant to act on the final treaty. It feared that ratification

---

[80] Plesur, "Looking Outward," 63–64. *Foreign Relations, 1881,* 761–762, gives Blaine's view; see also Blaine's statement in Callahan, *American Foreign Policy in Mexican Relations,* 494–497, also 420–421, 507, 516–517, 519.

[81] Plesur, "Looking Outward," ch. viii; Stolberg-Wernigerode, *Germany and the United States,* 204.

would contradict the Monroe Doctrine's dogma of no American interference in Europe and so invite European meddling in Latin America.[82]

Frelinghuysen had devoted most of his attention to Latin America, and here he had made an important contribution. Five years later Blaine would make Frelinghuysen's reciprocity treaties a successful part of his own Latin-American policies. Frelinghuysen had exemplified the new expansive attitude of the United States toward its southern neighbors. The New York *Herald* summed up this attitude in 1882 when it informed England that if she had to be active outside British borders, she should "take another turn" at the Zulus or Boers. "She need not bother about this side of the sea. We are a good enough England for this hemisphere." [83]

Bayard and the Pacific

The Cleveland administration halted Frelinghuysen's expansive plans for American involvement in darkest Africa and the reciprocity treaties with Latin-American nations. But Cleveland and his Secretary of State, Thomas F. Bayard, replaced Frelinghuysen's plans with expansive ideas of their own. Compared with his predecessor's policies, Bayard made one major change in the course of the new empire: he switched State Department attention from Latin America to the Pacific.

The reciprocity treaty signed with Hawaii in 1875 had been renewed in 1884, but eastern sugar interests had combined with high tariff advocates to prevent Senate ratification. These groups were fighting a losing cause. Between 1876 and 1885 Hawaiian sugar production had rocketed from 26,000,000 pounds and $1,300,000 in value to 171,000,000 pounds and $8,400,000. Under the 1875 treaty the islands' sugar producers had become utterly dependent

[82] Pletcher, "Awkward Years," ch. xvii; Younger, *Kasson*, 292–295, 334; Bald, "Expansionist Sentiment," 144–146.
[83] Plesur, "Looking Outward," 79.

upon the American market. Blaine correctly considered Hawaii "a part of the productive and commercial system of the American states."[84]

The Cleveland administration condemned reciprocity as the handmaiden of high tariffs. Bayard nevertheless pressured the Senate to ratify the Hawaiian reciprocity treaty quickly. A consistent open-door expansionist, Bayard wanted nothing to do with Hawaii's internal political problems, but he determined, first, that no foreign power should ever be allowed to acquire dominant interest in the islands, and, second, that Hawaii would serve as a base for exploiting the Asiatic market: "The vast importance and our close and manifest interest in the commerce of the Pacific Ocean upon which we now hold the most important seaboard, renders the Hawaiian group of essential importance to us on every score." Cleveland called the islands the "outpost of American commerce and the stepping-stone to the growing trade of the Pacific." "America's commercial competitors," the President warned, could never be allowed this "valuable ground." The treaty finally passed, however, only after the Senate Foreign Relations Committee included a provision giving the United States the Pearl Harbor naval base. At first cool, Bayard soon accepted the amendment wholeheartedly.[85]

Looking back on this episode, Bayard could use John Quincy Adams' classic analogy: the United States only had "to wait quietly and patiently and let the islands fill up with American planters and American industries until they should be wholly identified with the United States. It was simply a matter of waiting until the apple should fall."[86]

[84] Donald Marquand Dozer, "Opposition to Hawaiian Reciprocity, 1876–1888," *Pacific Historical Review*, XIV (June, 1945), 157–183; Stevens, *American Expansion in Hawaii*, 141–147, 159. Blaine's views are in *Foreign Relations, 1881*, 635–639.

[85] Charles Callan Tansill, *The Foreign Policy of Thomas F. Bayard, 1885–1897* (New York, 1940), 373–374; *Messages and Papers of the Presidents*, VIII, 500–501; Stevens, *American Expansion in Hawaii*, ch. viii.

[86] The statement was made in 1888 (Tansill, *Foreign Policy of Bayard*, 400).

Though less certain about the future of Samoa, Bayard maintained and enlarged American rights in these islands in the far-off South Pacific. The United States had become officially involved in 1878. The following year England and Germany established their own treaty rights with the Samoan chiefs. In the mid-1880's Germany, which had developed the largest interests on the islands, began to threaten the use of force to make itself sole ruler. Bayard warned Germany and Great Britain that the United States would never allow a single power to dominate the islands. Conditions grew worse. In 1887 the Secretary of State met with the German and British ministers to Washington in an attempt to find a solution before war broke out. During a period when the United States was supposedly providing the classic example of a nonentangling, nonexpansive foreign policy, it had actually jumped into the middle of a tumultuous power conflict in the Pacific.[87]

At the second meeting of the three men, the German Minister pressed Bayard for the reason why the United States cared so about Samoa. The Secretary of State replied that the United States had the moral responsibility for maintaining native independence and sovereignty on the islands. Bayard also added another reason. The islands were on the highway of a great commerce which was still in its early stages. The transcontinental railroad, he continued, had opened the west coast of North America to commerce and civilization, and this area now looked out upon the great Pacific theater. When an Isthmian canal was constructed, Bayard concluded, Samoa would assume crucial importance. The German Foreign Office grumbled that the Secretary of State was interpreting "the Monroe Doctrine as though the Pacific Ocean were to be treated as an American Lake." [88]

[87] Ryden, *United States and Samoa*, 173–321.
[88] *Ibid.*, 276–299, 301–316, 396; Tansill, *Foreign Policy of Bayard*, 30–31, 62–63, 72–73, 81, 92–93; memorandum read to cabinet meeting by Bayard, Nov. 19, 1888, Bayard MSS; "Protocol of Second Samoan Conference," July 2, 1887, Box 162, John Bassett Moore papers, Library of Congress, Washington, D.C.; Stevens, *American Expansion in Hawaii*, 183–186.

Unfortunately the conference could not reach agreement.[89]

As Bayard and Cleveland observed, Hawaii and Samoa were particularly valuable as way stations on the road to Asia. By centering his attention on Seward's favorite area, the Pacific, Bayard had also refocused on what Seward had considered "the prize"—millions of oriental consumers. The State Department and certain members of the business community cooperated during the 1880's to keep alive the vision of the fabled Asian market.

Some businessmen, especially the colorful and unscrupulous General James Harrison Wilson, who was on the boards of directors of several leading American railroads, conjured up great phantasms of American-built railroads in China and Korea. These, Wilson believed, would serve as the wedges to open this huge area to industrial goods from the United States. When Bayard named Colonel Charles Denby of Indiana as the new Minister to China, the Secretary of State had assured expansionists such as Wilson that the Cleveland administration had their interests in mind. Denby began to push his plan for an American-constructed railroad system which, he believed, would stop the progressive weakening of China. When one New York businessman asked Bayard for assurance on the State Department's China policy, the Secretary of State replied that Denby did not "lack friendly instruction in relation to American enterprises of the kind General Wilson alludes to," and that the new Minister was prepared "to rattle all the china in the National Cupboard." [90]

American policies in Korea exemplified the attempt to find new commercial opportunities through a more unilateral approach. China had long claimed suzerainty rights over the Hermit Kingdom, but the rising power of Japan became explicit in a

[89] For German and British reaction, see Stolberg-Wernigerode, *Germany and the United States*, 256–258.

[90] Denby to Bayard, Sept. 6, 1888, Bayard MSS; also Van Alstyne, *Rising American Empire*, 181; Dennett, *Americans in Eastern Asia*, 579–580; Pletcher, "Awkward Years," 179–180, 193–195; Tansill, *Foreign Policy of Bayard*, 422–431.

treaty between that country and Korea in 1876 in which Japan recognized Korean independence. In 1882 Commodore Shufeldt, working through Chinese officials after he had tried and failed to enter Korea through Japan, signed a treaty for the United States which opened Korea to the non-Asian world.

But Shufeldt's success soon proved to be a Pyrrhic victory. The United States had again pushed itself into a whirlpool of power politics in which it could exert little leverage. Russia believed the control of Korea necessary for the success of her Trans-Siberian Railroad; Japan, wanting no foreign-held Korean dagger hanging over her home islands, worked against both China and Russia; and Great Britain became alarmed because of Russian moves and the fear that China's loss of Korea might trigger other attempts to divide and annex Chinese territory.

The United States meanwhile insisted on creating a Korean vacuum which could be filled at least partially with American commerce and missionaries. The State Department feared that a Chinese-controlled Korea would weaken American trading rights, discourage the entry of missionaries, and bring into the picture too many pro-British Chinese officials. Frelinghuysen halted a Chinese attempt to obtain exclusive trade privileges in the Hermit Kingdom. This introduced Bayard's and Denby's attempts to fill the vacuum with American concessions. They were joined in this venture in 1884 by the fascinating figure of Horace Allen, a Presbyterian medical missionary from Ohio who used his intimate relations with the Korean court to sell American interests along with the Lord's. Bayard also attempted to weaken Chinese control by declaring that American policy was "not adverse to the autonomical independence of Corea," and then successfully exerting pressure on the Chinese to allow Korea to establish a separate legation in the United States.[91]

[91] Treat, *U.S. and Japan*, II, 218–219; Dennett, *Americans in Eastern Asia*, 450–474; Tansill, *Foreign Policy of Bayard*, 417–449; Fred Harvey Harrington, *God, Mammon and the Japanese: Dr. Horace Allen and Korean-American Relations, 1884–1905* (Madison, Wisc., 1944), 1–17.

Shufeldt had opened the door while Frelinghuysen and Bayard had tried to weaken the Chinese hold and fill the void with the open-door policy. It might have worked if all the claimants who scrambled to get through the Korean threshold had started from the same position, and if the State Department had demonstrated a willingness to pay a military price for the commercial benefits. As it was, the Japanese enjoyed a head start on the other powers. This fact became dramatically clear in 1894–1895.

The Beginning of the Modern American Navy

As the imbroglios in Central America, Samoa, and Korea proved, the United States needed a strong navy to protect its far-flung interests in the new empire. By 1880 the great American navy of the Civil War had decayed into a flotilla of death-traps and defenseless antiques. Of 1,942 vessels in the navy, only forty-eight could fire a gun. Political fights over Reconstruction policies, the decline of the merchant marine, the desire for financial retrenchment after the Civil War, and the fallacious belief held by some congressmen that the United States would stay out of entangling foreign affairs made impossible the creation of a modern navy in the 1870's. Oscar Wilde's Canterville Ghost could well reply to a young American lady who complained that her country had no ruins and no curiosities: "No ruins! No curiosities! You have your Navy and your manners!" [92]

In 1883, however, the modern American navy began to take form. It became a great navy only after 1890, when Congress authorized the building of the first battleships, but during the preceding seven years other classes of vessels rolled out of American shipyards, and a rationale developed to justify such a powerful naval establishment. A number of new developments made this break-through possible. Partial recovery from the depres-

---

[92] John D. Long, *The New American Navy* (New York, 1903), I 13–14; Harold and Margaret Sprout, *The Rise of American Naval Power, 1776–1918* (Princeton, 1939), 174–177; Elting E. Morison, *Admiral Sims and the Modern American Navy* (Boston, 1942), 19.

sion of the 1870's resulted in Treasury surpluses to pay for naval expenditures. By 1886 the Navy Department had ordered that all armor, steel, and ordnance for American ships be made in the United States, a move which put an important vested interest back of the "New Navy." [93]

But two additional factors were of most importance. In 1881 the Secretary of the Navy, William Hunt, established a naval advisory board to counsel him on matters of strategy and technology. A group of rising naval officers now began channeling their demands through this new board to a receptive Congress. Representative Benjamin W. Harris of Massachusetts recalled that at one meeting between the House Committee on Naval Affairs and the naval officers, "We . . . listened to the advice of naval officers, and our bill was changed in obedience to their views." Other naval officers obtained a sounding board with the opening of the Naval War College in 1884.

The second major factor was the knowledge that expanding American interests, especially in the Western Hemisphere, lay at the mercy of stronger European and even Latin-American fleets. More ambitious expansionists, as Representative William McAdoo of New Jersey and John Kasson, pleaded for a great navy to protect Americans in such distant areas as Samoa and the Congo. These factors meshed to produce appropriations in 1883 for the four steel vessels which mark the beginning of the New Navy. Between 1885 and 1889 Congress authorized thirty more ships while cooperating with the Secretary of the Navy, William Whitney, to improve the Navy Department's bureaucracy and the fleet's personnel.[94]

But just as American policy in Latin America proved more

[93] Robert Seager II, "Ten Years before Mahan: The Unofficial Case for the New Navy, 1880–1890," *Mississippi Valley Historical Review*, XL (December, 1953), 491–512; Sprout, *Rise of American Naval Power*, 183–184; *House Report No. 653*, 47th Cong., 1st Sess., xxii–xxiii.

[94] Seager, "Ten Years before Mahan," 491–500; *Annual Report of the Secretary of the Navy, 1881*, 27; *Congressional Record*, 50th Cong., 2nd Sess., 1437.

vigorous in the 1890's than in the preceding decade, so the building of the New Navy in the 1880's had little of the dynamic
quality it exhibited in the post-1890 period. The one element
lacking in the naval debates of the earlier decade was a consensus
on the need for a seagoing, offensive, battleship navy. Instead,
the United States built a lightly armored fleet of fast cruisers
suited for hit-and-run destroying of commerce, not for major
naval engagements with the great ships of Europe. Not even
such leading expansionists as McAdoo advised the building of
such capital ships. The lack of support for large battleships indicates the limited tactics and strategy of American foreign
policy in the 1880's, just as the creation of a great battleship fleet
after 1890 so revealingly typifies the more ambitious qualities of
American expansion in that decade.[95]

Conclusion: The Period of Preparation

The 1890's may correctly be called a major watershed in
American history, but this decade cannot be understood without
comprehending domestic and foreign policy in the 1850–1889
period. Spurred by a fantastic industrial revolution, which produced ever larger quantities of surplus goods, depressions, and
violence, and warned by a growing radical literature that the
system was not functioning properly, the United States prepared
to solve its dilemmas with foreign expansion. Displaying a notable
lack of any absentmindedness, Americans set out to solve their
problems by creating an empire whose dynamic and characteristics marked a new departure in their history. This would not
be a colonial empire. As the *Daily Alta California* phrased it in
1874 with a homey frontier metaphor, "Acquisition of territory
with us is . . . 'dead cock in the pit.' " But *Export and Finance*
noted in 1889 that, although the country was filled with self-

---

[95] Sprout, *Rise of American Naval Power*, 195; *Congressional Record*,
50th Cong., 2nd Sess., 1441; for the lack of consensus see the vote on an
important bill authorizing the construction of two warships of 15,000
tons, in *Congressional Record*, 50th Cong., 1st Sess., 6728.

styled "isolationists," it was impossible to find a single person who did not favor increased commercial entanglements. In due time these commercial ambitions would result in political and military entanglements also; affairs in Samoa and the growing navy provided ample proof of that.[96]

The years between 1850 and 1889 were a period of preparation for the 1890's. These years provided the roots of empire, not the fruit. The fruit of empire would not appear until the 1890's, when Frederick Jackson Turner, Josiah Strong, Brooks Adams, and Alfred Thayer Mahan systematically reformulated and publicized the nature of this empire, when the Harrison-Blaine policies outlined most explicitly the strategy of the empire, and, finally, when the depression of 1893 acted as the catalyst to these developments of a half century.

[96] Dozer, "Anti-Imperialism," 80–81; Plesur, "Looking Outward," 192.

II

The Intellectual Formulation

SOME intellectuals speak only for themselves. Theirs is often the later glory, but seldom the present power. Some, however, speak not only for themselves but for the guiding forces of their society. Discovering such men at crucial junctures in history, if such a discovery can be made, is of importance and value. These figures uncover the premises, reveal the approaches, provide the details, and often coherently arrange the ideas which are implicit in the dominant thought of their time and society.

The ordered, articulate writings of Frederick Jackson Turner, Josiah Strong, Brooks Adams, and Alfred Thayer Mahan typified the expansive tendencies of their generation. Little evidence exists that Turner and Strong directly influenced expansionists in the business community or the State Department during the 1890's, but their writings best exemplify certain beliefs which determined the nature of American foreign policy. Adams and Mahan participated more directly in the shaping of expansionist programs. It is, of course, impossible to estimate the number of Americans who accepted the arguments of these four men. What cannot be controverted is that the writings of these men typified

and in some specific instances directly influenc[ ]
American policy makers who created the new [ ]

This chapter does not pretend to explore a[ ]
corners in the intellectual realm of each man[ ]
areas which relate to the development of foreign [ ]
the policies of the 1890's. No attempt is made, for example, to
enter into all the shadowy labyrinths of the frontier thesis; but
it is legitimate and possible to extract certain parts of that thesis
to find their relationship to American expansion. In the conclud-
ing part of the chapter an attempt is made to cut across the
thoughts of these four men in order to ferret out a few commonly
shared ideas.

Frederick Jackson Turner and the American Frontier

In 1898 an angry British professor at Cambridge University
published a book which hotly disputed the right of an obstrep-
erous United States to act as if it dominated the entire Western
Hemisphere, especially since that area of the globe included
large chunks of British-owned territory. W. F. Reddaway admitted, however, that the new, bumptious policy had evolved
naturally out of the American past: "Hitherto, the internal development of the Union has been favoured by the existence of
relatively inexhaustible supplies of land. With fertile territories
crying out for settlement, a foreign policy has been superfluous."
But in the 1890's, Reddaway's argument continued, Americans
exhausted their supply of free land and a foreign policy became

---

[1] One of the weakest sections in the history of ideas is the relationship
between the new intellectual currents and American overseas expansion
during the last half of the nineteenth century. The background and some
of the general factors may be found in Alfred Kazin, *On Native Grounds:
An Interpretation of Modern American Prose Literature* (Garden City,
N.Y., 1942, 1956); Henry Steele Commager, *The American Mind: An
Interpretation of American Thought and Character since the 1880's* (New
Haven, 1950, 1959); Weinberg, *Manifest Destiny;* Julius W. Pratt, "The
Ideology of American Expansion," *Essays in Honor of William E. Dodd
. . .* , edited by Avery Craven (Chicago, 1935).

ary. Reddaway bitterly disapproved of the policy, but he
ought he understood the motivations.[2]

No such cause-and-effect relationship can, of course, be found
which so neatly links the closing of the frontier with American
expansionist activities in 1895 or 1898, especially since historians
have demonstrated that a larger number of original and ·final
homestead entries were registered after 1900 than during the
previous three hundred years. But there can be no doubt that
one important part of the rationale for an expansive foreign
policy in the 1890's was a fervent (though erroneous) belief held
by many American that their unique and beneficent internal
frontier no longer existed.[3]

The importance of the frontier will be associated with the
name of Frederick Jackson Turner as long as historians are able
to indent footnotes. Yet as Theodore Roosevelt told Turner in
a letter of admiration in 1894, "I think you . . . have put into
definite shape a good deal of thought which has been floating
around rather loosely." As has been amply shown by several
scholars, a number of observers warned of the frontier's disappearance and the possible consequences of this disappearance
long before Turner's epochal paper. The accelerating communication and transportation revolution, growing agrarian unrest,
violent labor strikes, and the problems arising from increasing
numbers of immigrants broke upon puzzled and frightened
Americans in a relatively short span of time. Many of them
clutched the belief of the closing or closed frontier in order to
explain their dilemma.[4]

[2] W. F. Reddaway, *The Monroe Doctrine* (Cambridge, Eng., 1898),
141.

[3] I am especially indebted to Professor Paul Gates of Cornell University, who not only improved this work with his criticism of several chapters but also aided me with statistics and information which gave me
a much clearer picture of the nature of the American frontier in the
late-nineteenth century.

[4] See especially Fulmer Mood, "The Concept of the Frontier, 1871–
1898," *Agricultural History*, XIX (January, 1945), 24–31; Lee Benson,
"The Historical Background of Turner's Frontier Essay," *Agricultural*

From the perspective of more than half a century, one can envy the timing of Turner's paper, though as far as he was concerned the timing was probably unintentional. Read before a solemn assemblage of American historians at the World's Fair in Chicago in mid-July, 1893, it came just as the panic of the spring transformed into a devastating four-year depression. It is interesting to note that many of the frontier theses which had presaged Turner's had appeared during or immediately after previous depressions. The 1883–1886 slump had produced the first spate of warnings about the frontier, though few went as far as James Bryce, who wrote gravely in his *American Commonwealth* that when Americans occupied all their western lands "it will be a time of trial for democratic institutions." But the depression of the 1890's destroyed whatever was left of "the myth of the garden." A conservative journal such as the *Commercial and Financial Chronicle* could imply a closed frontier in 1894 when it blamed the stagnation in the West on slackening railroad construction and fewer land sales. On the other end of the political spectrum, the most popular spokesman of the Populist forces, "Coin" Harvey, could use the same factor to explain why the "suffering race" battled the wealthy during the turbulent 1890's: "The unexplored portions of the world . . . were escape valves for the poorer people. . . . The damming up of the stream has now come. There is no unexplored part of the world left suitable for men to inhabit, and justice now stands at bay." [5]

History, XXV (April, 1951), 59–82; Herman Clarence Nixon, "The Precursors of Turner in the Interpretation of the American Frontier," *South Atlantic Quarterly*, XXVIII (January, 1929), 83–89. For the Roosevelt letter, see *The Letters of Theodore Roosevelt*, selected and edited by Elting E. Morison *et al.* (Cambridge, Mass., 1951), I, 363.

[5] For warnings issued during the middle and late 1880's, see especially Nixon, "Precursors of Turner in the Interpretation of the American Frontier," 83–89; *Congressional Record*, 49th Cong., 1st Sess., 7830–7831; Thomas P. Gill, "Landlordism in America," *North American Review*, CXLII (January, 1886), 52–67, especially 60; A. J. Desmond, "America's Land Question," *North American Review*, CXLII (February, 1886), 153–158, especially 153. Smith, *Virgin Land*, 219, mentions the effect of the

Turner's own introduction to his frontier thesis can be found in a most important paper published in the fall of 1891, "The Significance of History." Anticipating the twentieth-century theme that, as Turner phrased it, "each age writes the history of the past anew with reference to the conditions uppermost in its own time," the young Wisconsin professor provided notice of his own viewpoint: "Today the questions that are uppermost, and that will become increasingly important, are not so much political as economic questions. The age of machinery, of the factory system, is also the age of socialistic inquiry." Writing at that time, it is not strange that he interpreted the last part of the century as the age of Economic Man.[6]

Turner rested the central part of his frontier thesis on the economic power represented by free land. American individualism, nationalism, political institutions, and democracy depended on this power: "So long as free land exists, the opportunity for a competency exists, and economic power secures political power." Stated in these terms, landed expansion became the central factor, the dynamic of American progress. Without the economic power generated by expansion across free lands, American political institutions could stagnate.[7]

Such an analysis could be extremely meaningful to those persons who sought an explanation for the political and social troubles of the period. Few disputed that the social upheavals in both the urban and agrarian areas of the nation stemmed from

---

1893–1897 depression; also *Commercial and Financial Chronicle*, Dec. 22, 1894, 1082–1084; William H. Harvey, *Coin's Financial School* (Chicago, 1894), 79. For the Bryce quotation see James Bryce, *The American Commonwealth* (London, 1889), II, 701.

  [6] Frederick Jackson Turner, *The Early Writings of Frederick Jackson Turner . . . with an Introduction by Fulmer Mood* (Madison, Wisc., 1938), 51–52.

  [7] Frederick Jackson Turner, *The Frontier in American History* (New York, 1947), 32, 30; see also Per Sveaas Andersen, *Westward Is the Course of Empires: A Study in the Shaping of an American Idea: Frederick Jackson Turner's Frontier* (Oslo, Norway, 1956), 20–21; Smith, *Virgin Land*, 240.

economic troubles in the international grain markets, from the frequent industrial depressions, or, as the Populists averred, from the failure of the currency to match the pace of ever increasing productivity. This economic interpretation also fitted in nicely with the contemporary measurement of success in terms of material achievement. Perhaps most important, the frontier thesis not only defined the dilemma, but did so in tangible, concrete terms. It offered the hope that Americans could do something about their problems. Given the assumption that expansion across the western frontier explained past American successes, the solution for the present crisis now became apparent: either radically readjust the political institutions to a nonexpanding society or find new areas for expansion. When Americans seized the second alternative, the meaning for foreign policy became apparent—and immense.

With the appearance and definition of the fundamental problems in the 1880's and 1890's, these decades assumed vast importance. They became not a watershed of American history, but *the* watershed. Many writers emphasized the supremely critical nature of the 1890's, but no one did it better than Turner when he penned the dramatic final sentence of his 1893 paper: "And now, four centuries from the discovery of America, at the end of a hundred years of life under the Constitution, the frontier has gone, and with its going has closed the first period of American history." The American West no longer offered a unique escape from the intractable problems of a closed society. As another writer stated it four years after Turner's announcement in Chicago, "we are no longer a country exceptional and apart." History had finally caught up with the United States.[8]

The first solution that came to some minds suggested the open-

---

[8] Turner, *Frontier in American History*, 38; Eugene V. Smalley, "What Are Normal Times?" *The Forum*, XXIII (March, 1897), 98–99; see also Turner, *Frontier in American History*, 311–312. For a brilliant criticism of Turner's closed-space concepts, see James C. Malin, *The Contriving Brain and the Skillful Hand in the United States* . . . (Lawrence, Kan., 1955), the entire essay, but especially ch. xi.

ing of new landed frontiers in Latin America or Canada. Yet
was further expansion in a landed sense the answer? Top policy
makers, as Secretaries of State James G. Blaine, Thomas F.
Bayard, and Walter Quintin Gresham, opposed the addition of
noncontiguous territory to the Union. Some Americans interpreted the labor violence of 1877, 1886, and 1894 as indications
that the federal government could no longer harmonize and
control the far-flung reaches of the continental empire. Labor
and agrarian groups discovered they could not command the
necessary political power to solve their mushrooming problems.
The sprouting of such factions as the Molly Maguires, Populists,
Eugene Debs' Railroad Union, and several varieties of Socialist
parties raised doubts in many minds about the ameliorating and
controlling qualities which had formerly been a part of the
American system.

Perhaps the political theories of *The Federalist*, No. 10, had
worked too well. Madison had dreamed of a vast landed empire
which would divide various factions so that no one faction could
become dominant. But in a single century the Founding Father's
plan of landed expansion had apparently been so successful that
the resulting continental empire not only prevented some factions from obtaining control of the nation's political institutions,
but threatened to prevent these institutions from adequately controlling the factions. If this condition persisted, Americans might
soon arrive at the forked road where one path led to an all-
powerful central government and the other to anarchy.[9]

This was a cruel dilemma. Nonexpansion threatened economic
and political stagnation, but further expansion could worsen the
abscesses already festering on a sick body politic. No one understood this dilemma better than Turner. In his 1893 paper he observed that free land provides the opportunity for competency,
"and economic power secures political power."

[9] For an outstanding example of this thesis, see *Banker's Magazine*,
XLVIII (February, 1894), 563–565.

But the democracy born of free land, strong in selfishness and individualism, intolerant of administrative experience and education, and pressing individual liberty beyond its proper bounds, has its dangers as well as its benefits. Individualism in America has allowed a laxity in regard to governmental affairs which has rendered possible the spoils system and all the evils that follow from the lack of a highly developed civic spirit. In this connection may be noted also the influence of frontier conditions in permitting lax business honor, inflated paper currency and wild-cat banking. . . . A primitive society can hardly be expected to show the intelligent appreciation of the complexity of business interests in a developed society.[10]

Expansion in the form of trade instead of landed settlement ultimately offered the answer to this dilemma. This solution, embodied in the open-door philosophy of American foreign policy, ameliorated the economic stagnation (which by Turner's reasoning led to the political discontent), but it did not pile new colonial areas on an already overburdened governmental structure. It provided the perfect answer to the problems of the 1890's.

Turner, however, wrote of past American expansion in colonial terms: "the advance of American *settlement* westward." With his fixation on this historical landed development, he might have missed the amazing new cure-all of the open-door doctrine. But Turner did not miss this crucial change in the nature of American expansion. Unlike most policy makers, in fact, he saw far beyond it. In his 1891 paper, "The Significance of History," he made a statement which offers to historians the Ariadne thread for unraveling American foreign policy after 1890. Turner began by noting that the United States believed itself isolated politically from Europe.

But it is one of the profoundest lessons that history has to teach, that political relations, in a highly developed civilization, are inextricably connected with economic relations. Already there are signs of a relaxation of our policy of commercial isolation. Reci-

[10] Turner, *Frontier in American History*, 32.

procity is a word that meets with increasing favor from all parties. But once fully afloat on the sea of worldwide economic interests, we shall soon develop political interests. Our fishery disputes furnish one example; our Samoan interests another; our Congo relations a third. But perhaps most important are our present and future relations with South America, coupled with our Monroe Doctrine. It is a settled maxim of international law that the government of a foreign state whose subjects have lent money to another state may interfere to protect the rights of the bondholders, if they are endangered by the borrowing state.[11]

It is difficult to overemphasize the significance of this statement and unnecessary to elaborate upon it.

At the request of the editor of the *Atlantic Monthly*, Walter Hines Page, Turner published an article in September, 1896, during the heat of the Bryan-McKinley campaign, entitled "The Problem of the West." It is probably the best statement on the subject written during the decade. In one paragraph Turner assembled his thought on the relationship of the closing frontier to the new, vigorous American foreign policy:

For nearly three hundred years the dominant fact in American life has been expansion. With the settlement of the Pacific Coast and the occupation of the free lands, this movement has come to a check. That these energies of expansion will no longer operate would be a rash prediction; and the demands for a vigorous foreign policy, for an interoceanic canal, for a revival of our power upon the seas, and for the extension of American influence to outlying islands and adjoining countries, are indications that the movement will continue. The stronghold of these demands lies west of the Alleghenies.[12]

When writing his presidential address for the meeting of the American Historical Association fourteen years later, Turner saw no need to change this interpretation. The American in-

---

[11] Turner, *Early Writings*, 61–62.

[12] Frederick Jackson Turner, "The Problem of the West," *Atlantic Monthly*, LXXVIII (September, 1896), 289–297. This essay is reprinted in *Frontier in American History*, 205–221.

volvement in the Far East "to engage in the world-politics of the Pacific Ocean," the "extension of power" and "entry into the sisterhood of world-states," were not isolated events. They were, "indeed, in some respects the logical outcome of the nation's march to the Pacific." [13]

It is difficult to measure Turner's influence on expansionists in the 1890's, although he certainly affected Theodore Roosevelt's view of American history. He also played a major part in shaping the ideas of a future American statesman, Woodrow Wilson. In the 1890's, however, Wilson was more than a potential Chief Executive; as a well-known political scientist he enjoyed an influential reading public. In books and reviews he echoed Turner's theme that, since the closing of the continental frontier, Americans searched for "new frontiers in the Indies and in the Far Pacific." A close friend of Turner's, Wilson was not reticent in admitting, "All I ever wrote on the subject came from him." [14]

The ideas which Turner publicized exerted much force in the 1890's. The previous chapter mentioned the frontier theme, and the remainder of this work will note an increasing number of references after 1893 to a filled West. Such references were especially noticeable in debates waged over the necessity for an enlarged foreign trade and for a battleship navy to protect that trade. Americans were not slow in translating the fact of the closed landed frontier into the necessity for discovering a new commercial frontier. [15]

Turner is of prime importance to the student of American

[13] *Ibid.*, 315.

[14] For a pioneer interpretation, see Lawrence S. Kaplan, "Frederick Jackson Turner and Imperialism," *Social Science*, XXVII (January, 1952), 12–16; and for an excellent analysis see William A. Williams, "The Frontier Thesis and American Foreign Policy," *Pacific Historical Review*, XXIV (November, 1955), 379–395. For Wilson's view see "Mr. Goldwin Smith's 'Views' on Our Political History," *Forum*, XVI (December, 1893), 489–499, especially 496–497.

[15] For examples of how the frontier thesis was included in debates on naval appropriations, see *Congressional Record*, 53d Cong., 3rd Sess., March 2, 1895, 3109; also Chapters IV, V, VI, below.

foreign policy. During a crisis period of his nation's history he provided an explanation of that crisis by uniting various ideas about the American frontier, ideas which, as Roosevelt remarked, were "floating around rather loosely." His formulations best exemplify the thinking that was concerned with the disappearing frontier, the relationship of this frontier to the turbulent society of the 1890's, and the implications for foreign policy. In his crucial observation that an open-door form of economic expansion made inevitable political responsibilities, Turner saw beyond the limited vision of most policy makers and businessmen. In doing so he provided the key to understanding American foreign policy in the first half of the twentieth century.

Josiah Strong and the Missionary Frontier

Josiah Strong shared Turner's views of the 1890's as a crisis decade and of the closing frontier as a matter for grave concern. Here the similarity between the two men becomes less evident. Strong did not approach Turner's intellectual powers, and Turner never blew a clarion call for American expansion as loudly as Strong did in his several books. Turner attempted to analyze the frontier in a cool, methodical manner, in order to gain insight into the past. But Strong attempted to find good reasons for something he desired passionately for the future: a thunderous Protestant missionary charge which would conquer the American West for Christ and then use this region as the home base for overpowering the world. Yet the ideas of the two men were in a sense complementary, for Strong stressed the necessity of finding a new world frontier to replace the internal frontier which Turner so eloquently described. In substituting a new frontier for the old, Strong offered his solution for the spiritual, economic, and political problems of his day.

Born in Naperville, Illinois, in 1847, Strong knew the West well; not only was he raised on its periphery, but after becoming a Congregational minister in 1871 he traveled extensively in the area for the Home Missionary Society. The turning point in his life came with the publication of *Our Country* in 1885. The Home Missionary Society had requested Strong to update a small manual which had stolidly pleaded for more Christian missions. But as a scholar of sorts, social reformer, and a keen observer who noted and feared the growing labor and agrarian discontent, Strong infused new life into the book. Within a decade 175,000 copies were sold in the United States, and many other issues of the work sold in European and oriental languages. At a time when exhortations for missionary work were much in vogue, the *Nation* called *Our Country* "a Home Missionary address raised to the nth power." In terms of popularity few books of the time could equal it. Strong became a national figure, spreading his ideas from innumerable lecture platforms and through other books. He later became involved in the Social Gospel movement and dedicated himself to making this movement a world-wide affair. Symbolically, he had entitled his first book *Our Country;* in 1913, four years before his death, he began a four-volume work entitled *Our World*. But the change in titles is misleading. The latter title could legitimately have been the name of his first work.[16]

Strong pleaded fervently for the expansion of Christian missions, but he framed his argument in terms which had vital implications for foreign policy. His goal was a Christianized world, but what is of primary concern here is that he perceived and discussed certain aspects of American society which, he believed, made the attainment of this goal absolutely necessary. He especially stressed the disappearance of the public lands; increasing industrialization, with its effect on the speeding up of social processes and the resulting plethora of wealth; and, finally, the characteristics of Anglo-Saxons which made them peculiarly suited to distribute the spiritual and economic values of western civilization throughout the heathen world.

[16] John Haynes Holmes, "Josiah Strong," *Dictionary of American Biography*, XVIII, 150–151; Bald, "Expansionist Sentiment," 7; *Nation*, Sept. 30, 1886, 273.

Strong posed as one of the intellectuals of his day. His books reflect wide and intensive reading in historical documents and contemporary publications, especially the census reports (one of Turner's favorite sources also). From his collage of reading Strong had extracted the fascinating idea that the centers of world empire had moved west since the beginning of recorded history. He gave Bishop Berkeley and Tocqueville (a source whom he frequently cited) credit for this insight, but drew his own conclusions. The center of empire, Strong believed, would settle "to our mighty West, there to remain, for there is no further West; beyond is the Orient." This West would be the greatest of all empires. Other nations would bring their offerings to "the cradle of the young empire of the West," as they had once taken their gifts to the cradle of Jesus.[17]

But this message was too sanguine for the depression-haunted 1880's, especially if the author hoped to sketch a picture that would attract sympathetic cash contributions. So Strong quickly added that the West could not be assured of ascending and maintaining the seat of world empire; in fact, he continued, the West was at that moment approaching a crisis partly because of the rapid disappearance of the public lands. In a passage which resembles Turner's statement of eight years later not only in content but in stately cadence as well, Strong concluded with the warning: "When the supply is exhausted, we shall enter upon a new era, and shall more rapidly approximate European conditions of life." [18]

This occurrence only partially explained why the West faced new and dangerous times. To round out the picture, Strong explored the many implications of the exhaustion of the western lands. He discovered secondary effects which almost overwhelmed him with their gravity. The East, he observed, had begun as farms and then slowly evolved over several centuries

[17] Josiah Strong, *Our Country: Its Possible Future and Its Present Crisis* (New York, 1885), 29.
[18] *Ibid.*, 153–158.

into urban, industrialized areas. But the West developed with the railroad, which immediately spawned industry. The farms, for the most part, followed or arrived concurrently with this industrialization. He concluded that the innumerable, complex problems inherent in an urban-industrialized society would strike the West much earlier in the process of its settlement and with a greater impact than when they had struck the East. The West had to be prepared or a social breakdown might result.[19]

This sense of urgency throbbed throughout Strong's writing, and it was intensified by the observation that modern history moved many times faster than ancient, "for the pulse and the pace of the world have been marvelously quickened during the nineteenth century." He outlined the communication and transportation revolutions, the astonishing changes in modern science, and the rapidity with which "great ideas" sprouted. The "western world in its progress is gathering momentum like a falling body." His view of history, like that of Henry Adams' "law," saw events moving ever faster. Out of this insight he evolved his own law: two "great principles" were at work in history—the development of the individual and the organization of society. The accelerated pace of history, caused by the discovery and uses of the steam engine and electricity, was creating a centripetal force that ever more rapidly transformed diversity into unity. This tendency toward centralization appeared not only in industry, but in politics and society as well. The effects of such a basic change in Man's history could be perilous since it was occurring so rapidly that Man could not adequately adjust to it. "Thoughtful men everywhere have become expectant of great social changes," Strong warned. "Many expect revolution," and "probably" the Christian church was all that stood in the path of such a revolution.[20]

[19] *Ibid.*; Smith, *Virgin Land*, 300, provides an analysis of a similar aspect of Turner's thought.

[20] Strong, *Our Country*, 1–7; Josiah Strong, *The New Era or the Coming Kingdom* (New York, 1893), 1–16, 26–27, 342–343, ch. vii.

He thought he saw this centralization occurring in another sphere also. Noting the opening of Japan, Korea, and parts of Africa to western civilization, he believed that these events "point unmistakably to one conclusion [:] The drawing of the peoples of the earth into ever closer relations, which will render isolation and, therefore, barbarism impossible, and will operate as a constant stimulus." He predicted that "the growth of freedom which removes the greatest barriers to progress, the social ferment and the evident tendency toward a new social organization" would lead to a "new era, for which the nineteenth century has been the John the Baptist." Thus he concluded that expansion and consolidation would result in further expansion and further consolidation. If he had correctly assessed the world situation, and no doubt many of his thousands of readers were confident that he had, then American foreign policy makers could only operate from the basic assumption of an ever increasing involvement in world politics. The policy makers had no choice, given the discoveries of steam and electricity and the resulting unity of the peoples of the world.[21]

The rapid industrialization, especially in the American West, laid another heavy burden on the American people—a tremendous amount of wealth which became the idol and also the oppressor of the nation. As a man whose main problem was to find financial backing for missionary activities, Strong had no illusions about the power of money: "Money is power in the concrete. It commands learning, skill, experience, wisdom, talent, influence, numbers." He hoped every cent of American money would "be employed in the way that will best honor God," but he expressed well-founded doubts. Too often unscrupulous politicians used money to purchase the "floating vote." Others spent their earnings on needless luxury. But overproduction which led to gluts of goods and to unemployment endangered America's great wealth most of all. The concentrated money power refused to improve the deplorable living and working conditions

21 *Ibid.*, 3–16.

of laborers. Strong wondered if the growing discontent rising out of this surfeit of wealth did not herald an event as epochal as the Reformation or the French Revolution. While the first destroyed spiritual despotism and the second political despotism, "perhaps the third indicates the fall of economic despotism." [22]

He could discover a number of threats to American society, including immigrants, Roman Catholicism, Mormonism, intemperance, and immoral city life; but all these perils could be grouped, for purposes of his analysis, under one indescribably evil force—socialism. In the second longest chapter of *Our Country*, he warned against socialists who attempted "to solve the problem of suffering without eliminating the factor of sin." Nowhere did the acid of socialism threaten the fabric of society more than in the American West, for here capitalism was developing full blown under the impetus provided by eastern capital. Class distinctions were already the rule. Destroying his readers' last hope for an easy salvation in this world, Strong concluded with the grave observation that the United States could not stave off socialism by giving more political freedoms for there were no more to offer; beyond lies "but anarchism." The solution had to be found elsewhere, in a more difficult and complicated realm than politics.[23]

The future could be America's, but she could not trust in a beneficent, inexorable manifest destiny. Strong quoted Professor Austin Phelps (who wrote the "Introduction" to *Our Country*) that although "we are the chosen people," Americans "can no longer *drift* with safety to our destiny. We are shut up to a perilous alternative." Salvation lay in the fulfillment of the Anglo-Saxon mission to reshape the world in the mold of western civilization. After modestly reminding the reader that he made public these thoughts in a public lecture three years before the appearance of John Fiske's popular "Manifest Destiny," "which contains some of the same ideas," Strong outlined this mission

[22] Strong, *Our Country*, 113–128, 181–185; Strong, *New Era*, ch. vii.
[23] Strong, *Our Country*, 85–112.

in detail. Because of the westward movement of empire he assumed that England would provide some help but necessarily be the junior partner. The Anglo-Saxon, with his two virtues of civil liberty and "pure spiritual Christianity," would employ his "genius for colonizing" to "move down upon Mexico, down upon Central and South America, out upon the islands of the sea, over Africa and beyond. And can any one doubt that the result of this competition of races will be the 'survival of the fittest'?" [24]

This expansion of Anglo-Saxon Christianity would also solve the fundamental question of overproduction. Noting that "steam and electricity have mightily compressed the earth" so that "our markets are to be greatly extended," he told how these markets could be conquered: "The world is to be Christianized and civilized. . . . Commerce follows the missionary. . . . A Christian civilization performs the miracle of the loaves and fishes, and feeds its thousands in a desert." He could not resist invoking Africa and especially the fabled Asian market as his examples: "What will be the wants of Asia a century hence?" [25]

Our Country combined a view of the religious and industrial manifest destiny of the Anglo-Saxons, but *The New Era*, published in 1893, reflected an immersion in the growing Social Gospel movement. Seven years later Strong published *Expansion*, which reassembled and elaborated his earlier thoughts on American foreign policy, especially the dynamics of this policy. In the preface he thanks two of the leading expansionists of the day, Senator William P. Frye of Maine and Alfred Thayer Mahan, for providing information and also for reading some of the chapters. Little of the Social Gospel can be found in this book. He began by restating his belief that the disappearing internal frontier had forced capital and "energy" to find foreign outlets. This overseas expansion had been further motivated by the great industrial capacity of American factories. (He entitled

---

[24] *Ibid.*, 159–180; Strong, *New Era*, 78–79; also *Our Country*, 218, 159.
[25] *Ibid.*, 7–15; Strong, *New Era*, 355–356.

one of his chapters, "Foreign Markets, a New Necessity.") If adequate markets could not be found, an internal revolution would result. After examining in detail the markets of China and the Pacific and the commercial importance of an Isthmian canal, Strong very significantly noted the revision of Washington's Farewell Address by Richard Olney in the Venezuelan note of July, 1895. He then concluded by spelling out once again the Anglo-Saxon mission, its virtues, and its inevitability.[26]

Brooks Adams hoped to create a world-wide American empire by increasing the nation's efficiency and restoring its martial spirit. Strong hoped to accomplish the same objective by making the country both efficient and Christian. Yet in spite of his religious principles, he had perhaps as brutal a view of the future as did Adams. Strong prophesied that with the closing of the frontier two events would follow: the West, if properly Christianized, would become the pivot of world empire; it would then "enter on a new stage of its history—the final competition of races." The peoples of the western world, advancing across the American continent for four hundred years, would now be thrown back upon themselves and find outlets no longer in open frontiers, but in populated areas of the world such as Asia, Africa, and Latin America. Strong hoped that the resulting conflict would be a peaceful one, fought with Christian principles and technology, but he did not hesitate to advocate the use of force whenever necessary. After all, time was short and the Anglo-Saxon destiny could not wait: "The closing years of the nineteenth century [are] second in importance to that . . . which must always remain first; viz., the birth of Christ." [27]

Strong's influence reached the masses and the mighty of American society. The sophisticated *Nation* blasted *The New Era* in a review in 1893, but grudgingly admitted that it had to devote space to the book "because it is doubtless destined to considerable

[26] Josiah Strong, *Expansion under New World Conditions* (New York, 1900). For an analysis of Olney's message, see Chapter VI, below.
[27] Strong, *New Era*, ch. vi, 79–80, 1–16; Strong, *Our Country*, 1–7.

vogue," since "it is the very flower of a kind of . . . writing . . . which is accepted by the multitudes in lieu of sounder thought." [28] The amazing sales of Strong's books justified such fears. But his books also reached the elite. On the sheet opposite the title page of the Cornell University Library's copy of *Our Country* appears the scrawl: "An exceedingly valuable and interesting little book. ADW, April 3, 1887." Andrew Dickson White may have carried the message of Strong to James Bryce.

Such striking popularity makes Strong an important historical figure. More to the point, much of his contemporary popularity and his later value to historians rests on Strong's success in uniting the frontier thesis of Turner, the themes of the westward movement of empire and the increasing concentration of society stressed by Brooks Adams, and the Anglo-Saxon commercial and military mission outlined by Alfred Thayer Mahan. Finally, Strong exemplified the fervent expansionism emphasized by the other three.

Brooks Adams, Alfred Thayer Mahan, and the Far Western Frontier

Strong, Adams, and Mahan flashed with equal intensity in their writing of history and in their calls to action. Strong and Adams fervently believed in their own personal version of the apocalypse, partly because of their study of history, but mostly because of their own emotional experiences. In this way they differed from Mahan, who with Brooks exerted more direct influence on policy makers in the 1890's than did any of the other intellectuals. Mahan had rifled the history books more than his soul or his past in order to construct what he believed to be the necessary world of the coming twentieth century. His writings can be understood when separated from the personality of the author.

Such judgment cannot be passed on the books and articles of Adams. As the grandsons of John Quincy Adams and the

[28] *Nation*, July 20, 1893, 52.

sons of Charles Francis Adams, the noted Civil War diplomat, Brooks and his brother Henry suffered from the seemingly utter hopelessness which they feared was inherent in being the fourth generation, the fag end, of a great family. This hopelessness turned to fright in 1893, when the depression forced Brooks and Henry to the verge of bankruptcy and then generated social upheavals which threatened with extinction the brothers' fundamental beliefs of class and politics. Just the year before, Brooks had predicted some sort of social and economic breakdown. He had warned that unless a solution could be found quickly, the division between the haves and have-nots would deepen until the latter would be driven to revolution in order to readjust the imbalance. But the crushing force of the 1893 crisis shocked even the pessimistic, prepared Adamses. As Henry later commented, he felt "that something new and curious was about to happen to the world." [29]

Brooks responded by working out a "law" of history which he believed gave a reading of the present position of the United States. His manuscript was notable for its thesis, not for its historical evidence. Not that Brooks particularly cared, for he loathed the antiquarian and he railed against footnote sloggers who lost their thesis in a morass of details. In his mind only the thesis counted, and he believed that he had thrown up adequate historical supports for his "law." [30]

---

[29] Arthur F. Beringause, *Brooks Adams: A Biography* (New York, 1955), 98–102; see also Thornton Anderson, *Brooks Adams: Constructive Conservative* (Ithaca, N.Y., 1951); Worthington Chauncey Ford, "Memoir of Brooks Adams," *Proceedings, Massachusetts Historical Society*, LX (May, 1927), 345–358. For an excellent analysis of Adams' foreign policy, see Charles Vevier, "Brooks Adams and the Ambivalence of American Foreign Policy," *World Affairs Quarterly*, XXX (April, 1959), 3–18; also Brooks Adams to Henry Cabot Lodge, April 23, 1894, Henry Cabot Lodge Papers, Massachusetts Historical Society, Boston, Mass.; Henry Adams, *The Education of Henry Adams: An Autobiography* (Boston and New York, 1930), 338.

[30] Brooks Adams, *The New Empire* (New York and London, 1902), xvii; for an excellent analysis of Brooks as a historian, see Timothy Paul

Brooks offered a hypothesis which attempted to classify the phases through which society passed "in its oscillations between barbarism and civilization, or, what amounts to the same thing, in its movement from a condition of physical dispersion to one of concentration." Barbarian societies worked under the impetus of fear, which produced the military and religious classes. These classes generated and conquered energy to keep the society on-going; ultimately they were able to store surplus energy. But since the social movement of a civilization is proportionate to its energy and mass and its centralization proportionate to its velocity, societies centralize as human movement accelerates. As this centralization occurs, greed replaces fear and the surplus energy comes under the control of the economic man (the banker) who expends more energy than can be produced. Once in control, the banker forces the use of a single standard which appreciates currency, pushes debtors to the wall, and eliminates the "elasticity of the age of expansion." The imaginative and martial man disappears and the store of surplus energy declines. Art and architecture decay. The society continues to disintegrate until invigoration occurs with the infusion of new barbarian blood. As one of Brooks's close friends noted, his writings "tended in one direction—to warn of the end of the economic world." [31]

Infuriated at a hostile review of the book, Brooks protested that his work was not "a sort of political pamphlet," but "scientific," and "from this standpoint political nostrums would be as misplaced as agitation for legislation to correct Mr. Darwin's theory of the 'Descent of man.'" This argument was disingenuous. Viewing history as a series of cycles, Brooks believed that one cycle would end about 1900; the 1893 panic bolstered this belief.

Donovan, *Henry Adams and Brooks Adams: The Education of Two American Historians* (Norman, Okla., 1961), 73–75.

[31] Brooks Adams, *The Law of Civilization and Decay: An Essay on History* (London and New York, 1895), 290–294, vi–viii; Ford, "Memoir," 350; see also Brooks's summary and defense of the book in *Journal of Commerce*, Sept. 28, 1897, 4:4.

He hated with bitter intensity the bankers on whom he placed the responsibility for the decay of the western part of the world in the 1890's, and he believed their selfish ambitions were driving a doomed United States down the path marked out by the "law." His protestations that the "law" was scientific and that the western world was well along the path to destruction to the contrary notwithstanding, Brooks set out to repeal the "law." [32]

His study of history had taught him that a particular society could rule its world for a time, but would sink into oblivion when it failed to retain adequate flexibility to cope with its rapidly changing environment. Translated into contemporary terms, Brooks interpreted this to mean that the gold standard, controlled and manipulated by the bankers, prevented the rapidly expanding United States from being able to deal with problems arising out of the nation's development, especially the problem of the distribution of wealth. Brooks consequently advocated bimetallism. In 1896 Adams supported the Democratic silver bloc to the extent that William Jennings Bryan sallied into the campaign with several hundred dollars from Brooks's and Henry's bank accounts. [33]

The results of that fevered campaign forced the Adamses to accept the ascendancy of McKinleyism and the bankers. Brooks changed his attention from domestic politics to foreign policy as he desperately continued his attempt to exempt the United States from the fate of the "law." If he could not wrench the surplus energy from the bankers, he had to discover stores of new energy. Expansion provided the answer. Genuflecting before the frontier thesis, Adams noted that "the continent which, when Washington lived, gave a boundless field for the expansion of Americans, has been filled; and the risk of isolation promises to

[32] *Ibid.*, 4:3; Beringause, *Brooks Adams*, 122; Henry Adams, *The Letters of Henry Adams*, edited by Worthington Chauncey Ford (Boston and New York, 1930–1938), II, 100.

[33] Brooks Adams to Lodge, April 3, 1896, Lodge MSS; Donovan, *Henry Adams and Brooks Adams*, 90–93; Ford, "Memoir," 348; Beringause, *Brooks Adams*, 152.

be more serious than the risk of an alliance." A replacement would have to be found for the frontier. Tracing the movement of world empires, Brooks claimed he had found their key in the changing locations of the center of commercial exchanges. As he developed this idea, these centers had moved ever westward until now they had settled in London and Paris. But they would not remain there long. These centers would next move either east toward Germany and Russia, or westward toward the United States.[34]

To ensure America's rise to economic supremacy and thus repeal the "law" which he feared was slowly crushing the United States of the 1890's, Adams developed three lines of policy: encourage American efficiency through centralization so that the nation could compete successfully with other powers for stores of energy; help the United States gain control of Asia, that Far West which contained the potential energy for which the powers would compete; and, finally, discover a man brimming with martial spirit who would be willing to lead the American people on this crusade. Brooks Adams did not concern himself with small problems.

He believed that he had found his man on horseback in Theodore Roosevelt. Throughout 1897 and early 1898 Adams and Roosevelt believed that the approaching war with Spain would give them the opportunities they needed to repeal the "law." Moving into Henry's empty house on Washington's H Street, Brooks found as frequent dinner guests Cushman Davis, Chairman of the Senate Foreign Relations Committee, Henry Cabot

---

[34] Brooks Adams, "The Spanish War and the Equilibrium of the World," *Forum*, XXV (August, 1898), 641–651. Brooks filled out the skeleton of this theme in his post-1898 writings. The history of this idea of the westward movement of world empire is one of the most fascinating and least explored facets of intellectual history. For an 1878 evaluation based on the thesis that industrial supremacy is the key to empire, see Leonard Courtney, "The Migration of Centres of Industrial Energy," *Fortnightly Review*, XXX (December, 1878), 801–820. See also the section on Josiah Strong in this chapter.

Lodge, and Mahan. The *Law of Civilization and Decay* had made a resounding impact, nowhere more than in Washington. The first printing had sold out in three months, and Henry had made certain that all the Supreme Court Justices and the Cleveland cabinet received copies. Now, as the United States gathered its immense economic strength and approached armed conflict with Spain, leading figures of the McKinley administration proclaimed Brooks a prophet.[35]

During this period Brooks Adams, Roosevelt, and Lodge were, in the words of Arthur F. Beringause, "three musketeers in a world of perpetual war." Alfred Thayer Mahan became a fourth in 1897. Agreeing with much of Brooks's grand strategy, Mahan suggested the tactical details with which Brooks did not concern himself. Because of his technical knowledge as a naval officer, Mahan became not only the best known of the so-called intellectual expansionists of his time, but the most influential. Unlike Turner, Strong, and Adams, his significance for American foreign policy can be measured in such tangible terms as the 15,000-ton battleships built in the post-1889 period, which initiated the modern United States battleship fleet.

Mahan's approach to American expansion in the 1890's was less personal and more scholarly yet scarcely less dynamic than was Adams'. The austere, scholarly, arm-chair sailor-turned-prophet constructed a tightly knit historical justification of why and how his country could expand beyond its continental limits. Recent American historians have defined his philosophy as "mercantilistic imperialism." [36] No doubt an intense study of

[35] Roosevelt to Cecil Spring-Rice, May 29, 1897, Letterbooks, Theodore Roosevelt Papers, Library of Congress, Washington, D.C.; Beringause, *Brooks Adams*, 131–132, 129, 143, 156–161, 164–165; Williams, "The Frontier Thesis and American Foreign Policy," 387.

[36] William Livezey, *Mahan on Sea Power* (Norman, Okla., 1947), 48–49, 294–295; Harold and Margaret Sprout, *The Rise of American Naval Power, 1776–1918* (Princeton, 1946), 203; Foster Rhea Dulles, *The Imperial Years* (New York, 1956), 42. The following section, which compares the writings of the early mercantilists with Mahan's views appeared

seventeenth- and eighteenth-century mercantile empires heavily influenced Mahan's thinking. But characterizing him as a mercantilist tends to taint American expansion in the 1890's with strong mercantilist colors too, for his writings both reflected the reasons for, and directly stimulated the movement into, Latin America and the Pacific. Yet clearly, the industrial, financial, Darwinian, and humanitarian impulses of this decade only slightly resembled the forces of seventeenth-century mercantile expansion. Likewise, Mahan's thinking had few similarities with the conclusions of Thomas Mun, George Berkeley, and Daniel Defoe two centuries before.

A comparison of Mahan's thought with that of the early mercantilists reveals several insights into the nature of American expansion in the 1890's. Some of his tenets meshed perfectly with mercantilist principles. Both philosophies agreed upon the necessity of expansion. Both desired a favorable balance of trade. But on most points Mahan differed, and in doing so he demonstrated his recognition of the peculiar crisis that the United States faced at the end of the century. The mercantilists believed tariffs were necessary in order to enjoy favorable balances of trade; but Mahan praised Blaine's and McKinley's policy of reciprocity and their efforts to lower tariff walls. Viewing high tariffs as "essentially a defensive measure," Mahan, always on the offensive, stressed that "reciprocity, increased freedom of movement, is the logical corollary of expansion." Nor did Mahan agree with the mercantilist view that the state was an economic unit rather than a moral or religious one, or that the welfare of the state rated a higher priority than the welfare of the individual. Mahan drank deeply of the "White Man's Burden" elixir of his day, and this did not mix with the view of an amoral state which relegated the individual to an inferior status. Few seventeenth-century mercantilists would have agreed with his dictum, "Personal

---

in slightly expanded form in the author's "A Note on the 'Mercantilistic Imperialism' of Alfred Thayer Mahan," *Mississippi Valley Historical Review*, XLVIII (March, 1962), 674–685.

liberty is a greater need than political independence, the chief value of which is to insure the freedom of the individual." [37]

The two philosophies differed most notably, however, on the three fundamental issues of production, the merchant marine, and the nature of colonial empires. The mercantilist solicitude for production did not arise originally from a fear of overproduction, underemployment, or overpopulation. The desire for a favorable balance of trade which would result in an inflow of bullion caused seventeenth-century thinkers to want increased production. Mahan, however, said little about production as a means of bringing bullion into the country, and though he viewed production as both a means and an end, he emphasized it as an end in itself. Industrial efficiency led to the creation of a strong naval arm, but stating the problem this way reverses Mahan's

[37] I am deeply indebted to Curtis P. Nettels of Cornell University and William Appleman Williams of the University of Wisconsin, who gave me much of their time and many insights into the relationship of mercantilistic concepts and American history. The following are helpful in understanding mercantilist thought, especially as it related to the diplomatic world of the 1890's: E. F. Heckscher, *Mercantilism*, translated by Mendel Shapiro and edited by E. F. Soderlund (2nd ed.; London, 1955); Gustav F. von Schmoller, *The Mercantile System and Its Historical Significance* . . . , translated and edited by William J. Ashley (New York, 1896); Philip W. Buck, *The Politics of Mercantilism* (New York, 1942); Curtis P. Nettels, "British Mercantilism and the Economic Development of the Thirteen Colonies," *Journal of Economic History*, XII (Spring, 1952), 105–114. Some of these interpretations have been challenged in a series of articles by William D. Grampp. See especially his "The Liberal Elements in English Mercantilism," *Quarterly Journal of Economics*, LXVI (November, 1952), 465–501. For Mahan's views on the topics discussed in this paragraph, see A. T. Mahan, "Retrospect and Prospect," *Retrospect and Prospect* . . . (Boston, 1902), 19–22; Captain A. T. Mahan, "The United States Looking Outward," *The Interest of America in Sea Power, Present and Future* (Boston, 1897), 5; Livezey, *Mahan on Sea Power*, 82–83; A. T. Mahan, *From Sail to Steam: Recollections of a Naval Life* (New York and London, 1907), 324–325. For the differing mercantilist view, see Buck, *Politics of Mercantilism*, 14, 184; and Heckscher, *Mercantilism*, II, 286–292. For a good discussion of Mahan's emphasis on morality and his concern for the welfare of the individual, see Livezey, *Mahan on Sea Power*, 258–262.

priorities. He did not define a battleship navy as his ultimate objective, nor did he want to create a navy merely for its own sake. In the 1890's he did not seek military power for the sake of military power.[38]

Mahan grounded his thesis on the central characteristic of the United States of his time: it was an industrial complex which produced, or would soon be capable of producing, vast surpluses. In the first paragraph of his classic, *The Influence of Sea Power upon History, 1660–1783*, Mahan explained how this industrial expansion led to a rivalry for markets and sources of raw materials and would ultimately result in the need for sea power. He summarized his theory in a postulate: "In these three things—production, with the necessity of exchanging products, shipping, whereby the exchange is carried on, and colonies . . . —is to be found the key to much of the history, as well as of the policy, of nations bordering upon the sea." The order is all-important. Production leads to a need for shipping, which in turn creates the need for colonies.[39]

Mahan's neat postulate was peculiarly applicable to his own time, for he clearly understood the United States of the 1890's. His concern, stated in 1890, that ever increasing production would soon make necessary wider trade and markets, anticipated the somber, depression-ridden years of post-1893. Writing three years before Frederick Jackson Turner analyzed the disappearance of the American frontier, Mahan hinted its disappearance and pointed out the implications for America's future economic and political structure. He observed that the policies of the American government since 1865 had been "directed solely to

[38] See Mahan to Gen. Francis V. Greene, Sept. 17, 1900, Alfred Thayer Mahan Papers, Library of Congress, Washington, D.C. James C. Malin has caught the importance of Mahan's writings for the technology of the late nineteenth century in *The Contriving Brain and the Skillful Hand in the United States*, 344.

[39] A. T. Mahan, *The Influence of Sea Power upon History, 1660–1783* (Boston, 1890), 53, 28. This postulate is mentioned two more times in the famous first chapter, pages 70 and 83–84.

what has been called the first link in the chain which makes sea power." But "the increase of home consumption . . . did not keep up with the increase of forth-putting and facility of distribution offered by steam." The United States would thus have to embark upon a new frontier, for "whether they will or no, Americans must now begin to look outward. The growing production of the country demands it. An increasing volume of public sentiment demands it." The theoretical and actual had met; the productive capacity of the United States, having finally grown too great for its continental container and having lost its landed frontier, had to turn to the sea, its omnipresent frontier. The mercantilists had viewed production as a faculty to be stimulated and consolidated in order to develop its full capabilities of pulling wealth into the country. But Mahan dealt with a productive complex which had been stimulated by the government for years and had been centralized and coordinated by corporate managers. He was now concerned with the problem of keeping this society ongoing without the problems of underemployment and resulting social upheavals.[40]

Reversing the traditional American idea of the oceans as a barrier against European intrigue, Mahan compared the sea to "a great highway; or better, perhaps . . . a wide common, over which men pass in all directions." To traverse this "highway" a nation needed a merchant marine; Mahan made this the second part of his postulate. In his 1890 volume he expressed doubts whether a navy could be erected without the solid foundation of a carrying fleet.[41] This, however, was one of the few times in the decade that Mahan emphasized the necessity of a merchant marine. As the 1890's progressed, he could look about him and

[40] *Ibid.*, 83–84; Mahan, "A Twentieth-Century Outlook," *Interest of America in Sea Power*, 220–222; Mahan, "The United States Looking Outward," *ibid.*, 21–22. In their work which traces this centralization movement, Thomas C. Cochran and William Miller call the result the "corporate society" (*The Age of Enterprise: A Social History of Industrial America* [New York, 1942], 331).

[41] Mahan, *Influence of Sea Power upon History*, 25, 87–88.

conclude that in this respect his theory did not correspond to reality. Congress constructed a new battleship fleet, American businessmen focused their attention on foreign markets, the impetus for building an Isthmian canal accelerated, and Mahan himself became a prophet with honor in his own country. And all this occurred in spite of the minuteness of the American merchant marine.

Mahan's early theory had been misleading, for a nation no longer had to ship its goods in its own bottoms to become commercially prosperous. The exporting country only needed warships capable of protecting the carrying fleet, whether it be domestic or foreign. This was a crucial result of the industrial revolution; modern machinery and technological inventions had replaced the merchant marine as the process which determined the victors in the markets of the world. It is tempting to speculate that Mahan realized this, because after his initial outburst in 1890 he de-emphasized the merchant marine theme. But it is more probable that he neglected the middle link in his theory simply because he could see the third part (military sea power) becoming a reality without the second factor. In any case, this de-emphasis sharply differentiated Mahan's ideas from those of the early mercantilists. The latter not only were concerned about carrying their own goods, but encouraged their own nations to develop an entrepôt trade between foreign powers. When Mahan implicitly subordinated his merchant marine theme, he eliminated the central part of early mercantilist theory.[42]

Most important, Mahan differed from the British and French

[42] For contemporary statements of the early mercantilist view, see Buck, *The Politics of Mercantilism*, 107–108; for the early view of the entrepôt trade, see William Cunningham, *Growth of English Industry and Commerce in Modern Times: The Mercantile System* (Cambridge, Eng., 1912), 471–479. Livezey believes that Mahan paid less attention to merchant shipping because of America's comparative isolation (which afforded natural geographic protection) and because seasoned sailors from a merchant marine were of little value in the new technological navy (241–242).

mercantilists in the final part of his theory—the definition and purpose of colonies. The early writers wanted colonies as sources of raw materials, markets for surplus goods, and as areas for the settlement of a surplus or discontented population. They simply assumed the establishment of naval bases in these colonies. Mahan, however, separated these functions of colonies. They could serve "as outlets for the home products and as a nursery for commerce and shipping." He then stressed the second aspect (colonies as strategic naval bases) and set aside the first part (colonies as markets).[43]

It is especially in this crucial area—the purpose of colonial possessions—that Mahan becomes so dissimilar to the mercantilists, but so representative of the special characteristics of American expansion in the 1890's. To Mahan, William McKinley, Theodore Roosevelt, and Henry Cabot Lodge, colonial possessions, as these men defined such possessions, served as stepping stones to the two great prizes: the Latin-American and Asian markets. This policy much less resembled traditional colonialism than it did the new financial and industrial expansion of the 1850–1914 period. These men did not envision "colonizing" either Latin America or Asia. They did want both to exploit these areas economically and give them (especially Asia) the benefits of western, Christian civilization. To do this, these expansionists needed strategic bases from which shipping lanes and interior interests in Asia and Latin America could be protected.

In outlining his tactics, Mahan first demanded that the United States build an Isthmian canal. This would be the channel through which the Atlantic coast could "compete with Europe, on equal terms as to distance, for the markets of eastern Asia" and the markets on the western coast of Latin America. He viewed Hawaii through the same lens. The islands, once in American hands, would not only offset British naval dominance in the Pa-

[43] Mahan, *Influence of Sea Power upon History*, 55–58, 82–87; Mahan to B. Clark, Nov. 5, 1892, Mahan MSS.

cific, but, viewed in a postive way, be a major step in the "natural, necessary, irrepressible" American expansion into this western theater. But nothing better demonstrates Mahan's nonmercantilistic colonialism, strategic-bases philosophy than his view of the Philippines in 1898. As late as July, 1898, he still entertained doubts about annexing all the islands. He proposed to Lodge that the United States take only the Ladrones and Luzon (including, of course, the port of Manila), and allow Spain to keep the Carolines and the remainder of the Philippines. With the achievement of his double objectives of a battleship fleet and the occupation of strategic bases leading to the Asian and Latin-American markets, plus the writing of the Open-Door Notes to protect American commerce in China (Mahan actively advised John Hay while the State Department formulated the notes), the United States could repudiate once and for all a colonial empire in the mercantilist sense.[44]

Mahan had actually supplied the rationale for the open-door philosophy several years before the State Department issued the notes. He foresaw the advantages which commercial expansion possessed over further landed expansion. Most important, perhaps, he believed that commercial expansion would not cause political upheaval. Using French policy in the eighteenth century as an abject example, Mahan condemned France for pursuing a policy of expansion through land warfare when it had outlets to the sea. He quickly pointed to the lesson:

A fair conclusion is, that States having a good seaboard . . . will find it to their advantage to seek prosperity and extension by the way of sea and of commerce, rather than in attempts to unsettle and modify existing political arrangements in countries where a more

[44] Livezey, *Mahan on Sea Power*, 90–94, 181–183, 190–191; for Mahan's hope for an active United States in Latin America, see *Influence of Sea Power upon History*, 33–35, 324–326; also Alfred T. Mahan, "The Isthmus and Sea Power," *The Interest of America in Sea Power*, 99–100. See also W. D. Puleston, *Mahan: The Life and Work of Captain Alfred Thayer Mahan, U.S.N.* (New Haven, 1939), 186–187, 194.

or less long possession of power has . . . created national allegiance or political ties.[45]

Following these ideas to their conclusion, Mahan declared that, while financial and commercial control, rather than political, would lessen possible points of dispute, international conflict would not end. Here military sea power entered the theory, for "when a question arises of control over distant regions . . . it must ultimately be decided by naval power." Mahan emphasized that giant battleships, not commerce destroyers as American planners had earlier believed, would decide such conflicts, for only battleships could gain and maintain control of the sea. Mahan thus closed his circle: the foundation of an expansive policy is a nation's productive capacities that produce vast surpluses; these surpluses should preferably be sold in non-colonial areas in order to lessen political irritations; and sea power in the form of battleships enters the scheme to provide and protect lines of communication and to settle the conflicts which inevitably erupt from commercial rivalry, thus ensuring access to foreign markets for the surplus goods.[46]

The policy makers and other influential Americans who embraced Mahan's teachings made them a central part of the expansionist ideology of the 1890's. Albert Shaw, a close friend of Lodge, Roosevelt, and Mahan, advanced the Captain's ideas through the widely read pages of his newly established *Review of Reviews*. Book reviewers in the most popular periodicals of the day warmly received Mahan's voluminous writings. Theodore Roosevelt, perhaps the most important of these reviewers, emphasized the Captain's basic ideas in the *Atlantic Monthly* and then put these ideas into practice as Assistant Secretary of the Navy in 1897–1898 and later as President. Mahan and Roosevelt were the closest of friends and could often be found in the company of Brooks Adams, John Hay, and Lodge. Congressmen

[45] Mahan, *Influence of Sea Power upon History*, 324; also "A Twentieth-Century Outlook," *Interest of America in Sea Power*, 220–222.
[46] Mahan, *Influence of Sea Power upon History*, 416.

paid homage by plagiarizing not only ideas but phrases and paragraphs from Mahan's works in order to substantiate their own arguments for expansion.[47]

One of the more notable of Mahan's converts was Hilary Herbert, congressman from Alabama and then Secretary of the Navy in Cleveland's second administration. Herbert had been a devotee of small commerce-destroying cruisers, and deprecated both giant battleships and the training of men to operate these battleships in the newly established War College. After reading Mahan's work in 1893, Herbert reversed his opinion and saved the War College just as it was about to close its doors. More important, Mahan's books demonstrated to Herbert the superiority which a battleship fleet enjoyed over commerce-destroyers. By pushing through the naval appropriation acts of 1895 and 1896, Herbert can share with Benjamin Tracy the honor of being the founding father of the modern American navy. Mahan, in turn, can justly receive much of the credit for both Herbert's and Tracy's activities.[48]

Mahan, both the man and his writings, continued to receive tribute at home and abroad until his death in 1914. The course of Brooks Adams was not as triumphant. Roosevelt and Adams continued to try to repeal the "law" by meddling in Asia until 1906, when a rising Japan and a revolutionary Russia brought second thoughts to the President's mind about his Asian policies.

[47] Livezey, *Mahan on Sea Power*, 116, 171; *Congressional Record*, 53rd Cong., 3rd Sess., Feb. 15, 1895, 2249–2250; for Roosevelt's reviews see *Atlantic Monthly*, LXVI (October, 1890), especially 567, and *ibid.*, LXXI (April, 1893), 559; see also Theodore Roosevelt, "The Naval Policy of America as Outlined in Messages of the Presidents of the United States, from the Beginning to the Present Day," *Proceedings of the United States Naval Institute*, XXIII (1897), 509–522; Bald, "Expansionist Sentiment," ch. v.

[48] F. G. Chadwick to Mahan, Aug. 10, 1893, and Hilary Herbert to Mahan, Oct. 4, 1893, Mahan MSS; Mahan, *From Sail to Steam*, 296–297; see especially Herbert's *Annual Report* as Secretary of Navy in 1893 and 1896.

Brooks returned to the Adams home in Quincy, there to bury himself in a study of John Quincy Adams in an attempt to discover the point where the United States had made its first turn onto the road which had led to San Juan Hill and the Portsmouth Peace Conference. In 1919, eight years before his death, he admitted, "Each day I live I am less able to withstand the suspicion that the universe, far from being an expression of law originating in a single primary cause, is a chaos which admits of reaching no equilibrium, and with which man is doomed eternally and hopelessly to contend." The recantation, of course, came too late to mitigate his part in setting the United States on the course of her new empire during the 1890's.[49]

The Ideological Consensus

These four men typified and/or stimulated the thought of American expansionists in the 1890's. Their views provide a start (and this chapter pretends to be no more than that) in understanding the avowed reasons for accelerating the development of the new empire at the end of the century. In some respects these men disagreed with each other. But on some of the most vital issues they reached a substantial consensus.

All agreed with Turner that the 1890's marked the closing of "the first period of American history" and the beginning of a new epoch. They defined this as a crucial period partly because they discerned the disappearance of the landed frontier. Turner, of course, made this central to his thesis, but the other three men also recognized to a lesser degree the importance of the frontier in their writings. This frontier, as Turner declared, provided the economic support for political and social democracy. The others, using as evidence either the economic importance of the frontier and/or the glut of material wealth produced by American factories and farms, also interpreted the cause of the crisis in economic terms. This was the age of Economic Man, and these

[49] Beringause, *Brooks Adams*, 376; Ford, "Memoir," 355–356.

writers, as they traced the crisis to economic causes, reflected the emphasis of their time.[50]

Many Americans displayed their anxiety in one particularly fascinating way; they constantly compared their era with the late stages of the Roman Empire. Turner's most influential teacher at Wisconsin, William F. Allen, published in 1890 a seminal book on the Roman Empire, which opened to Turner new insights into American history. Brooks Adams made an extensive study of Rome in order to trace the working of the "law," and both he and Henry, although they preferred medieval history, were not above buttressing their pessimism with references from the three centuries after Augustus. Mahan's study of the Punic Wars had amazingly transformed him from an anti-imperialist in the early 1880's to the foremost exponent of an offensive policy in the following decade. He compared the "barbarians" of Asia in his own time with the barbarians on the Roman frontiers who remained peaceful while Caesar held a strong hand over them, but who overran Rome once the Empire's desire for peace made it soft. Cecil Spring-Rice, Secretary of the British Embassy in Washington and a close friend of Roosevelt and both Adamses, justifiably complained to a close friend after reading *Law of Civilization and Decay:* "Everyone has a new prescription for humanity and a new diagnosis. They all begin with the Roman Empire and point out resemblances." [51]

Americans balanced the pessimism and fear implicit in this

[50] For Mahan's views especially, see "Twentieth-Century Outlook," *Interest of America in Sea Power*, 220–222, and "Isthmus and Sea Power," *ibid.*, 71–72; for an interesting review which interpreted Mahan's doctrine as a quest for a new frontier, see "Nauticus," "Sea Power: Its Past and Its Future," *Fortnightly Review*, reprinted in *Proceedings of the United States Naval Institute*, XIX (1893), 460–484, especially 483.

[51] Turner, *Early Writings*, 27; Mahan, *From Sail to Steam*, 274–277; Mahan, "The Possibility of an Anglo-American Reunion," *Interest of America in Sea Power*, 118–122; *The Letters and Friendships of Cecil Spring-Rice: A Record*, edited by Stephen Gwynn (Boston and New York, 1929), I, 214.

analogy with the optimism and hope contained in the American version of Social Darwinism. Perhaps Social Darwinism was not the primary source of the expansionist ideology, but as Mahan wrote, " 'the struggle of life,' 'the race of life,' are phrases so familiar that we do not feel their significance till we stop to think of them." Perhaps Turner's essay of 1891 provided the neatest summary of this influence: "Historians have accepted the doctrine of Herder. Society grows. They have accepted the doctrine of Comte. Society is an organism." But it must be noted that other leading Social Darwinists, including John W. Burgess, E. L. Godkin, and William Graham Sumner, could discuss an evolving American society, yet draw back from a belligerent foreign policy or a Mahanian interpretation of "the struggle of life." [52]

American businessmen were trapped between the concepts of these two groups of intellectuals. Few disagreed with Andrew Carnegie's application of Spencer's ideas to the business community. After all, the increasing flow of American industrial goods into foreign markets after 1893 seemed to indicate that the fittest would indeed survive. This cycle of competition and American victories could not continue unbroken, however. The more perceptive Social Darwinists warned that the victors were often decided by violent as well as by peaceful competition. Mahan and Brooks Adams especially emphasized this bloody but necessary fact. When such a climactic occasion arose in 1898, however, the business community became hesitant. Wanting no war to disrupt the accelerating American industrial processes which were setting the pace in the race for survival,

[52] Richard Hofstadter, *Social Darwinism in American Thought* (Boston, 1955), 172. There is an especially good discussion in Bald, "Expansionist Sentiment," 56–69. See also Mahan, "United States Looking Outward," *Interest of America in Sea Power*, 18, and Turner, *Early Writings*, 52, 58. For the influence of Social Darwinism on the thought of Brooks and Henry Adams, see Donovan, *Henry Adams and Brooks Adams*, 87–93, 99. Julius W. Pratt, *Expansionists of 1898 . . .* (Baltimore, 1936), 6–12, has a good discussion of Burgess.

businessmen discovered that only war would prevent such disruption. Mahan, Adams, and Strong illuminate this paradox; they had thought out the process and divined the conclusion while businessmen, such as Carnegie, were still enjoying the fruits but unsuccessfully trying to evade the violent climaxes of Social Darwinism.

Realizing that Spencer's ideas had such sordid aspects, several of the intellectuals who are discussed in this chapter did not hesitate to use Social Darwinism as a justification for two related ideas: the use of military force in the struggle for survival; and cooperation with Great Britain to pave the way for the future assumption of power by the most fit of all the species, the Anglo-Saxon. No doubt Mahan contributed most to the glorification of military power and war, but when Brooks Adams concluded that only through the valor of the soldier could the American people escape the fiat of the "law," he differed only in slight degree from Mahan's extreme view. Even Strong realized that force might be necessary if the Anglo-Saxon hoped to carry out the will of the Almighty. This apotheosis of military power had several sources: the Social Darwinist emphasis on struggle determining the fittest in primitive times, the discovery of Nietzsche, the success of Bismarckian methods in western Europe, and the fear of some Americans that with the disappearance of the rough-and-tumble frontier their fellow countrymen were becoming flabby. Whatever the source, this admiration of force and war offered something new in American history, for with the possible exceptions of some of the inhabitants of the Old South and the pioneer's notions of how to deal with Indians, Americans had generally viewed war as an evil to be avoided, not cultivated.[53]

[53] Curti, *Growth of American Thought*, 673; Mahan, "The Future in Relation to American Naval Power," *Interest of America in Sea Power*, 140–141; Puleston, *Mahan*, 262–263. For a pioneering essay on the rise of the military spirit in the United States during the 1890's, see James C. Malin, *Confounded Rot about Napoleon: Reflections upon Science and Technology, Nationalism, World Depression of the Eighteen-*

A virulent strain of Anglo-Saxonism emerged from American nationalism and romanticism, but men such as James K. Hosmer, John W. Burgess, Mahan, and Strong made it particularly active and meaningful within the context of Social Darwinism. Paradoxically the belief in the superiority of the Anglo-Saxon gained popularity as the nation's economy slid into an almost continual twenty-year depression marked by violent social outbreaks. Americans could justify disposing their glut of goods and capital with the argument that the United States, blessed with so many of God's gifts, had the right to spread them around the world. In doing so, some writers candidly admitted that this was necessary also to save their own system from either anarchy or socialism. This theme particularly runs through Mahan's and Strong's writings.[54]

This expansive Anglo-Saxonism found its champion in John Fiske, perhaps the most popular public lecturer in American history. Fiske mixed Anglo-Saxonism, Social Darwinism, and expansionism in his widely known lecture and article of 1885, "Manifest Destiny." He gloried in the magnificent future of American industrial productivity and anticipated Mahan with a statement on "that sovereignty of the sea and . . . commercial supremacy." But Fiske was primarily concerned with the bloodless world-wide triumph of American federal institutions. This jovial, three-hundred-pound popularizer of the Good Life deprecated naked force, praying that "the victory of the industrial over the military type of civilization" would be shortly forthcoming. Unlike Mahan, Fiske saw American industrial power creating a world of peace, not friction that would flame into wars. It is a little-noted but significant fact that, when Fiske had to follow his expansive ideas to their conclusions and

---

Nineties, and Afterwards (Lawrence, Kan., 1961), especially 1–16, 159–161.

[54] Hofstadter, *Social Darwinism*, 172, 174; Curti, *Growth of American Thought*, 670–671; Puleston, *Mahan*, 171.

decide for or against the extension of the beneficent American political institutions to the Philippines in 1898, he had an extremely difficult time making up his mind.[55]

The popularization of the Anglo-Saxon mystique through such writings as Fiske's was a harbinger of the increasing cooperation between the State Department and the British Foreign Office. Many expansionists in Congress could not resist twisting the Lion's tail to delight their constituents; but others, like Mahan and Adams, who were not bothered by biennial elections, recognized the value of the developing Anglo-American alliance. They found it easier to go along with British policy in other parts of the world, moreover, once the Foreign Office had granted recognition of United States dominance in Latin America during the Venezuelan affair in 1895–1896. Mahan would not agree to an Anglo-American arbitration treaty, since he feared this would weaken the military preparedness of both nations, but he eloquently described the importance of the two great "islands," England and North America, putting their sea power in tandem in order to civilize the rest of the world. Brooks Adams, though an avowed Anglophobe when discussing British bankers, agreed with Mahan's ideas of Anglo-American cooperation in world politics, especially affairs in Asia.[56]

As the United States became more certain of its dominance in Latin America, American policy makers could afford to concentrate more of their attention on Asia. Each of the four men discussed in this chapter believed that the Orient was destined to be the next great theater of American overseas expansion, though Adams and Mahan stressed this belief more than Turner

[55] John Fiske, *American Political Ideas Viewed from the Standpoint of Universal History* (New York, 1885), 125, 138–139, 143–146, 148–151, 152; John Fiske, *The Letters of John Fiske,* edited by his daughter Ethel F. Fiske (New York, 1940), 673; Hofstadter, *Social Darwinism,* 176–178; Higham, *Strangers in the Land,* 32–33.

[56] For Adams, see Beringause, *Brooks Adams,* 170; for Mahan's views, see Mahan to Colonel John Sterling, Feb. 13, 1896, April 27, 1897, and Mahan to B. Clark, Jan. 17, 1896, Mahan MSS.

or Strong. But they could not debate just the matter of Asia. They knew that the Orient could be controlled only after the United States had completed several very difficult intermediate steps. Turner, who wrote of this process less than the other three, believed the development of the frontier had already fulfilled the prerequisites, but the others were much less sanguine. They pleaded for spiritual regeneration at home, increased efficiency of farms and factories, the building of a strong military power, and the taking of outlying islands in order to build a solid base for America's Asian empire.

Like Seward, they demanded a stable and prosperous American continent to serve as a springboard for conquests beyond the seas. But they also trapped themselves in the same dilemma which had ruined Seward's plans in the 1850's. On the one hand, they wanted a new empire to solve domestic problems of crisis proportions. On the other hand, they realized that only a nation which was spiritually, economically, and politically sound could create and maintain such an empire. American history has many paradoxes, but perhaps none is more important —or strange—than this paradox of the 1890's.

Turner, Strong, Adams, and Mahan, faced with the necessity of providing an immediate solution, could offer only expansion. Although they disagreed with each other on some points, all agreed on this conclusion. Their answer might seem trite, since expansion of one type or another characterizes all periods of American history. As used by these four men, however, this solution masked internal dynamics in American society which indicated a turning point in the nation's history. At the same time, their answer led the United States into the international power politics of the early twentieth century. They defined the paradox, then offered a solution which, though inadequate, nevertheless made the 1890's the watershed period of American history.

III

The Strategic Formulation

IN the hundredth year after George Washington had taken the oath as President of a newly reorganized American government, Benjamin Harrison repeated the now hallowed words and assumed the responsibility for starting the nation on its second century of existence. As the first hundred years had been distinguished by fantastic continental expansion and internal economic development, so the second century would have as its primary characteristic the attempt of the American people to grapple with the whirling complexities of involvements around the globe. The first ten years of this new century, 1889–1899, indicated the course the nation would follow. During this decade the United States entered not only a new century chronologically speaking but a virtually new world which ripped up the assumptions of the previous century and forced the American people to face the inexorable consequences of a lost security and a forfeited freedom of action. Fittingly, the first administration of the new century expressed many of the motivations and outlined the foreign policies that characterized the nation's broadening involvement in world affairs. Benjamin Harrison and his ambitious Secretary of State, James G. Blaine, formulated the strategy the builders of the new empire followed during the remainder of the 1890's.

These two men agreed on the essentials of the new empire, though a growing personal estrangement deprived their policies of much of the ordered symmetry which the tidy historian might desire. Harrison, the grandson of President William Henry Harrison, had risen through the ranks of the Republican party primarily because of his splendid war record, an unshakable devotion to the party, and his ability as a conscientious, hard-working, and self-contained Indiana lawyer. His intelligence was matched only by a forbidding reserve, which led one un-thawed visitor to remark that Harrison was the only man he ever knew who could carry a piece of ice in each pants pocket on a July afternoon and never lose a drop. Blaine, on the other hand, had dominated the Republican party for nearly twenty years with warmth, charm, and a political acumen few men could match.

Because of Blaine's influential friends and political standing, Harrison named him to the premiership of the cabinet, but the new President did so only after much pressure was exerted by such powerful Republicans as Murat Halstead, Stephen B. Elkins, Patrick Ford, and Whitelaw Reid. Harrison's distrust of Blaine's political ambitions and disputes between the two men on matters of patronage cooled their relations as early as 1890. This estrangement, combined with crippling attacks of what Blaine called lumbago and the Secretary's intense suffering over the deaths of his three eldest children in 1891 and early 1892, led to the Secretary of State's resignation in June, 1892, nearly a year before the administration finished its duties.[1]

During the three previous years, however, their views had coincided so closely that during the long months when Blaine

---

[1] *The Correspondence between Benjamin Harrison and James G. Blaine, 1882–1893*, collected and edited by Albert T. Volwiler (Philadelphia, 1940), 2–4, 6–17, 296, 299; S. B. Elkins to Gen. L. T. Michener, March 21, 1888, Benjamin Harrison papers, Library of Congress, Washington, D.C.; Patrick Ford to Harrison, Nov. 29, 1888, and Whitelaw Reid to Harrison, Nov. 30, 1888, Harrison MSS; see also Hale to Blaine, Nov. 21, 1888, Blaine MSS.

lay bedridden, Harrison could conduct much of the diplomatic correspondence in a manner which would arouse few disputes between the two men. Many of the administration's ambitious, expansive policies which have been ascribed to Blaine should in fact be more rightly credited to the President. Harrison has never received proper recognition as a creator of the new empire. His realization of this at the time widened the breach between himself and his Secretary of State. The President remarked with asperity to Senator Shelby Cullom in early 1892 that, although the White House had prepared foreign policy for more than a year, Blaine had insisted on taking the credit.[2]

The Assumptions and Objectives

The search for foreign markets dominated the administration's foreign policies. Campaigning in Indiana in 1888, Harrison had emphasized the protective tariff as the guardian of the home market. He attacked low tariff advocates, who, he insisted, wanted to replace the more valuable domestic market with the cheaper foreign variety. But several days later he remarked that, although the American markets must be preserved for American producers, "we do not mean to be content with our own market. We should seek to promote closer and more friendly commercial relations with the Central and South American states."[3]

After a year in office, Harrison found his administration besieged by both a panic which had originated in Europe and the embittered western cries of the Farmers' Alliance. Warned by his campaign manager that depressed agricultural prices threatened Republican victory hopes in the 1890 and 1892 elections, Harrison further dedicated himself to the philosophy of an expanded foreign trade. In his 1890 annual message, he assured Congress that, since he had been inducted into office, he had

[2] *Correspondence of Harrison and Blaine*, 3–4; Shelby M. Cullom, *Fifty Years of Public Service: Personal Recollections of Shelby M. Cullom* (Chicago, 1911), 252–253.

[3] Benjamin Harrison, *Speeches of Benjamin Harrison* . . . (New York, 1892), 110, 66, 68.

spared no effort in "the development of larger markets for our products, especially our farm products." In his 1891 message he candidly informed Congress that the United States had been saved from severe economic troubles only by the quickened flow of surplus agricultural goods into foreign markets.[4]

Harrison's words in 1890 and 1891 sounded like an echo of the policies which Blaine had widely publicized during the previous decade. In accepting the Republican nomination for the White House in 1884, the Plumed Knight had belittled the foreign market as compared with the great American home market. But he sandwiched this paragraph between two sections that sketched the amazing growth of foreign commerce under previous Republican administrations. Blaine then contrasted the old colonialism of Europe and one facet of the new empire of the United States: "While the great powers of Europe are steadily enlarging their colonial domination in Asia and Africa it is the especial province of this country to improve and expand its trade with the nations of America."[5]

On other occasions Blaine warned his countrymen that they had little choice in this question of extending their foreign trade. As Secretary of State in 1881 he had stressed the necessity of extracontinental involvements since the nation's "own vast resources fail to give full scope for the untiring energy of its citizens." The following year he described his foreign policy as one which had attempted to bring peace to, and increase American trade in, Latin America: "To attain the second object the first must be accomplished." But he made his most direct statement on the motivations and tenets of the new empire in a speech at Waterville, Maine, on August 29, 1890:

[4] L. T. Michener to Halford, Nov. 26, 1889, Harrison MSS; *Messages and Papers of the Presidents*, IX, 122–123, 206–207. The Ocala Platform of the new Populist party asked for the abolition of all national banks, a revenue tariff, increased currency, and nationalized communication and transportation systems.

[5] James G. Blaine, *Political Discussions, Legislative, Diplomatic, and Popular, 1856–1886* (Norwich, Conn., 1887), 425–426.

I wish to declare the opinion that the United States has reached a point where one of its highest duties is to enlarge the area of its foreign trade. Under the beneficent policy of protection we have developed a volume of manufactures which, in many departments, overruns the demands of the home market. In the field of agriculture, with the immense propulsion given in it by agricultural implements, we can do far more than produce breadstuffs and provisions for our own people. . . . Our great demand is expansion. I mean expansion of trade with countries where we can find profitable exchanges. We are not seeking annexation of territory. . . . At the same time I think we should be unwisely content if we did not seek to engage in what the younger Pitt so well termed annexation of trade.[6]

Although both Blaine and Harrison agreed on the necessity of expansion into foreign markets because of domestic overproduction, the Plumed Knight moved beyond the President in formulating systematic policies which would secure these desired objectives, especially markets in Latin America. The Secretary of State considered not only commercial expansion but also the non-economic implications of such expansion. He thought in terms of a hemispheric system based on peaceful intercourse, arbitral procedures for the settlement of disputes, and conferences that would deal with general inter-American issues. Blaine, more than any other statesman, personified the momentous change of his nation's attitude toward Latin America. Formerly concerned primarily with the exclusion of European powers, the United States now assumed a positive and constructive role in order to garner the benefits of peace and prosperity for the entire hemisphere, and especially for itself.[7]

[6] David Saville Muzzey, *James G. Blaine: A Political Idol of Other Days* (New York, 1935), 365; Blaine to Morgan, June 1, 1881, *Foreign Relations, 1881,* 761–762; Blaine, *Political Discussions,* 411. For the Waterville speech see New York *Tribune,* Aug. 30, 1890, 1:6. Tyler, *Foreign Policy of Blaine,* 362–365 has an excellent assessment of Blaine as a transitional figure in American diplomatic history.

[7] Blaine, *Political Discussions,* 411–419.

Blaine also delineated the relationship which would have to ensue between Europe (especially England) and Latin America if the United States hoped to fulfill its manifest destiny in the hemisphere. He enjoyed a reputation as one of the most adroit twisters of the British Lion's tail in American politics, no mean achievement at this time. He once told a British Minister, "England as against the United States was always wrong," and Blaine's friends freely circulated this and similar remarks at election time, especially among the Irish.[8]

Blaine, however, carefully controlled his anti-British passion in order to obtain maximum results. In defining the British threat to Latin America in 1882, he slighted its strategic aspects and emphasized England's increasing hold on Latin-American commerce. He feared that this wedge could lead to a British-controlled Isthmian canal and a European-inspired hemispheric alliance against United States interests. "If these tendencies are to be averted," Blaine warned, "if the commercial empire that legitimately belongs to us is to be ours, we must not lie idle and witness its transfer to others." [9]

Since he defined this battle in commercial terms, he believed the battle would be won or lost through economic efficiency and commercial advantages, not by vigorous finger waving under the British nose. Immediately after the 1888 election, Blaine advised Harrison to deal with England peacefully and patiently on the thorny questions of the Canadian fisheries and the seals in the Bering Sea. The Bering Sea dispute was finally solved after Blaine refused to meet the threat of British force with American force and instead restrained American sealers until a *modus vivendi* could be agreed upon. British Minister Sir Julian Pauncefote informed Lord Salisbury, the British Prime Minister, of an even more shocking example of Blaine's attitude. After hearing so much about the Secretary of State's famed Anglophobia,

---

[8] Muzzey, *Blaine*, 425, n. 1; Murat Halstead to Harrison, Dec. 7, 1888, Harrison MSS.

[9] Blaine, *Politial Discussions*, 418–419; Muzzey, *Blaine*, 195–196.

Pauncefote was astounded when Blaine arranged a "splendid" and "brilliant" party at Mount Vernon, complete with British flag and British national anthem, in Sir Julian's honor. Blaine maintained this conciliatory policy in spite of urgent requests from politicians who demanded anti-British pronouncements for home consumption. Blaine's treatment of England, together with his more constructive approach to hemispheric problems, amply indicates how he was no longer implementing the Monroe Doctrine with belligerent threats, but with a peaceful yet energetic policy of commercial expansion.[10]

The Secretary of State shared with the President two other ideas for the enlargement of foreign markets for American goods. At the request of New York businessmen and "friends in Congress," Harrison sent an American agent abroad in 1890 to lay the ground work for an international bimetallist agreement. The administration hoped that such an agreement would increase the nation's foreign trade and thus raise domestic prices and solve American difficulties in international exchanges. Blaine had earlier observed that the increased use of silver would be necessary in view of the "increasing commerce of the world," especially in Asia. Harrison began to de-emphasize this policy in 1891, however. Not only had the European powers refused to negotiate such an agreement, but after the Sherman Silver Purchase Act failed to raise the price of the metal in the United States, silver advocates began to espouse more radical measures which were repugnant to the administration.[11]

Harrison and Blaine also argued that an enlarged, subsidized

[10] Blaine to Harrison, Nov. 9, 1888, Harrison MSS; Blaine to Harrison, April 29, 1891, and March 6, 1892, *Correspondence of Harrison and Blaine;* Charles S. Campbell, Jr., "The Anglo-American Crisis in the Bering Sea, 1890–1891, *Mississippi Valley Historical Review,* XLVIII (December, 1961), 393–414; Pauncefote to Salisbury, May 10, 1889, Salisbury papers, Christ Church College, Oxford, Eng.

[11] Harrison to Blaine, Aug. 15, 1890, *Correspondence of Harrison and Blaine;* Blaine, *Political Discussions,* 433; *Messages and Papers of the Presidents,* IX, 194; Harrison, *Speeches,* 288–289.

American merchant marine would greatly increase the flow of goods to foreign markets. The President reiterated this point in his 1888 campaign and in his four annual messages. As befitted a representative of Maine, Blaine had long championed the cause of an improved merchant marine. He believed that no matter how cheaply a nation produced its goods, it had to have "special trade relations by treaty" and a great carrying fleet in order to retain foreign markets. After meeting with a committee of steamship owners in October, 1889, Harrison supported two bills in Congress: one granted mail subsidies to American steamship lines; the other promised bounties to American-owned vessels of more than five hundred tons which were built in the United States and used in foreign trade. The bills encountered sneering remarks from free traders such as Senator George G. Vest of Missouri, who sarcastically asked the protectionist Harrison-Blaine supporters: "What has become of the home market . . . ? Now there is a change as sudden and marvelous as that which came upon the great Apostle Paul as he journeyed from Jerusalem to Damascus. Now we must have free trade, the home market will not do." Congress passed the mail subsidy bill, but the House killed the bounty measure. Harrison and Blaine continued to insist on the rejected proposal, warning that without a great merchant marine the new reciprocity agreements would be "retarded and diminished." [12]

All these measures envisioned commercial, not landed, empire. As Secretary of State in 1881, Blaine had clearly enunciated his belief that the United States now viewed landed expansion as incompatible with its general interests. There were, however, two exceptions to this rule. He continued to hope for the annexation of Canada. Harrison summarized the second ex-

[12] Blaine, *Political Discussions*, 423–424, 416–417, 300–310, 186–193; Aaron Vanderbilt to Harrison, Oct. 23, 1889, Harrison MSS; John G. B. Hutchins, *The American Maritime Industries and Public Policy 1789–1914: An Economic History* (Cambridge, Mass., 1941), 437–438; *Messages and Papers of the Presidents*, IX, 56–58, 124–125, 322; *Congressional Record*, 51st Cong., 1st Sess., 6907–6909, 6916–6918.

ception to the rule in a personal letter to Blaine in October, 1891: "You know I am not much of an annexationist; though I do feel that in some directions, as to naval stations and points of influence, we must look forward to a departure from the too conservative opinions which have been held heretofore." [13]

The President had first outlined this strategic bases philosophy in his Inaugural Address when he declared that the United States would not use "coercion" in obtaining "convenient coaling stations" and "other trading privileges," but "having fairly obtained them . . . our consent will be necessary to any modification or impairment of the concession." Blaine told Harrison that he fully agreed with this approach: "I think there are only three places that are of value enough to be taken, that are not continental," the Secretary of State wrote in 1891. "One is Hawaii and the others are Cuba and Porto Rico." The last two would not be taken "for a generation. Hawaii may come up for decision at any unexpected hour and I hope we shall be prepared to decide it in the affirmative." The administration also considered the acquisition of the Danish West Indies, Samaná Bay in Santo Domingo, Môle St. Nicolas in Haiti, and a naval base at Chimbote, Peru. But when the Minister to France, Whitelaw Reid, approached the administration with an offer from Portugal of naval bases in Africa and on the Indian Ocean in return for American protection of Portuguese interests, Harrison told Reid that "it would be so flagrant a departure from the settled and traditional policy of this Government" that it could not "be thought of." [14]

[13] Blaine to Morgan, June 21, 1881, *Foreign Relations, 1881*, 768; Blaine to Harrison, Sept. 23, 1891, and Harrison to Blaine, Oct. 1, 1891, *Correspondence of Harrison and Blaine.*

[14] *Messages and Papers of the Presidents*, IX, 10; A. T. Volwiler, "Harrison, Blaine, and American Foreign Policy, 1889–1893," *Proceedings of the American Philosophical Society*, LXXIX (November, 1938), 637–639; Blaine to Harrison, Aug. 10, 1891, *Correspondence of Harrison and Blaine;* Reid to Harrison, Oct. 9, 1891, Harrison to Reid, July 12, 1891, Harrison to Reid, Oct. 21, 1891, all in Harrison MSS. For Harrison's

These attempts to obtain strategic bases can be understood only in terms of the administration's belief that future American commercial expansion would largely depend upon an American-controlled Isthmian canal. A future passageway in Central America would be the crucial link in the American chain of being which began with the production of surplus goods and ended in the dependence on foreign markets. The Maritime Canal Company had been organized in 1887 to construct a canal through Nicaragua. Four years later, Harrison asked Congress to take the major step of giving governmental guarantee of the company's bonds. In his annual message of 1891, the President even quoted a leading Democrat, Senator John T. Morgan, who had said that, regardless of the risk and cost, "the canal is the most important subject now connected with the commercial growth and progress of the United States." It should be observed that Harrison spoke of the canal in commercial, not strategic, terms. To ensure a more flexible and efficient policy in the area, Blaine pushed through Congress a measure that authorized an additional American Minister for Central America. Now instead of a single minister for the entire area, one man was responsible for Costa Rica, El Salvador, and Nicaragua, and another for Guatemala and Honduras.[15]

The Harrison-Blaine approach posited American control of this hemisphere. The administration's policies, climaxing in the Cleveland-Olney success in the Venezuelan affair of 1895–1896, laid the necessary groundwork for the establishment of a strong home base and the requisite freedom of action in the Western Hemisphere which allowed the McKinley administration to

---

interest in opening up trade in the Congo basin in Africa, see Harrison to Morgan, Feb. 8, 1892, Harrison MSS; on the Chimbote negotiations see Seward W. Livermore, "American Strategy Diplomacy in the South Pacific, 1890–1914," *Pacific Historical Review*, XII (March, 1943), 33–52.

[15] Harrison to Blaine, Jan. 17, 1889, Harrison MSS; Blaine to Harrison, Aug. 16, 1890, *Correspondence of Harrison and Blaine; Messages and Papers of the Presidents*, IX, 188–189; Williams, *Anglo-American Isthmian Diplomacy*, 287.

move into Asia. The McKinley-Hay policies for the Orient could be seriously considered only after the Harrison-Blaine policies had achieved success in the Americas. The Môle St. Nicolas, Hawaii, and reciprocity were to Harrison what the Philippines and the Open Door were to McKinley.

Pan-Americanism: "The Battle for a Market"

The quest of the Harrison administration for a new empire may be adequately examined in its policies regarding the construction of a battleship navy, Haiti, Chile, Samoa, and Hawaii. But perhaps Harrison and Blaine best demonstrated their grasp of the industrial revolution's significance for American foreign affairs when they formulated their Pan-American and tariff policies. Blaine had called a meeting of the American nations (with the exception of Canada) in 1881, but Frelinghuysen had withdrawn the invitations. The idea of such a general conference gained adherents during the decade, however. Congressmen William McKinley of Ohio and James B. McCreary of Kentucky, Senators William Frye of Maine and John T. Morgan of Alabama, and such publicists as Hinton Helper and William E. Curtis kept the issue before Congress and the people. The idea rapidly received popular, bipartisan support. In 1888 President Cleveland issued a call for a conference of Western Hemispheric nations (except Canada) to meet the following year in Washington. He hoped that it would consider the possibility of a customs union, inter-American rail and steamship lines, trademark and copyright laws, common silver coins, and arbitration treaties.[16]

Harrison and Blaine entertained high hopes for the proposed conference. They chose the United States commission carefully;

[16] *International American Conference, Reports of Committees and Discussion Thereon* (Washington, D.C., 1890), I, 7–8 (V, 293–375, contains an excellent summary of speeches and resolutions in the United States Congress during the 1880's); Blaine, *Political Discussions*, 403–406; Tyler, *Foreign Policy of Blaine*, 166–174; Arthur P. Whitaker, *The Western Hemisphere Idea: Its Rise and Decline* (Ithaca, N.Y., 1954), 77.

Blaine, for example, rejected the name of William R. Grace, who had widespread banking and shipping interests in Latin America, because Grace was "too largely involved in Chilian and Peruvian affairs to act as *American* Commr." But the results of this first Inter-American Conference proved disappointing. The delegates early disposed of the customs union idea as impractical, and then only seven delegations agreed to Blaine's pet idea of an arbitration treaty. The conference did agree on recommending an inter-American bank (which Harrison unsuccessfully tried to sell to Congress); an intercontinental railroad commission (which after a slow start produced the beginnings of the railroad in the twentieth century); and the establishment of the Commercial Bureau of the American Republics, which, in the words of Blaine's contemporary biographer, "became a permanent branch of the State Department and a true intelligence office regarding the Western hemisphere." Goodwill also gushed from a 6,000-mile trip through forty-one American industrial centers. The delegates enjoyed this excursion on a special train which was modestly described as representing "a money value of $150,000," and "whose elegance, comfort, and luxury a fairy prince might covet." [17]

One final result proved to be of most importance for the Harrison administration. After rejecting the customs union idea, the conference suggested reciprocity treaties. Some delegates, especially those from Argentina and Chile, attacked this recommendation on the ground that the United States produced many of the same raw materials which Latin America possessed, and this similarity, they believed, made impossible any real reciprocal trade. Anyway, these delegates observed, at the very time the conference was meeting, committees in the House of Representatives were busily jacking up the American tariff wall in

[17] Blaine to Harrison, Aug. 25, 1889, *Correspondence of Harrison and Blaine;* see also *ibid.,* 101, 110–112; *International American Conference,* I, 73, and III, 3–4; *Public Opinion,* April 13, 1889, 16–17. The biographer quoted is Gail Hamilton [Mary Abigail Dodge], *Biography of James G. Blaine* (Norwich, Conn., 1895), 680.

order to discourage imports. The conference nevertheless recommended such treaties. Blaine seized on this opportunity to revive his decade-old dream of rechanneling the Latin-American–European current of goods into a Latin-American–United States stream—to make the flow of trade run uphill, as one critic observed. Anticipating a mid-twentieth-century dilemma, Blaine began worrying about his country's unfavorable trade balance with Latin America. The resulting deficit balance of payments was depleting the United States gold reserves. He believed increased exports to be the solution. American commercial journals agreed with him and heartily endorsed the reciprocity recommendations of the conference.[18]

But Congress proved less enthusiastic. Although Blaine made an impassioned plea for reciprocity to the House Ways and Means Committee in February, 1890, the House passed the tariff bill on May 21 without a reciprocity clause. The Secretary of State then joined battle in the Senate. On June 19, Senator Eugene Hale of Blaine's home state of Maine proposed a far-reaching measure (inspired by the Secretary of State) which if passed would have included Canada as well as Latin America, and also would have provided for virtually free trade in raw materials. The amendment gained few adherents, and Hale himself later disavowed it.[19]

Blaine began encountering problems which could not be solved by a simple amendment. To make advantageous reciprocity treaties he needed goods with which to bargain. Markets for wool and sugar would be especially attractive to the several Latin-American nations that exported large quantities of these

[18] See *International American Conference*, I, 103–265, for the debates and criticism of the American position on the tariff; Blaine, *Political Discussions*, 418; see the summary of press opinion on the Inter-American Conference in *Public Opinion*, Nov. 2, 1889, 77–80, and in Bald, "Expansionist Sentiment," 135–137.

[19] Laughlin and Willis, *Reciprocity*, 178–179; Muzzey, *Blaine*, 444; *Senate Executive Document No. 158*, 51st Cong., 1st Sess. (serial 2688), 2–6; Hale's position is given in *Congressional Record*, 51st Cong., 1st Sess., 6256, 6259; *ibid.*, 53rd Cong., 2nd Sess., 6987.

two products. But in response to powerful lobbies, McKinley, who managed the bill through the House, raised the wool tariff virtually out of sight, thus serving notice that this duty was not negotiable. This left only sugar as a possible bargaining card. Again McKinley dashed Blaine's hopes by putting sugar on the free list. This gave the Latin-American sugar-producing nations free entry into the rich American market without the exaction of any trade concessions in return. Blaine and Harrison believed this to be economic idiocy. But the gift of free sugar in an election year, plus the fact that sugar revenues were largely responsible for the embarrassingly huge Treasury surplus, led Congress to exalt its action as a choice example of political astuteness. Staunch protectionists, meanwhile, attacked reciprocity as subversion of high tariff principles. Free trade advocates, however, complained that Blaine's idea would not work extensively enough to suit their tastes. In early June the chances for reciprocity grew less and less.[20]

Making the last great political effort of his career, Blaine refused to give up. As Washington endured the dog days of July and early August, the Secretary's arguments slowly but perceptibly gained adherents. The major breakthrough occurred in mid-June when the Senate Finance Committee hit upon a way to obtain both free sugar and reciprocity. As Blaine phrased it in a letter of July 23, reciprocity could be reconciled with free sugar "by inserting a proviso that if . . . the States or Colonies from which we derive sugar shall not by their laws or by treaty give us reciprocal advantages a duty shall go upon sugar from such states." It is difficult to determine whether Harrison, Blaine, or a member of Congress divined this solution first. It was probably Blaine. But there can be no doubt that it passed the upper house principally because the President lobbied intensely for the

---

[20] Laughlin and Willis, *Reciprocity*, 180; Hamilton, *Blaine*, 683; McKinley to Blaine, Dec. 9, 1891, Blaine MSS; *Messages and Papers of the Presidents*, IX, 74; *Congressional Record*, 51st Congress, 1st Sess., 9005, 9549.

proviso. Harrison sweated through dinner parties and conferences planned to bring together congressmen chary of the reciprocity issue, while an ailing Blaine enjoyed the sea breezes at
Bar Harbor.[21]

The President received crucial support from three sources.
The Senate approved the amendment, but it still had to run the
gamut of obstacles in the House. Here McKinley took control
and shepherded the amendment safely around the many pitfalls.
The Ohio Republican had been impressed with Blaine's idea
after several meetings in the congressman's Ebbitt Hotel room.
As McKinley saw the tariff rates rocket upwards, he became
fearful of the possible political consequences. He ameliorated
conditions somewhat by including a proviso giving a 99 per cent
drawback on raw materials imported for the manufacture of
finished goods which would be, in turn, exported. Proclaiming
to foreign trade expansionists, "Here is the opportunity for
you," McKinley could naturally view reciprocity as the supplement of the free raw materials clause; it would provide the
markets for the final disposal of finished goods. Other protectionists in both houses lined up with the measure, including
Justin Morrill, who heretofore had sworn that the Executive
had no constitutional right to make reciprocity agreements. For
virtually the first time, high tariff advocates had taken reciprocity from the free trade arsenal (where European economists had
long assumed it belonged) and had forged it into a weapon
which projected surplus goods over the reinforced high tariff
wall and out into the markets of the world.[22]

[21] Blaine to Harrison, July 19, 21, 22, 23, 1890, and Harrison to Blaine,
Oct. 1, 1891, *Correspondence of Harrison and Blaine;* Laughlin and Willis,
Reciprocity, 178; Hamilton, *Blaine,* 687. For the contemporary debate
over who should have received credit for thinking of the reciprocity
amendment, see P. C. Cheyney to Gen. L. T. Michener, March 23, 1893,
Nelson Aldrich papers, Library of Congress, Washington, D.C.; also
comments of A. T. Volwiler in Aldrich MSS, notes of Jeanette Nichols.
[22] For a particularly effective speech on the values of reciprocity, see
Gilbert Pierce's long effort on Sept. 3, 1890, in *Congressional Record,*
51st Cong., 1st Sess., 9605–9613. Pierce, who proposed a reciprocity

Blaine had especially hoped that reciprocity would open markets for the glut of agricultural goods flooding out of the trans-Mississippi region. When agrarians realized the importance of the amendment, they provided a second major source of support. Concerned about the weakening of the Republican party among western farmers because of the silver issue, Blaine complained in an open letter that, as reported out by the House committee, not a line in the tariff bill would "open a market for another bushel of wheat or another barrel of pork." Instead, "our foreign market for breadstuffs grows narrower." Free traders such as Senator George Vest of Missouri assailed as ludicrous the idea that American farmers could find markets in the great wheat and beef areas of Latin America. "All this talk of reciprocity and pan-American conventions and brass bands and terrapin and champagne is the merest froth and rot," Vest blared. But another western free trader admitted, "Blaine's plan has run like a prairie fire all over my district." Officials of the Farmers' Alliance and other agrarian groups began to exert pressure on behalf of the bill. As one senator explained, the farmers wanted free sugar, but they also wanted wider markets. Reciprocity promised both.[23]

---

amendment on July 18, began his discussion by noting that "someone" had said: "Whoever commands the sea commands the trade, and whoever commands the trade of the world commands the riches of the world and consequently the world itself." Pierce believed the reciprocity amendment aimed at, "not to be too sanguine or hopeful, ultimately commanding the world." See also T. B. Reed to McKinley, Jan. 30, 1892, William McKinley papers, Library of Congress, Washington, D.C. There is a good discussion in H. Wayne Morgan, "The Congressional Career of William McKinley" (unpublished Ph.D. dissertation, University of California, Los Angeles, 1960), 145–146, 148, 178–183. On the vital issue of reconciling "most-favored-nation" clauses with reciprocity, see Harrison's pronouncement which settled the issue in *Messages and Papers of the Presidents*, IX, 123.

[23] New York *Tribune*, July 15, 1890, 2:1; July 26, 1890, 1:5; Muzzey, *Blaine*, 445–447; Hamilton, *Blaine*, 687–688; Laughlin and Willis, *Reciprocity*, 189–190; *Congressional Record*, 51st Cong., 1st Sess., 7803–7808, 9938.

One "prominent Western Republican," as the New York *Tribune* labeled him, insisted that reciprocity would not help the farmer, but noted that he had received a letter from a harvester manufacturer in his state who said that 2,800 of his company's harvesters had been sold in Argentina alone, and that the Latin-American demand should now steadily increase. Industrial journals agreed. *Iron Age*, The Chattanooga *Tradesman*, *American Manufacturer and Iron World*, and the *Dry Goods Economist* echoed the *Age of Steel's* virile belief that reciprocity would "annex territories and markets from under the muzzles of its competitors' guns," and be a "mapmaker" in expanding American industrial power. Even the arch anti-imperialist *Harper's Weekly* approved reciprocity because mature American industries "look out into the world, and feel ready for its strife and eager for its prizes." Blaine played to this sentiment of manufacturers in his open letters written during the summer of 1890. This third major source of support provided much-needed help when the bill reached its final stages in September.[24]

The reciprocity amendment was assured of passage when the support of these forces became apparent in August. The Senate passed the clause 37-28 with 19 abstentions. As McKinley prepared to drive the measure through the House, the bill seemed certain of success, but Blaine took no chances. In his most explosive and brilliant speech on the subject, the Secretary of State explained to a cheering Waterville, Maine, audience the facts of American industrial life. Bragging that protectionist policies had allowed the United States to reach "a point where one of its highest duties is to enlarge the area of its foreign

[24] See the testimonial signed by a long list of New York merchants representing $50,000,000 of investments which was given to Blaine in appreciation of the Secretary's fight for reciprocity, New York *Tribune*, Feb. 28, 1891, 1:4; also Chattanooga *Tradesman*, Feb. 15, 1891, 48–49; Bald, "Expansionist Sentiment," 161–162; Laughlin and Willis, *Reciprocity*, 111–112, 205; Blaine to Harrison, July 24, 1890, *Correspondence of Harrison and Blaine*. Blaine's letter to the editor of the Boston *Journal* in New York *Tribune*, Sept. 17, 1890, 1:6, stresses markets for leather products.

trade," Blaine graphically described how mechanization was producing a plethora of agricultural and industrial goods. Production could not be cut back; "it would not be an ambitious destiny for so great a country as ours to manufacture only what we consume, or to produce only what we eat." The United States wanted to find no more outlets through the annexation of territory, but only through the "annexation of trade." Moreover, Blaine concluded, unless its foreign trade expanded, the United States would have trouble with specie payments. Reciprocity treaties, especially with Latin America, would help to solve all of these problems. The Secretary's speech received a warm welcome from commercial journals.[25]

Harrison signed the tariff bill into law on October 1. The reciprocity provision gave him the power to suspend by proclamation the entrance of sugar, molasses, coffee, tea, and hides from another country into the United States whenever he found that the other country discriminated against American exports in a manner which "he may deem to be reciprocally unequal and unreasonable." Blaine immediately notified the Latin-American nations of the act. Under threat of exclusion of their staple exports from the American market unless they signed reciprocity treaties, all except Colombia, Haiti, and Venezuela entered into such pacts. Harrison promptly reimposed the former duties on the goods from these three nations.

Overall the agreements did little to increase American exports or imports, although exact assessment is difficult because the 1890 depression and bad crops in Latin America from 1891 to 1893 hurt buying power. But in certain areas the treaties had a most significant effect. Two classes of exports—flour, grains, and meat products, on the one hand, and railroad iron, building materials, and machinery, on the other—greatly benefited. Trade with Brazil and the West Indies became especially more important. But nowhere did reciprocity have greater effect than in

[25] New York *Tribune*, Aug. 30, 1890, 1:6. For a good summary of the reaction, see Bald, "Expansionist Sentiment," 122–123.

Cuba. Its exports to the United States jumped from $54,000,000 in 1891 to $79,000,000 in 1893. When the 1894 tariff removed the reciprocity provision, the Cuban economy collapsed and became the spawning ground for the revolution which climaxed in the Spanish-American War. The Harrison administration also achieved some notable successes in opening the west-European market to American goods. A reciprocity agreement with Germany allowed American pork into an area where it had previously faced stiff discriminations. Hawaii, however, lost its favored position granted by the reciprocity treaty of 1887. After Harrison and Blaine unsuccessfully tried to restore the former dispensation, Hawaii provided a preview of the later Cuban situation by sliding into economic chaos and then into revolution in 1893.[26]

One of the more interesting results of the reciprocity battle was its effect on Harrison's views. In defending the home market he had frequently declared, "If the farmer could deliver his surplus produce to the consumer out of his farm-wagon his independence and his profits would be larger and surer." In 1891 the President set out on a long cross-country trip during which this theme virtually disappeared in the wake of his enthusiasm for the expansion of foreign trade.

At Galveston, Texas, Harrison discussed the problem of taking Latin-American markets away from the European powers, bragged how the Inter-American Conference and reciprocity pacts made a good start toward this end, and then concluded that the job could be finished if the United States had a subsidized merchant marine and steamship lines. At San Francisco the President reiterated the need for a carrying fleet and put

---

[26] Laughlin and Willis, *Reciprocity*, 212–214, ch. vii; John L. Gignilliat, "Pigs, Politics, and Protection: The European Boycott of American Pork, 1879–1891," *Agricultural History*, XXXV (January, 1961), 3–12. There are many letters in the Harrison MSS on the European discriminations against American meat products; a summary is in Harrison to Reid, Oct. 21, 1891.

new emphasis on the Nicaraguan canal project. While traveling eastward, he constantly stressed the need to solve the problem of disposing of the nation's surplus goods. After using the farm wagon analogy when speaking to an Omaha, Nebraska, audience, he then added, "We have a surplus production in these great valleys for which we must seek foreign markets." By the time the Presidential Special had reached Vermont, Harrison was proclaiming the need to do "battle for a market" throughout the world. The United States coveted no territory, but "we have come to a time in our development" when surplus capital and an overabundance of goods forced the nation to demand a greater foreign commerce. "Larger foreign markets, . . . peaceful relations with all mankind, with naval and coast defences that will silently make an effective argument on the side of peace, are the policies that I would pursue." Harrison had confirmed the assessment of Sir Alexander Galt, Canada's leading financial expert: "The American tariff is . . . an act of commercial war." [27]

The Beginnings of the Modern Battleship Navy

Commercial war could easily flash into a military conflict. This was the lesson Alfred Thayer Mahan taught in his influential writings published after 1890. Between 1889 and 1892 other new empire expansionists arrived at the same conclusion in a series of significant congressional debates. The result was the creation of the United States battleship fleet.

Although the modern navy had its origins in the appropriation act of 1883, this and following measures authorized the building of small, unarmored cruisers in the range of 7,000 to 7,500 tons, vessels capable only of hit-and-run destruction of commerce. The argument, later associated with Mahan, for large

[27] Harrison, *Speeches*, 287, 325, 388, 409, 415, 467–468, 499–500, 522, 540–541; also see the President's commendation of reciprocity in *Messages and Papers of the Presidents*, IX, 313.

armored battleships which could enjoy a wide cruising range and hold their own in pitched major naval battles on the high seas found inadequate support.

A congressional consensus on the battleship theory occurred after the arrival of Benjamin F. Tracy as Harrison's Secretary of the Navy. The two events were directly related. The President-elect had named Tracy in an effort to mollify competing Republican factions in New York, but Harrison had done so only after receiving assurance from several close advisers that Tracy could handle a post which the Chief Executive regarded "as one of the most important in my Cabinet." As the Boston *Journal* reported, Congress was in a big-navy mood, and no cabinet post promised "more to statesmen who are ambitious to increase their reputations." A leading lawyer and judge in New York during the 1870's and 1880's, Tracy fully lived up to expectations. Besides initiating the battleship fleet, he organized the Bureau of Construction and Repair to eliminate much of the red tape which had restricted the designing and building of new ships. He also established the Naval Reserve in 1891, issued a contract for the first American submarine in 1893, presided over the production of the first heavy rapid-fire guns, smokeless powder, torpedoes, and heavy armor, and reversed a former Navy Department decision in order to save the Naval War College, where Mahan's *The Influence of Sea Power upon History* was gestating.[28]

Tracy's first annual report in December, 1889, set the new battleship navy on its course, but the Secretary received much help in properly arranging the stage for rapid congressional action. While writing the report, he worked closely with Senator Eugene Hale, a powerful big-navy advocate from Maine. The confrontation of American and German naval units at

[28] Harrison to Elkins, Jan. 18 and 21, 1889, Harrison MSS; "Private Memoranda" in *Correspondence of Harrison and Blaine*, 300; *Public Opinion*, Feb. 9, 1889, 364; *Annual Report of the Secretary of the Navy, 1892*, 6–7; Volwiler, "Harrison, Blaine . . . 1889–1893," 638.

Samoa earlier in the year made some reticent Americans realize the power implications of expansion into the closed frontiers of the South Pacific. Finally, Tracy's report was followed by a message from the Naval Policy Board, which made the Secretary's paper seem almost antiexpansionist. Reiterating the concepts of the new empire theory, the naval officers on the board noted that the United States wanted no colonies, but that the nation would have to protect its expanding foreign trade. The officers then asked for 200 ships, including a fleet of battleships with a cruising range of 15,000 miles. Extreme expansionists, including the leaders of the House Committee on Naval Affairs, found in this report much ammunition for their arguments; more moderate expansionists, such as Hale, disclaimed the paper and used it to illustrate to their conservative colleagues just how moderate Tracy's demands really were.[29]

Although it was moderate relative to the board's report, the Secretary's 1889 message was nevertheless epochal. Tracy demanded a fleet not for "conquest, but defense." He defined a defensive fleet, however, quite differently from those who advocated fast cruisers for purposes of hit-and-run destroying of commerce. In words that could (and might) have been plagiarized from Mahan's manuscript, Tracy wrote: "We must have the force to raise blockades. . . . Finally, we must be able" to attack an enemy's own coast, "for a war, though defensive in principle, may be conducted most effectively by being offensive in its operations."

He then easily switched to the offensive: "The nation that is ready to strike the first blow will gain an advantage which its antagonist can never offset." Tracy evidently believed defense meant deterrent first-strike capability. He realized such a navy would be expensive, but "it is the premium paid by the United

---

[29] Hale to Tracy, Oct. 20, 1889, Benjamin Tracy papers, Library of Congress, Washington, D.C.; Sprout, *Rise of American Naval Power*, 206–211; "Report of Policy Board," *Proceedings of the United States Naval Institute*, XVI (1890), 201–273.

States for the insurance of its acquired wealth and its growing industries." The Secretary predicted that the theaters of future naval action would be the Gulf of Mexico and the Pacific, areas where American interests had grown so rapidly and were "too important to be left longer unprotected." He demanded two fleets of battleships, eight in the Pacific and twelve in the Atlantic, and asked for eight such capital ships immediately. He also requested five more first-class cruisers and "at least five" torpedo boats.[30]

Tracy momentarily dropped his efforts to drive these measures through Congress when he lost his wife and younger daughter in a fire which swept their Washington home in February, 1890. But as Tracy grieved, big-navy advocates such as Hale and Representatives Charles A. Boutelle of Maine and Henry Cabot Lodge of Massachusetts rapidly took up the cudgels. In introducing the 1890 measure, which called for three armored battleships, Boutelle explained that the Naval Affairs Committee had had a choice of either larger, far-ranging armored vessels which could "go to any part of the world," or armored 8,500-ton ships which could capably protect the coasts of North and Central America. The committee chose the latter in the belief that there should be "evolution" toward greater battleships. This disarmed some opponents, as did Lodge's shrewd suggestion in committee that the ships be called "sea-going, *coastline* battleships." Opposition nevertheless appeared from several factions: those who rightly termed the bill a "new departure" and refused to strike out on a course which might have so many unpredictable consequences; those who believed that for defensive "coastline" purposes old-fashioned monitors would be more effective than battleships; those who stuck with the commerce-destroying thesis and so wanted only smaller, cheaper cruisers; those willing to vote only for land defenses in harbors;

[30] *Report of the Secretary of the Navy, 1889,* 3–50; *Sprout, Rise of American Naval Power,* 207.

and those wanting as little as possible on grounds of economy.[31]

But these arguments made few inroads on a Congress which had grown amazingly offensive-minded since 1888. Assuming extracontinental commercial expansion as a fact of life, the big-navy advocates proceeded to draw all the conclusions. They sketched horrible pictures of a possible war with the great commercial competitor, Great Britain. Hale pointed out several times that "we have got to be so that we can strike Bermuda, the West Indies, and Halifax . . . and the seas round about." Senator Joseph R. Hawley of Connecticut added that when in trouble with England "you can not negotiate without a gun." Hawley was also among those who based his argument for battleships on the necessity of safeguarding the future Isthmian commercial thoroughfare.

When some Populists arose to dispute the arguments for a powerful navy, they met quick challenges from other westerners who had a better grasp of the situation. "We have grown to first rank among commercial nations," proclaimed Jonathan Dolliver of Iowa. "We must have ships, not to make war on anybody, but to keep other people from disturbing either our prestige or our rights." The recalcitrant westerners also received a warning from William A. McAdoo of New Jersey (destined to be Assistant Secretary of the Navy under Cleveland, 1893–1897): "One month of blockade of our ports on the seacoast and you would burn more corn in Kansas than you now do. One month's blockade on the Pacific coast and you would find your trade with the Orient cut off." With obvious sectional and partisan divisions, Congress authorized the three first-class battleships and a 7,300-ton cruiser. The new empire expansionists had begun to acquire an adequate military arm.[32]

[31] *Congressional Record*, 51st Cong., 1st Sess., 3163–3164, 3166, 3170, 3258, 3267, 5175, 5296. See the minority report of the Senate Naval Affairs Committee in *Senate Report No. 174*, 51st Cong., 1st Sess. (serial 2703), especially 1–7.

[32] *Congressional Record*, 51st Cong., 1st Sess., 3167–3169, 5227–5228,

When Tracy returned to make similar requests in his 1890 report, he found a lame-duck Republican Congress reluctant to cooperate. But in 1891 the Secretary submitted a report which ranks with his famous 1889 paper. He warned: "Commercial supremacy by a European power in . . . the Western Hemisphere means the exclusion of American influence and the virtual destruction, as far as that state is concerned, of independent existence. With the great maritime powers it is only a step from commercial control to territorial control." Stressing the "rapid extension of commercial relations" in the area, Tracy predicted "a great rivalry of three or four nations in the Pacific for the commerce of those seas." In fact, he reported, "the rivalry has already begun, and the signs are evident on every hand of sharp competition." The Senate, led by Hale and Frank Hiscock of New York, forced the House to accept one battleship. The most significant result, however, was the type of ship appropriated. Tracy later called it "seagoing battleship No. 1" and noted how its increased coal supply gave it a much greater "radius of action" than the ships appropriated in 1890 enjoyed. The 1892 vessel, which gained fame as the "Iowa," was a most important step upward in what Boutelle had termed the "evolution" of the American navy.[33]

Harrison had fully backed his Secretary of the Navy, even rephrasing Tracy's commercial arguments for a larger navy in presidential messages. When Harrison and Tracy entered office in 1889, the United States ranked between the twelfth and seventeenth notches among the navies of the world. When they left Washington four years later, the United States occupied

5288. There is an interesting note on the committee infighting in A. C. Buell to Charles Cramp, Sept. 17, 1891, Tracy MSS.

[33] *Annual Report of the Secretary of the Navy, 1891,* 30–34. Andrew Carnegie was ecstatic over Tracy's 1891 message; see Carnegie to Tracy, Dec. 8, 1891, Tracy MSS. Tracy's comment on the 1892 battleship is in his *Annual Report, 1892,* 14, 4. Also *Congressional Record,* 52nd Cong., 1st Sess., 3222–3225, 3270, 3362, 4357–4358, 3329, 4258, 4266. See Hiscock's important speech in *ibid.,* 4321–4322.

seventh place and was climbing rapidly. Tracy had boasted in an interview in 1891: "The sea will be the future seat of empire. And we shall rule it as certainly as the sun doth rise." In preparing the United States to occupy this "seat of empire," Tracy had few equals.[34]

The Haitian Revolution

When it entered office, the Harrison administration inherited a marvelous opportunity to acquire a naval base in the Caribbean for the New Navy and to gain added advantages for American commerce as well. A revolution had erupted in Haiti, and the nation had divided into a northern faction, headed by the forces of Hyppolite, and the southern group, led by Legitime. The latter claimed control of the nation's government. As European, especially French, influence swung behind Legitime, the Cleveland administration began to show marked favor toward the northern movement. This favor increased in December, 1888, when Hyppolite's agents indicated to American representatives that, if sufficient aid could be gathered to put Hyppolite into control, the United States would be rewarded with a new commercial agreement and perhaps even the valuable Haitian naval base of Môle St. Nicolas. By January, 1889, the representative of the Legitime regime in Washington was complaining to Bayard that the State Department was not acting in a neutral fashion in handling the Haitian situation.[35]

In 1882 Blaine had publicized his Latin-American policy which, he claimed, aimed first at peace in the area and then commercial expansion. But in dealing with Haiti from 1889 to 1891, the Secretary of State demonstrated that he cared more about commercial expansion than about peace. In the early summer of 1889 Blaine bluntly demanded of the Legitime government a

---

[34] *Messages and Papers of the Presidents,* IX, 200–201; Volwiler, "Harrison, Blaine . . . 1889–1893," 638–639, 648.

[35] Nemours to Bayard, Dec. 21, 1888, Preston to Bayard, Jan. 2 and Jan. 25, 1889, in Notes from Haitian Legation, NA, RG 59; John Bassett Moore to Bayard, Nov. 15, 1888, Bayard MSS.

naval station and American representation of Haiti in European capitals. A stunned agent of Legitime's refused both requests. Blaine indicated his displeasure by refusing to deal any longer with the agent. The Secretary of State then instructed the commander of the considerable American fleet in Haitian waters to disregard the blockade with which Legitime had attempted to strangle the Hyppolite group. American supplies flowed unhindered to the northern forces. In October, 1889, Hyppolite gained control of the nation. The Harrison administration meanwhile prepared to collect for past favors.[36]

William P. Clyde, a wealthy American shipbuilder and merchant who enjoyed large interests in Haiti, also began his collection for favors rendered. Keeping closely in touch with the Harrison administration through Secretary of the Navy Tracy, Clyde had helped the Hyppolite forces in every possible way. He assured Tracy that "the successful party now recognize who their friends have been, and if our Government will go wisely about it . . . we can secure any thing, in my opinion, which we should in decency ask." For his reward in helping the victors, Clyde asked for a steamship-line monopoly between the United States and Haiti, accompanied by a subsidy of $480,000 spread over ten years, from the newly established government. Hyppolite, however, proved strangely reluctant to pay such a price for Clyde's help. He also dawdled in response to Blaine's hints for Môle St. Nicolas. Under pressure from Clyde and Tracy, and unnecessarily fearful of French intervention, the Secretary of State decided in December, 1890, to force a showdown with Hyppolite.[37]

[36] Memorandum, Adee to Harrison, Sept. 17, 1889, Tracy to Blaine, July 13, 1889, Gherardi to Tracy, July 10, 1889, all in Harrison MSS. See George Boutwell's condemnation of Harrison's course of action in his letter to the President, July 6, 1889; Preston to Blaine, March 28, March 30, April 18, 1889, Notes from Haitian Legation, NA, RG 59; Rayford W. Logan, *The Diplomatic Relations of the United States with Haiti, 1776–1891* (Chapel Hill, N.C., 1941), 408–425.

[37] Clyde to Tracy, Oct. 15, 1890, May 31, 1889, Tracy MSS; Blaine's

Blaine first verbally instructed the American Minister, Frederick Douglass, to sound out the Haitian Foreign Minister, Anténor Firmin, on the possibility of obtaining Môle St. Nicolas. The talks proved unfruitful, so in January, Blaine sent Rear Admiral Bancroft Gherardi with special powers to negotiate for a lease on the naval base. In return, Gherardi could guarantee that the United States would maintain the Hyppolite government in power against any enemy. Firmin again stalled. At this point Blaine sent the Squadron of Evolution, which included the most powerful ships in the navy, to make a show of force off Port-au-Prince. The Haitian Minister in Washington, however, hurried a telegram to Firmin assuring him that the administration would never use the force. Unfortunately for Blaine's well-laid plans, the cable message arrived before the warships. On April 22 Haiti firmly rejected Blaine's offer. Five days later Gherardi returned to the United States. Clyde panicked, reminded Tracy that "I have half a million of dollars at stake," and demanded a reopening of the negotiations. Under Clyde's pressure, Douglass resigned in July, 1891. But Tracy cabled to Clyde on September 10, "Can do nothing more." [38]

As Harrison had insisted during his campaign and after, the United States wanted naval bases, but the administration would not use coercion to obtain them. Coercion comes in several forms. In using the term Harrison evidently meant military coercion. In the Haitian incident his administration did not hesitate to use other types it had available. Nor did Blaine hesitate to encourage revolution in Haiti in order to bring a government to power which he considered more amenable to Ameri-

---

fear of France is displayed in Pauncefote to Salisbury, Jan. 10, 1890, Salisbury MSS.

[38] Logan, *United States and Haiti*, 427–457; Clyde to Tracy, April 25 and May 27, 1891, and Tracy to Clyde, Sept. 10, 1891, Tracy MSS. Oddly, Clyde had wanted Firmin to remain in the Haitian cabinet in mid-1890 to hold off pro-French influences; see Clyde to Tracy, May 26, 1890, Tracy MSS.

can interests. After failing in Haiti, the Secretary of State did
not give up his quest for a naval base. Blaine began negotiations
with Santo Domingo for Samaná Bay. When the mere rumors
of the talks spread across the small nation, Santo Domingo's
Foreign Minister had to flee into exile to escape the wrath of
his people. Whether measured by results or virtue, the story of
the Harrison administration's attempts to obtain strategic bases
in the Caribbean is not a creditable one.

The Chilean Revolution

Although stopping short of military coercion in Haiti, Harrison came very close to using such force against Chile in early
1892. Embittered at what he considered to be an inexcusable
Chilean attack on American sailors, the President nearly threw
over three years of patient building of the inter-American
system for a war to defend the national honor. But it is his earlier
course in dealing with the Chilean revolution, especially Blaine's
response to the rapidly moving events in that Latin-American
nation, which provides the important clues concerning the administration's expansive foreign policies. In focusing on the
drama of the "Baltimore" incident, historians have lost much of
the real importance of American-Chilean relations in 1890–1892.

Conditions were nearly perfect for trouble between the two
nations. As Secretary of State in 1881, Blaine had incurred
Chilean enmity by attempting to save Peruvian interests when
the War of the Pacific broke out between Chile and Peru. Then
and later Blaine publicly interpreted the conflict as British-
inspired, and during the 1880's he openly criticized the growing
English investments in Chile. In 1886 the Balmaceda government,
more prone to a favorable view of the United States than
former Chilean governments had been, came to power. Blaine
attempted to build on this advantage by naming as American
Minister, Patrick Egan, a shrewd manipulator of the Irish vote.
With this single move, the new Secretary of State paid off cer-

tain political debts and openly declared war upon British influence in Chile.[39]

In January, 1891, congressional forces revolted when Balmaceda attempted to usurp certain legislative powers. Egan made it a point in his reports to Blaine during the next six months to tie the rebels to European influences. The Minister had some justification. The insurgents displayed laudable foresight in first seizing rich nitrate fields and then establishing a most profitable trade with British and German buyers. German warships shortly appeared to ensure the continuance of this trade. Realizing that United States aid was his only hope, Balmaceda courted American favor until Chileans assumed that their President represented Yankee interests and vice versa. Egan praised the embattled government for taking "prompt and energetic steps" to protect United States citizens and property. The State Department refused to sell to Balmaceda a warship he had urgently requested, but Egan was able to procure additional shipping facilities for the President.[40]

The lines were more firmly drawn when the rebel steamer, the "Itata," stoked with coal from English and German ships, moved to the California coast to buy arms and ammunition. Blaine had previously taken the correct neutral position of allowing the United States to sell arms to both sides, but when news reached Washington of the "Itata" voyage in the first week of May, 1891, Attorney General Warner Miller and Secretary of the Navy Tracy ordered American naval units to pursue and capture the insurgent ship. Blaine meanwhile lay ill in the home of his son-in-law, Walter Damrosch, in New York

[39] Volwiler, "Harrison, Blaine . . . 1889–1893," 639; Tyler, *Foreign Policy of Blaine*, 128–131; Devoy, Breslin, and Carroll to Wharton Barker, June 24, 1888, Box 4, Wharton Barker papers, Library of Congress, Washington, D.C.

[40] Egan to Blaine, Feb. 13, March 17, April 21, April 23, 1891, Chile, Despatches, NA, RG 59; Henry Clay Evans, Jr., *Chile and Its Relations with the United States* (Durham, N.C., 1927), 138–139.

City. The Secretary of State might have followed a different policy had he been in touch with the situation. After an exciting pursuit down the coast of Central America, the insurgents handed the "Itata" stores over to the American naval commander off the rebel-held Chilean port of Iquique. The commander assured Tracy that "the appearance of a squadron of modern vessels on this coast" explained "the compliance with the Department's demands" by the insurgents. The Balmaceda government profusely thanked the State Department for its efforts.[41]

The rebels, however, became rather surly over the affair, and their displeasure with past American action grew more apparent as they marched closer to victory. In late spring the State Department considered offering its services in mediating the conflict. Significantly, the Second Assistant Secretary of State, Alvey Adee, advised against such a move on the grounds that it would help the rebels. But when the slipping Balmaceda government hinted to Egan that it would appreciate such mediation, the United States offered its friendly offices. The insurgents bluntly turned down the offer. Relations grew worse between the United States and the rebels when the American naval commander tipped off the location of an insurgent invasion force to Balmaceda's shore batteries. Nor did matters improve after the rebels triumphed in late August when a United States court confirmed their protests by declaring that the "Itata" should not have been stopped by American ships; when the State Department hesitated several days before recognizing the new Chilean government; and, finally, when Egan insisted on granting asylum

[41] Memorandum dated March 8, 1891, Harrison MSS, tells the "Itata" episode well; also Comm. G. E. Wingate to Chief of Bureau of Navigation, June 12, 1891, and McCann to Tracy, June 13, 1891, Area 9 file, Box 15, NA, RG 45. The response of the Balmaceda government is in Lieut. Harlow to W. E. Curtis, June 9, 1889, Harrison MSS; that of the rebels in McCann to Tracy, June 22 and May 12, 1891, Area 9 file, Box 15, NA, RG 45; there is a good background in Tyler, *Foreign Policy of Blaine*, 135–141.

to Balmaceda's supporters in spite of heated complaints from the new government.[42]

Harrison meanwhile had developed little liking for the new government. Greatly overworked during the sweltering Washington summer, the President had been forced to deal with the Bering Sea problem, the dangerous implications of the lynching of eleven Italians in New Orleans, and the revolution in Chile. He had coped with such perplexities while his Secretary of State lay incapacitated at Bar Harbor, while the Second Assistant Secretary was "unwell" most of the summer, and while the Third Assistant Secretary prepared to resign. As Harrison told Blaine with admirable understatement, these events have "made life here rather uncomfortable." In the same letter the President complained that the rebel government did not "know how to use victory with dignity and moderation; and sometime it may be necessary to instruct them." [43]

At the same time both Egan and the commander of the American squadron off Valparaiso frequently informed the State and Navy Departments of the intense hostility shown toward the United States because of the administration's support of the defeated Balmaceda faction. Conditions in both Chile and the United States could have been detonated at the slightest provocation. On October 16 fighting broke out between sailors from the U.S.S. "Baltimore" and Chileans in the True Blue Saloon in

[42] There is an excellent summary of mediation and peace negotiations in a memorandum dated March 8, 1891, Harrison MSS; Adee's comment is in letter to Harrison, May 28, 1891, Harrison MSS; Wharton to Egan, June 1, 1891, Chile, Instructions, and Egan to Blaine, June 9, 1891, Chile, Despatches, NA, RG 59; Brown to Tracy, Nov. 15, 1891, Area 9 file, Box 16, NA, RG 45; Egan to Wharton, Oct. 22, 1891, Harrison to Blaine, Sept. 26, 1891, John W. Foster to W. H. H. Miller, Sept. 2, 1891, all in Harrison MSS. For Chilean hatred for United States help to Balmaceda see Robley D. Evans, *A Sailor's Log: Recollections of Forty Years of Naval Life* (New York, 1901), 266–267.

[43] Harrison to Blaine, Sept. 26, 1891, *Correspondence of Harrison and Blaine.*

Valparaiso. Two Americans were stabbed to death and seventeen more injured. Six months of distrust and hatred had borne a tragic climax.[44]

Chile moved slowly in investigating the affair. Having no doubts that it had been a flagrantly unjust attack on the American uniform, Harrison warned in his annual message on December 9 that the United States "expect full and prompt reparation." Three days later the Chilean Foreign Minister answered with an inexcusable public note which maligned both Egan and Harrison. Viewing this act as an atrocious insult to the American government, Harrison ordered the navy to prepare for action. While hurrying the fleet into war preparations, Secretary Tracy also worked to unite the cabinet behind Harrison's ultimatum of immediate apologies or severed diplomatic relations. Blaine, however, stalled further presidential actions for several weeks with the argument that the present Chilean government was provisional and would shortly be replaced with, perhaps, a more conciliatory cabinet.[45]

During the first three weeks of January, 1892, Blaine stopped the sending of the ultimatum, although, as Harrison's private secretary recorded in his diary, "the President stated that all the members of the Cabinet are for war." Matters worsened on January 20 when Chile demanded Egan's recall. On January 21, bowing to Harrison's militancy, the Secretary of State sent the

[44] Schley to Tracy, Oct. 30, Nov. 2, Nov. 28, 1891, all in Area 9 file, Box 16, NA, RG 45. For Chilean animosity before the "Baltimore" incident see Evans, *A Sailor's Log;* also Egan to Blaine, Sept. 24, Chile, Despatches, NA, RG 59; Schley to Tracy, Sept. 25, 1891, Cipher Messages, Entry 19, 1888–1895, and Schley to Tracy, Dec. 18, 1891, Area 9 file, Box 16, NA, RG 45.

[45] *Messages and Papers of the Presidents*, IX, 185–186; Egan to Blaine, Dec. 12, 1891, Chile Despatches, NA, RG 59. For U.S. war preparations see Rear Admiral George Brown to Tracy, Dec. 14, 1891, Area 9 file, Box 16, and a series of Tracy's telegrams to various commanders and Navy Yard personnel between Dec. 22 and Jan. 13, in Cipher Messages Sent, 1888–1895, both in NA, RG 45. For Chilean preparation for war see Col. Frederick D. Grant to Blaine, Jan. 7, 1892, Harrison MSS; Evans to Tracy, Jan. 17, 1892, Cipher Messages, Entry 19, 1888–1895, NA, RG 45.

ultimatum. Four days passed without an answer. Then Harrison laid the matter before Congress with a ringing message which reviewed the assault upon the American sailors and the impudent Chilean message of December 12. The President concluded that Congress, which under the Constitution had the sole power to declare war, should take "such action as may be deemed appropriate." Evidence exists which indicates that Blaine punctured Harrison's effort to whip up congressional enthusiasm by leaking the news to several congressmen that Chile had virtually capitulated. If true, Blaine would not have had to resort to such tactics to stop the outbreak of war, for within twenty-four hours after Harrison sent the message, Chile backed down. She finally paid a $75,000 indemnity for the "Baltimore" episode.[46]

This close brush with war resulted from the attack on the American sailors in Valparaiso and Chile's reluctance to offer a suitable indemnity. These events, in turn, can be understood only in the context of the souring relations between the United States and the insurgents during the summer of 1891. Few historians have stopped to ask the legitimate question: Why did the United States get involved with this revolution?

The outbreak of the revolution posed the first major challenge to the good intentions of the Harrison-Blaine Pan-American policies. When suddenly faced with a European-supported, anti-American revolutionary force that was rapidly growing more powerful, these good intentions dissipated. The administration failed in its attempts to preserve the small foothold American

[46] Volwiler, "Harrison, Blaine . . . 1889–1893," 643–647; Adee to Halford, Jan. 13, 1892, Blaine to Egan, Jan. 16, 1892, Montt to Blaine, Jan. 20, 1892, and typewritten memorandum of Harrison's, not sent, same date, all in Harrison MSS; Blaine to Egan, Jan. 21, 1892, Chile, Instructions, NA, RG 59; *Messages and Papers of the Presidents*, IX, 215–216. For the fascinating story of the Blaine "leak" see Hilary Herbert's memoranda for an autobiography, 310–313, in Herbert papers, University of North Carolina Library, Chapel Hill, N.C. It should be recognized that Herbert wrote this a quarter century later. He makes several obvious errors in chronology. For the encouragement which W. R. Grace & Company gave Blaine's peaceful stand, see Evans, *A Sailor's Log*, 277–278.

interests had obtained since 1886 under Balmaceda. To solve
the resulting crisis, Harrison pushed for war. Blaine, however,
advocated a more moderate course in the hope that relations
could be restored and the United States could, as the Secretary
of State said later, "make a friend of Chili—if that is possible."
During the tense final week of the crisis, the New York *Tribune*,
the foremost administration mouthpiece, explained American
interest in Chile:

The danger to the United States in these crises arises from the disposition of Europeans to interfere, the while pretending that they
are merely defending their own commercial interests. In Chili and
the Argentine, the most progressive commercial countries of South
America, we have permitted England to obtain monopoly of trade.
We have talked lustily about the "Monroe Doctrine" while Great
Britain has been building ships and opening markets. British subjects to-day hold a chattel mortgage over Chili and the Argentine.
. . . No American who wishes his country to possess the influence
in commerce and affairs to which its position among the nations en-
titles it can be pleased with this situation.[47]

The Chilean episode provided an example of the crises that
could occur when the Harrison-Blaine Latin-American policies,
working through nascent but vigorous American interests, faced
a severe setback at the hands of European-supported revolutionaries. An expansive Pan-American policy could engender
great risks as well as fond hopes.

The New Empire in the Western Pacific, 1889–1892

These events in the Western Hemisphere dominated the administration's attention in foreign affairs, but Blaine found time
early in his term to advance the concepts of the new empire in
the far Pacific. In one instance, however, he changed one of

[47] New York *Tribune*, Jan. 22, 1891, 5:3. The Blaine quotation is in
Blaine to Harrison, Jan. 29, 1892; see also the letter of Jan. 30, 1892,
Correspondence of Harrison and Blaine.

Seward's tenets. For many years Blaine had outspokenly advocated the restriction of Chinese laborers from American shores. The resulting ill will reduced correspondence between the State Department and the Chinese legation to a trickle during the 1889–1892 period.[48]

But this anti-Chinese attitude also produced positive results for the Plumed Knight's foreign policies. While in Garfield's cabinet, Blaine had written the instructions which ordered Commodore Robert Shufeldt to open Korea. Frelinghuysen and Bayard had afterwards attempted to minimize Chinese influence in the Hermit Kingdom in order to open new opportunities for Americans. In 1888 and 1889 Horace Allen, the most active of these Americans in Korea, had been approaching New York capitalists to gather funds for the exploitation of the immense Korean mineral riches. He held out special hopes for help from Blaine, whom Allen called "my friend." In formulating his Korean policy, the new Secretary of State posited that nation's independence from China. He assured Allen that, if American concession hunters inveigled contracts from the King, the State Department would "guarantee the parties—if of good standing —to take measures looking to the success of their work." Blaine also indicated a readiness to work for a coaling station in order to head off the Chinese and the Russians. But the Secretary of State most tangibly demonstrated his interest by naming Allen Secretary of the American Legation in Seoul.[49]

Greatly encouraged by Blaine's actions and also by the promise of extensive financial help from the large Wall Street firm of Morton-Bliss (headed by newly elected Vice-President of the United States, Levi P. Morton), Allen sped back to Korea to gain control of the mineral wealth in north Pangyang, the

[48] Blaine, *Political Discussions*, 216–235; Tyler, *Foreign Policy of Blaine*, ch. x.
[49] Pletcher, "Awkward Years," 184; *Foreign Relations, 1881*, 638; Harrington, *God, Mammon, and the Japanese*, 134–135.

richest gold mines in Asia. It took him five years to accomplish his mission, but with Blaine's help he had jumped off to a rousing start.

The Secretary of State obtained more immediate results in Samoa. Here German-American animosities, aggravated to nearly the point of war, had suddenly lessened when a devastating hurricane destroyed the American and German warships which had been threatening each other in Apia harbor. At the tragic cost of many lives, the diplomatic atmosphere had cleared only a month before British, German, and American representatives were to meet in Berlin to negotiate the Samoan problem. Although Germany possessed the largest financial stake in the islands, Chancellor Otto von Bismarck had decided not to risk a war in order to protect them. Calling Samoa "this little matter," Bismarck began an orderly retreat from his previous militant position.[50]

It was fortunate that Bismarck could thus change his policies, for Blaine did not enjoy such freedom of action. In late January, Congress had launched into a tirade which had ended in an $100,000 appropriation for the strengthening of the United States position at Pago Pago. The American press, especially in the West, followed the lead of the ultraexpansionist San Francisco Chamber of Commerce, which demanded "a decided policy on Samoa." Realizing the intensity of public opinion on the issue, Blaine had spent long hours studying the Samoan situation before assuming office. Thus his instructions to the American commissioners on April 11, 1889, were not written in a spur-of-the-moment fashion.[51]

He principally demanded the harbor of Pago Pago, because "our interest in the Pacific is steadily increasing; . . . our commerce with the East is developing largely and rapidly"; and

[50] Stolberg-Wernigerode, *Germany and the United States*, 252–255, 260.

[51] *Ibid.*, 255–258; Sherman to Harrison, March 9, 1889, Harrison MSS; Muzzey, *Blaine*, 398, n. 3.

there is "the certainty of an early opening of an Isthmian Transit." But significantly, Blaine backed down from Bayard's former demand for a virtual three-power protectorate over the islands. The new Secretary of State called this idea a "joint protectorate" and wanted no part of such political obligations. Blaine had nothing better to offer, however, so instructed the commissioners to feel their way through the early negotiations.[52]

John Kasson, a leading exponent of "larger policies" in American foreign affairs, led the United States commission; but compared with the other two members, William W. Phelps and George H. Bates, Kasson could be termed a moderate expansionist. Count Herbert von Bismarck refused to shake hands with Bates because of an article which the American had written in *Century Magazine*. Bates had attacked German claims to Samoa and urged American control, since the islands provided the "key of maritime dominion in the Pacific" and would open up markets "more than sufficient to absorb our surplus production." With this tough-minded delegation working on Bismarck's earlier predilections of softening the German position, the Americans were assured of obtaining most of their demands. The final pact gave the United States its claims to Pago Pago and minimized German influence, but Blaine did have to accept a three-power protectorate. The only alternative was outright partition of the islands; this would have meant even greater political responsibilities.[53]

The press in Paris and London believed that the United States had scored a great victory. But in the United States some journals expressed grave reservations. *Harper's Weekly* feared the pact took "the first step" in the American attempt "to adjust the

[52] *Foreign Relations, 1889*, 201; Ryden, *U.S. and Samoa*, 434–442, 465–466.

[53] Younger, *Kasson*, 355–360; George H. Bates, "Some Aspects of the Samoan Question," *Century Magazine*, XXXVII (April, 1889), especially 947; Phelps to Blaine, May 24, 1889, Blaine MSS; Blaine to Harrison, May 20, 1889, Harrison MSS.

governments and settle the domestic troubles of other semi-civilized communities throughout the world." Within a year the Secretary of State learned that the Samoan business could indeed be irksome. Skirmishes broke out between native factions supported by German, British, and American officials. Blaine disgustedly told the German Minister in August, 1890, that he wished the United States could get out of Samoa—but retain Pago Pago. Unfortunately for the Secretary's peace of mind, the two desires were contradictory.[54]

Samoan troubles plagued Harrison's administration until its close. As late as November 21, 1892, Blaine's replacement, John W. Foster, received word from the islands that the British had their eyes on part of Pago Pago. Foster sent word to London that the British would be wise to keep their distance. This warning provided the fitting conclusion to the administration's Samoan policy.[55]

In a larger historical context, the meaning of the events in Berlin, Washington, and Samoa during these four years become clearer. John Bassett Moore, who was Third Assistant Secretary of State during the Berlin conference, looked back on the affair a generation later and noted its importance: "No incident in the history of the United States . . . [better] prepares us to understand the acquisition of the Philippines, than the course of our government toward the Samoan Islands." [56]

A Premature American Frontier in the Pacific

The United States now enjoyed two of the finest naval stations in the Pacific. To retain Pago Pago, Blaine, shouldering more political responsibility than he desired, had entered into a three-power protectorate. In an effort to consolidate American hold-

[54] Younger, *Kasson*, 360; Dozer, "Anti-Imperialism," 179; Phelps to Blaine, Sept. 4, 1889, Blaine MSS; Stolberg-Wernigerode, *Germany and the United States*, 267.

[55] Foster to White, Nov. 21, 1892, Great Britain, Instructions, NA, RG 59.

[56] "Autobiography," Envelope II, Folder C, Box 207, Moore MSS.

ings in Hawaii, including the magnificent Pearl Harbor base, the Secretary of State first attempted to obtain a protectorate in 1890. When this attempt failed, the Harrison administration encouraged a revolution which, Washington officials hoped, would result in the annexation of the islands. Since other scholars have revealed this story with all its details,[57] only the bare outlines will be related here. The major concerns of the present discussion are two: first, why did the Harrison administration abandon the tenets of the new empire and attempt to assume full political control over the islands; second, why did the administration fail in carrying through its annexationist plans. This failure reveals much about the progress of the new empire as of 1893.

When Blaine re-entered office in 1889, the United States enjoyed a firm hold on Hawaiian affairs but none of the day-to-day political burdens. As Secretary of State in 1881, he had emphasized that "the material possession of Hawaii is not desired by the United States," though he did foresee circumstances which might make American control necessary, such as the growing power of Great Britain and Japan or the disintegration of the native government. Blaine considered the islands as part of the "American system," a belief he made explicit when he unsuccessfully invited Hawaiian representatives to attend the Inter-American Conference in 1889. He further indicated his interest by naming John L. Stevens as American Minister in 1889. Stevens and Blaine had been close friends in Maine. They shared the same inclination for an active foreign policy. A paucity of instructions in the State Department Archives from Blaine to Stevens indicates the Secretary's concurrence and confidence in his Minister's views.[58]

Until the McKinley tariff of 1890 the United States effectively

[57] The most complete account is William Adam Russ, Jr., *The Hawaiian Revolution (1893–1894)* (Selinsgrove, Pa., 1959); see also Pratt, *Expansionists of 1898*, and Stevens, *American Expansion in Hawaii*.

[58] Blaine, *Political Discussions*, 388–396; Tyler, *Foreign Policy of Blaine*, 198–202.

controlled Hawaii through the reciprocity agreements which had begun in 1876. As the Senate Foreign Relations Committee reported later, the 1875 treaty had been negotiated in order to make the islands "industrially and commercially a part of the United States," and to prevent "any other great power from securing a foothold there." In these terms it had been brilliantly successful. In 1891, the last year before the McKinley measure became effective, Hawaii exported 274,982,295 pounds of sugar to the American mainland, but only 285 pounds to all other nations. Then the islands felt the heavy blow of the 1890 tariff. With Harrison's and Blaine's prodding, McKinley introduced a bill that helped some Hawaiian products re-enter the American market, but nothing could be done for sugar. The hold of the United States was further shaken when in February, 1890, a new native-backed, anti-American political party won a squeaky victory in island elections.[59]

When the free sugar provision became a probability, Blaine quickly acted. In late 1889 and early 1890 he attempted to negotiate a treaty that would have transformed the islands into a formal American protectorate. In return for complete commercial reciprocity and the possibility of enjoying any bounties American sugar growers might receive, Hawaii would promise to sign no treaties with foreign powers without American approval and to allow United States military units to land at the State Department's discretion. The cession of Pearl Harbor would be made permanent as well as exclusive. The pact presaged nearly all the famous articles of the later Platt Amendment except the latter's concern for Cuban sanitation. Evidence exists that Blaine especially urged the guarantee of Hawaiian political independence and autonomy, while at the same time he suggested the

[59] Russ, *Hawaiian Revolution*, 33, 12–15; Stevens to Blaine, Sept. 5, 1891, Harrison MSS. Note that American exports to Hawaii did not fall after 1890 as did American imports from Hawaii; see Laughlin and Willis, *Reciprocity*, 104; Stevens, *American Expansion in Hawaii*, 187–203.

limitation upon the islands' treaty powers and the provision allowing the United States to land troops.[60]

The later attempt of the Harrison administration to annex Hawaii, and thus assume the political responsibilities which this treaty avoided, can be understood only in the light of Hawaii's failure to agree to the pact. Anti-American and native factions amended the treaty until the United States found it unacceptable. Blaine, Harrison, and Stevens pinned the blame especially on certain Canadians who were close to both the Hawaiian monarchy and Canadian Pacific Railroad interests. The incident did nothing to alleviate Blaine's churlish distrust of Canadians.[61]

On January 29, 1891, the anti-American faction's hold on the islands' government became more secure when Queen Liliuokalani ascended to the throne. As Stevens warned the State Department, the new Queen possessed "extreme notions of sovereign authority." The American Minister had dinned the threat posed by foreign-supported groups into Harrison's and Blaine's ears for two years, and now the Minister's fears were rapidly being confirmed. "I feel sure that American interests there are in jeopardy," the Chief Executive wrote Blaine in September, 1891, "but just how far we can go and what action we can take to thwart the schemes of those who are seeking to bring the islands under the control of European powers I do not yet see." Throughout 1892 Stevens and the various American naval commanders in Hawaii enhanced these fears of the European bogeymen with long dispatches vividly describing the various threats to American interests.[62]

[60] Blaine to Harrison, Sept. 16, 1891, Harrison MSS, also in *Correspondence of Harrison and Blaine;* Pauncefote to Salisbury, Jan. 10, 1890, Salisbury MSS; Stevens, *American Expansion in Hawaii,* 196–203.

[61] Blaine to Harrison, Sept. 16, 1891, Harrison MSS; Tyler, *Foreign Policy of Blaine,* 205.

[62] Harrison to Blaine, Sept. 18 and Oct. 14, 1891, *Correspondence of Harrison and Blaine.* See Pauncefote's summary of Blaine's attitude as the British Ambassador explained it to Gresham, March 16, 1893, Memo-

Stevens had the golden opportunity in mid-January, 1893, to free the islands forever from the threat of foreign domination. By the end of 1892 the Queen had succeeded in assuming some of the power formerly held by the legislature. Unsatisfied, she moved to gather more control in January, 1893, with a successful political coup which resulted in an antiplanter ministry. The conservative planter interests probably would not have been able to regain their former influence for some time if the Queen had not then made a major blunder. On January 14, she attempted to re-establish a constitution which would give her nearly absolute power. Two days later, after urgent advice from her ministers, she repudiated this attempt. But it was too late.

A group of radical annexationists had formed the Annexationist Club the previous year to prepare for the opportune moment, and they were prepared to use force to create the moment. The club's representative in Washington, Lorrin A. Thurston, received encouragement from Blaine and especially from Tracy. A month before the revolt occurred, both Tracy and the new Secretary of State, John W. Foster, assured Thurston that they realized the desirability of annexation. The final and most helpful encouragement came from American sailors of the U.S.S. "Boston," who landed on the evening of January 16 ostensibly to protect American property. Just a few hours before, the annexationists had whipped up public meetings to contest the Queen's grab for power. The following day the revolutionaries marched into the government buildings without opposition from the native forces, who feared that resistance would lead to a battle with the sailors. On January 18 the new government sent commissioners to Washington to work out the procedure for annexation. Harrison sent the treaty to the Senate on February 15 with the justification that the revolution had made it "quite evident that the monarchy had become . . . so

---

randum of Conversation, NA, RG 59; New York *Tribune*, Jan. 23, 1891, 6:4; Stevens, *American Expansion in Hawaii*, 193–203; Captain Wiltse to Tracy, Oct. 12, 1892, Area 9 file, Box 19, NA, RG 45.

weak and inadequate as to be the prey of designing and unscrupulous persons." Noting that the United States had a choice between establishing a protectorate and "full and complete" annexation, the President urged the latter.[63]

Harrison's change of mind between 1890 and 1893 was momentous. Moving away from the protectorate idea, he suddenly confronted the American people with a historic choice: would they assume political responsibilities over a chaotic population of about 88,000 natives and 2,000 white planters in order that the United States might continue to derive the commercial and strategic advantages which it had enjoyed without such political burdens? The President answered with an unequivocal "Yes" on his part. He based his decision on several factors. First, he and Blaine had unsuccessfully tried to establish a protectorate in 1890. Now a government much more amenable to American interests had assumed power. But in view of the kaleidoscopic events in Hawaiian politics during the previous three years, no one could be certain how long the revolutionaries could maintain their position. Only annexation would finally solve the problem.

Harrison especially feared that the downfall of the revolutionary government would bring renewed onslaughts from Canadian, British, and Japanese influences on the islands. Immediately after the revolution in mid-January, these powers had assured the United States that they had no designs on Hawaii, but the administration remained uneasy. On February 4, the American Minister in London sent the State Department a series of clippings which revealed that nearly every London newspaper had acquiesced to the inevitability of United States annexation. Only one, the *Daily Telegraph*, thought otherwise. Alvey Adee, the Second Assistant Secretary of State, passed over all the friendly editorials and marked the *Daily Telegraph*'s comments in double

[63] For the best rationale for the American position, see Foster to Lincoln, Feb. 1, 1893, Great Britain, Instructions, NA, RG 59; Wiltse to Tracy, Jan. 18 and Feb. 1, 1893, Area 9 file, Box 19, NA, RG 45; Russ, *Hawaiian Revolution*, 34–35; Stevens, *American Expansion in Hawaii*, 203–229.

red lines for the Department's perusal. Such important journals as the Washington *Post*, Baltimore *American*, and the New York *Sun* also exhibited such unfounded fears.[64]

More positively, the administration wanted Hawaii for its riches of sugar and rice. These, however, were viewed as of less importance than the islands' value as a naval base to protect the Isthmian route and as a coaling station on the avenues to Asia. It is significant that with Blaine's departure from the cabinet in June, 1892, Tracy became the leading figure in urging a firmer grasp on Hawaii. In order to round out his strategy of controlling the sea, "the future seat of empire," Tracy naturally looked upon Hawaii as a key objective. But again, the unstable political situation threatened the American hold on Pearl Harbor. The administration had urged modifying the 1890 tariff, because it feared that Hawaii might seize upon this change of commercial relations as an excuse to abrogate the 1887 cession of Pearl Harbor. The wildly fluctuating political scene offered too great an opportunity to the wily British and Canadians. This was the situation Foster referred to in his *Diplomatic Memoirs* when he recalled his fear that, if the United States did not annex Hawaii, "anarchy might have been created." This, combined with his belief that, if the "Islands did not soon become American territory, they would inevitably pass under the control of Great Britain or Japan" (and anarchy could too easily lead to the ascendancy of such anti-American influence), explains the administration's motives and haste in February, 1893. Some journals urged annexation for strategic reasons, that is, the necessity of controlling the approaches to the California coast. But many combined the commercial and strategic arguments by stressing Hawaii's excellent location for advancing America's foreign trade.[65]

The New York *Tribune* best summarized these positive com-

---

[64] Lincoln to Foster, Feb. 3, 4, 17, 1893, Great Britain, Despatches, NA, RG 59; *Public Opinion*, Feb. 4, 1893, 415–416.

[65] John W. Foster, *Diplomatic Memoirs* (Boston and New York, 1909), II, 166, 168; *Public Opinion*, Feb. 4, 1893, 415–417; Feb. 18, 1893, 464–465.

mercial-strategic reasons. It is useful to reiterate that the *Tribune* was the most important journal which spoke for the administration. The previous November its owner, Whitelaw Reid, had been the vice-presidential nominee on the Republican ticket with Harrison. On February 21 this journal wrote:

The views of the American people have grown with their growing empire. . . . Today we produce of manufactures more than any two nations of Europe; of agriculture more than any three, and of minerals more than all together. The necessity for new markets is now upon us, and with it the necessity for cultivating close commercial and political relations with the rapidly growing nations of South America and Australia and with the newly awakened empires of China and Japan. As a prime condition of this extending influence, the duty of controlling the Isthmian routes is clear to every intelligent mind. . . . To render that control sufficient, the sovereignty of Caribbean territory and of Hawaii is absolutely necessary.[66]

This editorial was particularly representative of the common view that the Isthmian passageway was important for commercial rather than military reasons.

There was, however, another answer to the question of whether the United States should assume such political burdens. Many antiannexationist journals are particularly valuable in detailing the reasons for a negative answer. Very few papers derided American interests in the islands. The vast majority offered a more realistic and subtle suggestion. "Annexation in any real sense is not now necessary or desirable," announced the New York *World* in early February, 1893. A protectorate could secure "the interests of our citizens there and the convenience of our commerce." The Chicago *Herald* agreed: "We are supreme at Hawaii in the only way we desire to be supreme; we control its trade and we will not suffer any other foreign power to invade or absorb the islands, as we do not need to absorb and shall not invade them ourselves. No jingoism!" The Boston *Herald*,

[66] New York *Tribune*, Feb. 21, 1893, 6:4; also in Stevens, *American Expansion in Hawaii*, 236.

Chicago *News Record,* Atlanta *Constitution,* and Boston *Journal,* among others, agreed. The New Orleans *Delta* added another reason: "It would seem that the United States has as much territory as can be properly handled." [67]

The large planters in Hawaii also preferred a protectorate rather than annexation. The wealthiest of them, Claus Spreckels, explained in May, 1893, that he would give the United States "a place at Pearl Harbor in fee simple" in order that Hawaii might be protected properly, but "the labor question is the all-important one and constitutes my only objection to annexation." Spreckles knew that after annexation the United States would exclude cheap oriental labor from the islands. This issue did not greatly influence the smaller planters, who were playing the major role in the annexationist movement. Finally, many Americans were not certain that the majority of Hawaiians, that is, the natives, wanted annexation. This question would especially trouble the conscience of the incoming Cleveland administration.[68]

By the end of February sufficient Democratic votes had gathered to stall the treaty of annexation until Grover Cleveland assumed power. In another eight months the treaty would be dead. In 1893 the United States refused to shoulder the burden of governing the multiracial Hawaiian population. This disinclination grew when the depression of 1893 struck. As economic chaos and social violence again upset the American scene, many people wondered what business the nation had in so assiduously searching for new problems.

And there was another point. Before the United States could enjoy the luxury of worrying about the highways to Asia, she had to solve the top priority problem of dominating the highways to Mexico City, Buenos Aires, and Caracas. Latin-American questions would be uppermost until the European powers, especially England, recognized that the Monroe Doctrine was

[67] *Public Opinion,* Feb. 4, 1893, 415–417; Feb. 11, 1893, 439–441; Feb. 18, 1893, 466–467; Feb. 25, 1893, 489; March 11, 1893, 540.
[68] Spreckels is quoted in Dozer, "Anti-Imperialism," 220.

not simply a half-century-old antique. The Harrison administration's Hawaiian policy is atypical when placed in the whole of its foreign policy. Before early 1893, it had emphasized commercial expansion and had focused on Latin America. The Inter-American Conference, Blaine's reciprocity, the attempt to obtain strategic bases in Haiti and Santo Domingo, and the striking at European interests in the Chilean revolution point up the principal features of the administration's policy in foreign affairs. Under the impetus of the depression, to which we shall now turn, the Cleveland administration would vigorously reassert the tenets of the new empire in Latin America.

Hawaii would have to wait until the Venezuelan episode and the war with Spain established American supremacy in the Western Hemisphere. Only then would the State Department be able to give the attention that area deserved. But as Frederick Jackson Turner observed, "it is one of the profoundest lessons that history has to teach, that political relations, in a highly developed civilization, are inextricably connected with economic relations." [69] The Hawaiian policies of the United States could not escape the logic of this dictum. Within six years after they left office, the United States achieved many of the strategic goals outlined by Harrison and Blaine in both Latin America and the Pacific.

[69] Turner, *Early Writings*, 61–62; see the analysis of Turner in Chapter II. Much the same comment is specifically applied to the administration's Hawaiian policy in Harrison's home-town newspaper, the Indianapolis *Journal*, as quoted in *Public Opinion*, Feb. 25, 1893, 188–189.

IV

The Economic Formulation

THE gap between outlining strategic objectives and obtaining those objectives is crucial and often extremely wide. Policy makers, no matter how astute, have frequently fallen in attempts to take the intermediate steps. In the 1890's, however, the United States quickly traversed these middle steps in attaining the empire envisioned by the Harrison administration. Of these steps, the most important were, first, the formation of a consensus by important political and business leaders on the necessity of a more expansive foreign policy; second, the Venezuelan boundary dispute of 1895–1896; and, third, the Spanish-American War. The first event was most important for, to continue the metaphor, if the first step had not been taken successfully, the second and third steps would not have followed.

This consensus resulted from the depression which struck the United States from 1893 to 1897. During these years concise and conscious economic analyses by the Cleveland administration, the business community, and leading congressional figures led these three groups to conclude that foreign markets were necessary for the prosperity and tranquillity of the United States. These groups also drew the corollary that British commercial competition, especially in Latin America, endangered America's economic well-being. The depression of the mid-1890's congealed the various explanations which had been offered for America's post-1873 economic and social problems into a consensus that directed the consummation of the new empire.

In their attempts to discover an antidote for the depression, the Cleveland administration and the business community could usefully draw on the facts of recent economic history. Crop failures and the collapse of the Baring Brothers banking house in England had sent western Europe spinning into a severe recession in 1890. Americans, however, had escaped the crisis by exporting an abnormally large amount of their agricultural products. These exports left at an opportune moment, for $70,000,000 of gold had fled the United States during the first six months of 1891. Again in 1892 European crops failed. American farm exports, finding excellent continental markets, once more reversed the gold flow. Observers in business periodicals and in the Harrison administration, including the President himself, warned that only these exports shielded the United States from economic embarrassment.[1]

During the first half of 1893 exports dropped below 1892 levels and imports soared. European investments, one of the cornerstones of the American industrial system, began to react to the strain on the Treasury's gold reserve by dropping off in volume. As large amounts of gold left New York banks to pay the nation's debts in Europe, Americans again turned to find economic salvation in their agricultural exports. But this time

[1] E. H. Phelps Brown with S. J. Handfield-Jones, "The Climacteric of the 1890's," *Oxford Economic Papers*, n.s. (October, 1952), 266–307; Seymour M. Lipset, "The Background of Agrarian Radicalism," *Class Status and Power: A Reader in Social Stratification*, edited by Richard Bendix and Seymour M. Lipset (Glencoe, Ill., 1953); Alexander Dana Noyes, *Thirty Years of American Finance* (New York, 1898), 1–6, 158–159, 182–183, 161–164, 200; Max Wirth, "The Crisis of 1890," *Journal of Political Economy*, I (March, 1893), 214–236; Albert H. Imlah, *Economic Elements in the Pax Britannica: Studies in Foreign Trade in the Nineteenth Century* (Cambridge, Mass., 1958), 157–198; Otto C. Lightner, *The History of Business Depressions* (New York, 1922), 188.

European crops promised to be sufficient. The collapse of the Philadelphia and Reading Railroad in February and the failure of the National Cordage Company in May touched off a wave of withdrawals from both western and eastern banks. Panic struck the nation.[2]

This business collapse had several important features. First, the blow climaxed a long period of deflation; unlike most previous panics it did not follow an era of inflation and speculation. Second, as James H. Eckels, Comptroller of the Currency, noted, "the assets reported of the failed concerns have been largely in excess of their liabilities." Those firms having a "very moderate or none" credit rating (according to *Bradstreet's* assessments) actually experienced a percentage drop in failures during the depression, while the failures of those having a "very good" rating or higher more than doubled. This commercial crisis did more than merely squeeze the "water" out of the system.[3]

A third feature of the panic appeared in the summer of 1893 when crops began moving toward eastern and European markets. Some gold began flowing back into the United States, yet money remained scarce. By the end of August, however, conditions changed. Forty-one million dollars' worth of the yellow metal entered New York that month. The premium on gold disappeared, and money flooded commercial channels. Now,

[2] Noyes, *Thirty Years of American Finance*, 200–201, 189–190; *The Commercial and Financial Chronicle*, Jan. 6, 1894, 4; Lightner, *History of Business Depressions*, 188; Albert C. Stevens, "Phenomenal Aspects of the Financial Crisis," *Forum*, XVI (September, 1893), 26–27; Horace Samuel Merrill, *Bourbon Leader: Grover Cleveland and the Democratic Party* (Boston, 1957), 146; John D. Hicks, *The Populist Revolt . . .* (Minneapolis, 1931), 309–310; W. Jett Lauck, *The Causes of the Panic of 1893* (Boston, 1907), 101–103; Frank S. Philbrick, "The Mercantile Conditions of the Crisis of 1893," *The University Studies of the University of Nebraska* (1894–1902), 304–306.

[3] Stevens, "Phenomenal Aspects," 26–29; *Commercial and Financial Chronicle*, Jan. 6, 1894, 4; Lightner, *History of Business Depressions*, 186; James H. Eckels, "The Financial Situation," *North American Review*, CLVII (August, 1893), 129–139; Philbrick, "Mercantile Conditions of the Crisis of 1893," 300.

however, no outlet could be found for surplus capital. Loan rates dropped drastically, demand almost disappeared, and a deep depression replaced the panic. The home market had collapsed. Secretary of the Treasury Carlisle noted in his annual report of 1893 that the country contained over $112,000,000 more in circulating money than on December 1, 1892. He reminded the nation that "money does not create business, but business creates a demand for money." [4]

The Goldbugs and Foreign Markets

The embattled administration first hoped to pry apart the closing fingers of the depression by repealing the Sherman Silver Purchase Act.[5] The repeal bill became law in early November, and businessmen waited for the supposedly inevitable change for the better to occur. But as one observer phrased it, the "stark, irrefutable fact" was that the repeal did not restore prosperity or even confidence.[6]

---

[4] *The Bankers' Magazine and Statistical Register*, XLVIII (September, 1893), 184–185—cited hereafter as *Bankers' Magazine*. Also Galveston Export Commission Company to Grover Cleveland, June 26, 1893, Grover Cleveland papers, Library of Congress, Washington, D.C.; James A. Barnes, *John G. Carlisle: Financial Statesman* (New York, 1931), 295; Alexander D. Noyes, "The Financial Record of the Second Cleveland Administration," *Political Science Quarterly*, XII (December, 1897), 561; Lauck, *The Causes of the Panic of 1893*, 108; Gerald Taylor White, "The United States and the Problem of Recovery after 1893" (unpublished Ph.D. dissertation, University of California, Berkeley, 1938), 28; Noyes, *Thirty Years of American Finance*, 194–196; *Commercial and Financial Chronicle*, Sept. 16, 1893, 446; *Annual Report of the Secretary of the Treasury, 1893*, lxxiv–lxxv.

[5] This act provided for an automatic issue of $50,000,000 in Treasury notes annually, based on silver. These notes could be exchanged for either silver or gold, but so far they had been redeemed only in gold. After being exchanged, the notes recirculated and again were redeemed in gold. The March, 1893, reserve in the Treasury amounted to barely over the supposedly magic $100,000,000 figure. When the reserve dropped below this figure, many financial observers believed the Treasury on the brink of bankruptcy.

[6] *Messages and Papers of the Presidents*, IX, 390–391. *Commercial and*

The repeal had another consequence. The heated infighting which occurred during the congressional debates revived the intensive struggle between goldbugs and silverites, a struggle which would reach its climax in the Bryan campaign in 1896. The conflict contained far-reaching implications for foreign policy, for it forced the Cleveland administration and other goldbugs to claim that overproduction, not the lack of money, was the prime cause of the depression. This glut of goods could be dissolved either through a redistribution of products in the United States or through finding additional foreign markets. When the administration and the business community chose the second alternative, they also influenced the course of American foreign policy.

Before the 1893 panic, the silver-versus-gold argument had largely revolved around two questions: the amount of circulating money needed in the economy and the plea of debtors for money to inflate prices, especially those of farm products. This second question led naturally to another debate. If the ultimate aim was to drive prices upward, this could also be accomplished by finding additional markets for the overproductive grain lands of the West. Goldbugs and silver advocates both made this assumption. But the debate continued bitterly on the question of whether the gold or silver standard would provide the most help in finding and keeping these necessary foreign markets.[7]

The Cleveland administration, and others who advocated the gold standard, used a two-edged sword; first, they argued that the panic had demonstrated that the fear of a silver standard would frighten vital European investment away from the United States; second, they believed that the gold standard best main-

---

Financial Chronicle, Jan. 6, 1894, 13; Merrill, *Bourbon Leader,* 183; *Bankers' Magazine,* XLVIII (December, 1893), 405. One of the few humorous incidents of the year occurred on Oct. 2, 1893, when W. H. "Coin" Harvey invited Cleveland to become a subscriber to Harvey's silverite magazine (Harvey to Cleveland, Oct. 2, 1893, Cleveland MSS).

[7] Davis Rich Dewey, *Financial History of the United States* (10th ed.; New York, 1928), 460–462; Edward C. Kirkland, *A History of American Economic Life* (New York, 1951), 434–438.

tained a high credit rating in international trade and so enhanced that trade. The silverites did not dispute the first point, for they wanted the United States to exile foreign capital anyway.[8]

No one better explained the second part of the argument than the Secretary of the Treasury, John G. Carlisle. At a banquet of the New York Chamber of Commerce in late November, 1893, the Secretary left no doubt that the administration thoroughly understood the relationship between the money question and international trade. He told his distinguished audience: "Our commercial interests are not confined to our own country; they extend to every quarter of the globe. . . . Without exception these prices are fixed in the markets of countries having a gold standard." The Secretary observed that American trade with the silver countries of Latin America (excluding Brazil) and Asia amounted to a comparatively smaller figure.[9]

Two aspects of the goldbug stand are important. First, since their argument defined overproduction as the predominant cause of the depression, the remedy could be found in the markets of the world. This conclusion tied the monometalists to a policy of finding and keeping foreign markets, and, in turn, this became an intimate concern of the Cleveland administration's foreign policy. Second, by refusing to move closer to a silver standard the goldbugs lessened the possibility of increased American trade with Asian and Latin-American markets which operated on the silver standard. By changing from a gold to a silver or bimetallic basis, the United States could have more easily undersold gold nations (as Great Britain and France) in these silver standard

[8] Roger V. Clements, "The Farmers' Attitude toward British Investment in American Industry," *Journal of Economic History*, XV (June, 1955), 151–159.

[9] Barnes, *Carlisle*, 299–302. It should be noted that Carlisle referred to an American trade based on agricultural exports, not manufactures. For a similar view of the relationship of gold to international commerce and the American industrial glut, see Michael D. Harter, "Free Coinage, the Blight of Our Commerce," *Forum*, XIII (May, 1892), 283–284; David A. Wells, "The Downfall of Certain Financial Fallacies," *Forum*, XVI (October, 1893), 131–149.

areas. In voluntarily refusing this advantage, the Cleveland administration had to find other means of encouraging and protecting American interests in these nations.[10]

Many persons, including prominent businessmen, scorned both the silver and gold arguments and advocated bimetallism by international agreement. This group emphasized, however, that it did not want the United States to go on a bimetallist standard alone, as most of the silverites desired. Henry Clews, head of one of New York's largest banking houses, propounded the bimetallism-by-international-agreement case to Cleveland himself. Senator George F. Hoar represented the conservative politician's viewpoint, proclaiming in 1893 that bimetallism provided a happy solution since outright repeal of the Sherman Silver Purchase Act would lead to increased imports and would further distress American manufacturers in world markets. Unfortunately for these bimetallist advocates, Great Britain blocked an international agreement. J. Pierpont Morgan attempted to negotiate a secret bimetallist arrangement with the Chancellor of the Exchequer, Sir William Harcourt, in the spring of 1893. When Morgan asked Harcourt what Great Britain could do, however, Sir William bluntly replied, "Nothing." Morgan reported to Cleveland that continued negotiations were useless. In his 1893 annual message the President excluded the possibility of any international bimetallist conference in the immediate future.[11]

[10] For a summary of how the silverites believed their standard would lead to increased international trade, see Henry B. Russell, *International Monetary Conferences* . . . (New York, 1898), 449–450; Barnes, *Carlisle*, 283–284; Nancy L. O'Connor, "The Influence of Populist Legislators upon American Foreign Policy, 1892–1898" (unpublished Master's thesis, University of Oregon, Eugene, 1958), 39–40.

[11] Charles Stewart Smith, Charles G. Wilson, James O. Bloss, Henry Hentz, "The Business Outlook," *North American Review*, CLVII (October, 1893), 392; Henry Clews to Cleveland, April 20, 1893, Cleveland MSS; Joseph Dorfman, *The Economic Mind in American Civilization* (New York, 1949), III, 225, 230; Henry White to Secretary of State Walter Quintin Gresham, personal and confidential, May 31, 1893, NA, RG 59. See also J. P. Nichols, "Silver Diplomacy," *Political Science Quarterly*, XLVIII (December, 1933), 583–584; Elmer Ellis, *Henry*

The bimetallists refused to concede. In fact, they picked up influential support in 1894 and 1895. William C. Whitney, a paramount member of Cleveland's first cabinet and the "Warwick" of the 1892 election victory, constantly urged the President to enter into a bimetallic agreement with England during the mid-1890's. A strong goldbug in 1893, Whitney became converted when Robert Barclay, a British economist, convinced him that a bimetallic standard could best exploit the oriental trade. Interestingly, when Cleveland coolly received these ideas and when the American silver movement turned to more radical solutions, Whitney began to soft-pedal his monetary theories and urged instead a militant foreign policy in Venezuela and Cuba.[12]

Henry Cabot Lodge and Thomas B. Reed also advocated a bimetallic agreement on the grounds that it would stimulate exports to Asia. This proposal can only be fully understood within the context of Lodge's delight in twisting the Lion's tail, Reed's presidential aspirations, and both men's desire to avoid the low Wilson tariff at all costs. But it is important to note that Lodge and Reed did not devise this plan themselves. They merely advocated it. The idea and the supporting arguments came from Brooks Adams' bimetallist club in Boston. Adams was "amused" at the way Boston merchants had discovered "that there is money in this thing after all." When Brooks informed Lodge that "about half of State Street" had joined the organization, the Senator also applied for membership.[13]

Moore Teller: Defender of the West (Caldwell, Idaho, 1941), 228; *Messages and Papers of the Presidents*, IX, 444–445.

[12] Mark D. Hirsch, *William C. Whitney: Modern Warwick* (New York, 1948), 475–481; W. C. Whitney to Cleveland, Oct. 31 and Nov. 22, 1894, Cleveland MSS; Whitney to Olney, Sept. 28, 1895, Richard Olney papers, Library of Congress, Washington, D.C.

[13] "Will There Be a Union of Protectionist and Free-Silver Forces?" *Literary Digest*, June 16, 1894, 181; Reed's interview is in *Fortnightly Review* (London), LXI (June, 1894), 837–838; Nevins, *Grover Cleveland*, 608–609; William A. Robinson, *Thomas B. Reed, Parliamentarian* (New York, 1930), 315–316; Brooks Adams to Lodge, May 6, April 11, 1894,

Several aspects of the bimetallist scheme were of particular significance. First, it appealed to Republican protectionists as a means of selling surplus goods abroad without a modification of high tariff principles; second, since this selling could most easily be done in the silver standard nations in Latin America and Asia, commercial attention focused on these areas; third, the proposal singled out Great Britain as the obstacle to an international bimetallist agreement. Believing foreign markets to be a tonic for the nation's economic illness, the bimetallists blamed England for the inability of the United States to reach these markets through a bimetallist standard. This conclusion carried sharp connotations for the bimetallists' foreign policy.[14]

The Cleveland administration answered such arguments by also relating the monetary standard to international trade. In a letter to the Chicago Business Men's meeting in April, 1895, the President emphasized that debased money would work only if the United States was "isolated from all others." But if it became commercially isolated, "American civilization . . . would abjectly fail in its high and noble mission." He wrote a southern governor, "I have never ceased to wonder why the people of the South, furnishing so largely as they do products which are exported for gold, should be willing to submit to the disadvantages and loss of silver monometallism." [15]

Secretary Carlisle rephrased Cleveland's arguments when he gave the Secretary of the Interior, Hoke Smith, a lesson in international finance in August, 1894. Smith, a Georgian who would leave the Cleveland cabinet over the silver issue in 1896, asked Carlisle why the government could not adopt free coinage of silver. Carlisle wrote a long reply, of which more than half ex-

---

Nov. 24, 1893, Jan. 13, April 23, 1894, Lodge MSS. See also E. Benjamin Andrews, "The Bimetallist Committee of Boston and New England," *Quarterly Journal of Economics*, VIII (April, 1894), 319–327.

[14] See, for example, *Textile Record*, April, 1894, quoted in *Nation*, April 26, 1894, 303.

[15] *Commercial and Financial Chronicle*, April 20, 1895, 690; Cleveland to Hon. J. M. Stone, April 26, 1895, Cleveland MSS.

plained the international trading aspects of the silver-gold controversy. If America went on a silver basis, Carlisle insisted, the nation would receive payment for its goods in silver, but would have to pay for purchases with gold. Carlisle repeated this same argument in his annual report of 1894.[16]

The Tariff of 1894

As the argument continued, the depression worsened. The repeal of the Sherman Silver Purchase Act had not even acted as an ameliorant, let alone as a cure-all. By itself the goldbug argument, no matter how handsomely dressed, was only a syllogism whose attractiveness depended largely on whether the listeners were creditors or debtors. As the goldbugs outlined the monometallist argument, their favorite standard had value, since it attracted foreign investment to the United States and increased American exports. In late 1893, when the monometallist standard had little positive effect in helping the nation dispose quickly of its plethora of goods, the Cleveland administration turned to the idea of a tariff measure whose predominant purpose would be obtaining foreign markets for depression-plagued industries.[17]

In the 1892 campaign the Democrats had discussed the tariff as a redistributive device rather than as a wealth-producing agency. This approach was, of course, politically attractive. Moreover, the Republicans claimed that their policy of reciprocity had already solved the problem of obtaining foreign markets for American surplus goods. The Republican tariff plank attacked the Democrats for opposing reciprocity, "this practical business measure." In reality, the Democrats did not oppose

[16] Carlisle to Smith, Aug. 11, 1894, Cleveland MSS; see also Carlisle's views in his *Annual Report, 1894*, lxxiii.

[17] Prof. Frank W. Taussig has observed that most tariff controversies in American history have been "concerned with the production of wealth rather than its distribution" ("Rabbeno's American Commercial Policy," *Quarterly Journal of Economics*, X [October, 1895], 109). For an excellent summary of this type of tariff argument, see article by David Ames Wells in the New York *World*, Aug. 8, 1893, in Bayard MSS.

reciprocity. They simply criticized the Republicans for not taking the idea to its logical conclusions. The Cleveland forces attacked "sham reciprocity" with the two telling points that, first, the United States as an agricultural nation was, under Republican reciprocity, encouraging trade relations with other agricultural nations, and little could be gained from this; second, that the retaliatory provision of the 1890 tariff had created ill will for the United States in Latin America. But the Democratic tariff plank was most emphatic in proclaiming that the Republican tariff had been "a fraud" in that it enriched the very few. The Democrats espoused a revenue-only tariff.[18]

Cleveland's letter of acceptance dealt largely with the tariff issue, but the statement displayed little concern with foreign markets. Other Democratic spokesmen, including William L. Wilson of West Virginia, who would lead the Cleveland forces in the House should the Democrats win the election, also slighted the foreign trade aspects of the tariff.[19]

The onslaught of the depression, however, drastically changed these viewpoints. The three men most responsible for the success of the administration's tariff plan, Cleveland, Wilson, and Senator Roger Q. Mills of Texas, began to emphasize in late 1893 that the tariff's main objective would be to help American manufacturers compete in foreign markets. The President stressed this aspect of the tariff measure in his annual message of 1893.

[18] *Republican Campaign Text-Book for 1892*, 9; *Official Proceedings of the Democratic National Convention, 1892*, 95–97; Laughlin and Willis, *Reciprocity*, 233–234.

[19] *Democratic Campaign Book: Congressional Elections, 1894* (Washington, D.C., 1894), 208–210; G. G. Vest, "The Real Issue," *North American Review*, CLV (October, 1892), 401–406; Hilary A. Herbert, "Reciprocity and the Farmer," *North American Review*, CLIV (April, 1892), 414–423; William L. Wilson, "The Tariff Plank at Chicago," *North American Review*, CLV (September, 1892), 280–286. An exception to this generalization about Wilson's views is his article, "The Republican Policy of Reciprocity," *Forum*, XIV (October, 1892), 255–256. This article looked forward to an extension of foreign trade, but Wilson mostly emphasized his objections to reciprocity for partisan and constitutional reasons.

He began by declaring that one of the measure's "most obvious features should be a reduction . . . upon the necessaries of life." This argument occupied one paragraph of his paper. The next three paragraphs then delineated Cleveland's request that tariff legislation provide free raw materials. "The world should be open to our national ingenuity and enterprise," the President declared, and this would not occur as long as a "high tariff forbids to American manufacturers as cheap materials as those used by their competitors." Cleveland tied this argument in with the growing unemployment problem, pointing out that "the limited demand for . . . goods" on a "narrow market" inevitably led to the closing of shops and industries. This declaration that foreign markets were to solve the double problem of economic stagnation and labor unrest was all the more remarkable since Cleveland had never before emphasized this argument in an official message.[20]

Just as remarkable was William L. Wilson's change of emphasis. In an article published in January, 1894, shortly after he had introduced the tariff bill in the House, Wilson declared that the measure served two purposes: it enabled American producers to acquire foreign markets, and it reduced taxation on products of home consumption. He mentioned first and most emphatically the foreign trade aspect. Like Cleveland, he organized his argument around the raw materials question, and also like the President, he stressed that the labor problem could be solved by such a program:

[The laborer's] wages, his steady employment and his personal ability to influence both are dependent on a full and expanding market for the products of his labor and his skill. The remark of a great

[20] *Messages and Papers of the Presidents,* IX, 459. Robert McElroy, *Grover Cleveland: The Man and the Statesman* (New York, 1923), II, 109, gives Cleveland's views of the income tax amendment. See also Nevins, *Grover Cleveland,* 380–387. Cleveland mentioned the tariff as a means to expand foreign trade only in passing during his first administration and never developed the theme at any length. See *Messages and Papers of the Presidents,* VIII, 589–776.

American statesman seventy years ago, that "the greatest want of civilized society is a market for the sale and exchange of the surplus of the produce of the labor of its members" was never as true of any people as it is to-day true of the people of the United States. There is not one of our leading industries that can find free and healthful play within the limits of our home markets.

Wilson concluded by denying the charge that lower tariffs would lose the home market for American industries. He believed that if an industry could invade the markets of other countries, it certainly could hold its home market.[21] Such an argument marked a radical change from Wilson's campaign statements.

In an article which appeared a month after Wilson's, Senator Mills, who was expected to guide the tariff bill through the upper house, also explored the advantages of free raw materials for labor. He noted that the "first thought" in the public mind was to protect labor from excessive imports. Mills then abruptly dropped the subject of imports and emphasized the place of exports in the American economy. He believed that "instead of fencing in the genius and skill of our laborers we should throw wide the gate-ways and permit them to enter every market." Mills wanted "every obstruction . . . swept out of the way of our products as they go to seek markets for their consumption." The first objective would be to obtain free raw materials. The Senator went beyond Cleveland and Wilson by insisting that the United States would also have to remove British interests in order to acquire those markets. Mills believed that, since England had but a "slender hold" on her markets, she "saw with alarm the triumph of Mr. Cleveland as the representative of commercial expansion."[22]

Many American industrialists did not agree with such argu-

[21] William L. Wilson, "The Principle and Method of the New Tariff Bill," *Forum*, XVI (January, 1894), 544–546.
[22] Roger Q. Mills, "The Wilson Bill," *North American Review*, CLVIII (February, 1894), 235–244.

ments. In hearings held in late 1893, some business representatives, notably those from the iron, steel, and agricultural implement sectors, preferred the McKinley tariff to anything the Democrats might offer. The iron and steel representatives emphasized that they wanted the McKinley tariff retained, since they valued the home market more than the foreign market. The latter was "always trifling." But several other comments throw a revealing light on such statements. G. M. Laughlin of the Jones & Laughlin Steel Corporation wanted the tariff kept as it was, declaring that its real effect was to put iron and steel products on a more favored basis in world trade. Andrew Carnegie afterward filled in the details which Laughlin omitted. Carnegie pointed out that the 1890 measure provided that 99 per cent of duty collected from raw material imports would be refunded if these materials were used in manufacturing articles for export. The 1890 tariff also reduced the duty on steel rails, beams, nails, and other items from 20 to 30 per cent. Carnegie concluded that the tariff "gave American manufacturers all the benefits of free trade in their contests with foreign manufacturers through the world," and that "all things considered, the McKinley bill was the wisest tariff reform measure ever framed." [23]

Wilson nevertheless argued that the Republican bill did not go far enough. His viewpoint appeared when he cross-examined Joseph Wharton, Vice-President of the American Iron and Steel Association. Wharton declared that he preferred the McKinley tariff, since it protected American steel mills against the advantage of the cheap labor which foreign steel manufacturers employed. Wilson recalled Wharton's statement that the United States consumed one-third of the world's steel. Wharton corrected Wilson, saying, "No, we produce it." Wilson retorted, "That is a pretty far advanced civilization." Wharton admitted

[23] *House Miscellaneous Document No. 443*, 53rd Cong., 1st Sess. (serial 3156), 257–260, 324, 327, 329, 326; Andrew Carnegie, *The Miscellaneous Writings of Andrew Carnegie*, ed. Burton J. Hendrick (Garden City, N.Y., 1933), II, 31–32.

that he had fallen into the trap by agreeing, "It is satisfactory."²⁴

In spite of Wilson's arguments, the majority of those appearing before the committee wanted to retain the 1890 measure. High tariff arguments so loaded down the testimony, in fact, that Wilson insisted that only a small portion of the hearings be published.²⁵ But the hearings had little bearing on the bill as it was introduced into the House. Wilson and Cleveland had carefully decided what would cure the illness of the American economy. The medicine was going to be given whether the patient liked it or not.

The pall of economic stagnation overhung all the tariff debates. In presenting the measure on the House floor, Wilson admitted that it had been devised "in the shadow and depression of a great commercial crisis." He did not wish to discuss the causes of the trouble, though "there seems to be some recurring cycle," but he asserted without a hint of doubt that the stagnation could be lifted by lightening taxation and loosening "the fetters of trade." ²⁶ The bill he presented promised to do just that.

The proposed tariff helped the sugar trust by reimposing a duty of one-fourth cent per pound on refined sugar, and the bill protected American petroleum with the only reciprocity clause embodied in the bill. One distinct change appeared in the replacement of specific rates with ad valorem tariffs. But most important, the measure levied no duty on many raw materials needed for manufacturing. This free list contained more than 340 subdivisions, including coal, lumber, iron ore, hides, raw sugar, cotton, wool, raw silk, and salt. Wilson indicated the extent of reform when he noted that the average rate on imports would drop about 18 per cent under these new provisions.²⁷

²⁴ *House Miscellaneous Document No. 443,* 53rd Cong., 1st Sess. (serial 3156), 268–273.

²⁵ Festus P. Summers, *William L. Wilson and Tariff Reform* (New Brunswick, N.J., 1953), 167–170; *House Report No. 234,* 53rd Cong., 2nd Sess. (serial 3269), 1.

²⁶ *Congressional Record,* Appendix, 53rd Cong., 2nd Sess., 193.

²⁷ In introducing the bill, Wilson said that his committee was not

To regain this lost revenue, and as a sop to the Populists, an income tax was imposed on earnings above $4,000 annually. This clause was the main target when the Senate later mutilated the bill.

As explained by Wilson, the measure was based on two assumptions: that the United States now enjoyed a mature farm and industrial economy, and that trade expansion would solve the three major problems of the current stagnation—labor unrest, farm surpluses, and inadequate revenue. Free raw materials provided the key, since they would enable this mature industrial system to acquire the necessary markets. Wilson summarized the argument when he stated that free raw materials would result in "the enlargement of markets for our products in other countries, the increase in the internal commerce and in the carrying trade of our own country." All these factors would "insure a growing home market." In effect, Wilson was forecasting that the United States would build its home market by enlarging its foreign market. He used iron and steel as an example. As far as this industry was concerned, "We could throw down to-day our tariff walls and defy the world's competition." With better tariff provisions "we will not only supply our own country, but we will go out and build up other great countries with our products." This campaign need not be limited to iron and steel, however, as the United States possesses "in many lines of production, the manufacturing supremacy of the world." [28]

Focusing upon this free raw materials clause, the minority on the Ways and Means Committee launched a strong attack against Wilson. These dissenters alleged that the provision would injure laborers. Not only would workers in industries which

"under any illusion as to its true character." He observed, "Reform is beautiful upon the mountain top or in the clouds, but oft times very unwelcome as it approaches our own threshold" (*ibid.*). See also Summers, *Wilson*, 175–176.

[28] F. W. Taussig, *Tariff History of the United States* (7th ed.; New York, 1923), 308; Summers, *Wilson*, 172–174; *Congressional Record*, Appendix, 53rd Cong., 2nd Sess., 195–196.

used raw materials suffer, but the lost revenue would have to be found in other areas where the tax "could only fall on the consumers and laborers." Vigorously disagreeing, Wilson viewed trade expansion as the solution for the unemployment problem. Concern with labor unrest formed the center of the House debate on the tariff, so Wilson's views are instructive:

What hope is there, Mr. Chairman, for a labor strike when production has outrun the demands of the home market . . . ? Do we not know when supply has outrun remunerative demand, the employer welcomes a strike . . . ? But with the world for a market, with hundreds of millions of consumers for our iron and steel and other products, with all our mills running and orders ahead, labor can achieve its own emancipation and treat on equal terms for its own wages.[29]

He asserted that commercial expansion would also solve the problems of farm surpluses and revenue. By reducing the costs of the farmers' necessary expenses, they could compete more cheaply in world markets. Farmers received no benefit from tariffs, Wilson believed, for "the prices of their products are fixed in the world's market in competition with like products produced by the cheapest labor of the world." Wilson stressed that the revenue deficit also would be cured by trade expansion, for experience had proven that tariff reductions led to "such an enlargement of commerce, or production and consumption, as rapidly to make up any apparent loss of revenue threatened by these reductions." [30]

Wilson's statements regarding labor unrest, the agricultural problem, and the inadequacy of reciprocity were debated vigorously and at length on the House floor. Democrat Bourke Cockran of New York and Populist Jerry Simpson of Kansas

[29] *House Report No. 234,* 53rd Cong., 2nd Sess. (serial 3269), 5, 16, 20; *Congressional Record,* Appendix, 53rd Cong., 2nd Sess., 196–197.

[30] *House Report No. 234,* 53rd Cong., 2nd Sess. (serial 3269), 8, 10.

explained that freer trade would raise laborers' wages. Cockran declared: "We want to raise the value of labor in this country by increasing its production. We want to stimulate production so that we can get into the markets of the world and command tribute from the people of every nation that finds a dwelling place upon this globe." But it was the Populist, Simpson, who gave the most sophisticated argument for the reformers. He based his case on the fact that there had once been a "great and boundless West" where "surplus labor . . . could find an outlet." Now, however, since the frontier had closed, "there is no more new country to be thus opened, and the great tide of population is turned back again upon the East." Fortunately this occurred at a time when no other world power could match American economic might. Now "we can safely tear down the custom-houses and challenge the world for competition in its markets." Democrats Josiah Patterson and James C. McDearmon, both from Tennessee, followed with passages even more purple. Patterson concluded his speech by exclaiming, "Sir, restriction is not progress; liberty is progress, and free trade points the way to achieve the manifest destiny of the American people."[31]

Protectionist representatives declared that if Wilson really wanted to help the farmers he should strengthen, not abolish, reciprocity. They believed that "the achievements of reciprocity mark the triumph of American trade in the markets of the world." Wilson and his backers disagreed. They dissented, not because they liked Republican reciprocity less, but because they loved unlimited reciprocity more. Democrats attacked this "sham" on three counts. They charged that it helped manufacturers, but not farmers, since it was aimed at Latin-American nations whose products were largely agrarian. Second, its retaliatory measures had provoked ill will from several nations, notably Colombia. Third, the President had been given this

[31] *Congressional Record*, 53rd Cong., 2nd Sess., 945, 776, Appendix, 79.

power of retaliation to use at his discretion. The Democrats claimed this gave him "the power to establish the commercial policy of the first Napoleon." [32]

The bill passed 204-140 on February 1, 1894. As it left the House, the measure specifically exempted all previous reciprocity treaties from abrogation. Moreover, it kept and strengthened the reciprocity principle; raw sugar remained on the free list, and this item had been the basis of most of America's reciprocity treaties. In effect, the Democrats tried to extract the trade benefits from reciprocity without straining diplomatic relations and enlarging executive power. It was not a radical tariff. Senator Mills called it "only a Sabbath Day's journey on the way to reform." Perhaps the best description was the nickname attached when Wilson first introduced it: "The New England Manufacturing Bill." [33]

During the next five months the Senate mangled the Wilson measure beyond recognition. When it emerged from the upper house, the over-all protection rates had risen only slightly, but the free raw materials list contained only three items: wool, lumber, and copper. Most of the reasons for this result were political. Five can be singled out. First, leadership in the Senate passed out of the hands of Cleveland's followers. Roger Q. Mills and Daniel W. Voorhees agreed with the President and Wilson as to the role free raw materials were to play in American foreign trade. But due to Mills' ineffectiveness and Voorhees' age and illness, other men, many of whom were enemies of Cleveland, assumed the leadership.[34] Second, Cleveland made crucial political mistakes. His refusal to compromise on the silver repeal and his determination to use all the patronage at his disposal to pass the repeal, sadly depleted his power. He alienated the two sena-

[32] *Congressional Record,* 53rd Cong., 2nd Sess., 1417–1418, Appendix, 826; *Congressional Record,* 53rd Cong., 2nd Sess., 681, 1422.

[33] *Ibid.,* 659; Laughlin and Willis, *Reciprocity,* 242; Barnes, *Carlisle,* 323; Nevins, *Grover Cleveland,* 564, Summers, *Wilson,* 174–175.

[34] John R. Lambert, *Arthur Pue Gorman* (Baton Rouge, La., 1953), 201–203.

tors from New York because of personal incidents. An attempt to ram a Supreme Court nomination down Senate throats led to a rebellion and to Cleveland's ultimate defeat on the nomination. After rejecting conciliation late in the fight, the President wrote a bitter letter, which was made public and consequently stiffened the back of the Senate. After this Wilson found it impossible to obtain compromises in the Senate-House conferences.[35]

Third, representatives of the Sugar Trust, the National Lead Trust, coal interests, Standard Oil, and other opponents of the bill exerted their considerable influence on key senators. Wilson had ignored these interests when writing the House measure, but senators were more susceptible.[36] The result was a hodgepodge of amendments protecting varied private interests, which the depleted Cleveland forces were unable to override. Fourth, the income tax provision alienated many influential businessmen who could have exerted considerable pressure. Powerful Senator David B. Hill of New York intensely disliked this part of the tariff bill. Fifth, Arthur Pue Gorman of Maryland opposed Cleveland more bitterly as the fight progressed. Gorman did not rewrite the bill's provisions in the Senate (James K. Jones of Arkansas handled this), but he did control the votes, and so was the man to win if Cleveland hoped to have his way. Gorman's golden rule was to keep the Democratic party united whatever the cost. Believing that compromises on the measure were permissible if in the end it could be passed by a majority of Democrats, Gorman climaxed the struggle when he castigated the President on the Senate floor because Cleveland would not moderate his adamant stand for free raw materials.[37]

[35] *Ibid.*, 200–203; Nevins, *Grover Cleveland*, 568–572; Merrill, *Bourbon Leader*, 176, 186; J. B. Moore recollected several interesting points in a letter to C. C. Tansill, Sept. 16, 1940, Box 148, Moore MSS.

[36] White, "United States and the Problem of Recovery after 1893," 66–67; Lambert, *Gorman*, 215; Summers, *Wilson*, 191.

[37] *Congressional Record*, 53rd Cong., 2nd Sess., 5132; Barnes, *Carlisle*, 326; Lambert, *Gorman*, 210–213, 181, 199.

While the Senate droned on, Democratic leaders worked behind the scenes to find acceptable compromises.[38] In several conferences Cleveland insisted upon free coal and free iron ore. On July 3 the Senate voted on the tariff. All free raw materials had been removed except wool, copper, and lumber. That morning Senator Isham Harris told the President that the bill had to be taken as it was or it would be tabled and killed. Cleveland again requested free coal, free iron ore, and lower sugar rates, but Harris said that such amendments could not be passed. According to Harris, Cleveland capitulated. The measure squeaked by the Senate 39-34 with twelve members abstaining.[39]

Wilson refused to budge in the Senate-House conference committee. Then on July 19 came the bomb from the White House. On July 2 (one day before Cleveland allegedly gave his approval of the Senate bill to Harris), the President had written a letter to Wilson. Its famous sentence that abandonment of tariff reform principles by Senate Democrats "means party perfidy and party dishonor" created an uproar. But it is the remainder of the message which should interest historians. First and foremost, Cleveland devoted four paragraphs to the need of American industry for free raw materials. He concluded that on this subject there "does not admit of adjustment on any middle ground." Second, Cleveland asked for a higher tariff on raw sugar. This, he believed, would adequately replace that lost from raw materials admitted without duty.[40]

The letter enraged leading Senate Democrats. Shortly after, an amendment was proposed in the upper house providing for

[38] For some of the several Senate speeches which extolled reciprocity and proclaimed the need for more foreign markets, especially in Latin America, see *Congressional Record*, 53rd Cong., 2nd Sess., 3621–3622, 3962–3993, 5436, 6995.

[39] Nevins, *Grover Cleveland*, 572–574, 579; Lambert, *Gorman*, 217–218; *Congressional Record*, 53rd Cong., 2nd Sess., 7136.

[40] *Ibid.*, 7191, 7712; Grover Cleveland, *Letters of Grover Cleveland, 1850–1908*, selected and edited by Allan Nevins (New York and Boston, 1933), 354–357.

free iron, coal, wool, and lumber; it was crushed 65-6. By the middle of August, Wilson and the House Democrats had given up the fight. The only remaining question was whether Cleveland would sign the measure. His concern for free raw materials did not lessen. He told a close friend in late July that "my wonder constantly increases at the seeming lack of appreciation of the importance of being right on the free raw materials question." But he allowed the bill to become law without his signature. He revealed the reasons for his refusal to sign the measure in a letter of August 27. The last third of the letter lamented the loss of the free raw material provisions. He concluded that "when we give to our manufacturers free raw materials we unshackle American enterprise and ingenuity, and these will open the doors of foreign markets . . . and give opportunity for the continuous and re-munerative employment of American labor." [41]

Everything considered, the 1894 tariff fulfilled the hopes of most moderate tariff reformers. Wool, copper, and lumber went on the free list, while the tariff dropped to 39.9 per cent. The Supreme Court declared the income tax amendment uncon-stitutional the following year. Several business journals which appraised the measure in terms of what it would do for American exports approved of the final result.[42] Moreover, figures soon demonstrated that with the exception of one or two special cases, trade with South American countries did not fall off under the new tariff. Trade increased in spite of a general price decline on

[41] *Congressional Record*, 53rd Cong., 2nd Sess., 7804, 7891; Lambert, *Gorman*, 232–237; *Letters of Grover Cleveland*, 363, 365–366; McElroy, *Grover Cleveland*, II, 114–115.

[42] *Commercial and Financial Chronicle*, Aug. 18, 1894, 253–254; *Bankers' Magazine*, XLIX (September, 1894), 170–171; "American Products Abroad," *The Literary Digest*, July 20, 1895, 331. After an extensive analysis, William Hill believed that the income tax amendment had to bear the blame for the Senate's mutilation of the bill. Hill concluded, "No sort of combination, comparison or analysis of this vote can be made to yield encouragement to the protectionists" ("Comparison of the Votes on the McKinley and Wilson Bills," *Journal of Political Econ-omy*, II [March, 1894], 290–292).

both continents. Even Cleveland praised the tariff in this respect. In his final annual message he claimed that the bill "opened the way to a freer and greater exchange of commodities between us and other countries, and thus furnished a wider market for our products and manufactures." [43]

The business journals and the President agreed on another point. They believed that the tariff would provide a powerful lever for the immediate revival of American factories.[44] But such hopes quickly withered. A minor wave of orders rippled through the economy, and then the system sank into the deepest part of the entire depression. Labor violence erupted. Questions began to be raised about the fundamental assumptions of the American political and economic system.

"Symptoms of Revolution"

On the first day of November, 1894, Cleveland's good friend, New York banker James Stillman, told the President that "contrary to general expectation," the tariff bill had "not produced any great revival in business." The depression was entering into its deepest trough. Looking back a decade later, Cleveland commented that after December 1, 1894, there "followed a time of bitter disappointment and miserable depression, greater than any that had before darkened the struggles of the Executive branch of the Government to save our nation's financial integrity." Conditions improved in February, 1895, when the Morgan-Belmont syndicate stepped in to save the Treasury's gold reserve. This move ushered in several months of business improvement including a boom in iron and steel. But as the New York correspondent of the London *Economist* warned in early fall, "business conditions in the United States have not even approximately returned to their normal level." Overproduction in iron and steel triggered

[43] Laughlin and Willis, *Reciprocity*, 266; *Messages and Papers of the Presidents*, IX, 552–553, 741.
[44] For the opinions of business journals, see White, "United States and the Problem of Recovery after 1893," 68–69.

a serious reaction in October. The American economy again faced the task of rebuilding itself.[45]

Against this somber and darkening background, the unemployed and discontented acted out what the Secretary of State, Walter Quintin Gresham, called "symptoms of revolution." In the three years of 1893 to 1895, almost everything occurred in the way of class conflict which conservatives and liberals alike had feared from the time of the Founding Fathers; almost everything, that is, except actual organized revolution. Laborers' wages had dropped drastically since 1890, and in 1894 one out of every six laborers received no wages at all. A basic change had occurred in American society which made it particularly vulnerable to such a depression. The United States was no longer the nation of self-sufficient farmers. Although the trend toward urbanization had been evident for decades, in the ten years after 1880 the number of individuals engaged in manufacturing and mechanical industries more than doubled to the figure of 4,712,000.[46]

[45] Stillman to Cleveland, Nov. 1, 1894, Cleveland MSS; *Letters of Henry Adams* prints Adams' opinion of April 28, 1894, that "the trouble is quite different from any previous experience . . . but nobody diagnoses it." And then a typical Adams twist: "I prefer my Cuba, which is frankly subsiding into savagery. At least the problems there are simple." See also *Economist* (London), March 30, 1895, 421; June 29, 1895, 852; Sept. 28, 1895, 1275–1276; Sept. 21, 1895, 1237; Oct. 26, 1895, 1404; Charles Hoffmann, "The Depression of the Nineties," *Journal of Economic History*, XVI (June, 1956), 137–149; White, "United States and the Problem of Recovery," 92–94; Grover Cleveland, *Presidential Problems* (New York, 1904), 142–143; Nevins, *Grover Cleveland*, 649.

[46] Paul H. Douglas, *Real Wages in the United States, 1890–1926* (Boston and New York, 1930), 389–391, 440; Bernard Weber and S. J. Handfield-Jones, "Variations in the Rate of Economic Growth in the U.S.A., 1869–1939," *Oxford Economic Papers*, n.s. (June, 1954), 101–131; Arthur Mier Schlesinger, *The Rise of the City, 1878–1898* (New York, 1933), 77–80, 426; White, "United States and the Problem of Recovery after 1893," 37. Concern over the unemployed was great. In one volume of the *Literary Digest* covering November, 1893, to May, 1894, there are references to at least sixteen articles on the problem and the possible danger.

The depression struck this wage-earning class with devastating force. One contemporary observer later wrote: "Through some curious psychological impulse, the notion of a general crusade of squalor spread all through the country; and from every quarter of the West and the Southwest, bands of ragged, hungry, homeless men appeared." Symbolically, labor armies, as the Coxey and Hogan groups, began their slow march eastward to Washington—the movement which signaled that the great American frontier no longer attracted but now repelled the discontented of the nation. The *Nation* exclaimed that "mobs" controlled the entire state of California. The socialist wing came within a breath of taking the control of the American Federation of Labor away from Samuel Gompers' moderate followers. One business reporter cried, "The greatest industrial struggle ever begun in this country, if not in the world, is in progress here." [47]

The depression thus not only forced the Cleveland administration to face the towering problem of invigorating the economy, but to do so before serious political and social upheavals occurred. The administration became the focal point for the fire of radicals and the fears of conservatives. Washington went into a turmoil. Officers had leaves cancelled, the War Department, in the words of one official, was "in a ferment," and the Treasury ordered special troops for its subtreasuries in Chicago and New York.

[47] Harry Thurston Peck, *Twenty Years of the Republic, 1885–1905* (New York, 1907), 373; Alexander Dana Noyes, *The Market Place: Reminiscences of a Financial Editor* (Boston, 1938), 107–108; Samuel Rezneck, "Unemployment, Unrest and Relief in the United States during the Depression of 1893–1897," *Journal of Political Economy*, LXI (August, 1953), 326; American Federation of Labor, *Reports of Proceedings of the Annual Convention . . . 1893* (New York, 1894), 9; Samuel Gompers, *Seventy Years of Life and Labor: An Autobiography* (New York, 1925), II, 4–5, 7, 522; George H. Knowles, "Populism and Socialism with Special Reference to the Elections of 1892," *Pacific Historical Review*, XII (September, 1943), 295–304; *Economist*, July 21, 1894, 893; the best article on the uprisings in the West is Frederick Jackson Turner, "The Problem of the West," *Atlantic Monthly*, LXXVIII (September, 1896), 296.

Railroad magnate James J. Hill wrote the Secretary of War, Daniel Lamont, that "the reign of terror . . . exists in the large centres." But when federal and state troops crushed several strikes, leading businessmen and conservatives expressed a fear of such methods. The *Bankers' Magazine* gravely pointed out that Cleveland's action in stopping the Pullman strike by force extended the national power to its fullest. The President's conduct provided "a very dangerous precedent," and the journal shuddered to think how the precedent might be extended should the "corporate combinations" or the "new Populist party" gain control. The journal believed class conflict could result. Others, however, advocated the use of force. David Starr Jordan, though a leader in the world peace movement, congratulated the President for "having done his plain duty" in smashing the Chicago strike. The President of the Farmers Loan and Trust Company of New York notified Cleveland that in view of the recent "destructive disturbances," the standing army should be increased from 25,000 "to at least two hundred thousand men." [48]

Unaffected by the repeal of the Sherman Silver Purchase Act and only temporarily slowed by the tariff bill, the depression hurtled along, splintering and inflaming every economic, political, and social unit it touched. The administration, having failed to blunt the destructive force with the well-worn weapons of the gold standard and the tariff, had reverted to armed force. But Cleveland, Gresham, and Carlisle also believed that the ultimate solution lay in large measure in the discovery of more foreign markets. In 1894 and 1895 the American business community engaged in a momentous debate which concluded in an agreement with the administration on the causes, solutions, and the foreign policy implications of the depression.

[48] Barnes, *Carlisle*, 332–333; A. B. Farquhar to Cleveland, June 1, 1894, David S. Jordan to Cleveland, July 18, 1894, R. G. Rolston to Cleveland, July 27, 1894, all in Cleveland MSS; James J. Hill to Daniel Lamont, July 7, Daniel Lamont papers, Library of Congress, Washington, D.C.; *Bankers' Magazine*, XLIX (August, 1894), 85–86, and XLVIII (May, 1894), 809.

The American Business Community: Analysis

Social upheavals and labor violence intensified as the depression entered its most critical period during the last months of 1894 and the first half of 1895. By the end of 1895, however, the American business community had reached a consensus on the causes of and solutions for the depression. Spokesmen for this community displayed special concern with two immediate problems: stopping the outflow of gold and halting the inflow of American securities from Europe. These problems were, in turn, subsumed in the larger challenge of increasing exports so that plants could dispose of their surplus goods and resume full productivity and regular employment. The administration demonstrated its agreement with this analysis when Secretary of the Treasury, John G. Carlisle, submitted a remarkable annual report in 1894 which held that American exports were the chief hope of restoring economic prosperity in the United States.

Halting the outflow of gold and the inflow of American securities from Europe were two sides of the same problem. Much of the gold that left the New York subtreasuries went into the pockets of panicky European investors. Business and political experts soon viewed exports of merchandise as the solution for both problems. Merchandise exports would stop gold exports by bringing so much money to the United States that the flow inward would overbalance the gold flow outward. Exports would also solve the foreign investment dilemma: first, they would invigorate American industries and so make the system attractive to foreign investors; second, the exports would provide the capital to replace any foreign investment which refused to take another plunge into American securities.

This last point became a particularly fascinating feature of the mid-1890's. In his message requesting the repeal of the Sherman Silver Purchase Act, Cleveland expressed the hope that repeal would revive interest in American investments and increase the amount of money available. But after the repeal, European money could not be found in any quantity. Instead, assistance came from an unexpected source—American banking houses. Capital, scarce in early summer of 1893, became so plentiful during the latter part of the year that loan rates dropped to very low levels. Some of this money bought out European investors and put American firms, especially railroads, into American banking hands.[49]

The growing power of American bankers also affected United States relations with other countries. The nation became steadily more independent of foreign capital. Some American investors, moreover, found the home market too narrow and unprofitable. By 1896 their capital was moving into Caribbean and South and Central American money markets. Financial spokesmen also began noticing the relation of exports to investment capital. In the few years before 1893, exports had managed to balance the nation's international debts, but had failed to help the country's economy expand, since withdrawals of European investments more than offset the export gains. To maintain an expanding industrial economy, these amounts of exports were not enough. Either exports had to be increased or European capital found; otherwise the industrial expansion which had occurred since 1865 could not be maintained. When Europeans neglected the American investment market from 1893 to 1896, business spokesmen expected exports to be important means of obtaining needed capital.[50] In other words, the United States would have to sell enough merchandise on the international market so that the nation could balance the debt it owed to that same market and have

---

[49] *Messages and Papers of the Presidents,* IX, 402; *Commercial and Financial Chronicle,* Jan. 6, 1894, 13; C. K. Hobson, *The Export of Capital* (New York, 1914), 150–151; W. Wetherell, "British Investors and American Currency Legislation," *Forum,* XVI (January, 1894), 606–615; A. D. Noyes, "Methods and Leadership in Wall Street Since 1893," *Journal of Economic and Business History,* IV (November, 1931), 9.

[50] Hobson, *The Export of Capital,* 152–155; see especially Carlisle's *Annual Report, 1894,* lxxii, lxxiii; also Hoffmann, "The Depression of the Nineties," 152–153.

sufficient capital left over to finance the expansion of home industry.

This presented a gargantuan task. The dimensions of the problem became strikingly evident in mid-1894, when business journals noted that during the 1894 fiscal year exports exceeded imports by $259,567,000, yet gold had left the country in increasing amounts since January 1. Statistics for the 1894 calendar year told the same story. Although exports of merchandise, gold, and silver reached an enormous sum of $250,000,000, the *Commercial and Financial Chronicle* lamented, "Yet even at this moment the outflow of gold is still in progress." *Bradstreet's* paradoxically termed such an enormous export surplus as "Our Disappointing Foreign Trade." The gold exports halted in mid-1895 because of the manipulations of the Morgan-Belmont bond syndicate, which was helping the Treasury maintain its reserve by buying gold abroad. Business circles harbored no illusions, however. They frankly admitted that the syndicate had "certain limits" in supplying "the deficiency in natural media of exchange." [51]

Businessmen believed their chief hope lay in autumn crop exports taking up where the syndicate left off. There were still fond memories of the 1891 and 1892 export years. But, as one business journal warned, if these exports failed to materialize there would probably result "unfortunate consequences which some of our contemporaries [the silverites] apparently delight to describe." By November, 1895, it became obvious that exports were not sufficient to handle the job. The New York correspondent for the *Economist* outlined the situation in detail. Over $7,300,000 had left the Treasury's gold reserve during the week of November 23, and "most . . . has gone to pay our debts." If exports of cotton, wheat, provisions, and other staples could continue in large amounts, gold would return to the country.

[51] *Bradstreet's*, Jan. 19, 1895, 36; May 26, 1894, 322–323; Aug. 31, 1895, 546; *Commercial and Financial Chronicle*, Jan. 19, 1895, 107–109; *Economist*, Aug. 3, 1895, 1022; *Public Opinion*, Sept. 26, 1895, 397.

But when these exports could not match the import of foreign goods and American securities returned by European investors, "it is inevitable that gold will leave this country." [52]

As gold continued to flow outward, business circles cried that they would have "to continue to suffer this sort of financial nightmare every time our international trade statistics indicate an unfavourable trade balance." One authority publicly prescribed the cure which many businessmen were considering. A. S. Heidelbach, the senior member of a large international banking firm in New York, declared that in order to end the gold out-flow, the balance of trade in merchandise would have to reach "at least" $350,000,000 a year. Some disputed his figures, but few disputed his solution.[53]

The selling of American securities not only endangered the gold reserve but also threatened to stunt the growth of the industrial economy through financial starvation. Reports issued by *Bankers' Magazine* and Worthington C. Ford, Chief of the Bureau of Statistics, clearly explained the relationship between foreign funds and American economic strength. The irony of this situation lay in the fact that surplus money glutted American banks. Secretary Carlisle noted in his 1895 report that money had been hoarded "until it nearly reached the proportions of a panic." Business magazines concurred with this view. Much of this money abjured depression-ridden domestic securities and moved into foreign markets. Americans actually increased their investments abroad by almost $250,000,000 during the depression. Most of this money went to Canada and Latin America. Not only did this movement of capital leave American industries in their stagnant condition, but it greatly aggravated the

---

[52] *Bradstreet's*, June 29, 1895, 403; *Economist*, Oct. 12, 1895, 1339–1340; Dec. 7, 1895, 1592.

[53] *Economist*, Nov. 2, 1895, 1435; Alfred S. Heidelbach, "Why Gold Is Exported," *Forum*, XVIII (February, 1895), 647–651; Worthington C. Ford, "Foreign Exchanges and the Movement of Gold, 1894–1895," *Yale Review*, IV (August, 1895), 137–138; *Commercial and Financial Chronicle*, March 30, 1895, 542–543.

balance of payments by enlarging the American demand for foreign exchange.[54]

Industrialists began to realize a harsh fact. As *Bradstreet's* commented, money would flow into American factories only when there would be "developments of commercial activity and legitimate business in lines which, up to the moment, cannot be clearly foreseen." This journal added that "if business becomes active," European investors would also "at once come back to the market." *Bankers' Magazine* agreed with this analysis. To restore this commercial activity, however, demand had to be found.[55]

By late 1895 the business community and the Cleveland administration agreed that exports provided one solution for the economic problems. In the business community no one summarized this agreement better than Henry W. Cannon, President of the Chase National Bank. Writing in February, 1895, Cannon stated that in order to prove to European investors that the United States could maintain gold payments, "it is necessary . . . that we should compete in the markets of the world with our goods and commodities, and also reconstruct our currency

[54] *Bankers' Magazine*, XLIX (August, 1894), 97–98; XLIX (January, 1895), 156; Hoffmann, "Depression of the Nineties," 156–157; James A. Stillman to William E. Curtis of the Treasury Department, July 31, 1894, Cleveland MSS; Noyes, *Thirty Years of American Finance*, 217–218; *Bradstreet's*, June 22, 1895, 388; Worthington C. Ford, "The Turning of the Tide," *North American Review*, CLXI (August, 1895), 188; *Annual Report of the Secretary of the Treasury, 1895*, lxix; *Messages and Papers of the Presidents*, IX, 650; *Commercial and Financial Chronicle*, Jan. 5, 1895, 10; Robert W. Dunn, *American Foreign Investments* (New York, 1926), 2.

[55] *Bradstreet's*, Sept. 29, 1894, 609; May 26, 1894, 323; Aug. 11, 1894, 499; *Bankers' Magazine*, XLIX (October, 1894), 245. For evidence of the recognition in 1894–1895 that the glut of both goods and money was deepening the depression, see W. P. Clough to Cleveland, March 23, 1894, Cleveland MSS; Charles Stewart Smith *et al.*, "Home Industries and the Wilson Bill," *North American Review*, CLVIII (March, 1894), 312–324; New York *Journal of Commerce* quoted in *Public Opinion*, Sept. 27, 1894, 623–624; *Bankers' Magazine*, XLIX (January, 1894), 489; *Bradstreet's*, Oct. 19, 1895, 659; the first three condensed articles in *Literary Digest*, Jan. 6, 1894, 189–191.

system." The New York reporter for the *Economist* stated the proposition tersely in September, 1895: "Either goods or gold must go abroad to pay for our purchases there, and thus far this autumn our shipments . . . have not equalled expectations." [56]

The most significant and influential statement of this sort, however, came from Secretary Carlisle in his annual report of 1894. He noted at the outset that the United States had been kept "almost constantly in the position of debtors." Then in a striking analysis of what he considered to be the American system's dynamic, Carlisle observed that the nation's "prosperity . . . depends largely upon [its] ability to sell [its] surplus products in foreign markets at remunerative prices" in order to pay off loans and interest and to secure credit abroad. The American economy, Carlisle warned, could survive the selling of securities by foreign investors in only two ways: "One is for our people to export and sell their commodities in foreign markets to a sufficient amount to create a balance of credit in their favor equal to the amount to be withdrawn, and the other is to ship gold, that being the only money recognized in the settlement of international balances." The latter course had been resorted to since 1893, and the results had been disastrous. The Secretary's either/or alternative appeared to be the only escape out of the depression.[57]

With recovery defined in such terms, the responsibility upon American exporters was great. Unfortunately, this responsibility came at a time when they could ill bear the burden. Exports for the 1894 fiscal year had been surpassed only twice before in American history, but ominously, the four leading staples—breadstuffs, provisions, cotton, and petroleum—had fallen off

[56] J. Sterling Morton, William M. Springer, Henry W. Cannon, "The Financial Muddle," *North American Review*, CLX (February, 1895), 129–156, especially 151; another banker, A. B. Farquhar, said essentially the same thing to his good friend Grover Cleveland, Nov. 9, 1894, Cleveland MSS; *Economist*, Sept. 21, 1895, 1244; "Comment," *Yale Review*, III (November, 1895), 225–228.

[57] *Annual Report of the Secretary of Treasury, 1894*, lxxii, lxxiii.

in value almost six million dollars. In order to find outlets, their producers had to accept very low prices, "in some cases," one journal declared, "the lowest ever made." The *Commercial and Financial Chronicle* and the *Economist* agreed with *Bankers' Magazine* that "there has been a natural cause" for the worsening depression; "small exports and agricultural depression, are . . . now the chief remaining obstacles to a return of general prosperity." [58] Unlike 1891 and 1892, cotton and wheat exports could not restore normal conditions.

Amid this gloom, Worthington C. Ford published an article, "The Turning of the Tide," in the summer of 1895. He entitled it thus although exports had declined $75,651,000, although the export balance had greatly decreased in comparison with 1894, and although the export staples, especially wheat and cotton, had suffered disastrous setbacks in the 1895 fiscal year. But Ford was correct in terming it a "Turn," for the figures in the export tables of fiscal 1895 marked not only a turn in the depression but a pivotal point in American commercial history. These figures indicated that, although farm exports had slumped, industrial exports had reached all-time highs. Iron and steel had especially topped their previous high levels of 1894 by nearly a million dollars. Ford emphasized this change further by noting that the nation imported less food in 1895, but that "more raw materials for domestic industries, more partly manufactured articles and more manufactures for consumption" arrived.[59]

In making this analysis, Ford simply repeated what some business journals had been proclaiming since early 1894. *Bankers' Magazine* and the *Commercial and Financial Chronicle* echoed *Bradstreet's* conclusion that the agricultural depression formed "the worst obstacle to our general business recovery." Another

[58] *Commercial and Financial Chronicle*, July 21, 1894, 93–95; Jan. 5, 1895, 9; *Bankers' Magazine*, XLIX (November, 1894), 326; *Bradstreet's*, Feb. 16, 1895, 99; *Economist*, July 27, 1895, 985; Aug. 31, 1895, 1148; Noyes, *Thirty Years of American Finance*, 245–246; *Annual Report of the Secretary of the Treasury, 1895*, xxxi.

[59] Ford, "Turning of the Tide," 188, 193–195.

journal observed that because of newly opened wheat lands in Latin America and Russia "it is practically impossible for the United States to compete with foreign exports of wheat." Out of this analysis arose a new evaluation of international trade. Several articles printed in *Bankers' Magazine* during the fall of 1894 best illustrate the new conclusions formed by these business spokesmen.[60]

These articles postulated that a "great revolution in prices" had occurred which made impossible a return to former price levels. Now "the cheapest" country would "win in the great National, and International race for the commerce of its own people [and] for that of the world." The journal lamented that the nation's agriculture, "hitherto regarded as the source of our National prosperity," would have to be sacrificed in this race. But clearly, the American farmer could no longer compete in world markets. He could perform an even more vital function, however, for the cheapness of foodstuffs, "together with cheaper raw materials," would provide "the foundation . . . of our future manufacturing supremacy over Europe." Upon this new industrial base "we must soon depend for our nation's prosperity, instead of upon her producers of food, feed, and raw materials." The visions arising from this premise were grandiose. There would be no more boom times followed by depression, but "slow and steady improvement . . . and our surplus manufacturing capacity turned to the production of goods we may be able to export hereafter, at reduced cost and thus keep all our industries permanently employed, as England does, having the world's markets in which to unload any accumulation." [61]

[60] *Bradstreet's*, Oct. 26, 1895, 674; April 27, 1895, 259; Dec. 22, 1894, 802; Dec. 1, 1894, 754; Nov. 2, 1894, 693; *Commercial and Financial Chronicle*, July 21, 1894, 95; Jan. 5, 1895, 10; July 29, 1895, 90–91; *Bankers' Magazine*, XLVIII (March, 1894), 649–650, and XLIX (December, 1894), 31–32; *Economist*, March 3, 1894, 273; Sept. 22, 1894, 1169; Dec. 1, 1894, 1473; Supplement, Oct. 13, 1894, 8.

[61] *Bankers' Magazine*, XLIX (November, 1894), 326–328; XLIX (October, 1894), 249; Worthington C. Ford, "Commerce and Industry under

Corroborating this reasoning, industrial goods slowly edged upward on the export charts, accounting for 15.61 per cent of the total exports in the fiscal year 1892, 19.02 per cent in 1893, 21.14 per cent in 1894, and jumping to 23.14 per cent in 1895. This, plus the announcement in mid-1895 that a large shipment of United States steel was to go abroad to compete in the highly competitive European market, "attracted considerable attention," in the words of *Literary Digest.* Examining these events, the New York *Journal of Commerce*, the New York *Herald*, and the antijingoist Louisville *Courier-Journal* had their views well summed up by the London *Iron and Coal Trades Review:* "The Americans themselves argue . . . that they must continue to increase the export of their manufactured goods, since their exports of food and other raw products must inevitably decline." [62]

Businessmen saw foreign markets as vitally important for their economic welfare, but they also clearly saw and feared the social consequences which would follow should their programs of commercial expansion fail to restore prosperity. Nowhere was this stated better than in *Bankers' Magazine* of February, 1894. This article is certainly one of the most interesting printed during the 1890's in business or popular journals. Written during the time when Populism was reaching its peak and labor uprisings threatened, the article re-evaluated American society along the classic lines of James Madison's *The Federalist*, No. 10.

The article opened by noting that business was severely depressed, and that destitute tramps symbolized the United States of 1894. It then asked bluntly whether the American political system had reached the end of its usefulness. The United States

Depression," *Bankers' Magazine*, XLIX (March, 1895), 480–486. See also Charles Stewart Smith and Francis B. Thurber, "What Will Bring Prosperity?" *North American Review*, CLXIV (April, 1897), 428–430.

[62] "Growth of Our Manufactured Exports," *Literary Digest*, Sept. 7, 1895, 549; "American Products Abroad," *Literary Digest*, July 20, 1895, 331–332; New York *Journal of Commerce* quoted in *Public Opinion*, Sept. 5, 1895, 315; *Bradstreet's*, July 20, 1895, 462.

had become sectionalized not only politically, but even more dangerously, "on business and economic questions." These "sectional differences are growing greater" as the people's interests grow more diversified. The article searched for the source of this trouble: "Have we grown too fast to consolidate our strength; or, are the interests of new communities naturally antagonistic to those of older ones?" The political economist would answer that "the greater the general good and prosperity, the greater that of the individual." But "neither the economics, nor the ethics of our times are founded upon Humanitarianism," but "upon the cornerstone of self, self-interest, self-aggrandizement, power and wealth, at the expense of everybody else."

These selfish interests have "become irreconcilable, by becoming so diversified" and so "have brought our National Government into its present impotency." The journal did not believe that Americans would admit that "we have grown too great, to hold our wide Empire intact, by the bond of commonweal." But after all, the Roman Empire had disintegrated when it failed to govern well a vast expanse of territory. The lesson was plain. If the depression and its attendant economic discontent continued to clog the political machine erected by the Founding Fathers, only two possible alternatives presented themselves: follow the British Empire and allow more local autonomy, or centralize to a great extent so that the majority may govern without hindrance.[63] This was an analysis of a crisis. It rested on the hope that improved economic conditions would end Populist and labor unrest and enable the machine of 1787 to continue with few repairs. But the importance of the article lay in the fact that the spokesman for a vital segment of the business community realized that the political penalty would be severe if the American economy continued to appear bankrupt.

[63] *Bankers' Magazine*, XLVIII (February, 1894), 563–565. For a British observer's analysis of a growing split between East and West in the United States "until they are now fairly in the attitude of hostile communities," see W. L. Alden, "War to the Knife," *The Nineteenth Century*, XL (August, 1896), 199–204.

The American Business Community: Solutions

Worthington C. Ford's article, "The Turning of the Tide," not only observed the slow change from foodstuffs to manufactured products in American exports, but calculated that such a change would switch the focus of the nation's commercial interest. Ford noted that "the political consequences" of the change were displayed in the increasing trade with underindustrialized areas such as South America, Oceania, and Africa and a corresponding decrease of trade with Europe. Again, Ford only summarized what American business and political circles had realized for some time.

This did not mean that American manufacturers refused to compete in European markets. In 1895 the entry of United States iron ore and steel in British and continental markets excited Wall Street. American paper products invaded established European markets. Even United States investment capital began flowing to Europe in increased amounts. But challenging European manufacturers in their own backyards was risky business. South America and Central America, on the other hand, not only provided a natural outlet for manufactures, but possessed geographical advantages and also came under the political protection of the Monroe Doctrine. True, American trade with the nations to the south approximated only one-seventh of the entire trade which the Latin-American nations carried on, but this fact merely strengthened American desires to obtain this market. Latin America appeared to be a virgin prize well located for an easy seduction.[64] United States interest in Asian markets also

[64] See especially the statement of General I. W. Avery, the commissioner sent by the Cotton States and International Exposition to South America in early 1895, in *Public Opinion*, April 25, 1895, 436–437; Ford, "Turning of the Tide," 187–188; see also the observations of an acute French observer, Maurice D. de Beaumarchais, *La Doctrine de Monroe* (Paris, 1898), 208–210. Also *Bradstreet's*, June 29, 1895, 413–414; May 11, 1895, 296; Nov. 2, 1895, 702. For American business and diplomatic correspondence which shows how much pressure certain European nations

increased after 1895, but this movement would not influence State Department policy makers in an important way until 1897.[65]

American financiers and manufacturers moved into Latin America with a conscious, concerted effort. As the *Bankers' Magazine* insisted in early 1894, if "we could wrest the South American markets from Germany and England and permanently hold them, this would be indeed a conquest worth perhaps a heavy sacrifice." The "sacrifice" this journal had in mind was probably the American farmer. In any case, increasing numbers of investors moved into the Latin-American area to make this conquest after 1893. In early 1894 a New York steamship company opened a regular trade route between New York and the Pacific coast of South America. By 1896 business had grown so profitable that the line increased its fleet, and a rival American company entered the field. A group of Chicago railroad capitalists signed a contract in 1895 to construct an important railway in Mexico. Several Denver financiers completed an important Costa Rican railway line in 1895. In Colombia a company composed entirely of Americans built and operated a railway along the Atlantic coast. It purchased its locomotives and cars in the United States. Another American-financed railway was under construction in Guatemala. One railroad official noted the American interest in Mexico when he remarked in early 1895 that "there are fully three times as many Americans in Mexico this winter looking up lands as were there last winter." [66]

A group of New York City bankers obtained a dominant share

were exerting on American insurance companies and farm exports, see John B. Jackson to Adee, Aug. 8, 1895, Olney MSS, and the correspondence with France and Germany in *Foreign Relations, 1894*, I, 402–413, 428–453, 497–504.

[65] For the Asian situation, see Chapter VII, below.

[66] *Bankers' Magazine*, XLVIII (January, 1894), 483–484; Bureau of American Republics, *Special [Monthly] Bulletin*, August, 1896, 842, 839; May, 1896, 626–627; September, 1895, 145; Callahan, *American Foreign Policy in Mexican Relations*, 508; *Bradstreet's*, Jan. 5, 1895, 14.

of Santo Domingo's finances in 1893 when they purchased the nation's debt from a Dutch company. Receiving the right to collect all customs revenues, this syndicate could exert a powerful influence on the Santo Domingo government. American capitalists controlled a Salvadoran company which obtained a government monopoly over the Bay of Jiquilisco and built a new port (El Triunfo) in 1894–1895. The port soon exacted the trade of the entire region, and by early 1896 coffee exports were nearly doubling each month. United States capital in Mexico, Cuba, and the Caribbean area alone amounted to $350,000,000 by 1898.[67]

The investor moved southward with a minimum of fanfare. The merchant and manufacturer, however, invaded Latin America with the cheers of commercial manifest destiny ringing in his ears. In 1889 James G. Blaine had led, and the businessmen had willingly followed. But after 1893 the businessmen played at least an equal role in focusing attention southward and in some instances blazed paths which the State Department followed in formulating Latin-American policies. *The Age of Steel* echoed Brooks Adams by declaring in 1895 that "there is no fixedness in commercial supremacy. It has come and gone from one nation to another." *Bankers' Magazine* added, "There is no reason why our manufactures should not find an enlarged market in the southern half of this hemisphere." *Bradstreet's* noted that the industrialists were responding with an aroused interest in Latin America by late 1894.[68] This interest took many forms—renewed demands for an Isthmian canal, increased attention given to reciprocity, the enthusiasm displayed by cotton and woolen tex-

[67] When news spread in Santo Domingo of the concession to the Americans, the population grew restless and a revolution seemed imminent. None occurred, however. See New York *Tribune*, Feb. 21, 1893, 1:2; David Y. Thomas, *One Hundred Years of the Monroe Doctrine* (New York, 1927), 219–220; Lewis Baker, American Minister to Nicaragua, to Olney, Feb. 22, 1897, Area 9 file, NA, RG 45; Hoffmann, "Depression of the Nineties," 156–157; Dunn, *American Foreign Investment*, 2.

[68] *Bradstreet's*, April 27, 1895, 270; Nov. 10, 1894, 711; *Bankers' Magazine*, XLIX (March, 1895), 498; *Public Opinion*, May 17, 1894, 159.

tile manufacturers in developing Latin-American markets, the growth of and interest in industrial expositions held in the southern United States, the development of commercial museums, and, finally, the formation and growth of the National Association of Manufacturers.

Bradstreet's mirrored much business opinion when it wrote that the Clayton-Bulwer Treaty should be formally abrogated as soon as possible, though this should be done "within the bounds of international courtesy." The *Economist's* New York correspondent observed that "considerable interest is taken in the outlook for the construction of the Nicaragua Canal," and then added an anti-British note that became more prominent as the depression progressed, "and particularly because of the attention directed to the control of that canal in recent British publications." *Bradstreet's* published a long summary of a paper by Emory R. Johnson, which emphasized the commercial, not the strategic, advantages of such a passageway. A canal, Johnson reported, would give the United States "a decided advantage over other nations" in "the future development of the South American and Oriental countries." [69]

A renewed interest in reciprocity appeared in early 1895 just as the Wilson-Gorman tariff went into operation. Three key business organizations especially displayed some inquisitiveness in the possibility of renewing the reciprocity amendment of 1890. The newly organized National Association of Manufacturers and the National Board of Trade expressed particular interest in negotiating reciprocity pacts with Mexico, Central America and South America, and the Spanish-American colonies. Andrew Carnegie published an article in which he termed reciprocity "the best step" in obtaining foreign trade otherwise unobtainable. [70]

[69] *Economist*, Sept. 7, 1895, 1179; *Bradstreet's*, Dec. 28, 1895, 820. A further discussion of the canal is found in Chapter V, below.

[70] *Bradstreet's*, Nov. 10, 1894, 711; "Legislative Demands by Business Interests," *Literary Digest*, Feb. 8, 1896, 423; Andrew Carnegie, "What Would I Do with the Tariff," *Forum*, XIX (March, 1895), 18–28.

Cotton and woolen textile manufacturers displayed intense interest in southern markets. Worthington C. Ford noted that the cotton industry was moving into the southern United States not only for cheaper labor, but because "geographically the South is nearer what are considered the natural markets of the United States—Central and South America." Ford further observed that in the past twenty years (1874–1894), the output of American cotton mills had jumped in volume five times. The greatest increase in exports had gone to South America and Asia, and this trade had expanded in spite of stiff competition from British and German agents. Meanwhile, the Boston *Commercial Bulletin* reported that woolen manufacturers worried about the "falling off of the export demand" which set the mills to "manufacturing for the home rather than the foreign market." These industrialists regretted especially the abrogation of reciprocity. Their exports were 11,000,000 yards less than in the previous several years, and 8,000,000 yards of this had formerly gone under reciprocity treaties to Cuba, Santo Domingo, and Brazil.[71]

Southern businessmen hoped to alleviate the depression in their section by developing Latin-American markets. Believing it to be "only a question of time when the United States will hold a practical monopoly of the trade of South America," the Chattanooga *Tradesman* urged that if "the South shall push her advantages . . . her ports will soon have a monopoly of many lines of trade" with Central America and South America. Good reasons for such optimism could be found in several industrial expositions held in the South during the mid-1890's. The largest and most publicized of these was the Atlanta Exposition of 1895. President Cleveland and several members of his cabinet found time to visit this affair. In inviting Secretary of State Richard Olney, Chairman J. W. Avery commented, "The foreign trade idea

[71] Ford, "Commerce and Industry," 483–484. Secretary of the Treasury Carlisle agreed with Ford's observations; see Carlisle's *Annual Report, 1896*, xc; Ford, "Turning of the Tide," 190–191; Boston *Commercial Journal* quoted in *Bradstreet's*, Sept. 28, 1895, 622.

is the basic and uppermost feature of the Exposition, both with our own people and the foreigners." Earlier, Avery had been sent to Latin America by the Atlanta business community to drum up interest in the exposition. Secretary of State Gresham, Olney's predecessor, assisted Avery's expedition by writing letters of introduction for the agent to all the United States ministers in South America. The letters instructed the ministers "to cooperate in his purposes." Commercial ties between Atlanta businessmen and groups in Costa Rica, Guatemala, and Mexico soon appeared.[72]

American commercial museums provided another approach to obtaining more Latin-American trade. Stimulated by the exhibits at the Chicago World's Fair in 1893, the full bloom of this movement appeared in the flowering of the Philadelphia Commercial Museum in the 1894–1897 period. Secretaries of State Gresham and Olney displayed active interest in this undertaking. William Pepper, the President of the museum, wrote Olney in 1895 that he had "been surprised and gratified at the rapid spread of interests" shown by American manufacturers for the project. Speaking at the museum's national opening in June, 1897, Olney outlined the inevitability of Western Hemispheric economic solidarity. "Trade does not of course go, like kissing, by favor," the Secretary declared. "Its sure and only basis is selfish interest." "Intimate commercial intercourse" between North and South America, he insisted, was "inevitable." New York City soon followed Philadelphia's example and constructed its own commercial museum.[73]

Perhaps the most publicized and concerted movement for the extension of foreign markets and control of Latin-American

[72] *Bradstreet's*, July 7, 1894, 430; Dec. 21, 1895, 808; J. W. Avery to Olney, Nov. 8, 1895, Olney MSS; *Public Opinion*, April 25, 1895, 436–437.
[73] William Pepper to Olney, Aug. 2 and Nov. 29, 1895, Olney MSS; *Bradstreet's*, Nov. 2, 1895, 693; Philadelphia Commercial Museum, *The Philadelphia Commercial Museum: What It Is, Why It Is* (Philadelphia, 1899); Philadelphia Commercial Museum, *Proceedings of the International Advisory Board* (Philadelphia, 1897), 6; June 2, 1897, Olney MSS.

trade began with the formation of the National Association of Manufacturers in January, 1895. The depression operated as a direct cause of this movement. As one student of the organization has written, "it was apparent to the manufacturers who had struggled through the depression years of 1893 and 1894 that some positive action was necessary to enlarge domestic and foreign markets." [74] The opportunity for such positive action came in the fall of 1894 when a southern trade paper, *Dixie*, threw out a suggestion to manufacturers to display their wares in a Mexico City industrial exhibition. *Dixie* was deluged with letters. The response so overwhelmed the journal's owners that they suggested that interested manufacturers band together and "have a meeting . . . in some central city." Several southern and several Cincinnati firms planned a convention for January, 1895. The invitations outlined a basic seven-point program, with three of these points directly related to foreign trade: a thorough development of foreign commerce including exhibition warehouses, a merchant marine, and reciprocity.[75]

When the convention opened in Cincinnati, Warner Miller, former Senator and President of the Nicaragua Canal Company, set the tone by noting that the panic of 1893 and the ensuing depression had created much interest in new markets outside the United States.[76] The featured speaker of the convention, Governor William McKinley of Ohio, brought the delegates to their feet with a trade pronouncement which embodied nearly everything the nascent organization desired.

We want our own markets for our manufactures and agricultural products; we want a tariff for our surplus products which will not surrender our markets and will not degrade our labor to hold our markets. We want a reciprocity which will give us foreign markets

[74] Albert Kleckner Steigerwalt, "The National Association of Manufacturers: Organization and Policies, 1895–1914" (unpublished Ph.D. dissertation on microfilm, University of Michigan, 1953), 24.

[75] *Bradstreet's*, Dec. 1, 1894, 759; Steigerwalt, "N.A.M.," 25–26, 28–29.

[76] *Ibid.*, 38.

for our surplus products and in turn that will open our markets to foreigners for those products which they produce and which we do not.[77]

Charles Heber Clarke, Secretary of the Manufacturers' Club of Philadelphia, followed McKinley and localized the new organization's interest. Devoting his speech almost exclusively to Latin America, he concluded that this area "ought to belong to us in a commercial sense." He highlighted his speech by asking for an international money order system to replace the payments which now went through London. This statement was significant, for it implied that the United States now believed that it had sufficient economic power to assume control of international payments from Great Britain. Clarke also asked for bimetallism, for he believed that the gold standard drove up the prices of American manufactured goods in South American silver areas.[78]

M. E. Ingalls, President of the "Big Four" railroad system, stressed another point at the convention, a point that has been noted earlier in this chapter. Since the American farmer was losing the European market, Ingalls explained, outlets for industrial goods would have to be found in Latin America and the Far East. Ingalls proposed raising the tariff so high that American manufacturers would be able to dump their surplus at rock-bottom prices in foreign markets. This, in effect, repeated the *Bankers' Magazine*'s idea that the nation's farmers would have to be sacrificed on the altar of American industry.[79]

Several general themes emerged as the convention proceeded. One emphasized the need for foreign and especially Latin-American markets. A second motif was a strong anti-British feeling. Pointed references were made to Britain's control of international trade and finance. The N.A.M. asked the federal government for assistance which would enable American industries to compete on more equal terms with the British. A third theme appeared as the organization also requested other extensive favors from the national government. *Iron Age* later criticized the con-

[77] *Ibid.*, 32.　　[78] *Ibid.*, 32–34.　　[79] *Ibid.*, 34–37.

vention for "relying solely upon extraneous help." A pro-N.A.M. journal sarcastically informed *Iron Age* that, after all, the government *was* "the servant of the people." These three themes were embodied in the preamble to the N.A.M. Constitution. Every objective in this preamble looked to the government to improve market conditions and trade, as it asked for reciprocity, a "judicious system of subsidies" to build a merchant fleet, a Nicaraguan canal, and the rebuilding of internal waterways.[80]

After the convention, a series of circulars were sent to influential industrialists and politicians. The first circular outlined the association's "Purposes." It listed fourteen of these, eight of them directly connected with foreign trade. One large section stressed the importance of "The Promotion of Spanish-American Trade." This part noted, "The trade centres of Central and South America are natural markets for American products," and the development of this trade "promises to be one of the most effective and most valuable lines of work undertaken by the National Association of Manufacturers." In early 1896 the N.A.M. sponsored a "party of representative American business men" who visited Argentina, Uruguay, and Brazil. The visitors hoped to learn more of the "resources of the countries" and "to indicate the means by which the trade between the nations interested can be enlarged and extended." Venezuela attracted special attention as the N.A.M. erected its first sample warehouse in Caracas. This occurred during and immediately after the United States settlement of the Venezuelan boundary dispute with England.[81]

The purposes of the N.A.M. were not lost on the business world. The St. Louis *Age of Steel* and the Pittsburgh *American Manufacturer* believed this organization to be "the beginning of an intelligent, organized effort to extend our foreign trade in

[80] *Ibid.*, 51–53, 41–42.
[81] National Association of Manufacturers, *Purposes of the National Association of Manufacturers*, June 15, 1896; National Association of Manufacturers, *A Commercial Tour to South America*, April 25, 1896; National Association of Manufacturers, *Sample Warehouse for American Goods in Caracas, Venezuela* (2nd ed.), May 25, 1897.

manufactures . . . with the neighboring nations of Spanish America." The Chattanooga *Tradesman*, however, pointedly remarked that several of the leading exporting interests—cotton and woolen manufacturers, coal mine owners, and lumbermen— had not attended the N.A.M. meeting. By omitting these three interests, the *Tradesman* commented, the discussion at Cincinnati "was not as wise as it might have been." [82]

Great Britain watched these movements with unconcealed fear. The London *Chamber of Commerce Journal* noted that even in British colonies American goods were becoming dominant; everywhere "the markets are flooded with all descriptions of American manufactures" which endeavor to drive out British goods with "what amounts to quite an alarming promise of success." This journal could have especially pointed to the changes which had only recently occurred in Honduras' trade. American commercial influence had grown so large in that British colony that Honduras adopted the United States gold dollar as its monetary unit in 1894. Among the several British papers which noted the revival of the Monroe Doctrine fetish in America during the summer and fall of 1895, the *British Trade Journal* observed that "it is all very well to ignore and ridicule America's Monroe Doctrine in its purely political aspects," but there is "surely an unwritten Monroeism working like yeast in the commercial world of America," and this "we must combat—or take the consequences of our fatuity." French observers also noted the growth of this "unwritten Monroeism." [83]

[82] Quoted in *Public Opinion*, Jan. 31, 1895, 101; quoted in *Bradstreet's*, Dec. 1, 1894, 766, and March 23, 1895, 190.

[83] Bureau of American Republics, *Special [Monthly] Bulletin*, October, 1896, 1011; July, 1896, 3; *Bradstreet's*, March 16, 1895, 168; April 20, 1895, 254; Sept. 1, 1895, 548; Oct. 26, 1895, 686; Bureau of American Republics, *Special [Monthly] Bulletin*, August, 1895, 96. Beaumarchais noted the new emphasis on the Doctrine in his chapter, "La Doctrine de Monroe sur le terrain économique" in *La Doctrine de Monroe*, 191–211. He noted especially the growth of the N.A.M. and the Philadelphia Commercial Museum. See also "Diplomatic Complications and the Monroe Doctrine," *Literary Digest*, April 6, 1895, 661–663.

American newspapers quickly replied in kind to such remarks. The New York *Tribune* proclaimed that, while the United States had depended on "a phrase" in the Monroe Doctrine, Europeans had moved into South America and converted these nations "into commercial dependencies." The Atlanta *Constitution* warned that the United States had to draw the line or "suffer imperialism to overrun Central and South America." But vastly more important, the Cleveland administration formulated a foreign policy which attempted to obtain and protect the objectives that the American business community's spokesmen had delineated. This policy climaxed in the Venezuelan crisis of 1895.

V

Reaction: Depression Diplomacy, 1893-1895

AS the depression worsened after 1893, important spokesmen for the American business community agreed with the solution advocated by the Cleveland administration during the tariff fight in early 1894. The stagnation could be ameliorated, the administration forces claimed, by shipping the industrial and agricultural surpluses into world markets. This, it was agreed, would have to be accomplished quickly if the labor and agrarian discontent was not to burst into a social revolution. If foreign markets were to provide the remedy, the State Department must help and protect American interests in these markets. Walter Quintin Gresham, who was Cleveland's Secretary of State from March, 1893, until May, 1895, was by nature, experience, and political philosophy cognizant of both the crises of these years and the necessity of finding markets for the nation's glut of goods.

Born near Lanesville, Indiana, in 1832, Gresham had been a Civil War hero at Vicksburg and again at Atlanta, a distinguished lawyer and judge, and a member of President Arthur's cabinet.

Until 1892, political observers usually categorized him as a Republican. He had endorsed Cleveland in 1892, but Gresham's nomination to the State Department nevertheless came as a surprise. The President-elect had first considered his name for the Treasury, but Cleveland's close adviser, Daniel Lamont, doubted whether the former Republican would accept any office in a Democratic administration. The President offered Gresham the State Department portfolio after William C. Whitney and Arthur Pue Gorman strongly urged the nomination.[1]

Gresham's sense of the 1890's as a crisis period in American history largely explains the motivations of the administration's foreign policy during its first two years in office. In a key position as United States District Court Judge during the strikes of 1877, Gresham had moved rapidly to end the tie-up. Shortly afterwards he freely expressed his fear of the degradation of American political democracy and the threat which irresponsible and unemployed laborers posed to the nation's institutions.[2] Throughout the 1880's he attempted to allay labor discontent. As a federal judge in the latter part of that decade, Gresham was conspicuously considerate of labor, so much so that the workers' representatives at the Populist convention in 1892 hoped to present his name for the convention's presidential nomination. Gresham rejected this offer, but the event presaged a turning point in his life. Four years before, he had been a leading contender for the Republican nomination. By late 1892, however, he believed so fervently that American economic salvation lay in a low tariff that he endorsed Cleveland. He believed that in so doing, as he said, "I have committed political suicide. Some people are unable to understand that a man can deliberately do that." Gresham's actions are understandable only when placed in the

---

[1] Memorandum, Dec. 7, 1892, Daniel Lamont papers, Library of Congress, Washington, D.C.; Diary-Memoranda, 1894, Moore MSS; Matilda Gresham, *The Life of Walter Quintin Gresham, 1832–1895* (Chicago, 1919), II, 685–687.

[2] See page 14, above.

context of his long-time apprehension of violent la
conflicts.[3]

The 1893 economic disaster set in motion the forces w
most feared. As early as July, 1893, he insisted that the She
Silver Purchase Act was not the only cause of the depressio
Gresham believed that "there is plenty of money. . . . Our
country is richer than it ever was." It was, in fact, this glutted
wealth that nearly obsessed him. In August, 1892, he had observed, "We are living under new conditions utterly unlike
anything in the past" because "labor-saving machinery" gives
"capital an advantage that it never possessed before." The great
problem is: "What is an equitable division of the joint product
of capital and labor, and who is to decide the question?" He
feared that "the settlement of the controversy will be attended
with serious consequences." This question constantly played on
his mind after he became Secretary of State. In long discussions
with British Ambassador Sir Julian Pauncefote, Gresham came
back again and again to the "greatest question of the age . . .
that of capital and labor." He parried with Pauncefote the problem of the surplus and how full employment could be maintained in the face of such conditions.[4]

During the first year of the depression, Gresham received letters from friends in the Midwest which warned him that "the
President and Congress do not comprehend even in a moderate
degree, the threatening and portentous conditions of the country." On a cool Sunday morning in May, 1894, Gresham sat on a
park bench near the Arlington Hotel and gravely informed

[3] Frederick E. Haynes, *James Beard Weaver* (Iowa City, 1919), 313;
Gresham to W. B. Slemons [?], Oct. 1, 1894, Gresham to Joseph Medill,
Nov. 7, 1892, Gresham MSS.

[4] *Letters of Grover Cleveland*, 466; Gresham to Judge D. P. Baldwin,
Aug. 17, 1893, Gresham to F. P. Schmitt, Aug. 16, 1893, Gresham to
General F. M. Force, Aug. 30, 1893, all in Letterbook (March 9, 1893–
April 12, 1895)—cited hereafter as Letterbook—Gresham MSS; Gresham
to Morris Ross, Aug. 1, 1892, Gresham MSS; Gresham, *Life of Gresham*,
II, 802–803.

that "the assembling of bands of men
d to him "to portend revolution." "If
ssume leadership of them, there was
le might end." The Secretary wrote
t a pessimist, but I think I see danger
his country. What is transpiring in
na, Illinois, and in regions west of
d as symptoms of revolution." [5]

It was by this route that Gresham arrived at a conclusion similar to that of the business community's. He analyzed the problem
and the solution in two remarkable letters written in July and
May respectively of 1894.

Sparse as our population is, compared with that of other countries,
we can not afford constant employment for our labor. . . . Our
mills and factories can supply the demand by running seven or eight
months out of twelve. It is surprising to me that thoughtful men do
not see the danger in the present conditions.[6]

Then Gresham presented his solution.

There is undoubtedly an element of danger in the present condition
of society. . . . Our manufactures of all kinds should have free raw
materials. . . . This would lower the cost of the manufactured
article and enable our people to compete in foreign markets with
Great Britain. Sir Julian Pauncefote said to me the other day that
he feared it would be an evil day for Great Britain when the United
States changed its economic policy.[7]

The Secretary of State thus had concluded that foreign markets would provide in large measure the cure for the depression
and its attendant labor troubles. To say that he was a commercial expansionist, however, does not mean that Gresham was a
colonialist. He did not favor the annexation of Hawaii or other

[5] Judge S. R. Davis to Gresham, March 23, 1894, Gresham MSS; Diary-
Memoranda, May, 1894, Moore MSS; Gresham to Wayne MacVeagh,
May 7, 1894, "Personal and Confidential," Letterbook.

[6] Gresham to Colonel John S. Cooper, July 26, 1894, Letterbook.

[7] Gresham to Judge Charles E. Dyer, May 2, 1894, Letterbook.

outlying territories. In this respect, Gresham provides the purest example of the economic expansionist, anticolonial attitude of the new empire. He gave political reasons for his anticolonialism: "A free government cannot pursue an imperial policy. We acquire territory with the sole expectation of bringing it into the Union as a State." Reiterating a common theme of the period,[8] he feared that noncontiguous possessions would kill the American republic just as they had destroyed the Roman republic. He did, however, like most anticolonialists and procolonialists of his day, see the "inevitable drift" of Canada into the American orbit.[9]

The primary problem nevertheless remained the averting of economic and political disaster at home by commercial expansion abroad. Carl Schurz, a friend of Gresham's, most effectively described this idea in an article entitled "Manifest Destiny," in *Harper's New Monthly Magazine* in October, 1893. Frequently alluded to as a prime example of the antiexpansionist attitude which emerged from the debates over Hawaii during 1893, the article was actually nothing of the kind. Schurz summarized his position this way:

There is little doubt that we can secure by amicable negotiation sites for coaling stations which will serve us as well as if we possessed the countries in which they are situated. In the same manner we can obtain from and within all sorts of commercial advantages. . . . [And] all this without taking those countries into our national household on an equal footing, . . . without assuming any responsibilities for them.[10]

Gresham wrote Schurz, "It is the best article of the kind that I have seen." [11]

[8] See the conclusion of Chapter II, above.
[9] Gresham, *Life of Gresham*, II, 797–798; Bluford Wilson to Gresham, July 24, 1893, Gresham MSS.
[10] Carl Schurz, "Manifest Destiny," *Harper's New Monthly Magazine*, LXXXVII (October, 1893), 737–746.
[11] Gresham to Schurz, Oct. 6, 1893, Gresham MSS. For an opposing

Besides Gresham, other members of the administration recognized the need for commercial expansion. One of the more important groups was the Bureau of American Republics which had been established by the Inter-American Conference to coordinate commercial relations in the Western Hemisphere. By 1891 the bureau had become an integrated part of the State Department and served principally as a collector of commercial information for American businessmen. The director of the bureau reminisced in 1895 that the United States had originally backed the bureau in 1890 in order "to extend what was aptly termed 'Reciprocity with a Club.'" In its December, 1893, report, the bureau noted the "increased interest" displayed by American businessmen in Latin-American trade during the past year. The demand for its informational pamphlets was so great, in fact, that the bureau had to begin charging a "slight expense" because of its mounting printing costs.[12]

Cleveland's 1893 annual message evidenced the increased interest of the United States in its southern neighbors. The President noted that "during the past six months the demands for cruising vessels have been many and urgent." Revolutions had endangered "American interests in Nicaragua, Guatemala, Costa Rica, Honduras, Argentina and Brazil." Ships were even taken from the Bering Sea fleet for service in Latin-American waters.[13]

For many decades the United States had been attacking British commercial supremacy in Latin America with nothing more than verbal brickbats. Now, however, as American business and diplomatic attention turned increasingly to the areas to the south, a direct confrontation became possible. In January, 1894, a London journal declared that Britain's "chief danger for the moment" came from the intense American efforts "to monopolize

---

view of Gresham, see Alfred Vagts, *Deutschland und die Vereinigten Staaten in der Weltpolitik* (New York, 1935), 1918.

[12] Clinton Furbush to Olney, Oct. 1, 1895, Olney MSS; Bureau of American Republics, *Annual Report of the Director of the Bureau of American Republics, 1893* (Washington, D.C., 1893), 15, 10–11.

[13] *Messages and Papers of the Presidents*, IX, 450.

the trade of South America." The anti-British attitude of such business groups as the National Association of Manufacturers confirmed the fears of this journal.[14]

These, then, were the elements which were mixing into a potion highly explosive for American foreign policy: Gresham's views of the necessity for economic expansion into foreign areas, views with which the business community could agree; increased official State Department support of such commercial ventures; and the depiction of Great Britain as the harridan who blocked the approaches to the sorely needed Latin-American markets. As will become evident in this chapter, Gresham's views exemplified not only the first characteristic but the other two as well. The second Cleveland administration, far from being a hiatus in the development of American empire, formed a vital, natural, and most interesting link between the blueprints of Harrison and Blaine and the achievements of McKinley and Hay.

Hawaii

Cleveland's and Gresham's attitude toward Hawaii well illustrated the tenets of the new empire. By discounting Harrison's fears of British encroachment or a successful native uprising against the provisional government, the President and his Secretary of State could enjoy the luxury of preserving and even tightening the American hold on the islands while at the same time righteously rejecting the burdens of governing a polyglot population located two thousand miles from the mainland. Moreover, when the United States would annex Hawaii in 1898, it would occur within the pattern of expanding American interests in Asia. In 1893 these interests were still nascent. During the Cleveland administration attention focused southward, not westward.

Shortly after entering office in March, 1893, Cleveland withdrew Harrison's annexation treaty from the Senate. The Presi-

[14] Bureau of American Republics, *Special [Monthly] Bulletin* (January, 1894), 30.

dent told close friends that he had not decided for or against
annexation, but that "we ought to stop, look and think."
Gresham, however, was already averse to annexation, partly because of his intense personal dislike of Benjamin Harrison.
Gresham expressed a second and stronger reason for his opinion
in a personal conversation with the Russian Minister to Washington on March 16, 1893. The administration, the Secretary of
State said, "would not favor principles and policy looking to
the acquisition of foreign territory." [15] That Gresham made such
an unequivocal statement at this early date is particularly interesting in view of Cleveland's indecisiveness.

Five days before, the President had named James H. Blount of
Georgia, former congressman and chairman of the Foreign Affairs Committee, to investigate the situation on the islands. In
early August, Blount informed Cleveland and Gresham that the
Harrison administration and the American naval units had acted
unjustly during the January revolution, and that without this
help the Queen would not have been overthrown. This information settled the annexation matter in Cleveland's mind. After two
more months of Gresham's prodding, the President decided to
help the Queen regain her throne *if* this could be accomplished
without bloodshed and *if* the Queen would promise to abide by
"all obligations created by the Provisional Government."

When the American Minister informed the former ruler of
this offer, she astounded the diplomat with the reply that she
would settle for nothing less than the heads of the provisional
government's leaders. After several more sessions, however, she
agreed to Cleveland's offer. But when the American Minister
then approached the Dole government, that regime, assured by
its representative in Washington that the Cleveland administration would not resort to force, flatly refused to discuss the proposition. Faced with this impasse, Cleveland dumped the matter

[15] Memoranda of Conversations, March 16, 1893, June 16, 1893, NA,
RG 59; Gresham, *Life of Gresham*, II, 732; Stevens, *American Expansion
in Hawaii*, 245–246, 267–269.

(but not the annexation treaty) back into the hands of Congress on December 18, 1893. Here the issue reposed, though frequently responding fitfully when touched by certain expansive-minded congressmen, until it was resurrected by the McKinley administration.[16]

Gresham was the key figure in the administration's Hawaiian policy; he held firm when the President wavered. The Secretary of State constantly reiterated that annexation should not be carried through because such a transaction would corrupt the republic by transforming the United States into an imperial power. Annexation would, moreover, condone a government which had assumed power with the unlawful aid of American forces. Gresham was buttressed in these beliefs by a long letter from Alvey Adee, Second Assistant Secretary of State, which, after an exhaustive survey of the situation in Hawaii, concluded that "the islands will never maintain a voting population sufficient to confer a rightful claim to state-hood." [17] Advanced in the context of the labor and agrarian upheavals of Homestead, the Pullman Strike, and Coxey's Army, this was a persuasive argument.

But it is crucial to note that Gresham did not follow a hands-off policy in Hawaii. As Carl Schurz had pointed out in his *Harper's* article, a refusal to assume political responsibilities did not mean a refusal or abnegation of strategic and commercial

[16] Gresham to Willis, Dec. 2, 1893, Cipher Messages Sent, 1888–1895, NA, RG 45; Willis to Gresham, Nov. 16, 1893, and Dec. 9, 1894, Cleveland MSS; Willis to Gresham, Dec. 20, 1893, Hawaii, Despatches, NA, RG 59; *Messages and Papers of the Presidents*, IX, 460–463. Olney had some influence in shaping Hawaiian policy; see Olney to Gresham, Oct. 9, 1893, Gresham MSS.

[17] Gresham to Colonel John S. Cooper, Feb. 5, 1894, and Gresham to John Overmeyer, July 25, 1894, Letterbook; Personal letter from Adee to Gresham, March 10, 1893, Memoranda of Conversations, NA, RG 59; Gresham to Senator Roger Q. Mills, Jan. 23, 1895, Gresham MSS. Ernest R. May has noted that Cleveland's "message against the annexation . . . had not been a brief against imperialism so much as an indictment of the methods used" (*Imperial Democracy* . . . [New York, 1961], 37).

benefits. It is obvious but significant that, though the Secretary of State hastily withdrew in a political sense, he did not withdraw or even weaken the American grasp on Pearl Harbor; nor did he want to loosen the commercial connection with Hawaii. In fact, both claims were reaffirmed.[18]

In the light of this observation, several other events become more significant. When the administration approached the Queen with its offer of restoration, Gresham not only hedged the offer by demanding a promise from the Queen that she would assume the obligations of the provisional government (which meant guaranteeing the supremacy of the planters), but he also informed her that she would have to include in her ministry members of the provisional government, including President Dole. Another of Gresham's actions is important in this context. When the American Minister approached the Dole government with the plan of restoring the Queen, the Hawaiian Foreign Minister bluntly told the State Department that the United States could not exert such authority over Hawaiian officials. Gresham retorted that the State Department could remonstrate with Hawaii, since American force had "subverted" the Queen. Given this assumption, Gresham could logically conclude that the United States could interfere in the affairs of the provisional government as long as the latter remained in power.[19]

[18] After losing their sugar bounty in the 1894 tariff bill, domestic sugar growers attempted to abrogate the Hawaiian treaties of 1875 and 1887. Senators Morgan, Chandler, and Perkins led a fight to retain the treaties. They effectively argued that Bayard had remarked in 1887 that if the treaty of reciprocity was repudiated, the United States would lose its rights to Pearl Harbor. The Morgan forces maintained the reciprocity treaty with a crushing 57–11 vote of confidence (Dozer, "Anti-Imperialism," 234–236).

[19] Gresham did not hesitate to interfere and threaten the use of force to protect American citizens implicated in revolutionary activities against the Hawaiian government during an 1895 uprising; see Gresham to Willis, Feb. 26, 1895, Hawaii, Instructions, NA, RG 59; Stevens, *American Expansion in Hawaii*, 276–277; Willis to Gresham, Dec. 9, 1893, Cleveland MSS.

The 1894 tariff considerably simplified Gresham's task. By abolishing the sugar bounty and restoring the Hawaiian planters' favored position in the American market, the Wilson-Gorman bill alleviated the islands' economic problems. The measure had also tightened the economic interdependence of the two nations. Realizing the importance of these developments, many planters who had warmly endorsed or equivocated on the question of annexation, now strongly opposed the union. Benefiting from both the American market and the immigration of coolie labor (which annexation would terminate), the influential planters had the best of both worlds. The American Minister informed Gresham of these developments in 1894.[20]

Gresham and the planters enjoyed such latitude in their actions only because outside powers did not pose a threat to the *de facto* American protectorate. Jingoist congressmen, expansionist-minded naval officers, and militant-minded newspaper editors frequently attempted to conjure up the specter of British, Japanese, or even Russian control of the islands. The State Department was not alarmed. In a series of private conversations conducted shortly after he entered office, Gresham told the British Ambassador and the Japanese and Russian Ministers that the United States would tolerate no outside interference in the islands. They, in turn, remarked that they had been directed by their foreign offices to assure the Secretary that their respective governments had no aspirations regarding Hawaii.[21]

When the British Minister to Hawaii became too ambitious in advancing English and Canadian interests, Gresham promptly asked Great Britain to replace its representative with someone "who had no entangling relations with the natives or with *aliens,*

---

[20] Willis to Gresham, May 24, 1894, July 21, 1894, Sept. 20, 1894, all in Gresham MSS; Scrapbook, Box 240, Moore MSS; Stevens, *American Expansion in Hawaii,* 281.

[21] Pauncefote to Rosebery, May 6, 1893, Archives of the Foreign Office, Public Record Office, London—cited hereafter as F.O. followed by record and message number—5/2189; Memoranda of Conversations, March 16, 1893, NA, RG 59; Pratt, *Expansionists of 1898,* 125–127.

prosecuting business at Honolulu" (italics added). Gresham and the Secretary of the Navy, Hilary Herbert, also shrewdly kept British warships away from Hawaii by assuring London that the United States would protect British lives and properties on the islands. When one American naval officer misunderstood his instructions, refused to guarantee British property, and then reported a British warship steaming back into the Hawaiian area, Herbert gave the officer a severe reprimand.[22] The United States wanted a monopoly in those waters.

Richard Olney took much the same approach when he became Secretary of State after Gresham's death in May, 1895. When the Japanese began exerting pressure on Hawaii because of immigration problems in 1896, the Hawaiian Minister to the United States asked Olney for help. The Secretary of State replied that he doubted whether Japan would push too far in the face of strong American claims to priority on the islands, but if the Japanese did do so, the United States would, Olney intimated, become directly involved. The Hawaiian Minister reported to Honolulu that the Secretary had, in effect, stretched the Monroe Doctrine to touch Hawaii.[23]

The New York *Evening Post* had given a good summary of the administration's policies in 1893 when the journal advised Hawaiians, "Go on, therefore, sending us your sugar and other tropical products, and sitting under your own fig-trees, in the full assurance that none will dare make you afraid." The rationale for this policy was outlined two years later, in 1895, by a State Department official. Writing a series of anonymous articles on Cleveland's foreign policy, Frederic Emory devoted special attention to Hawaii. He recalled that during the President's first term, Bayard and Cleveland had persevered to advance "American influence" there. "The obvious course was to wait quietly

[22] Memoranda of Conversations, March 16, 1893, NA, RG 59; Willis to Gresham, December, 1893, Cleveland MSS.

[23] William A. Russ, Jr., *The Hawaiian Republic, 1894–1898* (Selinsgrove, Pa., 1961), 132.

and patiently, and let the islands fill up with American planters and American industries until they should be wholly identified" economically and politically with the mainland. But "a handful of adventurers" had upset the calculation. Without political democracy the "islands have nothing in common with this country . . . ; at best, they could be only a colonial dependency, and that is something entirely alien to our institutions." [24]

The United States had refused to annex Hawaii in 1893 for three reasons. First, the administration believed that the provisional government had assumed power undemocratically and with the illegal aid of American naval units. Second, annexation would break the hallowed tradition of not attempting to stretch American political institutions over extracontinental territory. This tradition became especially important during the political and social turbulence suffered by the United States during the depression. Many Americans, especially Gresham, feared that so much flexibility had gone out of these institutions that further stretching would snap them completely. Third, Hawaii's only value lay as a sugar producer and defensive outpost. These values the United States already enjoyed without assuming tiresome political burdens.

Within five years each of these reasons would be cancelled out. By mid-1894 Cleveland recognized the provisional government as a strong body, "clearly entitled to our recognition without regard to any of the incidents which accompanied or preceded its inauguration." [25] Three years later, the disappearance of the depression would re-establish Americans' confidence in their political institutions. Four years later, Hawaii would obtain a new value in the eyes of the State Department and the business community; it would be viewed as a way station to China. The islands would then be annexed.

---

[24] Stevens, *American Expansion in Hawaii*, 236–239; Clipping from Baltimore *Sun*, May 27, 1895, Bayard MSS.

[25] Interview given by Cleveland in 1894, dated Jan. 6, 1895, Cleveland MSS.

The Brazilian Revolution of 1894

Gresham had preserved American interests in Hawaii by warning the provisional government and the major powers that the United States would brook no interference in its rights, either commercial or strategic, on the islands. All parties had respected his wishes. During the winter of 1893–1894, however, the Secretary of State tried to preserve increasing American commercial interests in Brazil while a European-supported revolutionary movement attempted to terminate these interests. When the moment of truth arrived, as it does during all revolutions, Gresham did not hesitate to use United States warships to defeat the insurgents and maintain in power the pro-American, established Brazilian government.[26]

Although it has since faded in importance in American diplomatic history, this rebellion was front-page news at the time. The United States was particularly interested because it had signed a reciprocity agreement with the newly formed Brazilian republic on February 5, 1891. This agreement became one of the most important reciprocity treaties signed under the McKinley tariff. The pact, however, received a cool reception in Brazil. Only resolute stands taken by several Brazilian presidents, especially Floriano Peixoto, had prevented that nation's legislature from repudiating the agreement. The rebellion was led by political enemies of Peixoto, some of whom bitterly opposed him on the issue of this treaty.[27]

[26] This section of the present study was first published in more detailed form as "United States Depression Diplomacy and the Brazilian Revolution, 1893–1894," in the *Hispanic American Historical Review*, XL (February, 1960), 107–118.

[27] Gresham, *Life of Gresham*, II, 777; Laughlin and Willis, *Reciprocity*, 208, João Pandiá Calógeras, *A History of Brazil*, translated and edited by Percy Alvin Martin (Chapel Hill, 1939), 290–291; Lawrence F. Hill, *Diplomatic Relations between the United States and Brazil* (Durham, N.C., 1932), 265–272. The best account of the revolution and American participation in it is in Hill, *United States and Brazil*, 265–281. John Bassett Moore, *A Digest of International Law* . . . (Washington, D.C.,

Elements of the Brazilian navy formed the core of the insurgents. Led by Admiral Custodio de Mello, the rebels boarded three warships and a number of merchant vessels and set siege to the harbor of Rio de Janeiro. Land forces fought pitched battles in southern Brazil, but the rebellion was to be decided in this harbor. Admiral de Mello's strategy was simple: keep as many foreign ships as possible away from the harbor so that the customs houses, upon which the government largely depended for revenue, would soon become bankrupt. Gresham thus had to do two things. He had to get American ships into the harbor for the double purpose of keeping American trade flowing and strengthening the pro-United States elements in Brazil. Further, he had to withhold belligerent status from de Mello or else the United States would be forced, by declaring a position of legal neutrality, to allow de Mello to blockade the harbor, stop trade, and probably overthrow the Peixoto government. Gresham's trouble was compounded when it appeared that several European nations, especially Great Britain, were clandestinely helping the insurgents.

The American Minister to Brazil, Thomas S. Thompson, observed strict neutrality at the outset. He refused to confer with

1906), II, 1113–1120, covers the period from Jan. 11 through Feb. 1, 1894, in detail. Adequate accounts are Charles A. Timm, "The Diplomatic Relations between the United States and Brazil During the Naval Revolt of 1893," *Southwestern Political and Social Science Quarterly*, V (September, 1924), 119–138; also Charles E. Martin, *The Policy of the United States as Regards Intervention* (New York, 1921), 118–123. Timm relies on the printed volumes of *United States Foreign Relations*, while Martin uses Moore's *Digest* as his principal reference. A good Brazilian account is Calógeras, *History of Brazil*, 290–294. Also see Pedro Calmon, *Historia de la civilización brasileña*, traducción del original de Julio E. Payró (Buenos Aires, 1937), 390–392, which considers mostly the fighting on the mainland and neglects foreign participation. Pedro Calmon, *Brasil e America: Historia de uma politica* (Rio de Janeiro, 1944), 79, mentions and passes judgment on American actions during the revolt. See also citations in Hill, *United States and Brazil*, 280, 208–313. None of these accounts, American or Brazilian, attempts to explain the reason for the American policy adopted after Jan. 6, 1894.

Peixoto, but did call for American ships to protect United States commerce and citizens. This was the only time Thompson was neutral throughout the revolution, however, for, influenced by the American business interests in Rio, he soon took a strong pro-Peixoto position. He asked United States naval commanders to bring American goods to shore even if force had to be employed in accomplishing the task.

His requests were based upon instructions from Gresham which arrived on October 11, though the Secretary of State had carefully refrained from mentioning the use of any force. As a result of Thompson's requests, a split ensued between him and the American commander, Rear Admiral Oscar F. Stanton, who disagreed on the use of force to protect American goods. Stanton then overstepped his bounds when he visited de Mello on board an insurgent ship. He was promptly recalled.[28]

His replacement, Commander Henry Picking, followed Stanton's policy, splitting with Thompson and with the American Consul General in Rio, William T. Townes, over the attitude to be taken toward the insurgents. Gresham stepped into the breach. On October 25 he refused an insurgent request for belligerent status. This was followed by a statement of policy on November 1. Since there had been no belligerent status accorded, and since there was "no pretense" that Rio was blockaded, Gresham declared that American ships could land their cargo on lighters which could go on into shore provided that the lighter "in doing so does not cross or otherwise interfere with Mello's line of fire." In this note, Gresham developed the policy which could achieve both his objectives: he provided for the landing of American goods, but he also maintained at least a semblance of neutrality by saying that the goods should not

[28] Gresham to Minister Thomas S. Thompson, Oct. 11, 1893, Brazil, Instructions, NA, RG 59; Thompson to Gresham, Nov. 10, 1893, Brazil, Despatches, NA, RG 59; Secretary of Navy Hilary Herbert to Rear Admiral Oscar F. Stanton, Oct. 23, 1893, Cipher Messages Sent (1888–1895), NA, RG 45.

land if in landing they interfered with the course of the revolt. This loophole was to cause Gresham much trouble. For longer than a month, this policy worked satisfactorily. American vessels had little trouble landing their cargo, though other nations met some difficulty. As the goods rolled through the customs houses, de Mello's chances grew dim. By late November he had suffered losses in land skirmishes and had lost prestige.[29]

In general the American press backed up Gresham's attitude, though it put his policy in more active terms than he had himself. The Springfield *Republican*, the Boston *Daily Advertiser* and the Philadelphia *Recorder* agreed with the New York *Tribune*, which stated that the "plain duty of the Cleveland Administration" was to support the existing government and so discourage such "revolutionary outbreaks and political anarchy." But at least one newspaper, the Detroit *News*, believed that Washington was "not so neutral" as "it wanted the public to believe it was"; not only was the administration helping Peixoto through trade, but New York shipyards were busy building a "formidable" navy for him. This, the *News* feared, was "more suggestive of the way the Confederate Navy recruited its navy-yards during our war." [30]

In early December the rebel cause was suddenly strengthened by the defection of Admiral Saldanha da Gama. He previously had been a neutral, and, since he had strong monarchical tendencies, he brought with him many who wanted to restore the pre-1889 rule. Although the State Department knew about the strengthening of the insurgents through the defection of da

[29] United States Consul General William T. Townes to Commander Henry Picking, Nov. 6, 1893, Area 4 file, NA, RG 45; Gresham to Thompson, Oct. 25, Nov. 1, 1893, Brazil, Instructions, and Thompson to Gresham, Nov. 23, 1893, Brazil, Despatches, NA, RG 59.

[30] *Literary Digest*, Nov. 25, 1893, 277; *Public Opinion*, Nov. 2, 1893, 117; Jan. 11, 1894, 352. See also Hill's citations of newspaper opinion, *United States and Brazil*, 280; *Public Opinion*, Jan. 4, 1894, 329; Feb. 22, 1894, 495; *Literary Digest*, Nov. 25, 1893, 277; and the *Nation*'s strong denunciation of any possible American intervention, Jan. 4, 1894, 3.

Gama, Gresham did little until January 6, 1894. The Secretary of State evidently feared that the insurgents were gaining in power, and he wanted to be on the right side when the battle ended.[31]

But Gresham was soon shaken from this wait-and-see attitude. He received word from Thompson that the Brazilian government had two affidavits showing that Great Britain was helping the rebels, and that this pro-da Gama policy was being followed in the hope that the insurgent leader would reinstall the monarchy once he overthrew the Peixoto regime. The Brazilian Minister in Washington confirmed this information. Gresham especially feared the withdrawal of the British fleet protection, for he believed it would be a prelude to recognizing da Gama's belligerency.[32]

This rumored British action only pointed up a more important threat to American interests, however. If the insurgents, encouraged directly and indirectly by British elements, eventually overthrew the Peixoto government, American trading interests would be in serious danger. Many of the insurgent leaders could not see advantages for Brazil in the 1891 reciprocity agreement. If helped to power by European interests, these leaders would certainly discriminate against American products. At this same time, December, 1893, this agreement was being abrogated in the United States Congress. The proposed substitute, however, the so-called Wilson tariff, was being framed with the express intention of obtaining even more South American markets. Gresham's beliefs coincided with the philosophy of the Wilson

[31] On that day, he again refused da Gama's request for belligerent status (Gresham to Thompson, Jan. 6, 1894, Brazil, Instructions, NA, RG 59).

[32] Gresham to Ambassador to Great Britain, Thomas F. Bayard, Dec. 18, 1893, Great Britain, Instructions, NA, RG 59. Also, Montgomery Schuyler, "Walter Quintin Gresham," *The American Secretaries of State and Their Diplomacy*, edited by Samuel Flagg Bemis (New York, 1928), VIII, 253–254.

tariff. The success of the Brazilian insurgents and the loss of much of the Brazilian market would be a serious setback if Gresham's remedy was to revive American industry.[33]

American exporters to Brazil concurred with the Secretary's analysis of the situation. In late December and early January the State Department received numerous letters and telegrams from these exporting firms. One of the most influential requests for aid came from W. S. Crossman & Brothers. This had a personal letter attached from Isidor Straus, one of Gresham's close friends. Perhaps the most urgent request was a message received from William Rockefeller, President of the Standard Oil Company. Rockefeller's company was undergoing a vigorous and bitter competitive war with Russian oil throughout the world. Standard Oil's attention had turned southward, especially to Cuba and Brazil. Now the trade with Brazil was threatened.[34]

On January 6, Gresham assured Straus that American interests in Brazil would be protected. The Standard Oil request arrived at the State Department on January 8. On January 10, Gresham sent instructions to Thompson which stated that unless all foreign shipping suffered common restrictions, "no substantial interference with our vessels, however few, will be acquiesced in." These orders were coupled with a change of naval commanders, Rear Admiral Andrew E. K. Benham replacing Picking. The "San Francisco" (Benham's flagship) and the "New York" arrived shortly after, and the American navy became the most powerful fleet in the harbor.[35]

[33] See discussion of the tariff in Chapter IV, above. For Gresham's views of the need for expanding trade to ameliorate the depression conditions, see the first section of this chapter. For an excellent analysis of how Gresham viewed the relation of the new tariff to increased trade with Brazil see Emory's article in Baltimore *Sun*, May 27, 1895, also in Bayard MSS.

[34] Gresham to Isidor Straus, Jan. 6, 1894, Letterbook; William Rockefeller to Gresham, Jan. 4, 1894, Area 4 file, NA, RG 45.

[35] Gresham to Isidor Straus, Jan. 6, 1894, Letterbook; Herbert to Picking, Jan. 6, 1894, Cipher Messages Sent (1888–1895), NA, RG 45;

Benham told da Gama on January 24 that the rebels had no right to establish a blockade and warned that "American vessels shall not be molested in any manner whatever." The new United States commander then told American merchants to begin landing their goods. On January 29, da Gama challenged this new policy. Benham, warned of da Gama's move, sent the "Detroit" alongside a merchant vessel which was moving for shore. An insurgent ship fired a blank shell at the bow of the merchant vessel, and the "Detroit" responded with a shell, not a blank, into the side of the rebel ship. The "Detroit" commander then told the insurgents if they fired again, "I will sink you." There was no more firing. On February 1, Gresham approved Benham's action, cabling Thompson, "I trust you are in accord with Benham for he has acted within his instructions." [36]

From this point on, the rebellion drifted into oblivion. Benham's action brought the other naval commanders into accord with his policy. They had no choice, for it was either get on the side which was obviously being strengthened by the American policy, or stop the United States convoying by force. Two more times da Gama asked for belligerent status, but the requests were refused by Gresham. The European powers, led by Britain, fol-

Gresham to Thompson, Jan. 9, 1894, Brazil, Instructions, NA, RG 59; Gresham to Thompson, Jan. 10, 1894, Area 4 file, NA, RG 45. In Moore, *Digest*, II, 1113, this instruction is dated Jan. 11, 1894.

[36] Benham to da Gama, Jan. 24, 1894, Area 4 file, and Benham to Herbert, Feb. 1, 1894, Cipher Messages Received (1888–1895), NA, RG 45; Gresham to Thompson, Feb. 1, 1894, Brazil, Instructions, NA, RG 59. Benham's policy (and Gresham's approval of it) has been condemned in all the accounts which pass judgment on American policy that this writer has found. On the vital point of the United States in reality ending the rebellion, see Calmon, *Brasil e America*, 79; John W. Foster, *A Century of American Diplomacy* (Boston and New York, 1902), 466–467; Hill, *United States and Brazil*, 291; A. Curtis Wilgus, *The Development of Hispanic America* (New York, 1941), 327. Admiral de Mello later declared that Benham's interference provided the turning-point of the revolt. See *Public Opinion*, March 29, 1894, 615. See Adee's detailed discussion in a memorandum of 1901 in J. B. Moore MSS, Box 214.

lowed Gresham's example. The State Department, however, took no chances. During the month of February, five of the American South Atlantic Squadron's fleet of six ships were stationed in Rio harbor, remaining there in spite of yellow fever which was scourging the area and which had forced all the other foreign ships, with the exception of one Portuguese vessel, to leave. The insurgents put up token resistance throughout April, then left for refuge in Portugal.[37]

Two interpretations have been suggested regarding this action. President Cleveland, in his annual message in 1894, asserted that from the revolution's outbreak, the administration realized that the situation called "for unusual watchfulness." Consequently, the American naval force was strengthened, and "this precaution, I am satisfied, tended to restrict the issue to a simple trial of strength between the Brazilian Government and the insurgents." Cleveland believed that "our firm attitude of neutrality was maintained to the end." [38]

Historians and international lawyers who studied this episode in later years disagreed with Cleveland. They concluded that the American action taken during January, 1894, determined the winner of the Brazilian revolt. In the five days of January 6 to January 10, there took place an almost complete reversal in the American wait-and-see policy of September through December, 1893. Mrs. Gresham in her biography is clear in attributing the cause of this policy change to business pressure.[39] The Secretary of State realized in early January that American trade was suffering and that, if the insurgents won, it would suffer

[37] Thompson to Gresham, Feb. 1, 1894, Brazil, Despatches, Gresham to Thompson, Feb. 5, 1894, Brazil, Instructions, Bayard to Gresham, Feb. 7, 1894, Great Britain, Despatches, NA, RG 59; newspaper clipping, London *Times*, March 2, 1894, enclosed in Bayard to Gresham, March 2, 1894, Great Britain, Despatches, NA, RG 59.

[38] *Messages and Papers of the Presidents*, IX, 524.

[39] Hill, *United States and Brazil*, 280; Foster, *A Century of American Diplomacy*, 466–467; see also authorities listed in note 35 and Gresham, *The Life of Walter Quintin Gresham*, II, 778.

even more. Such an occurrence could impair and discourage vital segments of the American economy, hamper recovery, and breed those "symptoms of revolution" which Gresham feared.

Thompson agreed with this assessment. He wrote Gresham on February 1, 1894, that Europeans, especially the English, sympathized with the insurgents. He accounted for this "partly through the gradual increase of American trade with Brazil, and the corresponding decrease of their own." He believed that it could not be denied that the reciprocity agreement between the United States and Brazil had given American merchants "a leverage of which all Europeans are extremely jealous." [40]

The Bureau of American Republics issued similar statements to the American business community. It noted that the American naval action in Brazil would "lead to still closer commercial relations between the two nations, and to a considerable increase in their commerce with each other." It concluded that "American merchants and manufacturers have now an undisputed advantage in the competition" for Brazilian markets. The German Minister to Brazil phrased the same thought more tersely: "The American dollar started to roll in order to break off the monarchist point of the revolution." [41]

Replacing the British in Nicaragua

Several months after ending the Brazilian revolt, Gresham became deeply involved in Nicaragua's domestic problems. One aspect of this affair centered around the importance of the proposed Nicaraguan canal. Another aspect was more subtle, yet more important; Gresham maneuvered England out of its strategic position in Nicaragua and led the United States into the

[40] Thompson to Gresham, Feb. 1, 1894, Brazil, Despatches, NA, RG 59.
[41] Bureau of American Republics, *Special [Monthly] Bulletin*, II (March, 1894), 22–26; Vagts, *Deutschland und die Vereinigten Staaten*, 1699–1700; Pauncefote to Rosebery, Feb. 9, 1894, F.O. 5/2234. See also David N. Burke, Minister to Brazil, to Cleveland, June 11, 1894, Cleveland MSS; Burke fully agreed with the bureau's opinions.

newly created political vacuum to replace the British. A third feature of this policy defined the relationship of the State Department to American business interests in Nicaragua. The department assumed a protective role, one which burdened it with explicit responsibilities. Finally, the bitter reaction from the American press and Congress to these affairs illustrated that public opinion was becoming very tender about European actions in strategic areas of the Western Hemisphere.

The Nicaraguan affair was played out in the midst of increasing American interest in an Isthmian canal. In 1887 the Maritime Canal Company had obtained from Nicaragua a concession for the construction of a canal. General J. S. Zelaya, who became Nicaragua's President after the revolution of 1893, opposed this scheme because he wanted the American government, not a private company, to do the job. Under a measure proposed by Senator John Morgan of Alabama, the government would practically do this by guaranteeing the bonds of the subsidiary Maritime Canal Company, the company which would handle the actual construction. Morgan's plan enjoyed much public sympathy. Chambers of Commerce passed numerous favorable resolutions, while a National Nicaragua Canal Convention met in St. Louis in 1893 with three hundred delegates from thirty states and territories. A similar convention was held in New Orleans.[42]

Morgan and other congressmen were not reticent in explaining their interest. The Alabama Senator stressed that "there can not be anything done for the Southern people of equal advantage to the building of the Nicaragua canal, so as to give us access to the eastern Asiatic countries for our cotton." If this trade could be taken from the British, "we shall find that we shall harvest that wealth of the Indies about which we have heard so many romantic statements made in past times." Morgan supported his point by reading similar arguments in letters sent to him by the

[42] *Congressional Record*, 52nd Cong., 2nd Sess., 1526, 1529, 1530; Lindley Miller Keasbey, *The Nicaragua Canal and the Monroe Doctrine* . . . (New York, 1896), 455–461.

President of the New Orleans Board of Trade and the Secretary of the New Orleans Cotton Exchange. These letters declared that increased trade with Asia provided the solution to ending the depression in the South. In the House, Congressman George D. Wise of Virginia proposed a special canal committee, noting that a canal would solve "the burning question of a foreign market for surplus home production." When the House Committee on Interstate and Foreign Commerce reported on the canal bill in early 1894, it declared, "We seek to found no colonies, we covet no dependencies," but the United States could not "lag superfluous" while her rivals staked claims to "the rich commercial territory of the Western Pacific." Congress finally dispatched a commission to gather further information on the canal companies and the feasibility of the Nicaraguan project itself.[43]

Before the commission could act, a serious dispute arose between the United States and Great Britain in the Mosquito Reservation in Nicaragua. This reservation was a key strategic area, for it controlled the eastern entranceway to the proposed canal. The native Mosquito Indians were ostensibly independent, but they actually had been controlled by the British since the Treaty of Managua in 1860 and a subsequent arbitration in 1881. But a third force had entered the picture in the form of American commercial interests. United States citizens established flourishing banana plantations and a lucrative trade with the interior of Nicaragua. By 1893, ten years after the first shipment of American bananas had left the reservation, American interests had

[43] *Congressional Record*, 52nd Cong., 2nd Sess., 561–562, 650–662; 1513–1518; *House Report No. 226*, 53rd Cong., 2nd Sess. (serial 3269), 1–4; *House Report No. 1201*, 53rd Cong., 2nd Sess. (serial 3272), 11–12; *Senate Report No. 331*, 53rd Cong., 2nd Sess. (serial 3183), 7–13; Keasbey, *The Nicaragua Canal*, 470–472; August C. Radke, "Senator Morgan and the Nicaraguan Canal," *Alabama Review*, XII (January, 1959), 5–34. For the Cleveland administration's view of the validity of the Clayton-Bulwer Treaty, see a memorandum prepared by Olney in June, 1894, Olney MSS. Olney wanted the pact abrogated only with England's consent.

mounted to $2,000,000, while the over-all trade with the United States approximated $4,000,000 per year. The American Minister estimated that between 90 and 95 per cent of the total wealth of the reservation lay in American hands.[44]

Faced with an empty treasury after the 1893 revolution, President Zelaya coveted the rich reservation area. In early 1894 he sent troops into the territory for the ostensible purpose of protecting the Indians from Honduran troops. The Indian Chief Clarence promptly protested to the British Foreign Office, a development duly noted by the American State Department.[45] British troops promptly landed and disarmed the Nicaraguan soldiers. A provisional government was organized with several Americans occupying high official places. The Americans, however, withdrew from one government and expressed dissatisfaction with another. This reaction by American interests in Mosquito provides a key to the State Department actions taken from March through July, 1894. These interests preferred British to chaotic Nicaraguan control over the reservation, but the Americans desired United States protection even more.[46]

The American consul at Bluefields opposed Nicaraguan encroachment and struggled to regain the former autonomy of the reservation. Gresham, however, had more foresight. He cor-

---

[44] Lindley Miller Keasbey, "The Nicaragua Canal and the Monroe Doctrine," *Annals of the American Academy of Political Science*, VII (January, 1896), 21–23; Schuyler, "Walter Quintin Gresham," 254–256; Rising Lake Morrow, "A Conflict between the Commercial Interests of the United States and Its Foreign Policy," *Hispanic American Historical Review*, X (February, 1930), 2–13.

[45] *Foreign Relations, 1894, Appendix*, 287–288; Morrow, "Conflict between the Commercial Interests of the United States and Its Foreign Policy," 5; Baker to Gresham, Feb. 9, 1894, Nicaragua, Despatches, NA, RG 59.

[46] For a differing interpretation, see Morrow's article. See especially the State Department Memorandum, "Course of Events in Nicaragua," April 30, 1894, NA, RG 59—cited hereafter as "Course of Events in Nicaragua." See also *Foreign Relations, 1894, Appendix*, 238; Baker to Gresham, March 6 and 8, 1894, Nicaragua, Despatches, NA, RG 59.

rectly equated autonomy with the restoration of British supremacy. From this assumption the Secretary of State set out to achieve the double objectives of removing the British from the strategic area and at the same time assuring the American commercial interests in the reservation that they would be fully protected from unjust acts of the new Nicaraguan government.[47] One overtowering implication emerged from this policy. In achieving these objectives Gresham would commit the United States to interference in Nicaraguan affairs whenever American commercial or strategic interests were threatened.

This policy received strong support from the Americans in the reservation. Lewis Baker, the American Minister in Managua, revealed the American community's true feelings when he reported that though "no American here has denied to Nicaragua the sovereign power over this territory," the Americans nonetheless feared that the Zelaya government might take away certain navigational rights from them and give these rights to "a company of favorites, partly composed of foreigners but not Americans." Thus if Nicaraguan replaced British control, Baker wrote, the Americans believed that "they have a right to appeal to the Government of the United States . . . for the protection of their vested rights in this territory, and for securing to them a local government which shall protect them." [48]

With this support from the Americans in the reservation, Gresham began pressuring the Foreign Office in London. When the American Ambassador to London, Thomas F. Bayard, sanguinely reported that Great Britain coveted "no protectorate in substance or form," Gresham replied that this guarantee was not enough. The Secretary wanted neither "foreign intervention in the government of the reservation" nor resident aliens controlling the administration of affairs. Gresham also repeated his

[47] Baker to Gresham, March 8, April 1, June 5, 1894, Nicaragua, Despatches, NA, RG 59; "Course of Events in Nicaragua," NA, RG 59; *Foreign Relations, 1894, Appendix,* 243–244, 253, 256–258.
[48] *Ibid.,* 273–275.

view to Baker that Nicaragua had "paramount rights" in the region.[49]

Gresham's policy moved along smoothly and subtly in March and April. British influence was waning in the reservation. Then Nicaragua struck at the most fragile link in the American policy. Taking Gresham's affirmations of Nicaraguan sovereignty at face value, Zelaya's officials began to discriminate against American interests in the belief that they could do so with impunity. Gresham, moving quickly, initiated the second part of his policy, that of protecting American property and lives in the area with direct intervention if necessary. When in April an American was murdered in the reservation, Nicaraguan authorities displayed laxity and negligence in tracking down the killer. In mid-May a highly impatient Gresham ordered the American naval commander at Bluefields to inform Nicaragua that it must capture the murderer quickly. If the authorities failed to press the inquiry, the commander was to "use all the force at your command" to close the matter.[50]

More important than this crime, however, was the increasing danger to American canal interests. This danger appeared at a delicate time, for the State Department was trying to set an example for the British by refusing to interfere in Nicaraguan affairs. In April, Nicaragua issued notice of its intention to terminate the entire concession on grounds of nonfulfillment of contract. Gresham first shrewdly put the British on the defensive by intimating to Bayard that British intrigue had instigated this Nicaraguan act. The American Minister promptly reported this

[49] Bayard to Gresham, March 15 and 29, 1894, Great Britain, Despatches, and Gresham to Bayard, April 30, 1894, Great Britain, Instructions, NA, RG 59; *Foreign Relations, 1894, Appendix*, 271–272; Morrow, "Conflict between the Commercial Interests of the United States and Its Foreign Policy," 11–12; McAdoo to Watson, May, 1894, Cipher Messages Sent, 1888–1895, NA, RG 45; Gresham to Baker, June 13, 1894, Nicaragua, Instructions, NA, RG 59.

[50] McAdoo to Watson, May 14, 1894, Cipher Messages Sent, 1888–1895, NA, RG 45; Baker to Gresham, June 11, 1894, Nicaragua, Despatches, NA, RG 59.

to the Foreign Office and received assurance that Lord Kimberley, the Foreign Minister, wanted to "act in line" with the United States.[51]

With the immediate British danger lessened, Gresham conferred with the Nicaraguan Minister to Washington, while Baker exerted pressure on Zelaya and Foreign Minister José Madriz. In a conference with Madriz, Baker accused Nicaragua of jumping "on us with both feet and [spitting] in our faces." Baker emphasized his point by observing that State Department interest in regaining the concession "is evidenced by the presence of two powerful war steamers on your eastern coast." By the first of July, Nicaragua had withdrawn the threat of forfeiture.[52]

American diplomacy had thus achieved a notable double victory in removing the dominant British interest from Mosquito and giving the Maritime Canal Company another chance at building the canal. Then the scene again became complicated. On July 5 the Indians overthrew the Nicaraguan authorities. Significantly, this time American marines, not British troops, landed to keep order. When Americans entered into the new native government, Gresham was embarrassed, but Nicaragua was embittered. The Secretary reassured both the British and the Nicaraguan governments that "so far as American rights of person and property in the reservation are concerned, this Government can not distinguish them from like rights in any other part of Nicaragua, and should they be invaded we could only look to the territorial sovereign for redress."[53]

[51] The State Department knew that Baker was actively interested in overriding the Clayton-Bulwer Treaty and in building a canal controlled by the U.S. Government; see Gresham to Bayard, May 2, 1894, Letterbook; Bayard to Gresham, May 22 and 28, 1894, Great Britain, Despatches, NA, RG 59.

[52] *Senate Document No. 184*, 54th Cong., 2nd Sess. (serial 3471), 96–102; Gresham to Baker, June 2, 1894, Nicaragua, Instructions, and Baker to Gresham, June 3, 4, 5, 30, 1894, Nicaragua, Despatches, NA, RG 59.

[53] *Foreign Relations, 1894, Appendix*, 302–305, 316–318, 311–312; Keasbey, "Nicaragua Canal," 24; Commander Charles O'Neill to Herbert, July, 1894, Area 8 file, NA, RG 45; Gresham to Bayard, July 19, 1894,

When in August, Zelaya restored his control over the reservation, he also tested Gresham's new affirmations regarding Nicaraguan sovereignty. Madriz informed Baker that several Americans had been implicated in the revolt in July and then announced his intention of weeding out those Americans who had anti-Nicaraguan prejudices. Gresham showed his displeasure with this announcement by increasing the United States naval force at Bluefields. The Secretary then exerted pressure on the Zelaya government to allow two Americans, who had been exiled from Nicaragua for their participation in the revolution, to return to the reservation. Zelaya finally surrendered, despite the fact that substantial evidence, including the testimony of the American naval commander at Bluefields, directly implicated the two Americans in the revolt against Nicaraguan authority.[54]

Although Gresham was thus not consistent with his conception of Nicaraguan sovereignty, he had been consistent and successful in his anti-British policy. He obtained everything he wanted from both Great Britain and Nicaragua. The British had left the strategic entrance to the proposed waterway. Gresham had restored the rights of the Maritime Canal Company in spite of a recalcitrant Nicaraguan government. American commercial interests had been protected by the mere flourishing of the United States Navy. Lastly, Gresham had maneuvered the release of two Americans who had been leaders in the rebellion against the recognized sovereign government of the reservation. The Secretary's success was crowned when in December the reservation formally became incorporated into Nicaragua. The new munic-

Great Britain, Instructions, and Baker to Gresham, July 27, 1894, Nicaragua, Despatches, NA, RG 59.

[54] Baker to Gresham, Aug. 11, Aug. 29, Sept. 2, 1894, Nicaragua, Despatches, and Gresham to Baker, Aug. 4 and 29, 1894, Nicaragua, Instructions, NA, RG 59; *Foreign Relations, 1894, Appendix,* 326–327; Nicaraguan Minister of Foreign Affairs, M. C. Matus, to Captain Sumner enclosed in Sumner to Herbert, Aug. 28, 1894, Area 8 file; see the testimony of Commander O'Neill in O'Neill to Herbert, Oct. 30, 1894, Area 8 file, NA, RG 45.

ipal government included two American officials, one of whom was the *Alcalde,* or Mayor. The acceptance of offices by Americans signified that now American business interests were confident of United States protection from Nicaraguan injustice.[55]

By late 1894 only one matter still clouded the Nicaraguan picture. Along with the two Americans, the Zelaya regime had deported the British Pro-Consul. The British Foreign Office did not match Gresham's finesse in persuading Nicaragua to see the necessity of yielding. In late November, Gresham received word that British warships were steaming to Bluefields to demand an indemnity and apology for the Pro-Consul's arrest. The Secretary immediately realized that Britain could use this pretext to recover its lost authority in the reservation area. Matters drifted until February, 1895, when the Foreign Office suddenly broke off relations with Nicaragua and handed that country an ultimatum. When a panicked Nicaragua turned to the United States for help, it found only advice.[56]

Convinced that Great Britain had a good case, Gresham advised Nicaragua to end the crisis by paying the indemnity immediately. He refused to invoke the Monroe Doctrine. In a memorandum written during the height of the crisis in April, Gresham expressed fear of one thing: "Suppose Great Britain demands a money indemnity which Nicaragua is unable to pay, and, as a consequence, territory is then demanded." This would be a tight situation for the Monroe Doctrine and also for Gresham's own Nicaraguan policies. The Zelaya government tried unsuccessfully to stall off the demands. The result was the occupation of Corinto by British troops on April 27. Five days later

[55] O'Neill to Herbert, Oct. 30, 1894, Area 8 file, NA, RG 45; Baker to Gresham, Dec. 4, 1894, Nicaragua, Despatches, NA, RG 59; Mary Wilhelmine Williams, *Anglo-American Isthmian Diplomacy, 1815–1915* (Washington, 1916), 297–298.

[56] Bayard to Gresham, Nov. 24, 1894, Feb. 27, 1895, Nov. 27, 1894, Great Britain, Despatches, and Gresham to Bayard, Nov. 24, 1894, Great Britain, Instructions, NA, RG 59; Gresham to Bayard, Dec. 24, 1894, Letterbook, Gresham MSS.

the crisis ended when England accepted Salvador's offer of helping Nicaragua pay its indemnity within two weeks.[57]

The American press and expansionists in Congress enjoyed
a field day in blasting the British policies at Corinto. Albert Shaw
of the *Review of Reviews* wrote, "The Monroe doctrine has
never been so much discussed since its first promulgation." Senators Shelby Cullom of Illinois and William Stewart of Nevada
supported Senator John Morgan's statement to Richard Olney
that "I am not an Anglophobist, or anything like it [but British]
history in Central American diplomacy is only a series of ex-
ploits to gain the control of the Isthmus." Few could agree with
Morgan's definition of himself, but few Americans disagreed
with his view of Britain's diplomatic objectives.[58]

Watching the British-Nicaraguan dispute attentively from the
sidelines, the State Department believed that it saw a distinctively
anti-American trend in the diplomacy of Britain's new Prime
Minister and Foreign Minister, Lord Salisbury. In November,
1895, Salisbury refused to allow an American to become a third
member of the arbitral commission which was to settle the
Corinto problem; he did this in spite of earlier assurances to the
contrary. On the dispatch which informed Washington of Salisbury's decision, Alvey Adee wrote neatly in red ink: "Mr. Secretary: This is an important indication of the drift of British

[57] Memorandum enclosed in State Department's files with Baker to
Gresham cable of April 13, 1895, NA, RG 59; also Memorandum prepared by the State Department for Richard Olney, Aug. 10, 1895, Olney
MSS. In the two months after Olney replaced Gresham as Secretary of
State (July and August), State Department personnel compiled a series
of memoranda which filled in the minute details of the Nicaraguan
problem for Olney. See also Bayard to Gresham, Feb. 27, 1895, Great
Britain, Despatches, NA, RG 59; *Foreign Relations, 1895*, 696, 1033–
1034.

[58] *Review of Reviews*, XI (June, 1895), 621–622; *Public Opinion*,
May 9, 1895, 502; Nelson M. Blake, "Background of Cleveland's Vene-
zuelan Policy," *American Historical Review*, XLVII (January, 1942),
264; Archibald Ross Colquhuon, *The Key to the Pacific: The Nicaragua
Canal* (New York, 1898), 293; Morgan to Olney, March 6, 1895, Olney
MSS.

policy." [59] Although the problem was soon settled, Adee's note, written just two weeks before the Venezuelan crisis was made public, indicated State Department anxiety over British movements in Latin America.

The United States had gained much in Nicaragua in two years, and the State Department guarded these gains with care in 1896 and 1897. When Nicaragua threatened to reopen the whole Mosquito question over the British claims problem, Bayard lectured the Nicaraguan Minister to London so severely that the plan was squashed. In April and May of 1896 a revolt broke out in the Corinto area, but this time American marines landed to restore order, though British ships and troops were waiting offshore. When in January, 1897, Nicaragua again threatened to terminate the canal contract, Secretary of State Olney and Senator Morgan met with a Central American representative in Washington. Morgan ended the session by telling the stunned visitor: "Our people intended to have a water way . . . and no government, not even their own could refuse their demand on just grounds. They would even go to war to secure their rights." Shortly after, Zelaya sent assurance that the canal company would not be bothered.[60]

Perhaps most important to the understanding of American diplomatic history during this period was the fact that the State Department was willing to assume explicit responsibilities for the purpose of protecting and encouraging American commercial expansion into Latin America. Gresham revealed this policy during the peak of the Mosquito controversy. When the British Minister to Washington insisted that under the 1860 treaty England was bound to see that Nicaragua did not oppress the Mosquito Indians, the Secretary of State simply replied, "We will

[59] Baker to Olney, Nov. 18, 1895, Nicaragua, Despatches, NA, RG 59.
[60] Bayard to Olney, Dec. 2, 1895, Great Britain, Despatches, NA, RG 59; Memorandum of meeting between Rodriguez, Morgan, and Olney, Jan. 25, 1897, and Hiram Hitchcock, President of the Maritime Canal Company to Morgan, April 9, 1897, Morgan MSS.

see that she does not." [61] Gresham had replaced England's control of the crucial reservation area with a *de facto* American protectorate.

Depression, Expansion, and the Battleship Navy

Because of increased commercial interest and self-defined political responsibilities, the United States was becoming more and more involved in Latin-American affairs as the decade of the 1890's progressed. Such crises as the Chilean affair of 1891, the Brazilian and Nicaraguan problems of 1893–1895, and the more dangerous Venezuelan episode of 1895–1896 convinced administration and congressional leaders that American claims in Latin America would only be as strong as the military force behind them. Consequently, as American stakes in Central and South America increased, so also did American military strength. The most significant and revealing aspect of this developing military power was the rise of the American battleship navy between 1890 and 1896.

Congress had appropriated the funds for the first three battleships in 1890. Two years later a fourth such ship was authorized.[62] In view of later events, these debates are especially interesting, for they reveal the attitudes of Hilary Herbert of Alabama and William A. McAdoo of New Jersey. In 1893–1897 Herbert would serve as Secretary of the Navy, and McAdoo would be Herbert's chief assistant. In 1890 Herbert still preferred cruisers to battleships. McAdoo attempted to replace the proposed battleships with outdated low-board monitors, although he finally agreed on the battleship clause when his amendment was crushed. The ideas of both men were to change considerably in the next few years. In the Democratic Congress of 1892, Herbert, acting

[61] Wilfrid Hardy Callcott, *The Caribbean Policy of the United States, 1890–1920* (Baltimore, 1942), 77–78; Keasbey, "Nicaraguan Canal," 25–26.

[62] See Chapter III for a discussion of the origins of the battleship fleet in the 1890–1892 period.

as chairman of the House Committee on Naval Affairs, submitted a report cutting naval appropriations more than $3,500,000 from the level of the previous year. Ten months later Herbert submitted his first report as Secretary of the Navy. After paraphrasing Mahan's arguments for a battleship navy, the report concluded by requesting "at least one battle ship and six torpedo boats" and an increase of $3,000,000 over the 1893 appropriations, even though Treasury conditions had worsened during the year.[63]

This document unveiled the naval policy which the new Cleveland administration would follow, a policy of creating a large battleship navy which could protect not only home shores, but American commercial interests as far away as Asia. The report also revealed Hilary Herbert's rather startling transformation into an advocate of a battleship navy. The reasons for this metamorphosis appear to be several. First, and perhaps most important, he not only began reading Mahan's writings, but also carried on a correspondence with the distinguished Captain. In one of these personal letters Herbert assured Mahan that the Navy Department would follow the capital-ship (battleship) policy, the only policy which, as Mahan had taught, could provide sound protection for an expanding commercial empire. In his 1893 report the Secretary even retold the story of the naval battles of the French Revolution in phrases which Mahan had used in his epic *The Influence of Sea Power upon History*. Herbert had changed many of his ideas since his commerce-destroying days of 1889.[64]

Another aspect of Herbert's altered views was evident in the Secretary's concern with distant areas of the globe. He especially

[63] *Congressional Record*, 51st Cong., 1st Sess., 3271–3272, 3168, 3257, 3321, 3223–3224; *ibid.*, 52nd Cong., 2nd Sess., 1877; *Report of the Secretary of the Navy, 1891*, 33–34; *Report of the Secretary of the Navy, 1893*, 39, 59.

[64] Herbert to Mahan, Oct. 4, 1894, Mahan MSS; *Report of the Secretary of the Navy, 1893*, 37.

noted the Asian and Latin-American areas as places of immediate interest:

Our close interests with China and Japan; . . . our geographical and political relations with the islands of the Pacific; our multifarious interests along the whole South and Central American coasts, now more or less in a state of political unrest . . . would be sufficient to tax nearly all of our present naval strength in the Pacific Ocean alone. Indeed, the continent to the south of us, and both oceans, as I have said before, now demand the presence of American ships of war to a greater extent than ever before, and this demand is not, in my judgment, a temporary one, but one that will steadily increase.[65]

Herbert's expansive policies met an unmovable obstacle in the depression-scared Congress of 1894. Not only was Congress reluctant to appropriate additional funds at a time when the Treasury faced steep deficits, but President Cleveland emphasized in his annual message of 1893 that depression conditions made new shipbuilding unadvisable.[66]

In the following year Cleveland abruptly changed this opinion. When in 1894 Herbert moved far beyond his first report by recommending the building of three additional battleships and ten or twelve torpedo boats, Cleveland fully supported his Secretary. The President declared in his annual message of 1894, "If we are to have a navy for warlike operations, offensive and defensive, we certainly ought to increase both the number of battle ships and torpedo boats." [67] Congress cooperated by authorizing two battleships and narrowly missed the appropriation of money for a third. Since it occurred in just one year, this change of administration policy merits close analysis.

Four factors can be distinguished which caused this resurgence

---

[65] *Ibid.*, 41.

[66] *Messages and Papers of the Presidents*, IX, 451; *Congressional Record*, 53rd Cong., 2nd Sess., 4636–4637, 7210.

[67] *Messages and Papers of the Presidents*, IX, 540–541.

of interest in the navy. First, the American fleet in the South Atlantic and the Pacific had been remarkably busy during the previous two years. Cleveland noted in his 1893 message that ships had even been taken from the Fish Commission and the Revenue Marine to supply the demand "in Nicaragua, Guatemala, Costa Rica, Honduras, Argentina, Brazil" and Hawaii. Affairs in Brazil and Nicaragua could have alone fully occupied the navy. Mahan complained to a British friend that the American fleet could never get together for maneuvers, for "just as we expect them to begin, a bobbery starts up in Central or South America, or Hayti, or elsewhere, and away go one or two ships." [68]

A second general cause for the renewed interest centered around Mahan's growing influence and the increasing prestige of other naval officers. Mahan had followed his historic book of 1890 with a series of articles which applied the lessons of history to America of the 1890's. In 1893 he emphasized the need for control of the canal route. In 1895 Mahan analyzed the rising interest in the Monroe Doctrine. He emphasized that "reduced to its barest statement . . . the Monroe Doctrine . . . formulated an idea to which in the last resort effect could be given only through the instrumentality of a navy." Mahan believed that this laid bare the weakness of the frequently advanced argument that America needed a navy only "for the defence of our own coasts." [69]

In the mid-1890's naval officers enjoyed their most popular days since the Civil War. The navy exhibition at the World's Fair in Chicago in 1893 proved to be a tremendous attraction to visitors. When a navy review was held in New York in August, 1893, the New York *Herald* reported that "it was a sight to stir

[68] *Ibid.*, 450–451; Mahan to J. R. Thursfield, Nov. 21, 1895, Mahan MSS.

[69] Mahan, "The Isthmus and Sea Power," 102–105; Mahan, "The Future in Relation to American Naval Power," 152, 156, 158–159. Both articles are reprinted in *The Interest of America in Sea Power*. This work is discussed in Chapter II, above.

men's souls, to send the blood tingling through their veins." [70] Naval officers used this newly found popularity to advance their views on naval expansion.

In almost every instance these officers called for a battleship navy which would be able to protect America's growing commercial interests abroad. In 1896, Lieutenant John M. Ellicott published an article calling for strict enforcement of the Monroe Doctrine and a battleship fleet. He made the cardinal mistake, however, of declaring that the United States ought to be ready to fight a defensive war, that the best weapon in such a war was commerce destroying, and that a navy loaded with monitors (along with battleships) could best defend American coastlines. Commander C. F. Goodrich attacked this position vigorously, arguing Mahan's thesis that wars were decided only when battleships went far out to sea and destroyed entire fleets. Goodrich received strong support from Rear Admiral Stephen B. Luce, founder of the War College and in 1895 President of the Naval Institute at Annapolis. Luce believed that by 1898 the United States would need eighteen battleships, with "other classes of ships, in proportion." He justified such an estimate by repeating Mahan's history of commercial sea lanes.[71]

The depression provided the reason for the third and fourth causes of revived interest in the battleship navy—the need to provide jobs for American laborers, and the impulse to find and

[70] Frank M. Bennett, *The Steam Navy of the United States* . . . (Pittsburgh, 1897), 764–767; clippings of the New York *Tribune* and the New York *Herald,* both dated April 28, 1894, in Mahan MSS. If Charles A. Beard were alive in the present space age, he would no doubt be amused by a quotation he once used: "As a celebrated English statesman once remarked, if you give any service of a government a free rein it will exhaust the budget, and fightingmen, in their search for strategic frontiers and naval bases, will want to annex the moon" (quoted in *The Navy: Defense or Portent?* [New York and London, 1932], 74).

[71] John M. Ellicott, "The Composition of the Fleet," *Proceedings of the United States Naval Institute*, XXII (1896), 537–559; S. B. Luce, "As to Navy-Yards and Their Defense," *Proceedings of the United States Naval Institute*, XXI (1895), 688.

protect markets for American surplus goods. The last cause was frequently supplemented with the argument that commercial and territorial rivalry threatened to bring war with England. These were the two most immediate and important factors that affected Congress in 1895 and 1896.

When in his report of December, 1894, Herbert requested three battleships and twelve torpedo boats, he based this request on two factors—the need of domestic industries for work, and the belief that the battleship was necessarily superior over a cruiser in warfare. Speaking during the deepest trough of the entire depression, the Secretary disclaimed any intention of advocating paternalistic government, but he warned that unless Congress immediately authorized more ships many large shipyards would have to "be entirely disbanded." The navy would lose a large corps of skilled workmen, and the national defense would suffer.[72]

Congressmen happily realized that government contracts with home industries stimulated their chances of re-election, especially during depression, debt-ridden times. When the House Committee on Naval Affairs reported, it fully endorsed Herbert's three battleships and twelve torpedo boats. The committee emphasized that mechanics and skilled laborers working in shipbuilding should not be unemployed. Republican Jonathan Dolliver from Iowa fully backed this Democratic report, as he declared "that in these times of poverty, idleness and misfortune it is well for the country to continue" the machine shops which the New Navy had "called into existence." Remembering the plague of surplus Iowa farm products, Dolliver also advocated outright subsidization of American carrying trade. For such hearty cooperation, Dolliver succeeded in having two of the torpedo boats built at Dubuque, Iowa.[73]

[72] *Report of the Secretary of the Navy, 1894,* 49–51.
[73] A survey of the bill's passage through Congress can be found in *Congressional Record,* 53rd Cong., 3rd Sess., 2310, 3047, 3049, 3123–3124, 3232–3237; see especially 2248–2250, 2459.

More extended debate resulted when Congress discussed the commercial and political implications of the battleship provision. Several big-navy senators began their argument with an examination of the consequences arising from the closed frontier. Anthony Higgins of Delaware declared: "We have already arrived at the end of our land for homesteads. . . . To-day the needy American youth . . . will have to seek his fortune in some other field, and to manufacturers and to commerce, rather than to agriculture, will our growing population have to apply itself." Like Mahan, Higgins concluded that such commercial expansion would result in conflict with other commercial nations. He believed that this rivalry had already brought about the necessity of Benham's action at Rio de Janeiro. Senator Orville Platt of Connecticut declared, "It is to the ocean that our children must look, as they have once looked to the boundless West." He believed, "The future of this country, so far as growth, development, progress, and civilization are concerned, lies outside of us largely." [74]

Other senators and representatives left no doubt that they related American prosperity to a great battleship navy. Nelson Aldrich of Rhode Island believed that the navy did not exist for "any purpose of warfare," but for its "commercial uses." Senator John Morgan declared that Captain Mahan had established "as a proposition of universal political economy" that sea power provided great nations with "their principal wealth and progress."

Representative Thomas A. E. Weadock of Michigan defined future American prosperity as follows: "Our future growth lies in the success of our commerce, and no great commerce has ever been built up without the assistance of a navy to protect the merchant marine and enforce the rights of merchants and traders." Representative John O. Pendleton of West Virginia minced no words in stating that if American surplus farm produce and cotton exports suffered from a naval blockade, then

[74] *Ibid.*, 3109, 3045.

western and southern agrarians would find almshouses as their only source of relief.[75]

Latin America received special attention. Representative Robert Adams, Jr., of Pennsylvania emphasized that the Monroe Doctrine "has now become not merely a political principle, but a cardinal doctrine of the American people that we will brook no foreign interference either in the political affairs or the commercial relations of this hemisphere." He pointed to American interference in Brazil as a specific example: "When that shot was fired it was understood that the United States stood ready to maintain that doctrine; and thereupon the rebellion collapsed." When J. Fred Talbott of Maryland, chairman of the House Committee on Naval Affairs, defended his committee's bill, he also recalled Rear Admiral Benham's actions at Rio harbor. Talbott then added: "But I go beyond that; away beyond that. I claim that it is the province of good American citizenship and statesmanship that the American fleet shall dominate . . . the western waters of the Atlantic Ocean and the eastern waters of the Pacific." If any man disputed this fact, he was "not worthy to represent his people in this Congress." [76]

Many of the congressmen coupled Asia with Latin America as another aspect of the same problem. Weadock observed that not only had revolutions in Latin America involved American interests, but the war in Asia had "put in jeopardy the property and lives of our citizens and the large commerce we have in both these nations." Lodge viewed the upsurge of Japan with alarm. He quoted a London journal's report that the Japanese were building two battleships and planned to contract for two more. The Massachusetts Senator concluded, "There they are, our nearest neighbor on the Pacific; there they are, with Hawaii lying halfway between us." Higgins said that he feared not only Japan, but also China. The Delaware Senator prophesied that when China "shall have arisen out of the ashes of her defeat,"

[75] *Ibid.*, 1889, 1950, 3054, 3043, 2259, 3107, 2246–2247.
[76] *Ibid.*, 2307, 2311.

she would be "likely to become the dominant military power of the globe." [77]

As the principal threat to American interests, however, Japan and China ranked far behind Great Britain. Chairman Talbott proclaimed that "Great Britain never arbitrates with anybody except one who is ready to fight her." Representative Hernando de Soto Money of Mississippi admitted that in 1890 he had heatedly opposed the authorization of a single battleship. Since then, however, he had learned that war "is the inevitable thing. . . . There are no great nations of Quakers." Money warned that the principal threat would come from Great Britain. John Van Voorhis of New York stated that "we can take care of ourselves," but added that he wanted battleships to protect Latin America as well. He spent much time elaborating on the instances when Britain had insulted American interests in Honduras, Nicaragua, Venezuela, and Brazil during the previous thirty years. [78]

Populists led the opposition to additional battleships. "Sockless" Jerry Simpson believed a navy useless until the nation had its own merchant marine. Senator William Peffer, noting that fourteen American states had recently been under martial law because of labor discontent, feared that the naval armaments were being created "to suppress rebellion and insurrection and revolution amongst the common people." Non-Populist opposition came from Senators David B. Hill of New York and Redfield Proctor of Vermont. Hill did not care for increased taxation to pay for the ships, and Proctor observed that Mahan's theories were useless without colonies, a commodity the United States did not have. [79]

Despite such opposition, Congress appropriated the money for two battleships. The bill becomes most meaningful when viewed

[77] *Ibid.*, 2261, 3107–3110.

[78] *Ibid.*, 2310–2311, 2252–2255, 3105–3106, Appendix, 325–327; *Report of the Secretary of the Navy, 1894*, 17.

[79] *Congressional Record*, 53rd Cong., 3rd Sess., 2241–2244, 3095, 3044, 3112–3113, 3103.

as a complement of the American business community's contemporary conclusions regarding expansion. It should be emphasized, moreover, that these battleships were authorized *before* the Corinto and Venezuelan episodes. Thus, although the battleship measure in part emanated from past American involvement in far-flung areas of the world, the measure itself formed a part of a general, growing, and emphatic feeling that the political and commercial health of the United States depended on such distant areas as Latin America and Asia.

When Cleveland and Herbert again asked Congress for naval appropriations in December, 1895, Corinto had become history, but the Venezuelan crisis was still imminent. Cleveland again noted how, during the year, American vessels protected American interests in places as distant as Turkey. The President struck a new note by declaring that "Cuba is again greatly disturbed," thus pointing out another area in which American naval forces were needed. Herbert followed the President's message with a report requesting two more battleships "and at least twelve torpedo boats." Citing his previous arguments, Herbert also noted that "the lessons taught at Yalu and Wei Hai Wei" (battles of the Chinese-Japanese war) proved the value of these two types of vessels.[80]

When the House Committee on Naval Affairs submitted its report in March, the Venezuelan incident had occurred, though the report only briefly noted this event. The committee wanted to give Herbert $2,000,000 more than the Secretary had thought necessary. The committee also asked for four battleships and fifteen torpedo boats. Chairman Charles Boutelle justified this large increase by alluding to the "remarkable decrease in the cost of the construction of modern war ships," and to the need of "providing employment for vast numbers of our own people." But he closed his report with the comment that the United States should set "afloat a navy that . . . may prove in peace the mes-

[80] *Messages and Papers of the Presidents*, IX, 626–655, especially 640; *Report of the Secretary of the Navy, 1895*, xxxiv–xxx, lvii.

sengers of good will to other lands and show to us and to the world again that 'commerce follows the flag.' " [81]

In an amazing display of unanimity, the House supported Boutelle's request for four battleships. Phillip B. Low of New York admitted that "we are confronted with a depleted Treasury. But what has that to do with it?" Amos Cummings of New York spoke for the Democrats who backed Boutelle, as he stressed that "in view of the war cloud on the horizon . . . this is an exceedingly economical bill." [82]

The House measure ran into trouble in the Senate. Arthur Gorman proposed that the number of battleships be cut to two. Matthew Quay immediately asked that it be raised to six. Gorman had his way. With the aid of all the Populists plus men such as Proctor, who feared that a big navy would lead to taking colonies, Gorman squeezed his amendment through 31-27 with 31 abstentions. When the measure came back to the House, Boutelle became so bitter that the Speaker had to remind him that it was highly improper for one house of Congress to describe the other in such language.[83]

Despite the efforts by Lodge, Hawley, and Quay to persuade the Senate to agree with the House, the deadlock continued throughout May and early June. Another factor entered the controversy. The Senate wanted to limit the price of armor to $350 per ton, thus taking away much of the profit which the Bethlehem Steel and Carnegie works had received by selling armor to the government at figures as high as $550 per ton. The House objected to setting a definite limit. On June 9 the bill finally passed. It provided for three battleships and disposed of the armor controversy by directing the Secretary of the Navy to make an investigation and then recommend to Congress the price he believed to be fair.[84]

[81] *Congressional Record*, 54th Cong., 1st Sess., 3193–3194; *House Report No. 904*, 54th Cong., 1st Sess. (serial 3460), 1.

[82] *Congressional Record*, 54th Cong., 1st Sess., 3196, 3195.

[83] *Ibid.*, 4511–4512, 4519, 4565, 4653, 4799–4804.

[84] *Ibid.*, 6195, 6326.

In his last message as President, Cleveland boasted that in March, 1893, the United States Navy had only two armored vessels. Since then, three first-class and two second-class battleships and two armored cruisers had been placed in commission. The "Iowa" (the battleship authorized in 1892), would be ready in early 1897. Besides these, there had been five battleships authorized under his administration. But Herbert wanted more. In his 1896 report, the Secretary feared that the navy was not yet in "a satisfactory condition." He suggested three more battleships and twelve torpedo boats. Interestingly, Herbert asked for battleships which would have less than twenty-three feet draft so that they might enter American harbors in the Gulf of Mexico. All of the previously authorized battleships had drafts of twenty-three to twenty-five feet and so could not enter these ports.[85]

Congress did not grant Herbert's request, but for immediate American history this refusal was irrelevant.[86] The fleet that would defeat Spain in 1898 had been set afloat. It had been constructed at a time when the theme of overseas commercial expansion and conflicts arising from this expansion had stimulated Congress to accept Mahan's capital-ship theory and all that this theory implied for America's political and economic responsibilities for the future.

The environment in which the New Navy had been created was described by Richard Olney. In a speech which opened the Philadelphia Commercial Museum on June 2, 1897, Olney declared that American businessmen could ask the government for two favors: free access to the markets of the world, and the right to conduct foreign trade in American bottoms.

Sea-power—as an officer of the United States Navy demonstrates in a recent treatise conferring almost equal lustre upon himself and his country—sea-power is an essential element both of national

[85] *Messages and Papers of the Presidents*, IX, 733; *Report of the Secretary of the Navy, 1896*, 4–5, 7, 9, 56.

[86] Boutelle analyzed the reasons why Congress did not act in *Congressional Record*, 54th Cong., 2nd Sess., 2115.

security and national greatness. The fact seems to be now thoroughly implanted in the popular mind and is largely responsible for the birth of our navy. . . . Yet it is not to be forgotten that men-of-war for a nation that is without the vessels of commerce is almost an incongruity and that the true basis of a navy is a merchant marine. The business man of this country, therefore, who longs to see its foreign trade conducted to a reasonable extent at least under the stars and stripes, . . . who objects to one great power sequestering the highways of the ocean, . . . that man is not to be regarded as a mere sentimentalist.[87]

Olney missed the vital point that American bottoms were not necessary to stimulate American exports. All that was needed was the ability to outproduce other manufacturing or agricultural countries, plus a navy to protect both distant markets and the merchant ships that carried this surplus. This statement nevertheless shows that Olney appreciated Mahan. It also demonstrates that he realized the value of "free access to the markets of the world," and that he resented "one great power sequestering the highways" to these markets. That the Cleveland administration thought about these factors, and that it viewed any businessman who wanted to obtain overseas markets as more than "a mere sentimentalist," can be illustrated not only in this speech of its Secretary of State, but also in the way the administration countered British encroachments in Venezuela.

[87] Speech is dated June 2, 1897, Olney MSS. Dexter Perkins ties in the growing concern for the Monroe Doctrine with the growth of the navy in his *Monroe Doctrine, 1867–1907*, 225–226.

VI

Reaction: The Venezuelan Boundary

Crisis of 1895-1896

IN the development of the new empire, only the economic effects of the 1893–1897 depression and the battle of Manila Bay in 1898 rank in importance with the Venezuelan boundary crisis of 1895–1896. The boundary episode is crucial for several reasons. First, it indicated the explosive potential of the conclusion reached by American political and business leaders that overseas commercial expansion could solve the economic stagnation and the attendant social unrest. These leaders considered Latin America as the most promising area for this expansion to occur. Thus when the Cleveland administration enunciated the so-called "Olney extension" of the Monroe Doctrine in 1895, the administration emphasized the positive aspect of that doctrine; namely, that the Western Hemisphere was to be under American commercial and political control, not European.

Two aspects of the crisis substantiate this first conclusion. The State Department did what it thought would most benefit American interests, not what Venezuela necessarily wanted. The United States cared little for Venezuelan opinion or advice on the situation. Moreover, the timing is significant. Since this boundary dispute had simmered for over a half-century, it should be noted why the United States chose 1895 as the opportune moment to end the controversy and assert its control over the Western Hemisphere.

These observations lead to another conclusion. American action came as a direct answer to British encroachments in Latin America. Congressional critics, American businessmen, and the press had made Great Britain the scapegoat for troubles in the United States. The depression of 1893 quickened this tendency when English investors worsened the panic by unloading their American securities. This was followed by ominous British moves in Brazil, Nicaragua, and the small island of Trinidad, which was located off the Brazilian coast. The State Department became anxious over these movements and finally forced a showdown struggle on the issue of the Venezuelan boundary.

Lighting the Fuse

The boundary difficulties had begun in 1841 when a British surveyor, Robert Schomburgk, mapped the western limits of British Guiana. He included Point Barima inside Guiana's boundaries. Venezuela immediately protested, for Point Barima controlled the mouth of the Orinoco River, and that river was the trade artery for the northern third of South America. In the 1840's and again in the 1880's, Great Britain offered to relinquish its claims to Point Barima if Venezuela would concede much of the remaining area within the Schomburgk line. Venezuela refused, asking that the entire disputed territory be settled by arbitration.

Venezuela had unsuccessfully attempted to bring the United States into the argument·while Hamilton Fish was in the State Department. In the late 1880's, however, the Secretary of State, Thomas F. Bayard, became interested. The British Foreign Office increased its claim in the disputed area from 76,000 square miles to 108,000 square miles and capped its new demand by announcing that Point Barima was British territory. Venezuela broke off diplomatic relations with England. Bayard then sent America's first emphatic protest to Great Britain, but E. J. Phelps, the American Minister in London, thought the time inopportune and did not deliver the message.[1]

The United States did little else until Venezuela began pleading its case with the newly installed Cleveland administration in 1893. By this time Venezuela was desperate. Her government was tottering and her economy was in shambles. She could not reopen diplomatic relations with England because of the fear that this would force the payment of huge debts to British citizens, debts which the bankrupt Venezuelan Treasury could not afford to honor. Finally, acute unrest permeated the eastern section of the country where the boundary dispute lay. If the government surrendered the boundary claim, open revolution would be sure to follow. These growing pressures forced Venezuela to step up its appeals to the State Department. Gresham responded with a message of July 13, 1894, to Bayard, now American Ambassador to England. The Secretary of State noted that British claims had "been silently increased by some 33,000 square miles" and now embraced "the rich mining district of the Yuruari," one of the wealthiest gold stores on the continent. The American Ambassador, who had grown to dislike the Venezuelan character as

[1] Paul R. Fossum, "The Anglo-Venezuelan Boundary Controversy," *Hispanic American Historical Review*, VIII (August, 1928), 300–304; Theodore Clarke Smith, "Secretary Olney's Real Credit in the Venezuela Affair," *Proceedings of the Massachusetts Historical Society*, LXV (1932–1936), 112–147; Henry James, *Richard Olney and His Public Service* (Boston, 1923), 221–222; *Foreign Relations, 1888*, I, 698–702. Parts of this chapter were presented in greatly condensed form in "The Background of Cleveland's Venezuelan Policy: A Reinterpretation," *American Historical Review*, XLVI (July, 1961), 947–967. Venezuela gave concessions to American speculators in the middle of these gold fields. Vagts believed that the monetary situation affected Cleveland's Venezuelan policy, for the policy not only silenced silverite expansionists temporarily, but also kept England away from gold stores which the U.S. Treasury could use (*Deutschland und die Vereinigten Staaten in der Weltpolitik* [New York, 1935], 510, 1257).

much as he loved the Anglo-Saxon cultural tradition, delayed taking the instruction to the Foreign Office and finally presented a weakened version of the note.[2]

American interest markedly increased in December, 1894. Gresham again asked Bayard to protest England's new claim. Cleveland followed by declaring in his annual message that he would "renew the efforts heretofore made to bring about a restoration of diplomatic relations . . . and to induce a reference to arbitration." In January, 1895, Gresham sent several instructions to Bayard asking him to sound out Great Britain on the two points Cleveland had mentioned. These incidents in December and January marked the beginnings of full-fledged American participation in the boundary dispute. Events soon occurred in the United States and Latin America which picked up the momentum of American interest and speeded it first to Olney's epochal declaration of July, 1895, and finally to Cleveland's dramatic pronouncement in December.[3]

Five general factors can be analyzed to indicate the background and immediate causes of these two messages: (1) new European encroachments in Latin America; (2) vigorous reaction by American public opinion to these encroachments; (3) the entry of commercial arguments into the American case, especially (4) the view that the Orinoco River was the vital pawn in the dispute; (5) the arrivals of Richard Olney into the United States State Department and Lord Salisbury into the dominating position in British politics.

Commercial interests and politicians in the United States had interpreted the Brazilian incident of 1893–1894 as an American action to halt European commercial and political infiltration of

[2] *Foreign Relations, 1894,* 803–805; Tansill, *Foreign Policy of Bayard,* 661–663; Partridge to Gresham, Nov. 15, Oct. 17, 1893, Venezuela, Despatches, and Gresham to Bayard, July 13, 1894, Great Britain, Instructions, NA, RG 59.

[3] Gresham to Bayard, Dec. 1, 1894, Jan. 3, 1895, Great Britain, NA, RG 59; Bayard to Gresham, April 5, 1895, Cleveland MSS; *Messages and Papers of the Presidents,* IX, 526.

Brazil. The Mosquito incident in 1894 seemed to be another instance of British interests appearing in an area where they had no right to appear. Both these events, however, paled beside the potential threat posed by the Corinto episode. The landing of British troops on Nicaraguan soil incited American public opinion and official circles to strong anti-British sentiments. This feeling became explicit during the naval debates of 1895 and 1896 and during the discussions carried on by the business community in 1894 and 1895. The outbreak of the Cuban revolution in the spring of 1895 heightened American interest in the Caribbean area.[4]

Other European threats to the rights of nations in the Western Hemisphere appeared in 1895. England alone was staking out so many claims that the Second Assistant Secretary of State, Alvey A. Adee, exclaimed to Olney in August, 1895, that the British were playing a "grab game" throughout North and South America. In December, 1894, the United States received word that the legislative chamber of British Guiana had passed a measure which authorized the construction of a road uniting the upper Barima with either the Cuyuni or the Yuruari areas in the heart of the disputed territory. The Cuyuni and the Yuruari had been the scenes of recent gold rushes. In mid-summer Great Britain occupied a small island six hundred miles off the coast of Brazil for use as a cable station. Although the island was small and uninhabited, Brazil had claimed it. American public opinion quickly became interested in this trivial affair. Adee told Olney that "the newspaper men are wild about the Trinidad business." The State Department maintained its interest until the dispute was settled in mid-1896.[5]

The United States also viewed France as a threat in Latin America. A large area encompassing 155,000 square miles of

[4] See Chapters IV and V, above; also "Did England Assist the Brazilian Insurgents?" in *Literary Digest*, May 26, 1894, 115.

[5] Adee to Olney Aug. 2 and 19, 1895, Olney MSS; Adee to Bayard, Aug. 30, 1895, Great Britain, Instructions, NA, RG 59; *Foreign Relations, 1894*, 841–843.

Brazil had been claimed by France, though she had never attempted to occupy it until gold was found there in 1894 and 1895. When French soldiers tried to move into the area, fighting broke out in May, 1895. The dispute paralleled the Venezuelan-British controversy in several respects. Both areas not only contained gold, but also provided a valuable entrance into the interior of South America. In Brazil the disputed area controlled the northern estuary of the Amazon River. Although the United States did not become immediately involved, both Bayard and Olney closely watched French-Brazilian relations. Bayard, in fact, wrote Olney regarding the contingencies which might occur "in the assumption of the United States of a supervision of Brazilian boundaries, should French interests or ambitions prompt their invasion." Bayard further warned the French Ambassador in London that the United States had a "serious interest" in Latin America and that these states would not be allowed to "become an element in European politics." From this single incident it is plain that American interest in the Venezuelan boundary dispute did not develop in a diplomatic vacuum.[6]

France also became involved in two other areas of the hemisphere. Venezuela had broken off diplomatic relations with France over alleged insults by the French Minister to the Venezuelan government. The United States stepped into the argument and worked to restore relations. Bayard revealed the importance of the dispute: it was "of present interest especially when viewed in [its] connection with the status of the existing Anglo-Venezuelan Boundary dispute." The United States became more actively interested in French claims in an affair over the Santo Domingo customs houses in 1894 and 1895. There the French threatened to use force to obtain reparation for the murder of a French citizen. The State Department became involved when the Santo Domingo Improvement Company of New York requested help. This company had been incorporated by a

[6] Bayard to Olney, Oct. 25, 1895, Great Britain, Despatches, NA, RG 59.

group of New York bankers and had bought Santo Domingo's debt. It had then taken over the customs houses in order to guarantee payment of the debt. The French delivered an ultimatum demanding that these customs houses "must respond . . . and guarantee the payment of the sums specified." A French squadron arrived at Santo Domingo. The United States responded by sending an American ship to the scene with instructions to "watch carefully" over American interests. Fortunately, the matter was soon adjusted.[7]

An observer writing in *Forum* noted the significance of these several conflicts. Looking back at Olney's and Cleveland's actions in the Venezuelan dispute from the perspective of April, 1896, this writer aptly commented: "The thunderbolt of last December may have come out of a seemingly clear sky, but nimbus clouds had long been hovering over Mexico, Nicaragua, Panama, and the Spanish Main. Wise international weather prophets had discerned the threatening storm." [8]

Aggressive public and congressional opinion in the United States provided more thunder and lightning for international weather in the spring of 1895. Congressional critics of the administration displayed the most interest in foreign affairs. In almost every issue of foreign relations—Hawaii, the battleship navy, Nicaragua, an Isthmian canal—Great Britain was the target for the congressional onslaught.[9]

Henry Cabot Lodge exemplified this sentiment. In two articles written during the first half of 1895, Lodge warned that, although England, Germany, and France were attempting to sur-

---

[7] Bayard to Olney, Aug. 8, 1895, Great Britain, Despatches, NA, RG 59; Explanatory Memorandum sent by Dominican Chargé in Washington to the State Department, Feb. 5, 1894, Acting Secretary of State Edwin Uhl to Secretary of Navy Hilary Herbert, Feb. 13, 1895, and Herbert to Rear Admiral R. W. Meade, March 9, 1895, Confidential Correspondence, NA, RG 45. For the background see *Foreign Relations, 1895*, I, 397–402.

[8] J. W. Miller, "Rumors of War and Resultant Duties," *Forum*, XXI (April, 1896), 239.

[9] Blake, "Background of Cleveland's Venezuelan Policy," 260–262; also Chapter V, above.

round the United States with colonial dependencies, the American people would not "give up their rightful supremacy in the Western Hemisphere." Interestingly, Lodge attacked Cleveland for trying to end the depression by expanding overseas commerce through the means of free trade. Lodge believed that the President had devoted so much time to trade expansion that the administration had ignored vital foreign policy problems. The Massachusetts Senator wanted to use the Monroe Doctrine in Venezuela to exclude British interests, but he quickly made a caveat concerning the Doctrine: "The Monroe Doctrine has no bearing on the extension of the United States, but simply holds that no European power shall establish itself in the Americas or interfere with American governments." [10]

In February, 1895, Congress officially announced its opposition to the British claims in Venezuela. Representative Leonidas F. Livingston of Georgia proposed a resolution on February 6, 1895, which asked for "friendly arbitration" in the boundary dispute. When some weak opposition appeared, it was quickly stilled by the remark that "large American interests will be promoted by a friendly settlement of this question." Livingston emphasized the threat posed to the Orinoco River; if Great Britain controlled that artery, she would "revolutionize the commerce and political institutions of at least three of the South American Republics." Livingston clinched his argument by remarking bluntly: "This relates to a matter on our [*sic*] continent. Our trade and other relations with those people are involved in this settlement." [11] It is difficult to find much altruistic concern for Venezuela in this debate.

Other Americans also noted the European movements in Latin America. R. A. Alger wrote Lodge that he read the Sen-

[10] Henry Cabot Lodge, "England, Venezuela and the Monroe Doctrine," *North American Review*, CLX (June, 1895), 657–658; Lodge, "Our Blundering Foreign Policy," *Forum*, XIX (March, 1895), 13–16. Dexter Perkins offers some excellent observations on Lodge's place in the history of the 1890's in *The Monroe Doctrine, 1867–1907*, 149.

[11] *Congressional Record*, 53rd Cong., 3rd Sess., 1832–1834.

ator's articles to a Cincinnati audience, and "could you have
heard the noise . . . you would know that [foreign policy]
more than anything else, touches the public pulse of today."
From his Washington social parlors, Henry Adams prophesied
that "a direct trial of strength with England" was imminent.
Adams thought "it time that the political existence of England
should cease in North America," and "particularly on the
Orinoco." Toward that, "all my little social buzz has been directed since September, 1893." [12]

An important and vocal part of American public opinion
believed that European threats to commercial markets in Latin
America provided an adequate reason for American intervention. Economic arguments played a large part in successfully
passing the congressional resolution on Venezuela in February,
1895. A speech by Don Dickinson in May, 1895, was perhaps the
most widely publicized commercial argument for American intervention in Latin America. Dickinson controlled the Democratic party in Michigan. He was, moreover, a close friend of
President Cleveland, and it is significant that he made the address immediately after a long conference with the President.
It thus should be emphasized that this speech was one of the most
blatant expressions of American commercial manifest destiny
made in the 1890's. Dickinson's words were more than a play to
the jingoes in the galleries; they exemplified a wide and strongly
held opinion that the United States needed additional foreign
markets for its prosperity.

Dickinson began his speech by noting that the danger of war
would always be with the world. Like Mahan, he believed that
wars arose out of commercial competition. Dickinson emphasized that this meant that the United States would have to face
the danger of many conflicts, for America stood "in the way of
the settled policy of Great Britain." Since the United States
assumed this position, English actions would have to be watched

[12] R. A. Alger to Lodge, June 11, 1895, Lodge MSS; *Letters of Henry
Adams*, II, 69.

closely, especially "the most extraordinary claims and movements . . . in Nicaragua and Venezuela." After reviewing the
several bloody chapters of Anglo-American history, Dickinson
reached a flaming peroration:

We are a great nation of producers; we need and must have open
markets throughout the world to maintain and increase our prosperity. . . . Whereas our interests in the early days were largely
at home, our material interests today depend upon the markets
abroad. We have entered the lists in the great contest of live and
let live with commercial Europe, and our diplomacy should be alert
to secure and protect favors and advantage from all peoples that
buy and sell or have a port our ships can enter.[13]

Since Dickinson's intimacy with Cleveland was well known,
the speech aroused much comment. Most revealing, however, is
the President's reaction. He wrote Dickinson on July 31, 1895
(eleven days after Olney sent his note to England), that he had
read the speech "with much interest" and was "glad you wrote
it." Cleveland sagely added, "In due time it will be found that
the Administration has not been asleep." [14]

A key factor in such commercial arguments, and indeed a
vital influence in the shaping of American diplomacy during the
Venezuelan troubles, was the controversy over the control of
the Orinoco River. Oddly, historians have paid little attention to
this important aspect of the negotiations.[15] It appears from study-
ing the chronology of events, however, that the British extension of their claim to the mouth of this river triggered the more
vigorous policy which the State Department pursued from the
spring of 1895 to Cleveland's message in December. As early
as 1885, Great Britain hinted that the Schomburgk line included

[13] Blake, "Background of Cleveland's Venezuelan Policy," 267; clipping
in Cleveland MSS from the Detroit *Free Press*, May 10, 1895.
[14] Nevins, *Grover Cleveland*, 632; Cleveland to Dickinson, July 31, 1895,
Cleveland MSS. Dickinson summed up the favorable public opinion which
greeted his speech in a letter to Cleveland, May 15, 1895, Cleveland MSS.
[15] An exception is Nevins' *Grover Cleveland*, 631, which mentions the
Orinoco question without elaboration.

the Orinoco's mouth, but England's first overt move into the area occurred in 1894, when British Guiana began to build a railroad into the Cuyuni gold fields. The rumor that England claimed this area was confirmed on April 5, 1895, when Lord Kimberley, the British Foreign Minister, showed Bayard a map on which the terminal point of the Schomburgk line ran a short distance inside the mouth of the river. Kimberley stated that this area had been "conclusively proven and established as a British possession, and would not be submitted to arbitration." Finally, on May 13, 1895, the State Department received a note from the Venezuelan Foreign Minister reporting that England had withdrawn her offer of 1890 to renounce her claim to the mouth of the Orinoco in exchange for other concessions.[16]

The United States had shown interest in keeping the Orinoco open to American shipping during the early months of 1895. In October, 1894, Venezuela unconditionally closed all but one of the river's entrances in an alleged effort to end smuggling. Gresham exerted pressure to reopen the river, and Venezuela finally complied in early 1895 by opening one of the key ports on the Orinoco. American official circles wondered whether Venezuela had closed the ports to show the United States how American interests would suffer if England controlled the river. *Bradstreet's* printed the story and added the comment that "the fact is made clear, however . . . that Venezuela relies largely upon the mediation of the United States" in the boundary dispute.[17]

Venezuela played its Orinoco trump card for all it was worth. In notes to the State Department, the Venezuelan Foreign Minister, P. Ezequiel Rojas, emphasized that the boundary trouble "is almost as serious and important to the great Republic of the

<hr />

[16] Fossum, "The Anglo-Venezuelan Boundary Controversy," 322–323; Bayard to Gresham, April 5, 1895, Great Britain, Despatches, NA, RG 59; see also *British and Foreign State Papers*, 1894–1895, LXXXVII (London, 1900), 1062–1063; *Foreign Relations*, 1895, II, 1482–1483.

[17] P. F. Fenton, "The Diplomatic Relations of the United States and Venezuela," *Hispanic American Historical Review*, VIII (August, 1928), 299–329; *Foreign Relations*, 1894, 800; *Bradstreet's*, April 27, 1895, 257

North as it is to Venezuela herself." Not only was the Monroe Doctrine at stake, but, Rojas believed, "England's control over the mouth of our great fluvial artery, and over some of its tributaries, will be the cause of permanent danger to industry and commerce throughout a large portion of the New World." Venezuela next granted a concession of land 125 miles by 15 miles located at the mouth of the Orinoco to a group of wealthy Americans. The concession, enormously rich in minerals and wood, lay in the heart of the disputed area.[18]

William L. Scruggs, former American Minister to Venezuela, had been hired as special agent by Venezuela for the purpose of interesting American opinion in the boundary controversy. Scruggs stressed the importance of the Orinoco in an influential pamphlet, *British Aggressions in Venezuela or the Monroe Doctrine on Trial*. After reviewing the history of the dispute, Scruggs concluded that Great Britain had unlawfully encroached on two areas. One of these was the mouth of the Orinoco, "the key to more than a quarter of the whole continent," which England could use "to work radical changes in the commercial relations and political institutions of at least three of the South American republics." The second place of British encroachment was the small island of Patos which controlled "the most available entrance" to the Orinoco and was "the key to the gulf which commands the Orinoco delta." The pamphlet went through four printings. Scruggs sent copies to congressmen, governors, public libraries, and newsstands. Olney received a copy in June, 1895, while Scruggs wrote Cleveland to remind the President that the controversy was not settled. It was Scruggs, moreover, who induced Leonidas Livingston to propose the Venezuelan resolution in Congress in February, 1895.[19]

[18] Haselton to Gresham, Jan. 15, 1895, Venezuela, Despatches, and Bayard to Gresham, April 5, 1895, Great Britain, Despatches NA, RG 59; G. H. D. Gossip, "England in Nicaragua from an American Point of View," *Fortnightly Review*, LVIII (December, 1895), 829–842.

[19] William L. Scruggs, *The Monroe Doctrine on Trial* (2nd ed.; Atlanta, Ga., 1895), 24–25; Theodore D. Jervey, "William Lindsay

Venezuela and Scruggs could have conserved their energies. Cleveland and other leading Americans fully realized the value of the Orinoco. Just before his speech in May, Don Dickinson made a midnight call on the hard-working Chief Executive. Cleveland went to the trouble of displaying a large map which showed the area of the boundary dispute. The President told Dickinson that Great Britain had previously offered to negotiate its claim to the mouth of the Orinoco, but now Kimberley had retracted that offer, and that he (Cleveland) was alarmed since the control of the river meant the control of the interior.[20] Considering the tenaciousness of Dickinson's speech, Cleveland must have made a forceful impression on the Michigan Democrat.

This new British claim stimulated Gresham to urge again arbitration of the dispute. On January 16, 1895, the Secretary of State wrote Bayard that recent information indicated that "the British boundary claim is variable and is expanded westward from time to time as expedience or interest may counsel." Again on the last day of March, and after the State Department had received rumors that Britain claimed the Orinoco's mouth, Gresham told his Ambassador in London that the British position was "contradictory and palpably unjust." The Secretary of State added, "If Great Britain undertakes to maintain her position on that question, we will be obliged, in view of the almost uniform attitude and policy of our government to call a halt." Written eleven days after the cabinet discussed the situation, Gresham's letter reflected the administration's opinion.[21] Interesting also is the indication that, as early as January and March, Gresham

Scruggs—A Forgotten Diplomat," *South Atlantic Quarterly*, XXVII (July, 1928), 292–309; Scruggs to Olney, June 17, 1895, Olney MSS.

[20] Nevins, *Grover Cleveland*, 631; for other references to the Orinoco see Lodge, "England, Venezuela and the Monroe Doctrine," 657–658; Gossip, "England in Nicaragua," 833.

[21] Gresham to Bayard, Jan. 16, 1895, Great Britain, Instructions, NA, RG 59; Perkins, *The Monroe Doctrine, 1867–1907,* 145.

showed the same disgust with the British position as Olney displayed in July.

Gresham initiated a two-point policy. In May he exerted pressure on Venezuela to renew diplomatic relations with Great Britain; the United States would then "be in a position" to urge Great Britain to arbitrate the problem. Venezuela finally informed the State Department in August that it had decided to follow Gresham's wishes. By this time, however, the Olney note had rendered meaningless the Venezuelan decision. Second, Gresham began composing a note to the British Foreign Office. His untimely death on May 28 prevented the sending of this note. The contents of the message are unknown since it cannot be found in his papers or his biography. Mrs. Gresham remarks that "there was to be no ultimatum as my husband had prepared it." Judging, however, from the Secretary of State's growing impatience with the British position, it was no doubt a stern note and might well have produced the same results as Olney's July 20 dispatch.[22]

Cleveland clearly expected some trouble to arise from the situation. In April and May he asked friends for suggestions of candidates to fill the vacated ministerial post to Venezuela. He noted that Venezuelan affairs were "liable to assume a condition calling on our part for the greatest care and good management," and he wanted "to send someone there of a much higher grade than is usually thought good enough for such a situation." After several men refused the offer, the post was given to Allen Thomas, the American Consul at La Guayra.[23]

Shortly after Gresham's death, Richard Olney became Secretary of State. Olney had been one of the best-paid railroad lawyers in New England before he accepted the post of Attorney General in 1892. He possessed two beliefs which must be under-

[22] Acting Secretary of State Uhl to José Andrade, May 25, 1895, and Andrade to Olney, Aug. 10, 1895, Olney MSS; Gresham, *Life of Gresham*, II, 794–795.

[23] *Letters of Grover Cleveland*, 392; John E. Russell to Cleveland, April 12, 1895, and G. L. Rives to Cleveland, May 9, 1895, Cleveland MSS.

stood in order to comprehend American actions in the dispute. He had changed his views concerning the cause of the depression during the course of 1893 and 1894. In 1893 he attributed the depression to a normal turn of the business cycle. By June, 1894, however, his understanding of the economic picture had matured to the point where he interpreted the depression as a great "labor revolution" resulting from the introduction of machine technology into the economy. He hoped that this revolution would be confined to "peaceful and moderate channels." When, during the Pullman strike a month later, labor violence overflowed these channels, Olney did not hesitate to use force to end the strike. The Attorney General regarded Eugene Debs, the leader of the Pullman strikers, with contempt. Olney declared that "no punishment he is likely to get . . . will be commensurate with his offense." [24]

Olney's second major belief concerned his view of the course of American history. He believed that the United States of the 1890's had emerged from its century of internal development into a full-fledged world power. Olney holds a prominent place in American history because he believed that the United States in 1895 was by necessity expanding outward, and that it was rapidly developing the power to clear away obstacles which lay in its path. From 1895 to March, 1897, Olney possessed and vigorously used the instruments of power which could remove these obstacles. He fervently believed that the American Century began during his years as Secretary of State.

In several notable statements that Olney issued after leaving the State Department, he outlined the philosophy of his foreign policy. In an article for *Atlantic Monthly*, Olney attacked the common belief that Washington's Farewell Address envisioned eternal isolation for the United States. He pointed out that Wash-

---

[24] New York *Tribune*, June 8, 1895, 1:2; remarks prepared for Harvard Commencement Dinner, June 28, 1893, and clipping from Philadelphia *Daily Evening Telegraph*, June 20, 1894, Olney MSS; Olney to Edwin Walker, Aug., 1894, Olney Letterbook, Olney MSS.

ington had said merely that America should stay out of world affairs until it was strong enough to command its own fortunes. Olney believed that this time had arrived. He declared that "it behooves us to accept the commanding position" the United States had "among the Powers of the earth." He noted that "this country was once the pioneer and is now the millionaire." After asking what is "the present crying need of our commercial interests," Olney answered, "It is more markets and larger markets for the consumption and products of the industry and inventive genius of the American people." In his address at the opening of the Philadelphia Commercial Museum on June 2, 1897, Olney emphasized his belief that Latin America provided the natural market for American products.[25]

In a remarkable article written after 1900, he predicted that future historians would call the events of 1898 the turning point of American history. He then flatly stated that these chroniclers would be mistaken. Olney believed that the change had occurred earlier in the 1890's, and that "the change was inevitable, had long been preparing, and could not have been long delayed." He observed that the American people

had begun to realize that their industrial and commercial development should not be checked by the limitation to the demands of the home market, but must be furthered by free access to all markets; that to secure such access the nation must be formidable not merely in its wants and wishes and latent capabilities but in the means at hand wherewith to readily exert and enforce them.[26]

[25] Richard Olney "International Isolation of the United States," *Atlantic Monthly*, LXXXI (May, 1898), 577–588. After the outbreak of the Spanish-American War, Olney wrote Cleveland that American expansionist sentiment had gone too far (*Letters of Grover Cleveland*, 503). But Cleveland told a friend in 1900 that Olney "is largely responsible through his 'Atlantic' article for the doctrine of expansion and consequent imperialism" (James, *Olney*, 187). See also "Speech at National Opening of the Philadelphia Commercial Museum," June 2, 1897, Olney MSS.

[26] Richard Olney, "The Nation's Parting of the Ways," *Harvard Graduate Magazine*, XIII (September, 1904), 48–51.

These remarks do not place Olney in the colonialist camp. Like Gresham, he despised the thought of a colonial empire and strenuously opposed the acquisition of the Philippines.[27] The attempt to ensure America's "free access to all markets" and the flexing of the fully developed muscles of one of the "powers of the earth" nevertheless envisioned a kind of vigorous foreign policy which even Lodge and Roosevelt could heartily endorse, as they did after Olney's July 20 note became public. Such a philosophy furthermore envisioned the extension of American responsibility abroad far beyond any previous limits.

Not the least of Olney's characteristics were his bluntness and stubbornness. As early as 1894 his vigorous statements and determination made him the most powerful member of Cleveland's cabinet. Shortly after he became Secretary of State, a man with similar characteristics rose to power in England. Lord Salisbury re-entered office in July, 1895, as both Prime Minister and Foreign Minister. Since the retirement of Bismarck, he was the dominant European statesman. Swept into office in July, 1895, with the largest majority any government had enjoyed in the House of Commons since 1832, Salisbury's vigor was abetted by the power both to carry out his decisions and to compel Parliament to abide by them.[28] The clashing on the international diplomatic scene of two men such as Olney and Salisbury promised to be not only exciting, but explosive.

Olney's interesting personal traits and the blustering language of the July 20 note often make one lose sight of the fact that President Cleveland greatly influenced the formulation of the Venezuela policy. Some historians claim that Cleveland made the key decision of sending the July message and that he outlined the tone of the policy. It is definitely known that the President warmly endorsed Olney's first draft of the message, though he

[27] Richard Olney, "Growth of Our Foreign Policy," *Atlantic Monthly*, LXXXV (March, 1900), 289–290.
[28] Aubrey Leo Kennedy, *Salisbury, 1830–1903* . . . (London, 1953), 251–257.

proposed "a little more softened verbiage here and there." In a letter to his Secretary of State, Cleveland called the message "the best thing of the kind I have ever read and it leads to a conclusion that one cannot escape if he tries—that is if there is anything of the Monroe Doctrine at all." The President declared in this letter that Olney had shown that there was "a great deal" in the Monroe Doctrine, and that the Secretary of State had placed "it I think on better and more defensible ground than any of your predecessors—*or mine.*" This letter indicates that Cleveland endorsed not only the language of the note, but also Olney's key point that the United States could intervene in the dispute because it was affected by events occurring elsewhere in the Western Hemisphere. Other than the President, the Secretary of the Navy, Hilary Herbert, the Secretary of the Treasury, John Carlisle, and the new Attorney General, Judson Harmon, read and endorsed the message before it was sent to Salisbury. Several weeks later the Secretary of War, Daniel Lamont, added his blessings. No record has been found of any cabinet member who disagreed with the note.[29]

The Explosion

Olney began the July 20 message by reviewing the respective claims.[30] He concluded that neither party stood for a boundary line "predicated upon strict legal right." The Secretary of State then turned his fire directly on Great Britain for its attempt to move "the frontier of British Guiana farther and farther to the westward" of the Schomburgk line. Olney noted the vital point

[29] George Roscoe Dulebohn, *Principles of Foreign Policy under the Cleveland Administration* (Philadelphia, 1941), 20; Alfred L. P. Dennis, *Adventures in American Diplomacy, 1896–1906* (New York, 1928), 22; Cleveland to Olney, July 7, 1895, Cleveland MSS (italics used in the original); telegrams from Olney to Harmon, Herbert, and Carlisle, July 18, 1895, Olney MSS.

[30] Olney to Bayard, July 20, 1895, Great Britain, Instructions, NA, RG 59; also in *Foreign Relations, 1895,* I, 545–562. The best historical criticism of the note is Perkins, *Monroe Doctrine, 1867–1907,* 153–168.

that these British moves included two recent advances: one by Salisbury in 1890 which "fixed the starting point of the line in the mouth of the Amacuro west of the Punta Barima on the Orinoco," and one by the Rosebery government in 1893.[31] Venezuela had offered to arbitrate these claims, but Great Britain, so Olney claimed, had consistently refused. The Secretary closed this first section of the message by noting that to all this "the United States has not been, and indeed, in view of its traditional policy, could not be indifferent."

Olney then reached the transition to the next section, which concerned the Monroe Doctrine:

By the frequent interposition of its good offices at the instance of Venezuela . . . the Government of the United States has made it clear to Great Britain and to the world that the controversy is one in which its honor and its interests are involved and the continuance of which it can not regard with indifference.

This phrase provides the key to the remainder of the note, for Olney then tried to fit the Monroe Doctrine into the meaning of this sentence. The Secretary of State made a bad fitting, but this is irrelevant to the understanding of Olney's intention and to the aims of the administration's foreign policy. Olney advanced the argument that American interests as well as Venezuelan territory were at stake. In essence he was interpreting the Monroe Doctrine as the catchall slogan which justified protecting what the United States considered as its own interests. If the Monroe Doctrine had not existed, Olney's note would have been written anyway, only the term American Self-Interest would have been used instead of the Monroe Doctrine.[32]

---

[31] In protesting against the advancement of British claims, Olney failed to note that the Venezuelan government had advanced claims which were also without foundation and, moreover, that Venezuela had granted concessions in the disputed area which violated former agreements with the British (*ibid.*, 154).

[32] Albert Bushnell Hart compared Olney's argument to an Oxford undergraduate's account of a football game: "It would have been just

Olney asked rhetorically whether the United States had a right to intervene in the dispute. He emphatically answered that it did and gave the involvement of American interests as the reason: according to "the admitted canon of international law," the United States could interfere in a controversy concerning two or more other nations "whenever what is done or proposed by any of the parties primarily concerned is a serious and direct menace to its [the United States] own integrity, tranquillity or welfare." Olney believed this right was spelled out in two forms "peculiarly and distinctively American," Washington's Farewell Address and the Monroe Doctrine.

The note emphasized that the Monroe Doctrine was positive as well as negative. Monroe's declaration did "not content itself with formulating a correct rule for the regulation of the relations between Europe and America. It aimed at also securing the practical benefits to result from the application of the rule." Further, the Doctrine was a "distinctively American doctrine of great import to the safety and welfare of the United States." Olney advanced the thesis that the "safety and welfare of the United States" could be affected in two ways. One stemmed from the fact that the Latin-American nations were "friends and allies, commercially and politically, of the United States." Thus, "the subjugation of any of them by an European power . . . signifies the loss of all the advantages incident of their natural relations to us." Olney then moved beyond this in elaborating his second point: "But that is not all. The people of the United States have a vital interest in the cause of popular self-government." Using sentences which sound much like the phrases Woodrow Wilson used in 1917 when he proclaimed the ideal of extending the American form of democratic self-government to the world, Olney pronounced the extension of this form of government to Latin America as the most important factor to be protected if the self-interest of the United States was to remain unharmed. A

as good a fight without the ball; the ball was only in the way" (*The Monroe Doctrine: An Interpretation* [Boston, 1916], 203–204).

further insight into Olney's thinking can be gained from his implicit distinction between British democracy and American democracy.

Olney coupled this closing reference to political ideals, however, with the more mundane matter of the Orinoco River. First, however, he wrote the famous phrase:

Today the United States is practically sovereign on this continent, and its fiat is law upon the subjects to which it confines its interposition. Why? It is not because of the pure friendship or good will felt for it. . . . It is because, in addition to all other grounds, its infinite resources combined with its isolated position render it master of the situation and practically invulnerable as against any or all other powers.

Olney did not include this declaration in the message as a debating technique. As his speeches prove, he earnestly believed that the United States possessed a commanding position among the powers of the world. From this double assumption that the United States had the right to intervene in Latin-American affairs whenever its rights were endangered, and further, that it had the power to protect its rights, Olney asked the crucial question whether American interests were involved in the Venezuelan boundary dispute to the extent that the United States could legitimately intervene. He answered with an emphatic affirmative: "The political control at stake . . . is of no mean importance, but concerns a domain of great extent . . . and if it also directly involves the command of the mouth of the Orinoco, is of immense consequence in connection with the whole river navigation of the interior of South America." After denying that Great Britain could qualify as an American state, Olney concluded the message by declaring that "peaceful arbitration" was the "one feasible mode" of determining the boundaries.

Bayard did not relish the task of reading the note to Salisbury. He nevertheless impressed upon the Prime Minister that Olney wanted a reply as quickly as possible. The Secretary of State's notes to Bayard during the fall revealed an increasing nervousness over the coming diplomatic battle. Due partly to a misunderstanding of the time Cleveland's message was to be sent to Congress, partly to the fact that Salisbury was inundated by other matters, and partly to the Foreign Office's underestimation of the dispute's significance in American minds, the British reply did not arrive at the State Department until five days after the President's annual message had been delivered.[33]

The State Department, meanwhile, endeavored to keep the note secret. Vigilant journalists nevertheless began reporting rumors of the message as early as September 2. The American public became especially aroused over these rumors when, in October, Great Britain sent an ultimatum to Venezuela. In January, Venezuela had seized and held for questioning eight members of the British Guiana police stationed on the right bank of the Cuyuni River. Salisbury demanded a reparation of fifteen hundred pounds. He gave Venezuela three months to comply or Britain would "adopt other means for obtaining satisfaction." The British press interpreted the Foreign Office as saying in effect that "Venezuela is to run on all fours with Nicaragua," and that like Corinto, the Monroe Doctrine would be "evaded, not defied." Bayard sent these clippings to Washington for Olney's attention. The British Foreign Office quickly assured Olney, however, that the ultimatum had "no reference whatever" to the boundary dispute.[34]

Two other events further disconcerted the State Department in the autumn of 1895. In October, the British Ambassador to the United States, Sir Julian Pauncefote, told a reporter that Great Britain would not think of submitting its "well-defined"

[33] Bayard to Cleveland, Sept. 10, 1895, Cleveland MSS; pencil notation to Adee, undated, probably August, 1895, Adee to Olney, Aug. 14, 1895, Bayard to Olney, Nov., 1895, Olney MSS; *Public Opinion*, Oct. 31, 1895, 554.
[34] Adee to Olney, Sept. 2, Aug. 30, 1895, Andrade to Olney, Dec. 11, 1895, Bayard to Olney, Oct. 21, 1895, Olney MSS; Cleveland to Olney, Oct. 16, 1895, Cleveland MSS; Bayard to Olney, Oct. 22, 1895, Great Britain, Despatches, NA, RG 59. Venezuelan pleas to the State Department can be found in *Foreign Relations, 1895*, II, 1483–1488.

territory in Venezuela to arbitration, especially that area which contained British settlements. Olney feared that this interview was a "foreshadowing" of the British reply from Salisbury on Venezuela.[35]

Olney also became concerned over British actions in Nicaragua. Bayard reported in early November that the British had *"reserved their rights"* in the whole Nicaraguan affair. Later in November, the British-Nicaraguan indemnity treaty was made public. The pact expressly stipulated that no American could serve as the third commissioner on the arbitration board. England wanted to settle directly with Nicaragua. Adee believed that such an obviously anti-American provision was "an important indication of the drift of British policy." [36]

Adee's fear was mirrored in the American press and political circles throughout the fall and early winter of 1895. During October and November journals freely expressed the opinion that Cleveland would present a vigorous interpretation of the Monroe Doctrine in his December address. Many of these papers fervently hoped for such a message. Politicians recognized that many constituents were intensely concerned with Latin-American affairs. Representative Thomas M. Paschal from Texas wrote Olney, "Turn this Venazuelan [*sic*] question up or down, North, South, East or West, and it is a 'winner.'" "Why, Mr. Secretary," Paschal exclaimed, "just think of how angry the anarchistic, socialistic, and populistic boil appears, on our political surface. . . . One cannon shot across the bow of a British boat in defense of this principle will knock more pus out of it than would suffice to inoculate and corrupt our people for the next two centuries." Other congressmen, as Representatives Joe Wheeler of Alabama and Charles H. Grosvenor of Ohio and Senator William E. Chandler of New Hampshire, published ar-

[35] Olney to Bayard, Oct. 8, 1895, Great Britain, Instructions, NA, RG 59.

[36] Bayard to Olney, Dec. 2, 1895, Great Britain, Despatches, and Adee's notation on Baker's despatch to Olney, Nov. 18, 1895, Nicaragua, Despatches, NA, RG 59.

ticles stressing the importance of the Orinoco River within the context of the necessity to expand the foreign commerce of the United States.[37]

Salisbury's reply finally arrived at the State Department on December 7, five days too late for Cleveland's annual message. The answer consisted of two letters. One message bluntly refuted the validity of the Monroe Doctrine as international law, while the other answered Olney's defense of the Venezuelan position and the Secretary of State's request for arbitration.

In his consideration of the Monroe Doctrine, Salisbury simply disclaimed the relation of the hallowed dogma "to the state of things in which we live at the present day." But he went beyond this generalization. Olney's "novel prerogative," the Prime Minister observed, in effect asserted an American protectorate over Latin America. This was something which Monroe's "sagacious foresight would have led him energetically to deprecate."

Salisbury emphasized this vital point in another way. He challenged Olney and Cleveland to admit explicitly that the American economic and political system could not remain a viable system if it was forced to remain within the continental bounds of the United States. Salisbury declared that "the United States have no apparent practical concern" with the controversy. The adjectives are important. Olney had mentioned that American "honor and . . . interests" were involved. Salisbury had demonstrated that historically the Monroe Doctrine had no relevance to the affair. If the United States then rested its case on some-

---

[37] *Bradstreet's*, Oct. 19, 1895, 657; *Economist*, Nov. 30, 1895, 1563; quotations in Perkins, *Monroe Doctrine, 1867–1907*, 169–171; Henry M. Stanley, "Issues between Great Britain and America," *Nineteenth Century*, XXXIX (January, 1896), 1; New York *Tribune*, Nov. 26, 1895, 6:3; *Public Opinion*, Nov. 7, 1895, 585–586; Blake, "Background of Cleveland's Venezuelan Policy," 270–271; Thomas M. Paschal to Olney, Oct. 23, 1895, Olney MSS; Joseph Wheeler and Charles H. Grosvenor, "Our Duty in the Venezuelan Crisis," *North American Review*, CLXI (November, 1895), 628–633; Nevins, *Grover Cleveland*, 637. See also the stormy congressional debates in early December in *Congressional Record*, 54th Cong., 1st Sess., 24–25, 28, 36, 114–126.

thing beyond the tradition of the Doctrine, namely the nation's honor and interests, Salisbury demanded to know what these interests were. The Prime Minister emphasized this point with a touch of sarcasm. The United States, he wrote, "is not entitled to affirm as a universal proposition, with reference to a number of independent States for whose conduct it assumes no responsibility, that its interests are necessarily concerned in whatever may befall those States simply because they are situated in the Western Hemisphere."

Salisbury capped his argument by making a tactical concession. He admitted that, if American interests were involved or threatened, the United States had a right, "like any other nation, to interpose in any controversy" which endangered these rights. The Prime Minister granted that the United States was entitled to "judge whether those interests are touched, and in what measure they should be sustained." He merely wanted Olney and Cleveland to define these interests. Unless his allegations could be controverted, Salisbury denied that the United States had a right to demand arbitration in the dispute.[38]

The second note, dealing with the boundary controversy proper, began by again declaring that the British government believed the boundary dispute "had no direct bearing on the material interests of any other country." Salisbury cited historical facts which ripped apart Olney's argument for the Venezuelan case. At one point Salisbury sarcastically commented, "It may reasonably be asked whether Mr. Olney would consent to refer to the arbitration of another Power pretensions raised by the Government of Mexico on such a foundation to large tracts of territory which had long been comprised in the Federation [of the United States]." The Prime Minister steadfastly refused to submit to arbitration those claims of British subjects "who have for many years enjoyed the settled rule of a British Colony." [39]

Bayard immediately wrote Cleveland to praise Salisbury's

---

[38] Salisbury's first note is printed in *Foreign Relations, 1895*, I, 563–567.
[39] Salisbury's second note is in *ibid.*, 567–576.

notes as being "in good temper and moderate in tone." The American Ambassador believed that "our difficulty lies in the wholly unreliable character of the Venezuelan rulers and people." Neither Cleveland nor Olney, however, was in a frame of mind to listen to Bayard's eulogies of Salisbury's diplomacy. Cleveland was "mad clean through." He later wrote that it would have been "depressing" and "unpleasant" for the United States to learn that the great Monroe Doctrine was really "a mere plaything with which we might amuse ourselves." [40]

Olney released his anger by drafting the President's message of December 17. Cleveland later asserted that Olney's draft "entirely satisfied my critical requirements"; in fact, "I have never been able to adequately express my pleasure and satisfaction over the assertion of our position." The draft was never submitted to the other members of the cabinet. This was unfortunate, for Carlisle and the Secretary of Agriculture, Sterling Morton, later expressed disagreement with the bluntness of the message. [41] Olney and Cleveland thus unloaded their fury unmolested, and on December 17 the world heard of the American challenge to the British Empire.

The President's message was, in essence, a succinct summary of Olney's July 20 note. Cleveland's declaration is significant, however, because it emphasized and amplified Olney's crucial point that the United States was becoming involved in the controversy not for the sake of Venezuela, but for the welfare of the United States. It directly replied to Lord Salisbury's charge that, since the Monroe Doctrine was inapplicable "to the state of things in which we live at the present day," the United States had no right to become involved in the dispute.

At the beginning of his message Cleveland quoted and then

[40] Bayard to Cleveland, Dec. 4, 1895, Cleveland MSS; Perkins, *Monroe Doctrine, 1867–1907*, 183; Grover Cleveland, *Presidential Problems* (New York, 1904), 268; Olney to Pauncefote, Dec. 10, 1895, Olney MSS.

[41] Cleveland to Olney, Dec. 3, 1895, Cleveland MSS; George F. Parker, *Recollections of Cleveland* (New York, 1909), 197, 199; Nevins, *Grover Cleveland*, 641.

attacked these words of the British Prime Minister. The Monroe Doctrine was "strong and sound," the President declared, "because its enforcement is important to our peace and safety as a nation and is essential to the integrity of our free institutions and the tranquil maintenance of our distinctive form of government." Such a principle could "not become obsolete while our Republic endures." This was an emphatic definition of the Monroe Doctrine as a doctrine of self-interest. Cleveland so defined the Doctrine explicitly: "The Monroe doctrine finds its recognition in those principles of international law which are based upon the theory that every nation shall have its rights protected and its just claims enforced."

Cleveland and his Secretary of State did believe that American interests were greatly endangered. Nothing better illustrates their beliefs than Cleveland's statements in the closing part of his December 17 message: "The duty of the United States [is] to resist by every means in its power, *as a willful aggression upon its rights and interests*, the appropriation by Great Britain of any lands or the exercise of governmental jurisdiction over any territory which after investigation we have determined of right belongs to Venezuela." Cleveland emphasized the importance he placed on this sentence by then declaring, "In making these recommendations I am fully alive to the responsibility incurred and keenly realize all the consequences that may follow." [42] He italicized the sentence, as it were, by saying that the United States would risk war in order to preserve the principle contained in the statement.

In a letter to Ambassador Bayard in late December, Cleveland again underscored the fact that the United States was entering into the boundary imbroglio to protect its own interests. The President also emphasized that the controversy had been germinating for some time. The administration had not suddenly leaped upon the issue in mid-1895 for domestic political gains. Cleveland wrote:

[42] *Messages and Papers of the Presidents*, IX, 656–658—italics added.

Events accompanying the growth of this Venezuelan question have recently forced a fuller examination of this question upon me and have also compelled us to assume a position in regard to it.

I am entirely clear that the doctrine is not obsolete, that it should be defended and maintained for its value and importance *to our government and welfare*, and that its defense and maintenance involve its application when a state of facts arises requiring it.

The President assured Bayard that no political motives lay behind the message. Cleveland admitted that he could not understand why Great Britain had not "yielded or rather conceded something" to "stem the tide of 'jingoism' " in the United States. The President carefully prefaced these remarks, however, with the comment that Great Britain's failure to do this was "entirely irrelevant to the case and . . . has had absolutely nothing to do with any action I have taken." [43]

In failing to consult Venezuela's wishes in the affair, Cleveland and Olney further emphasized that they entered into the boundary controversy to protect American interests. Venezuelan authorities learned the contents of Olney's July note only after newspapers published the message on December 18, 1895. No evidence has been found which indicates that Olney consulted Venezuelan officials in Washington before or during the time he drafted the President's message. A British observer, writing during the peak of the dispute, informed his countrymen that they would be wrong if they thought "that any partiality for Venezuela has inspired these utterances" by Cleveland.[44]

Although the President intimated that he would risk war to protect American interests, he neither wanted war nor believed

[43] Cleveland to Bayard, Dec. 29, 1895, Cleveland MSS; also in *Letters of Grover Cleveland*, 417–420—italics in the original.

[44] George B. Young, "Intervention under the Monroe Doctrine: The Olney Corollary," *Political Science Quarterly*, LVII (June, 1942), 251–252, 260; Thomas M. Spaulding, "Allen Thomas," *Dictionary of American Biography*, XVIII, 420; Arthur P. Whitaker, *The United States and South America: The Western Republics* (Cambridge, Mass., 1948), 160–161; Stanley, "Issue between Great Britain and America," 4.

that war would result from the dispute. The December message embraced many qualifications and opportunities for retreat. Cleveland's declaration that an American commission would investigate the boundary controversy was a diplomatic means to gain time and allow tempers to cool. It would take the commission at least one year, and probably several years, to investigate all the relevant facts and write a report. On the other side of the Atlantic, Salisbury and his leading cabinet members appreciated the safety-valve features of Cleveland's address. The British officials did not react in haste or panic. But they did at last react, and this was what Cleveland and Olney wanted.[45]

Aftermath

Expansionist-minded Americans heartily endorsed the President's message, though most of them also fully shared his hopes that no war would result. In its lead editorial *Public Opinion* declared, "It is doubtful if there was ever before witnessed in the United States so nearly unanimous an expression of press approval of any Administration." [46] In Senate proceedings, however, Henry Cabot Lodge and other ultraexpansionists toned down their belligerence. The House had responded to Cleveland's message by quickly whipping through an appropriation measure for a boundary commission. The Senate, while standing firm on the principles of the Monroe Doctrine, nevertheless asked that the Committee on Foreign Relations carefully consider the measure before the entire upper house voted upon it. There was a minimum of indulgence in the popular congressional game of

[45] See especially the last three paragraphs of the message; also Young, "Intervention under the Monroe Doctrine," 259–260. Both nations alerted their military planning experts. See Rear Admiral H. C. Taylor, "The Fleet," *Proceedings of the United States Naval Institute*, XXIX (December, 1903), 799–808; and J. A. S. Grenville, "Great Britain and the Isthmian Canal, 1898–1901," *American Historical Review*, LXI (October, 1955), 51, for relevant comment.

[46] *Public Opinion*, Dec. 26, 1895, 837; New York *Tribune*, Dec. 18, 1895, 6:5; for midwestern opinion, see Chicago *Times Herald*, Dec. 18, 1895, 6:2; New York *World*, Dec. 18, 1895, 2:2–8, and Dec. 19, 1895, 3:3–4.

twisting the Lion's tail. Two factors probably account for this attitude. As Senator Roger Q. Mills of Texas declared, "It will be no child's play, Mr. President, when we engage in a conflict with Great Britain." The impending stock market break provided a second moderating influence.[47]

The effect on the stock market and the reaction of the American business community to Cleveland's message deserves detailed analysis. Historians have pictured this reaction as one of panic. From this, it may be inferred that businessmen vigorously opposed extending American control or responsibility in Latin America, especially when such action would run the risk of conflicting with European interests in the area. In reality, business opinion was more complex.[48]

Some financial leaders, especially bankers in New York, Boston, and Chicago angrily criticized the Chief Executive's statement as ending any hope of immediate business recovery. Peter B. Olney reported from New York to his brother in the State Department that "there is an undercurrent of sentiment among bankers and businessmen of considerable strength, that censures" the message. Critics included Charles Stewart Smith, former President of the New York Chamber of Commerce, Frederick D. Tappen, President of the Gallatin National Bank, and J. Edward Simmons, President of the Fourth National Bank. In an informal poll taken at the Union League Club "practically everybody" expressed disgust "over the whole business." In Boston, the New England Free Trade League and important members of the Boston Stock Exchange agreed with Edward Atkinson's views. Atkinson, President of the Boston Manufacturers Mutual Fire Insurance Company and one of the popular economists of the day, shouted to an inquiring reporter, "This is ridiculous,

---

[47] *Congressional Record,* 54th Cong., 1st Sess., 234–235, 240–247, 255–265, 420, 529–531, 294.

[48] The following section appeared in a revised and enlarged version as "The American Business Community and Cleveland's Venezuelan Message," in *Business History Review,* XXXIV (Winter, 1960), 393–402.

ridiculous, ridiculous!" At each word his voice rose until he almost shrieked.[49]

These were influential voices, but they were soon balanced by the views of business leaders in New York, Boston, and the Midwest. Two opinion polls, one published by the New York *World* and one conducted by *Bradstreet's*, outlined this fact. After interviewing twenty-three boards of trade, chambers of commerce, and commercial exchanges, the *World* concluded that all but one group approved the message. The single organization which did not, the Richmond, Virginia, Chamber of Commerce, had not polled its members and thus refused to comment. *Bradstreet's* survey of leading merchants and manufacturers in twenty cities revealed an identical trend of opinion.[50]

Even on Wall Street imperfect unanimity existed. John A. Stewart of the United States Trust Company, Oscar Straus, and Chauncey Depew endorsed the President's stand on the Monroe Doctrine. Andrew Carnegie was especially pleased, since the crisis provided him with the perfect opportunity to publicize two of his pet projects: the disposal by Great Britain of her colonial empire in the Western Hemisphere, and international arbitration. Many members of the Boston business community, including the Boston Board of Trade, approved the message. The President of the Massachusetts State Board of Trade proclaimed, "I believe that this nation has reached a period in its history when it is of sufficient importance that no national wrong or injustice should be disregarded, and we should demand, in justice to our mercantile interests, that respect to which we are entitled." The

[49] Peter B. Olney to Richard Olney, Dec. 20, 1895, Abram S. Hewitt to Olney, Jan. 8, 1896, Olney MSS; New York *World*, Dec. 21, 1895, 1:8, 4:1, and Dec. 20, 1895, 1:8, 2:1; *Wall Street Journal*, Dec. 19, 1895, 1:4; Boston *Morning Journal*, Dec. 18, 1895, 4:6; *Wall Street Journal*, Dec. 20, 1895, 1:2; New York *World*, Dec. 21, 1895, 5:1.

[50] New York *World*, Dec. 20, 1895, 2:3–5; *Bradstreet's*, Dec. 21, 1895, 813. The *World* denounced Cleveland's course of action on its editorial pages and displayed its bias by headlining this survey, "TRADE DEPRESSED BY MESSAGE," although not a single reply to the opinion poll could be construed in this manner.

rush of many Boston bankers to Cleveland's support provided a most surprising occurrence. H. J. Jaquith, President of the Traders' National Bank, N. P. Hallowell, President of the National Bank of Commerce, and Eben Bacon, President of the Washington National Bank, expressed views more common to their ardent Massachusetts expansionist, Henry Cabot Lodge, or to western silverite jingoists.[51]

The absence of immediate panic on the New York Stock Exchange indicated a lack of concern in financial circles over Cleveland's policy. When word of the message reached the floor of the Exchange, the bear contingent cried "War! War!" and selling began. In a very few minutes, however, market prices began to climb. The bears rushed to cover their shares. One disgusted bear trader was heard to complain, "Ugh! Is this the whole bloody war?" The next day the market actually strengthened. Industrials led the way upward while the investors neglected the bond market. This was not the way a frightened financial community usually acted.[52]

The crash finally occurred on the morning of December 20. Losses ran upward to $170,000,000. Five firms failed, though all of them were small. A new shipload of gold totaling $3,400,000 left the depleted Treasury stocks for Europe. But the panic lasted less than one day. By the afternoon of December 20, "good buying" featured the trading. Other than its short duration, two other factors of the crash deserve notice. First, British investors,

[51] New York *World*, Dec. 20, 1895, 1:8, 2:1, and Dec. 18, 1895, 1:7, 2:3; Boston *Morning Journal*, Dec. 18, 1895, 4:6, 5:3, and Dec. 19, 1895, 4:3; *Bradstreet's*, Dec. 21, 1895, 813; Straus to Cleveland, undated, but probably Dec. 18, 1895, Oscar Straus papers, Library of Congress; Carnegie to the Duke of Devonshire, Dec. 26, 1895, Andrew Carnegie papers, Library of Congress, Washington, D.C. Carnegie saw the crisis as an opportunity to obtain a large order for steel from the United States Navy. See Carnegie to John G. A. Leishman, President of the Carnegie Steel Company [no specific date, but after the Cleveland message], Dec., 1895, Carnegie MSS.

[52] New York *World*, Dec. 18, 1895, 2:2, 13:1, and Dec. 19, 1895, 11:1; *Wall Street Journal*, Dec. 19, 1895, 2:1.

not American, touched off the downward surge of stock prices. But it was American buyers who firmed the prices in the afternoon. The New York *World* examined the day's activities and bragged that the afternoon events demonstrated the "ability of American finance to take care of itself." The rapidly maturing New York financial community was beginning to demonstrate that it could play an important independent role in international finance.[53]

Second, factors other than the diplomatic crisis undermined the stock market. In his annual message of December 2, 1895, Cleveland had warned that the gold reserve in the Treasury had dwindled to a dangerous point. When on December 20 the President asked Congress for emergency measures to deal with this gold crisis, he thus dealt with a long-term problem which had been accelerated by the Venezuelan crisis. Business magazines realized this. Financial periodicals agreed with R. G. Dun & Company's *Weekly Review of Trade*, which reported that the Venezuelan message had little direct effect on the market, since "business was remarkably dull" anyway.[54]

Farther removed from the hypnotic influence of the New York exchanges, business groups in Fall River, Massachusetts, Pittsburgh, Buffalo, Baltimore, and Trenton warmly approved the President's stand. Commercial bodies speaking for the midwestern business communities of Kansas City (Missouri), St. Paul, Milwaukee, and Indianapolis also expressed wholehearted support of the message. Most interesting was the Chicago scene, where the bankers attacked Cleveland, but men in the industrial-merchant group, such as Marshall Field and P. D. Armour, gave equally strong endorsements. Armour even added, "In fact,

[53] New York *World*, Dec. 21, 1895, 1:7–8; *Wall Street Journal*, Dec. 20, 1895, 2:1; New York *Journal of Commerce*, Dec. 19, 1895, 5:1, and Dec. 23, 1895, 1:3. By Dec. 24 the gold exports had dwindled, buying of gilt-edged securities had increased, and general optimism prevailed.

[54] *Messages and Papers of the Presidents*, IX, 645; New York *World*, Dec. 17, 1895, 1:1; Chicago *Times Herald*, Dec. 21, 1895, 14:3; *Bankers' Magazine*, LII (January, 1896), 107.

there are a great many of us republicans [*sic*] who like Mr. Cleveland." Cincinnati and Cleveland led midwestern support for the message. The Chambers of Commerce and conservative financial journals in both cities applauded the President's position. Southern and western commercial centers such as Memphis, Atlanta, San Francisco, and Helena backed the American policy also.[55]

Trade journals divided on the issue. Businesses whose stocks fluctuated with every smile and frown of British investors excoriated Cleveland's policy. The *Railway Gazette, American Wool and Cotton Reporter*, and *Engineering and Mining Journal* were among the spokesmen for these disenchanted groups. But many journals, especially those published in industrial and in iron and steel centers, supported the President. The *American Manufacturer*, published in Pittsburgh, was usually not a pro-Cleveland paper, since it advocated high tariffs. But in discussing the Venezuelan situation this journal reasoned that England was in a tight situation because "the markets of the world are being wrested from her," and so she "seeks to extend her commercial influence in South America." In this light the President's course was correct. The *Manufacturers' Record*, the *Farm Implement News* (a bimetallist journal), and the *Bulletin of the American Iron and Steel Association* warmly endorsed the President's message.[56]

[55] *Bradstreet's*, Dec. 21, 1895, 813; New York *World*, Dec. 20, 1895, 2:3–5; New York *Evening Post*, Dec. 23, 1895, 3:4; Chicago *Times Herald*, Dec. 19, 1895, 5:3, 4, and Dec. 21, 1895, 3:3, 4; New Orleans *Times-Democrat*, Dec. 20, 1895, 2:5; Milwaukee *Sentinel*, Dec. 18, 1895, 9:4; Cincinnati *Commercial Gazette*, Dec. 18, 1895, 4:1, Dec. 19, 1895, 4:2, and Dec. 21, 1895, 1:1–2; Memphis *Commercial Appeal*, Dec. 18, 1895, 4:1–2.

[56] *Literary Digest*, Jan. 4, 1896, 278; *Railway Gazette*, Dec. 27, 1895, 858; *Public Opinion*, Dec. 26, 1895, 843; *American Manufacturer and Iron World Weekly*, Dec. 28, 1895, 919; *Farm Implement News*, Dec. 26, 1895, 18; *Bulletin of the American Iron and Steel Association*, Jan. 10, 1896, 12:1, and Jan. 1, 1896, 1:1; *Northeastern Lumberman and Manufacturers's Gazette*, Dec. 28, 1895, 3:3.

This analysis of the business community suggests several conclusions. First, a split occurred between New York–Boston–
Chicago banking circles and the remainder of the business
community. Not even some leading Boston bankers agreed with
their fellow financiers. Industrialists and merchants almost unan-
imously backed the President. Second, several monetary weaknesses in the American economy contributed as much to the
panic of December 20 as did the Venezuelan crisis. Most important, British security holders triggered the decline, while
American investors displayed considerable financial power in
stemming the tide and stabilizing stock prices.

Two weeks after Cleveland's message, even the more appre-
hensive businessmen could begin to relax. On January 2, 1896,
the German Emperor sent a telegram to President Kruger of
the Transvaal Free State and offered congratulations for Kruger's
capture of the Jameson raiders. An intense anti-German feeling
erupted in Great Britain, and the Venezuelan difficulty was relegated to the background. Six days later the American Embassy
in London learned that Salisbury had "very considerably modified his views in regard to the Venezuelan question . . . and was
prepared to 'trim' his views" to meet the requests of the United
States.[57]

This new British attitude resulted in concrete proposals when
on January 12, Lord Playfair, a former Liberal cabinet minister,
came to see Bayard as an intermediary for Salisbury and Joseph
Chamberlain, the Colonial Secretary. Playfair offered three proposals. First, an international conference should be called to
clarify the Monroe Doctrine. Second, all British settlements in
the disputed area should be exempt from arbitration. Third, the
Court of Arbitration should consist of two or three persons from

---

[57] Tansill, *Foreign Policy of Bayard*, 738; Bayard to Cleveland, Jan.
29, 1896, Cleveland MSS. Bayard's despatches and letters indicate that
the Kruger telegram had a greater influence on British policy and opinion
than some historians have thought.

England and a like number from Venezuela and the United States.[58]

Olney's reply to these proposals is most revealing. He "highly appreciated" Playfair's suggestions, but flatly refused to submit the Monroe Doctrine to an international conference where a large number of European nations could outvote the United States. As for the settlements, Olney insisted that they be submitted to an arbitral board just like the remainder of the boundary line. Finally, the Secretary of State offered a counterproposal for the arbitral board by suggesting that two members from the American commission be joined by two named by Great Britain. These four could name a fifth member if necessary. Olney's proposal not only excluded Venezuela from the commission, but no evidence has been found which indicates that Olney consulted with Venezuela before making this suggestion.[59]

The American reply presaged the final settlement. Great Britain abandoned the idea of a conference on the Monroe Doctrine. A compromise was reached on the settled districts which exempted titles more than fifty years old or others which had been legally held for a reasonable number of years. Finally, the treaty which Pauncefote and Olney signed on November 12, 1896, established an arbitral tribunal consisting of two Americans, two British citizens, and a Russian authority in international law. No Venezuelan was included. Salisbury had not accepted these terms without a struggle. He had been especially adamant on the issue of the settled districts. But diplomatic difficulties elsewhere, especially in the Middle East, pressure from Sir William Harcourt, leader of the Liberal party, and the growing realization in Great Britain that the United States was a sizable power to be

[58] Bayard to Olney, Jan. 13 and 15, 1896, Great Britain, Despatches, NA, RG 59; Tansill, *Foreign Policy of Bayard*, 740–741; Wemyss Reid, *Memoirs and Correspondence of Lyon Playfair* (New York, 1900), 405–409.

[59] Olney to Bayard, Jan. 14, 1896, Great Britain, Instructions, NA, RG 59.

courted, not abused, forced the Prime Minister to accept most of Olney's points.[60]

One other aspect of the settlement merits attention. Venezuela ratified the treaty only after the police crushed threats of street rioting in Caracas. The cause of these riots could be traced to an early statement of Olney's. He did not wish, the Secretary wrote Bayard in January, 1896, to have Venezuela "consulted at every step." Olney had scarcely consulted Venezuela at all. Authorities in Caracas knew nothing of the treaty's contents until December 7, 1896, when the pact was published. Venezuelans were especially enraged when they learned that they were not to have a seat on the arbitral tribunal and that Olney had agreed on the fifty-year occupation clause in the settled areas dispute. Venezuela had fought for unrestricted arbitration since 1840; now her position had been compromised without her knowledge. The Latin-American nation finally was allowed to name a member to the tribunal, but the ill will resulting from the American actions played a large part in creating Venezuela's strong pro-Spanish attitude during the war in 1898.[61]

Venezuela's pained reaction strikingly illustrates the veracity of Cleveland's statement that the United States interfered in the controversy in order to protect its own rights and interests. For in the final settlement England received most of the disputed territory, but the United States obtained its two principal objectives: Venezuela retained control of the Orinoco River, and England submitted the dispute to an arbitral commission. By so doing, Great Britain recognized Olney's claim of American dominance in the Western Hemisphere.

American historians have offered three interpretations to ex-

[60] Tansill, *Foreign Policy of Bayard*, 776; Smith, "Olney's Real Credit," 145.

[61] Olney to Bayard, Jan. 22, 1896, Olney MSS; London *Times*, Feb. 5, 1897, 5:1, and Feb. 15, 1897, 6:1; Young, "Intervention under the Monroe Doctrine," 276–278; Olney to Pauncefote, Feb. 1, 1897, Olney Letterbook, Olney MSS; José Andrade to Olney, Dec. 7, 1896, Cleveland MSS; Fenton, "Diplomatic Relations of the United States and Venezuela," 354.

plain the Cleveland administration's policy in the boundary dispute. The most popular explanation states that Cleveland brought about the crisis in response to domestic political attacks on the general policies of his administration.[62] A second thesis traces the policy's roots to Olney's bellicose, stubborn temper.[63] A third interpretation declares that a "psychic crisis" struck influential segments of American opinion in the 1890's and that a new spirit of manifest destiny emerged from this "crisis." [64]

There can be little doubt that Cleveland took domestic political pressures into account, but defining these pressures as major causative elements leaves key questions unanswered and raises many others. Cleveland's bellicose policy could not have permanently won political enemies to his side. The Republican jingoists and the Democratic silver bloc led the cheering for the December 17 message. Neither of these groups would have agreed with the President on national political objectives. Cleveland actually alienated many of his strongest supporters, especially the eastern bankers who had once saved the gold reserve and who, at Cleveland's request, repeated the rescue operation shortly after the December message. In other words, the administration's Venezuelan policy attracted groups which were irreconcilable in domestic politics and repelled some of the administration's staunchest supporters. Cleveland obviously realized that such maneuvers did not win national elections. War might have united the nation behind him, but the President certainly did not plan to turn the controversy into a war.[65]

[62] Blake, "Background of Cleveland's Venezuelan Policy," 275–276; Vagts, *Deutschland und die Vereinigten Staaten,* 510–511.

[63] Tansill, *Foreign Policy of Bayard,* 776; also see Vagts, *Deutschland und die Vereinigten Staaten,* 1918.

[64] Richard Hofstadter, "Manifest Destiny and the Philippines," in *America in Crisis,* edited by Daniel Aaron (New York, 1952), 173–200, especially 176, 178.

[65] *Wall Street Journal,* Dec. 21, 1895, 2:3. Two weeks before the special Venezuelan message Henry Villard personally pleaded with the President to prevent American "arguments with Europe" until the treasury reserve was restored (Vagts, *Deutschland und die Vereinigten Staaten,* 512, 1702).

No reliable proof exists that Cleveland hoped the Venezuelan episode would rebound to his personal political benefit. It is extremely doubtful that with his conservative conception of the Chief Executive's duties and responsibilities he would have broken the third-term tradition even if he had possessed the support. E. C. Benedict, who handled Cleveland's investments in stocks and bonds, testified three weeks before the Venezuelan message that the President had repeatedly said that he was "impatient to lay aside all official cares and [was] utterly averse to their prolongation." [66]

An interpretation which stresses Olney's bellicose character misses two important points. First, Gresham worked on a diplomatic note which concerned the Venezuelan situation several months before Olney assumed the top position. Judging from Gresham's letters in the late winter and early spring of 1895, this note was probably quite militant. Second, Cleveland initiated the dispatch of the Olney note, reworked the draft, and heartily endorsed his Secretary of State's language. The President played an extremely important part in the formulation of the policy, especially during the crucial incubation period of April-July, 1895.[67]

A thesis which emphasizes that Cleveland bowed to the pressure of jingoism and a mass psychological need for vicarious excitement helps little in understanding the whole of the administration's foreign policy. After all, Cleveland defied these public pressures when they were exerted (often in even greater force) for Hawaiian annexation, the application of the Monroe Doctrine in the Corinto dispute, and compromises in the silver repeal act and the 1894 tariff. There is no reason to believe that he suddenly bent to the winds of jingoism in 1895, unless he had better reasons than pleasing irreconcilable political enemies. It

[66] *Wall Street Journal,* Nov. 27, 1895, 1:2.

[67] Cleveland, *Presidential Problems,* 257–259; *Letters of Grover Cleveland,* 392; Samuel Flagg Bemis, *The Latin American Policy of the United States: An Historical Interpretation* (New York, 1943), 119.

should be further noted that it is impossible to put Cleveland and Olney in those social groups which supposedly were undergoing this psychological dilemma.

Olney and Cleveland acted because they feared that United States interests were in jeopardy. Both men emphasized this point at the time, and there is no reason to doubt their word. The Venezuelan dispute threatened American interests in three areas. As Lodge noted in his Senate speech of December 30, 1895, British military control of the Orinoco would make the Caribbean a "British lake." Second, if England controlled the entrance to this river, she could regulate the commercial traffic flowing into and out of the upper third of the South American continent. Third, if Great Britain either militarily or diplomatically coerced Venezuela into accepting the British position, not only would the Monroe Doctrine have become an empty shell, but the United States would have moved far in forfeiting its rights to, what Olney termed in his July note, "the practical benefits" which resulted from the "application" of the Monroe Doctrine.

Obviously, neither domestic political pressure nor mass psychological complexes could have endangered such interests. Rather, the danger would have had to come in the explicit form of European encroachments and threats to Latin America. These occurred in 1894 and 1895. In this short space of time, Great Britain and France made ominous moves in Venezuela, Nicaragua, Trinidad, Santo Domingo, and Brazil. Cleveland, Olney, and Adee carefully studied these moves. Even Bayard, the foremost apostle of Anglo-American friendship, admitted in January, 1896, that there were good reasons to "fear that there was an indefinite plan of British occupation in the heart of America." [68]

The gravamen of the problem is, of course, that the Cleveland administration considered American interests to be endangered by such encroachments. Again, the time element is important. The United States had entered into the deepest trough of the

[68] Nevins, *Grover Cleveland*, 644.

depression in late 1894 and early 1895. Cleveland noted these factors in his annual message on December 2, 1895. The American commercial community believed that an expanding overseas commerce would revive the American economy. Cleveland and Secretary of the Treasury Carlisle expounded this commercial philosophy in its most detailed form throughout 1894. Secretary of State Gresham, who reopened the Venezuelan question in 1894, also emphasized the importance of foreign markets if the repressive weight of industrial glut was to be lifted from the American economy.[69]

Richard Olney entered the State Department in June, 1895, with the two elements needed to touch off the explosion. He had realized in 1894 that the depression was no ordinary turn of the business cycle, but a "labor revolution" which marked a new era in American economic history. Second, he had a profound sense that the United States had matured to a point where it could exert its influence on the world stage. Olney naturally wanted to use this power to benefit American interests.

The two currents of economic overseas expansion and Olney's realization that the United States possessed the means to protect its interests converged into the Venezuelan controversy. A feeling of manifest destiny existed, but it was not a type of mob excitement which Cleveland and Olney would have disparaged. It was a rational opinion that American interests in Latin America would have to be expanded and protected. An official in the State Department wrote several anonymous articles in the spring of 1895 which keenly analyzed this opinion. "The commercial instinct," Frederic Emory wrote, "is beginning to assert itself once more among the American people. Our manufacturers are reaching out, at last, for foreign trade." "The time has come," he concluded in his second article, "when our manufacturers must

[69] It is significant to note that contemporary observers saw Cleveland's Venezuelan policy as creating fertile grounds for American economic expansion into Latin America. Among these observers was the Bureau of American Republics in the State Department. See the bureau's *Special [Monthly] Bulletin*, March, 1896, 523; *Literary Digest*, May 30, 1896, 152.

help to swell the volume of our export trade. . . . It has been the task of Mr. Cleveland's foreign policy to prepare the way for them, to insure a hospitable reception for them." [70] One may speculate that Cleveland had the ideas of this article in mind when he told a close friend in late 1896 that the Venezuelan affair was not a foreign question, but the "most distinct of home questions." [71]

[70] Clippings from the Baltimore *Sun*, May 26, 27, 28, 1895, in Bayard MSS.

[71] Parker, *Recollections of Cleveland*, 195. This conclusion differs from Vagts's belief that Cleveland's policy was one of "negative imperialism," or what Vagts describes as "eager for rule but not for gain" (*Deutschland und die Vereinigten Staaten*, XI, 1416, 1701, 1702).

VII

Reaction: New Problems, New Friends, New Foes

THE Harrison-Blaine strategy, the consensus formed in 1894–1895 by the business community and political leaders, and the Venezuelan crisis of 1895–1896 are of paramount importance in understanding the expansive tendencies which swept the United States into war with Spain in 1898. In the three years immediately preceding that war, however, new factors appeared which built upon these earlier developments. A revolution in Cuba, as Cleveland noted in his annual message of 1895, once again disturbed hemispheric tranquillity. During this same year the balance of power in the Far East, ever teetering precariously, suddenly swung in the direction of Japan. Germany and Russia attempted not only to restore the balance, but to expand their own interests to the particular disadvantage of Japan, Great Britain, and the United States. When the State Department became more active in protecting American interests in the Far East, the United States found itself forced to sympathize with British policies and to condemn those of Russia and Germany. Such action strengthened the growing Anglo-American informal alliance and led to a historic break in the century-old Russian-American friendship and the decades-old German-American tics.

In this chapter these three new developments that affected post-1895 American policy formulation—the Cuban revolution, the threat to American interests in the far Pacific, and the momentous realignment of old enmities and friendships—will be briefly analyzed as they unfolded during the 1895 to March, 1897, period. In early 1897 two new agents appear, the newly elected McKinley administration and an American business community rapidly dredging itself up from the depths of the depression. Their reactions to events in Cuba and the Far East in 1897–1898 will be described in the next chapter. The point should be re-emphasized here that the actions of this new administration and the business community in 1897–1898 cannot be understood unless placed in the over-all framework of 1895–1898, and these last three years, in turn, are comprehensible only when inserted into the context of American foreign policy after the 1850's. The months of 1897 and early 1898 marked not a break but a culmination of nearly half a century of commercial expansion into extracontinental areas.

The Cuban Revolution, 1895–1897

A revolution erupted in Cuba's Santiago Province on February 24, 1895. During the next two years the Cleveland administration, motivated by the belief that the warfare gravely threatened American interests in Cuba and economic and political tranquillity in the United States, moved ever closer to a policy of intervention. The administration first hoped that Spain would retain its sovereignty but would grant to Cuba a large measure of autonomy. Olney initiated the next policy phase in April, 1896, when he offered to aid Spain in persuading the rebels to accept the reforms. The final stage was marked by Cleveland's annual message of 1896, in which the President warned that "higher obligations" than the maintenance of neutrality might compel the United States to use more vigorous means to end the revolt. Throughout the two years, however, two factors constantly restrained Cleveland and Olney. First, they refused to consider policies which might climax with the island's being annexed by the United States. The administration already had enough problems without assuming those of the Cubans. Second, throughout much of his final year in office, Cleveland realized that intervention would lead to a war which either silver Democrats (who had repudiated him) or Republicans would have the honor of finishing. Such a thought was not comforting to gold Democrats, who nursed the hope of regaining power in 1900.

A group of Cuban exiles in the United States had long awaited the proper moment to free their homeland from Spanish rule. The opportunity arose in 1895 when the Wilson-Gorman tariff suddenly removed Cuba's favored position in the American sugar market. Already ground between the millstones of Spanish taxes, corrupt governments, and bad transportation, the loss of this rich market was the final blow for the sugar growers. As plantations discharged workers in late 1894 and early 1895, discontent and rebel bands grew in force. In February sporadic uprisings were reported, and in April the Maceo brothers, José Martí and Máximo Gómez, assumed control of the insurgent groups. In the United States, the Cuban Junta with headquarters in New York and a "Cuban Legation" in the Raleigh Hotel in Washington supported the revolution with a bankroll supposedly amounting to almost $1,000,000. This war chest was constantly replenished with contributions from Cuban Leagues which spread throughout the country, Cuban exiles, and wealthy American supporters. The Junta received considerable help especially from the Cigar Makers' Union, which agreed to support Junta activities in return if the numerous Cuban workers in cigar factories joined the union. In 1895 the American Federation of Labor, led by Samuel Gompers, who had received his union initiation in the Cigar Makers' organization, passed a resolution at its national

convention which called for supporting the Cuban revolutionaries. Bolstered by such American encouragement, the revolution had progressed to such a point by September 13, 1895, that
delegates adopted a constitution for an independent Cuban government.[1]

At the outset of the revolution the Cleveland administration
wanted Spain to retain sovereignty of the island, but hoped that
Cuba would receive enough autonomy to puncture the rebel cry
that Spain ruled despotically. This policy found support from
many prominent Americans. Edwin F. Atkins, millionaire sugar
grower in Cuba and a close friend of fellow Bostonian Richard
Olney, urged that the administration refuse to recognize the
rebels as belligerents, since such recognition would free Spain
from the responsibility of protecting American property. This
factor of property protection was one major reason why American investors in Cuba opposed congressional attempts to give
the rebels belligerent status. Henry Clews, a New York banker
who frequently corresponded with Cleveland, publicly declared
that he did not desire American annexation of Cuba, since "we
really gain all the advantages through existing trade relations."
Former congressman John DeWitt Warner of New York agreed:
since "we practically control the trade, it strikes me that we have
the milk and the other nation the shell, of the cocoanut." William
Graham Sumner, having no taste for "Cuban Senators, either

[1] French Ensor Chadwick, *The Relations of the United States and
Spain: Diplomacy* (New York, 1909), 406–407; the causes of the revolt
are well outlined in Elbert J. Benton, *International Law and Diplomacy
of the Spanish-American War* (Baltimore, 1908), 22–24; and Hannis
Taylor, "A Review of the Cuban Question in Its Economic, Political
and Diplomatic Aspects," *North American Review*, CLXV (November,
1897), 610–635. Also *Bradstreet's*, Sept. 22, 1894, 593, and Sept. 29, 1894,
622, and Jan. 12, 1895, 17; Horatio S. Rubens, "The Insurgent Government in Cuba," *North American Review*, CLXVI (May, 1898), 561;
George W. Auxier, "The Propaganda Activities of the Cuban *Junta* in
Precipitating the Spanish-American War, 1895–1898," *Hispanic-Amer-
ican Historical Review*, XIX (August, 1939), 293–298.

native or carpet-bag," nevertheless wished for conditions which would be conducive to an expanding commerce with the island.[2]

Moving from these assumptions and having to devote much time to preparing its case on the Venezuelan boundary dispute, the administration steered a conservative course around the Cuban problem during the first half of 1895. On June 12, 1895, Cleveland issued a neutrality proclamation which recognized a state of insurgency. Although this appeared to be a formality, the pronouncement had certain obligations attached, for it declared that American relations with the insurgents would be regulated by the neutrality laws. Cleveland did not, of course, mention the more important step of belligerent status for the rebels. By late fall, however, the revolutionaries had formed a provisional government, expanded their base of military operations, and had clearly demonstrated that they possessed much greater strength than they had exhibited during the previous Ten Years' War of 1868–1878. This display of rebel strength compelled the Cleveland administration to re-evaluate its policies toward the rebellion. This re-evaluation led to Olney's April 4, 1896, offer of mediation, an offer which marked a distinct break with previous policies.[3]

The Secretary of State opened this new phase with a long letter to the President on September 25, 1895. Reporting that he had discussed the problem at length with "one of the largest landed proprietors of Cuba, a man of great wealth," Olney was now pre-

---

[2] Edwin F. Atkins, *Sixty Years in Cuba* . . . (Cambridge, Mass., 1926), 208–209; Callcott, *The Caribbean Policy of the United States*, 80; C. E. Akers to Olney, May 5, 1895, Olney MSS; "Ought We to Annex Cuba?" *Literary Digest*, July 20, 1895, 337–338; *Public Opinion*, July 11, 1895, 43; W. G. Sumner, "The Fallacy of Territorial Extension," *Forum*, XXI (June, 1896), 414–419. Not even leading jingo newspapers wanted to consider annexation in 1896; see Joseph E. Wisan, *The Cuban Crisis as Reflected in the New York Press, 1895–1898* (New York, 1934), 184–185.

[3] *Messages and Papers of the Presidents*, IX, 591–592; Benton, *International Law and Diplomacy*, 34–36; Adee to Ramon O. Williams, Consul General of the United States at Havana, Aug. 31, 1895, Olney MSS. A similar letter on Cuban belligerency went to Atkins.

pared to state flatly that "Spain cannot possibly succeed" in quelling the revolt. He insisted that the administration would have to assume a more active role in the Cuban situation in view of the "large and important commerce between the two countries" and the "large amounts of American capital . . . in Cuba." Olney therefore proposed that an agent be sent to the island to investigate the conditions there. If the rebels proved to be only "roving banditti," then the State Department would protest against the cruel warfare. But if, as Olney suspected, the revolutionaries had "a substantial portion of the community" with them, then the Americans should "put ourselves in a position to intelligently consider and pass upon the questions of according to the insurgents belligerent rights, or of recognizing their independence." [4]

Olney advocated taking a position which neither the Cleveland administration during its remaining months nor the McKinley cabinet in its first year in office dared to assume. He clearly believed than an agent would discover strong insurgent support and that a recognition of belligerency or even Cuban independence would follow. The Secretary of State refrained from mentioning that such recognition would almost certainly lead to war with Spain, but perhaps the letter is more remarkable because it so blandly neglected such a conclusion.

Replying on September 29, 1895, Cleveland wrote that he had also spoken with Peter Brooks, the Cuban planter to whom Olney had referred. Brooks's statements, the President remarked, "impressed me very much," but the Chief Executive wanted "to think your proposition over a little." After two weeks of reflection, Cleveland decided to reject Olney's idea. It was logical that the President did so. A war with Spain and the towering problems of annexation could not easily be glossed over. The Venezuelan dispute promised to provide enough excitement without searching for new diversions in Cuba. Finally, as Cleveland announced in his annual message in 1895, Spanish-American re-

[4] Olney to Cleveland, Sept. 25, 1895, Cleveland MSS.

lations were amiable. Several thorny problems involving American rights in Cuba had been settled in the administration's favor. The President saw no reason to modify his attitude toward Spain.[5] During the next twelve months, however, his views rapidly changed.

Several factors shaped the new administration position in 1896; among them were congressional pressure, public opinion, and changing conditions in Cuba. As Olney observed in his letter of September, politicians were "setting their sails . . . to catch the breeze" of rebel popularity in the United States. Prorebel arguments were stuffed into the *Congressional Record* by Populists who hoped that war with Spain would force the impoverished United States Treasury to coin silver to pay for the war. Congressmen such as Wilkinson Call of Florida and William Sulzer of New York, who had close ties with the Junta, supported the Populists' militancy.

These debates especially noted the growing involvement of American economic interests in the rebellion. Senators John T. Morgan of Alabama and Don Cameron of Pennsylvania introduced resolutions requesting recognition of Cuban belligerency and recognition of Cuban independence, respectively. Morgan, Cameron, and their supporters stressed the necessity of ending the conflict in order to allow American commerce and investments to operate safely on the island. Jefferson Caffery of Louisiana objected that the resolutions would open "the door to foreign conquest, and that opens the door to annihilation of the Republic," but the Senate swept the Morgan resolution over Caffery's objections by the vote of 64-5.[6]

[5] Cleveland to Olney, Sept. 29, 1895, Oct. 6 and 9, 1895, and Olney to Cleveland, Oct. 8, 1895, Cleveland MSS. All the letters cited in notes 4 and 5 may be found in *Letters of Grover Cleveland*. Also see *Messages and Papers of the Presidents*, IX, 636; Wisan, *The Cuban Crisis*, 100.

[6] *Congressional Record*, 54th Cong., 1st Sess., 1065–1066, 1970–1972, 1317, 2066, 2249–2250; *Senate Report No. 141*, 54th Cong., 1st Sess. (serial 3362), 1–3. John Bassett Moore publicly charged that the men who spon-

Morgan's proposal paled beside the resolution submitted to the House by Robert Hitt of Illinois, a Republican who was chairman of the Foreign Affairs Committee. Hitt asked for recognition of belligerent rights and "intervention if necessary." In arguing for this proposal of war, Hitt neglected humanitarian motives and mentioned the "immense commerce" and "enormous investments" of Americans which were being destroyed in Cuba. Hitt's resolution passed 262-17, and its passage threw both Washington and Madrid into a dilemma. Cánovas del Castillo, Prime Minister of the Spanish government, told the New York *World* that "the situation now is one of extreme delicacy." Cleveland considered moves to stall Senate action. But the upper house defeated the Hitt resolution, although the proposal found much support from such important legislators as John Sherman. The venerable Ohio Senator declared that if the resolution made it appear that "a money consideration" motivated American intervention, the House might change the language, but, he emphasized, "in substance it is true." "The only trouble," he candidly continued, "is it is better not always to speak of money and property and property interests when the rights of millions of people are involved." Under the threats of a filibuster, especially from some southern senators who feared the racial question which would arise from possible intervention, the Senate defeated the

---

sored the resolutions to recognize rebel belligerency realized that Spanish searching of American vessels would lead to open conflict between the two nations in short time. See Moore's "The Question of Cuban Belligerency," *Forum*, XXI (May, 1896), 298–299. In supporting the belligerency resolution, Lodge listed a number of reasons for American intervention and concluded that the most important was the "higher ground of humanity." In a private letter of March 12, 1896, he outlined five reasons why he wanted the United States to control Cuba, and none of them encompassed humanitarian motives. Three of them emphasized the economic rewards to be gained; one noted the threat of European intervention; the other mentioned the extension of democratic government (Lodge to Pickman, March 12, 1896, Lodge Letterbooks, Lodge MSS).

House resolutions. Both houses then agreed on a proposal which requested belligerent rights and the offering of friendly offices by the Executive.[7]

Pressure for intervention increased as conditions in Cuba worsened. General Valeriano Weyler y Nicolau replaced General Martínez Campos in February, 1896, and promptly announced that he would institute no reforms until peace had been restored. Fitzhugh Lee, the American Consul General in Havana, summarized the Cuban feeling when he reported that autonomy and home rule would no longer satisfy the rebels. He also observed that Spain was erecting new fortifications around Havana and that many of the guns "point to the sea and not to the insurgents." [8]

Searching for a compromise solution, Olney and Cleveland found some hope in a speech made by the leader of the Spanish opposition party which requested American aid in applying some reforms in Cuba. On April 4, 1896, Olney made such a proposal to Spain. Commenting caustically on "the inability of Spain to prolong the conflict," the Secretary of State nevertheless urged that the Spanish not abandon the island, since "a war of races would be precipitated." He then gave four reasons why the struggle concerned the United States: first, Americans' favor toward "any struggle anywhere for freer political institutions"; second, the inhumanity of the war; third, the desire of the United States for a "noninterruption of extensive trade relations"; and fourth, "the wholesale destruction of property," which "is utterly destroying American investments." Olney proposed a plan

[7] *Congressional Record*, 54th Cong., 1st Sess., 2342–2343, 2346–2347, 2355, 2359, 2485–2486, 2719–2720, 2728, 2826–2827, 2970–2971, 3541, 3628; Chadwick, *United States and Spain*, 439, 445, 446; Summers, *Cabinet Diary of William L. Wilson*, 35–37; Olney to Hale, March 17, 1896, Olney MSS.

[8] Recently named to the post, Lee had the approval of the jingo press in New York; see Wisan, *Cuban Crisis*, 141, 66–67; also Chapter VIII, below; Chadwick, *United States and Spain*, 431–432; Fitzhugh Lee to Olney, Jan. 24, 1896, Olney MSS.

of pacification which would retain Spanish sovereignty.[9] The administration was trying to stop the rebellion before one of two things occurred. Spain might be driven from the island and anarchy (or worse, a biracial war) ensue, or the United States might have to intervene to stop the revolution and then be forced to assume political responsibility for the island. As anticolonialists, Cleveland and Olney feared the latter alternative as much as the former. The April proposal, if accepted by Spain, would ingeniously short-circuit the possibility of American annexation.

Unfortunately for the administration's hopes, Spain rejected the offer in a note of May 22, 1895. The Duke of Tetuán, the Spanish Foreign Minister, moreover accused the American government of encouraging the revolution, since Tetuán claimed the administration refused to enforce adequately the neutrality laws. This Spanish reply angered Cleveland and Olney. When Dupuy de Lôme, the Spanish Minister in Washington, attempted to discuss Spain's reply with Olney, he found the Secretary of State "very reserved." Olney ominously hinted, "The situation here and in Cuba must be bettered." At this point, the administration entered the last phase of its Cuban policy.[10]

From July, 1896, when his record was repudiated by the silverite-controlled Democratic Convention, until the end of his term of office, Cleveland preserved American freedom of action until a new administration could assume the reins of foreign policy. But both the Chief Executive and his Secretary of State became more militant in their attitude toward Spain. In mid-July the President deprecated Fitzhugh Lee's "style of rolling intervention like a sweet morsel under his tongue," but several days before, Cleveland had written Olney, "I am thinking a great

[9] A copy of the note is in the Olney MSS and also in *Spanish Diplomatic Correspondence and Documents, 1896–1900* . . . [translation] (Washington, D.C., 1905), 4–8.

[10] Taylor to Olney, April 6 and 4, 1896, Olney MSS; *Spanish Diplomatic Correspondence and Documents*, 3–4, 8–13; de Lôme to Olney, June 17, July 2, 1896, Olney MSS.

deal about Cuba, but am as far as ever from seeing the place where we can get in." Purchasing Cuba might mean "incorporating" the island "into the United States system," and this, the President feared, "would be entering upon dangerous ground." On the other hand, "it would seem absurd for us to buy the Island" and allow the Cubans to run their country.[11]

During the summer and fall, Spanish actions further exasperated the President. Olney spent much of his time protesting against Spanish regulations which penalized American persons and property. In October, General Weyler announced the brutal *reconcentrado* policy. But the most spectacular threat to American interests came from the disclosure in August that the Duke of Tetuán had asked the European powers to help Spain prevent American intervention in Cuba. Learning of the proposal from the British Ambassador in Madrid, Hannis Taylor, the American Minister, immediately demanded an explanation from the embarrassed Spanish government. The Duke of Tetuán justified the move by explaining his fear of "future political changes which might take place in the United States" that would bring a less friendly government to power. This justification did little to lessen Olney's and Cleveland's anger. Taylor aptly handled the delicate situation and obtained from the Spanish Minister the promise that the notes would not be sent without further consultation with American authorities. In October, Spain dropped the scheme.[12]

A sidelight of this incident merits consideration. The Spanish note had attempted to win support from European powers by

[11] Cleveland to Olney, July 13, 1896, Olney MSS; Cleveland to Olney, July 16, 1896, Cleveland MSS. Both letters are in *Letters of Grover Cleveland*, 446, 448–449.

[12] For Olney's vigorous policies to protect American interests, see Olney to Taylor, July 9, Oct. 15, 1896, and Feb. 12, 1897, Spain, Instructions, NA, RG 59; Olney to Taylor, July 7, 1896, Olney MSS; Orestes Ferrara, *The Last Spanish War: Revelations in Diplomacy*, translated from the Spanish by William E. Shea (New York, 1937), 33–45, 59–62; Taylor to Olney, Aug. 8 and 13, 1896, Spain, Despatches, NA, RG 59; Taylor to Olney, Aug. 11, 1896, Olney MSS.

reminding them that the United States, relying on "the daily more absorbent and expansive Monroe Doctrine," threatened their interests as well as Spain's. But in assuming that the major European governments would unhesitatingly assist him, the Duke of Tetuán made a major miscalculation. If his plan was to succeed, he needed at least the passiveness of the British navy and the active participation of Russia. England, however, was revising her American policies in view of the Venezuelan incident and her growing isolation in the Far and Middle East. Russia also refused to become involved, since she had now turned her attention to the Far East and wanted nothing to harm Russian-American relations. Ironically, American expansion in the Caribbean and the Far East prevented Spain from obtaining the help of the two nations she needed for the success of her plan to halt just such American expansion.

Spain must have spent little time in considering the effect of this proposal on the volatile minds of Olney and Cleveland. Relations were not improved when Taylor informed the Secretary of State in a personal letter that Spain was hurrying its preparations for war. The United States responded in several ways. The Secretary of the Navy, Hilary Herbert, declared in late October, 1896, that "in the improbable contingency of a war with Spain plans will have been perfected and officers designated to carry them out" before the end of the year.[13]

Cleveland's annual message in December provided the most striking evidence of the administration's concern and anger. The President began by intimating that Spain was incapable of regaining complete control of Cuba. The rebels, however, provided "a government merely on paper." He warned that this condition could no longer continue, for the chaotic situation endangered American interests, which Cleveland described as "by no means of a wholly sentimental or philanthropic character." Enumer-

[13] Taylor to Olney, Aug. 18, 1896, Olney MSS; Olney to J. Walter Blandford, May 29, 1897; Herbert to William L. Wilson, Oct. 27, 1896, Cleveland MSS; Memoranda for Autobiography, 342, Herbert MSS.

ating in detail American investments in and trade with Cuba, the President demanded the cessation of the war, which threatened to ruin "the industrial value of the island." Rejecting any grant of belligerent rights to the rebels, the recognition of Cuban independence, or the possibility of purchasing the island (since Spain, Cleveland declared, refused to sell), the President added that outright intervention could not be considered at present. He advocated his favored solution of "genuine autonomy" and advised Spain to take advantage of this American offer. He warned that the past "expectant attitude of the United States will not be indefinitely maintained." Rather, "a time may arrive" when the desire to save Cuba "from complete devastation, will constrain our Government to such action as will subserve the interests thus involved and at the same time promise to Cuba . . . the blessings of peace." [14]

These closing passages were an explicit threat and warning to the Spanish, but it is significant that in the first draft of the message, Cleveland considered the use of even more belligerent phrases. The original draft included an ultimatum to Spain in the form of a time limit. Cleveland refused to define a time when the United States should undertake the restoration of the "blessings of peace" to the island, but he immediately added in this draft: "It would seem safe to say, however, that if by the coming of the New Year, no substantial progress has been made towards ending the insurrection either by force of arms or otherwise, the conclusion that Spain is incompetent to successfully deal with it would be almost inevitable." [15] Since Spain was "incompetent" to stop the bloodshed, Cleveland thus clearly indicated when "higher obligations" might force the United States to assume the task of restoring adequate protection to American interests.

[14] *Messages and Papers of the Presidents*, IX, 716–722. It is doubtful if Cleveland wanted to buy Cuba. The problems of annexation were still present. The President was on safe ground in saying that Spain would reject such an offer.

[15] The original draft was sent to Olney, who made pen corrections in November, 1896. This draft is in the Olney MSS.

Cleveland's message of December 2 is important for several reasons. The President clung to the hope that Cuban autonomy would be the best solution for "all concerned," though he ignored the aspirations of the Junta at this point. He recognized that Spain insisted on pacifying the island before granting autonomy; on this vital question he completely agreed with the insurgents' belief that the Spanish position was absurd and dangerous. The grave threats at the end of the message warned Spain that she must quickly change her policy and accede to the American request. It would be too late when either the rebellion completely devastated the island or American sentiment forced McKinley to intervene and possibly annex the island.

The message also preserved American freedom of action in case Spain refused to grant autonomy. The Chief Executive clearly and simply informed Spain that if she did not end the rebellion soon the United States would have to intervene. He might have declared this in order to pressure Spain into granting immediate reforms, but the fact remains that the message was an unveiled threat of intervention. Cleveland rationalized American intervention in Cuba and gave his administration's support for it (under certain conditions) two years before a Republican President led the nation into war. Olney re-emphasized this threat when he submitted his departmental report in 1896. After a detailed analysis of American commercial interests on the island, which Olney estimated as at least $50,000,000 ($33,000,000 would probably have been more accurate), the Secretary of State warned that "the time may not be far distant" when American "rights and interests" may call "for some decided change in the policy hitherto pursued." [16]

Militant members of Congress wanted an immediate change in policy. Shortly after the President's message, Lodge observed

---

[16] *Foreign Relations, 1896*, lxxxvi. The jingo press in New York nevertheless attacked Cleveland's views on Cuba, while the conservative, anti-jingo papers, along with the business community, approved the message; Wisan, *The Cuban Crisis*, 240–244.

that "an explosion may happen any day and force our hands." Lodge, Don Cameron, and Roger Mills of Texas led the interventionist forces. Cameron's resolution, which requested recognition of Cuban independence, aroused the most interest. Several factors evidently motivated Cameron's and Lodge's espousal of this measure. President-elect McKinley had informed Lodge of his desire that the crisis "be settled one way or the other" before the new administration entered office. Lodge agreed with McKinley, for he feared that the prolongation of the rebellion would further unsettle business conditions and undermine the Republican victory cry of coming prosperity. An unsettled economy would also increase the strength of the silver bloc. A final influence derived from Lodge's and Cameron's friendly ties with the Junta in New York City.[17]

On December 19, as Cameron prepared to introduce his measure on the Senate floor, Olney killed the resolution's chances of success by informing a Washington *Star* reporter that if passed the measure would have no binding effect on the administration. The Senate promptly dropped the resolution. Olney had made this dramatic move for two reasons. He feared that the debates on the measure would precipitate another financial panic. The administration also wanted to avert war with Spain. If the United States had recognized Cuba as independent, the Monroe Doctrine would have come into effect. The State Department would then have had to intervene in order to prevent a European power from acquiring territory in the Western Hemisphere. Olney realized that, after the administration's adamant stand on the Venezuelan dispute, the United States would be compelled to enforce the Doctrine in Cuba. The administration would go to war because

[17] Lodge to Fairchild, Dec. 11, 1896, Lodge to E. M. Weld, Dec. 19, 1896, Lodge to Henry Lee, Dec. 21, 1896, Lodge to E. A. Adams, Dec. 23, 1896, Lodge to Morgan, Dec. 21, 1896, Lodge Letterbooks, Lodge MSS; *Congressional Record*, 54th Cong., 2nd Sess., 39; Wisan, *The Cuban Crisis*, 251; Auxier, "The Propaganda Activities of the Cuban *Junta*," 290–291.

of "higher obligations," but not because the Senate forced the Executive's hand.[18]

Throughout January and February, 1897, Olney continued to seek a solution. On February 5, Cánovas sent a list of reforms which resembled the unacceptable suggestions of early 1895. The Cuban insurgents attacked Cánovas' offer with derision, and the Spanish press cried that the reforms gave "everything to the Cubans." During the last week of February, Cleveland asked Frederic R. Coudert to try to reach a solution with Spanish authorities in Cuba, but the distinguished New York lawyer refused the appointment.[19]

As he prepared to leave the White House, Cleveland could be satisfied that he had attempted to enforce the neutrality laws, protect American property, bring about Spanish reforms in Cuba, and, above all, that he had maintained the peace. The administration's actions were of more significance than this, however. Olney's April note had informed Spain that American interests were deeply involved in the rebellion and that the United States would be forced to protect those interests. The April offer of mediation was the first American effort to interject the United States officially into the struggle.

[18] Nevins, *Grover Cleveland*, 717; for press discussion of Olney's constitutional right to lay down such a rule, see *Literary Digest*, Dec. 26, 1896, 225–226; also Hale to Olney, Jan. 4, 1897, Olney to Clifton R. Beckinridge, Jan. 25, 1897, Olney to A. M. Straw, Dec. 24, 1896, Olney MSS; for the fears of businessmen, see The Commercial Club of Chicago to Henry T. Thurber, Cleveland's private secretary, Dec. 30, 1896, Cleveland MSS.

[19] Chadwick, *United States and Spain*, 487; Olney to Lee, Jan. 18, 1897, Taylor to Olney, Jan. 26, 1897, Olney MSS; Taylor to Olney, Jan. 27, 1897, Cleveland MSS; Lee to Olney, Feb. 18, 1897, Olney MSS; *Spanish Diplomatic Correspondence and Documents*, 19–24; Olney to de Lôme, March 7, 1897, Olney MSS. Coudert had been one of the earliest exponents of ending Spanish rule and annexing Cuba to the United States. Cleveland doubtless knew of Coudert's opinion. Coudert's view is in *Public Opinion*, July 11, 1895, 43; Cleveland's thoughts on the project are partially revealed in a letter to Olney, Feb. 28, 1897, Cleveland MSS.

In December, Cleveland had carried this policy one step farther. American interests were so involved in this conflict, he had declared, that the United States had an unquestioned right to intervene in order to pacify the island. Since Spain refused to grant the right of American intervention in any form, the carrying out of the President's policy could only have resulted in war. Cleveland and Olney thus restrained American intervention for a time, but they also contributed to the causes for war in 1898; they emphasized the involvement of American material interests and provided a rationale for the right to use force, if necessary, to protect these interests.[20]

The Far East

Any attempt to understand the background of the 1898 war with Spain and the immediate results of that war must include an analysis of the developing American interest in Asia during the early and middle 1890's.[21] To neglect the Far East, or to begin the study of United States relations with that area only with the Kiaochow incident in late 1897, distorts the picture of the new empire in the post-1890 period. The United States had large material interests in both Cuba and the Orient; a revolution threatened these interests in the former area, and internal discontent and the imperial grasp of European powers threatened holdings in the Far East. Cuba deserved primary attention, of course; but increased American trade, concession hunting, and

[20] See Chadwick, *United States and Spain*, 465–466, for a similar interpretation; also James, *Richard Olney*, 166; and Pratt, *Expansionists of 1898*, 212.

[21] No historian has adequately analyzed the links between American expansion in the Far East from 1895–1898 and the growing United States involvement in world affairs overall, especially the links between the Caribbean and Far Eastern policies. This work attempts to remedy this lack in a minor way. The definitive work on the topic should be available when Thomas McCormick of Ohio University publishes his "'Fair Field and No Favor'; American China Policy during the McKinley Administrations" (unpublished Ph.D. dissertation, University of Wisconsin, 1960).

missionary activity in China, Korea, Japan, and Manchuria forced the State Department to devote much attention to these growing interests. In 1899 and 1900, with the Cuban problem settled, the United States would give Asia top priority, but this would be merely an acceleration of a policy which had long characterized America's handling of its oriental affairs. Both Cuba and the Far East were different manifestations of the expansion of the new empire in the 1890's, and each was dealt with in turn by the State Department. Not the least important link between the two was the effect which the realignment of American interests in the Far East had upon United States relations with the major European powers in both the Orient and Cuba.

In a speech in 1894, the Assistant Secretary of the Navy, William McAdoo, noted that the demand for American ships in the Pacific area was so great "that we could almost use the entire fleet in those waters alone." In contrast, he noted, "We are represented by only one ship in Europe." [22] The American interests these ships protected in Asia fell into two categories, business and missionary.

The belief that the fabled and long-awaited Asiatic market was at last a reality dominated the United States' dealings with the Far East in the 1890's. After hovering around the 5 per cent mark of the nation's total trade during the last half of the century, American trade with Asia suddenly spiraled in the mid-1890's. Exports to China, which had approximated $4,000,000 annually in the early part of that decade, jumped to $6,900,000 in 1896 and soared to $11,900,000 in 1897. Exports to Japan evidenced the same inflationary figures; reaching $3,900,000 in 1894, they moved to $7,600,000 in 1896 and nearly doubled to $13,000,000 the following year. American exports led those of all other nations in the potentially rich Manchurian area. Such statistics were not lost on market-hungry American businessmen during these depression years. The *Commercial and Financial Chronicle* re-

[22] William McAdoo, "The Navy and the Nation," *Proceedings of the United States Naval Institute,* XX (1894), 420–421.

marked in the autumn of 1894 that the effects of the Sino-Japanese war on the Orient should "give an entirely new character to our Western coast." [23]

Concession seekers were as active as exporters, but they did not enjoy the same measure of success. Charles Denby, the American Minister to China, listed the Cramp Shipbuilding Company, Union Iron Company, American China Development Company, the Bethlehem Iron Company, and a railroad and banking syndicate as some of the American firms interested in obtaining concessions from China. The American Trading Company of New York City, headed by James R. Morse, was also active throughout the Far East. In order to help these companies as much as possible, Denby literally strained at the leash which the State Department held on him. These businessmen, the Minister reported, "expect that this legation will do everything necessary or conceivable to carry out their views, and they are not disappointed. Except that I do not take China by the throat and demand concessions" as the Europeans do. And Denby had no illusions about the Chinese. He had reported to the department earlier: "The foreigner in China holds his position by force alone. . . . We must therefore recognize the fact that kindness to this people goes for little." [24]

The State Department fully approved of all aid which Denby might provide American concessionaires, but Washington officials admonished him not to play favorites among the Americans. Gresham lectured him much as one would a young virgin about to go to the big city: "You will likely be beset by Americans

[23] Dennett, *Americans in the Far East*, 580–581; *Commercial and Financial Chronicle*, Sept. 22, 1894, 496–497; see also Thomas R. Jernigan, U.S. Consul General to China, "Commercial Trend of China," *North American Review*, CLXV (July, 1897), 63–69.

[24] Denby to Olney, May 25, 1896, China, Despatches, NA, RG 59; New York *Tribune*, Sept. 24, 1896, 7:4; Denby to Olney, Nov. 25, 1895, Olney MSS; for Denby's statement on the Chinese, see Denby to Bayard, Sept. 6, 1888, Bayard MSS. See also Vagts, *Deutschland und die Vereinigten Staaten*, II, 960–961.

anxious for valuable concessions from China, and knowing your generous and obliging nature I sent you the second telegram today. . . . You may compromise yourself in the minds of strangers. Of course, you will understand that this admonition is a friendly one." Since Washington would not allow Dénby more freedom to pick and choose, Americans were divided, then conquered, by European capitalists who enjoyed the full support of their own governments. Thus the American Trading Company lost the opportunity to loan China a large amount of the war indemnity to be paid to Japan in 1895–1896, and thus the American China Development Company lost a fat railroad concession to a Russian-Belgian group. The United States refused to follow the European methods of mixing business and politics. Denby reported on May 24, 1897, "The ominous suspicion that European politics are figuring in commercial concessions in China is not promising for Americans." The United States would somehow have to counter this European influence, and within two years the State Department decided upon a course of action—a reaffirmation of the open door bolstered by an avowed pro-British, pro-Japanese, and anti-Russian policy.[25]

Americans were more successful in Japan and Korea. As American trade with Japan rocketed upward after 1894, Japan doubled her purchases of American cotton in 1895 to 11,000,000 pounds; she approached Great Britain as the best customer of United States growers. Eleven American firms were conducting business in Kobe, and one of them, the China and Japan Trading Company, boasted the largest business in the city. When Japan began expanding her navy in the mid-1890's, agents from the Cramp Shipbuilding Company and the Union Iron Works were among the first on the scene, and, as the American Minister reported in

[25] Olney to Denby, Dec. 10, 1896, Letterbook, Olney MSS; Gresham to Denby, April 12, 1895, Letterbook, Gresham MSS; Denby to Gresham, May 12, 1895, and Uhl to Denby, May 14, 1895, Cleveland MSS; McCormick, " 'Fair Field and No Favor,' " 61–62, 68–74; Edward H. Zabriskie, *American-Russian Relations in the Far East: A Study in Diplomacy and Power Politics, 1895–1914* (Philadelphia, 1946), 33, 38–39.

late 1895, these "gentlemen left Japan fairly well satisfied with their reception," since they won several contracts. Secretary of State Olney cooperated by ordering a survey to find "the prospects of competition by American manufacturers for contracts in the Japanese Empire." Denby, among others, returned a detailed and highly encouraging report of the prospects.[26]

In the Hermit Kingdom, Horace Allen was energetically directing American economic and political moves from his post as Secretary of the American Legation in Seoul. In 1895, after he had plotted five years to win the concession, Allen was suddenly offered by the Korean King the Un-san mines, probably the richest gold mines in the Far East. Never one to let an opportunity slip by, Allen coolly directed an astonishing intrigue to reorganize the Korean cabinet so that pro-Japanese elements could not block the grant. Allen then gave the concession to James R. Morse, who in turn sold it in 1897 to another group of American financiers. For the next forty-two years this American company mined the Un-san concession to the tune of nearly fifteen million dollars in profits. For an encore Allen won the streetcar concession in Seoul for yet another American company.[27]

The Commercial and Financial Chronicle could point to these and similar events as substantiation for its sweeping statement, "We, more than any other Power, are to have the Pacific trade —the trade with China and Japan." But Horace Allen exemplified another side of American interest in the Far East, for he had been a missionary before becoming an intermediary for American entrepreneurs. An American naval officer reported in 1891, "Since my last visit to China, fourteen years ago, I find that the Missionary cause has made most extraordinary progress. . . . Their number is constantly increasing, and there seems to be no limit to the money that is behind them." Using the sharp wedge

[26] Area 10 file, Box 8, April-June folder, NA, RG 45; Ford, "Turning of the Tide," 190; Dun to Olney, Nov. 23, 1895, Japan, Despatches, NA, RG 59.
[27] Harrington, *God, Mammon, and the Japanese*, ch. ix.

provided by the 1858–1860 treaties, which opened the Chinese interior and the Yangtze River and included provisions for religious toleration, by 1898 the missionaries had touched all eighteen provinces plus Manchuria and had set the pattern their activities would follow for the next thirty years.[28]

The forces which intensified missionary activity in the Far East during the 1880's and 1890's emanated from several sources. Christianity had always been an expansive doctrine, a religion, as one missionary phrased it in 1896, "that will not keep." This characteristic was accentuated in the 1890's when, as a partial response to the onslaughts of Darwinism, the church reacted emotionally, yet confidently and expansively. College campuses were set ablaze with missionary fervor. An intercollegiate Student Volunteers for Foreign Missions mushroomed in membership. Henry Luce, Horace Pitkin and Sherwood Eddy were among the many who flocked under this society's unmodest slogan, "The Evangelization of the World in this Generation." The industrial revolution affected missions not only by providing angels of finance to pay costs, but also by spawning beliefs such as Andrew Carnegie's Gospel of Wealth, which urged men to gain as much wealth as possible in order to help others. Rev. Russell H. Conwell's *Acres of Diamonds*, one of the most popular lectures in American history, advanced the formula succinctly: "To secure wealth is an honorable ambition, and is one great test of a person's usefulness to others." Such a definition of blessings in a secular, rather than a religious, sense hid a subtle but significant danger to the missionary outlook. The strong racist beliefs of the day channeled this outpouring of emotion and finance especially into the nonwhite areas of the world. Such articles as "The Anglo-Saxon and the World's Redemption" were

[28] *Commercial and Financial Chronicle*, Aug. 18, 1894, 256–257; also see *Bradstreet's*, May 18, 1895, 311; Commander F. M. Barber to Belknap, Dec. 1, 1891, Area 10 file, Box 8, NA, RG 45; Kenneth Scott Latourette, *A History of Christian Missions in China* (New York, 1929), 360–361; Paul Varg, *Missionaries, Chinese, and Diplomats* . . . (Princeton, 1958), 12–14.

not uncommon, and Josiah Strong, Alfred Thayer Mahan, and John Fiske bolstered this racism with their popular writings.[29]

Increased American economic and political interests, the Sino-Japanese War of 1894–1895, and the fact that the area was non-white made the Far East a natural target for missionary enthusiasm. Reiterating the classic theme, mission advocates could claim in 1890, "As in all the past, so now the indications of Providence all point Westward." But the work would have to be accomplished quickly: "China is open to the Gospel now; it may not be so when she becomes strong enough to dictate the terms of her treaties." This sense of urgency was intensified by the fear that unless China assimilated Western morality quickly, she would either become an amoral industrial giant or would be absorbed by Russia to form, as one missionary wrote, "the most powerful Empire ever known among men." Alfred Thayer Mahan especially publicized his fear of these possibilities and helped to implant that fear into the minds of Theodore Roosevelt and Henry Cabot Lodge.[30]

These dynamic changes in American thought and action largely explained the burgeoning missionary success in China in the 1890's. In 1893 Protestant missionaries claimed 55,093 communicants; in five years the figure jumped 50 per cent to 80,682. Missionaries reported that they were embarrassed by the crowds who sought instruction. In 1890 the different Protestant groups had held their second general meeting (the first had been called to order in 1877) to coordinate their activities and to make a plea for saving "the present generation." The missionaries hoped that one thousand men would come to China to help the churches within the next five years; 1,153 actually arrived before 1895. Americans predominated in this Protestant movement. Of the

[29] *Ibid.*, 3, 51–57; Ralph Henry Gabriel, *The Course of American Democratic Thought* (2nd ed.; New York, 1956), 156–158. For a good discussion on the influence of racist beliefs, see Bald, "Expansionist Sentiment," ch. iii.

[30] Varg, *Missionaries*, 77–85; *Public Opinion*, Feb. 8, 1890, 432.

445 participants in the 1890 meeting, 230 were United States citizens and 193 were British.[31]

American political and economic influences often followed the missionaries. Some churchmen abroad desired protection only from nationals in case of outbreaks in the interior, but others demanded and received protection from American ships and troops. A few publicly claimed that they were trying not only to influence spiritual life, but also to "shape political life and development." With some help from Horace Allen, American missionaries in Korea devoted their considerable political skills to the maintenance of Korean independence in the face of Chinese, Japanese, and Russian incursions. When Allen became Minister to Korea in 1897, the missionary movement in that country had, in effect, received carte blanche from the State Department.[32]

Nor were the economic influences of the missionaries negligible. The fabled China market would become much greater as all Chinese adopted western food, clothes, and customs, as well as spiritual values; the missionaries dispensed all four. Missionaries bragged of their commercial prowess, partly no doubt in order to attract support from industrialists and financiers, but also because many believed what they were saying. The *Congregationalist* could tersely announce, "Commerce follows the missionary." One missionary who had labored in China in the 1890's spelled this out:

If I were asked to state what would be the best form of advertising for the great American Steel Trust or Standard Oil or the Baldwin Locomotive Works . . . or the Singer sewing machine . . . I should say, take up the support of one or two or a dozen mission stations. . . . Everyone thus helped would be, consciously or unconsciously, a drummer for your goods, and the great church they represent at home would be your advertising agents.

[31] Latourette, *History of Christian Missions*, 402–405, 413–415, 494–496.
[32] Bald, "Expansionist Sentiment," 92, 106–109; Harrington, *God, Mammon, and the Japanese*, 98–102.

Charles Denby, who wasted little love on the missionaries, nevertheless valued them precisely because of this economic influence.[33]

Within five years these various American interests were nearly engulfed by European ambitions and antiforeign movements in China. These threats had first become apparent to American policy makers during the Sino-Japanese War of 1894–1895. Secretary of State Gresham measured his reactions to this crisis with one rule of thumb; he feared, as he informed the Japanese Minister to Washington, that if Japan "continues to knock China to pieces, the powers, England, France, Germany and Russia, under the guise of preserving order, will partition China." If this occurred, the open door would be slammed shut. The doctrine of the new empire, moreover, had no provision for controlling a slice of China as an American protectorate. Gresham thus refused to cooperate in joint mediation efforts with the European powers. "When we act at all in such matters," the Secretary of State informed Pauncefote, "we prefer to act alone." Gresham had no intention of jeopardizing his nation's freedom of action in the Orient, especially if this meant giving consent to the undermining of traditional American interests. The United States did, however, offer its good offices and exert pressure on both belligerents to stop the fighting before the other powers could step in. When Japan finally agreed to peace, her surprisingly successful warfare had already frightened Russia, France, and Germany into taking drastic steps to check the claims Japan made on China. Gresham's fears had been well founded.[34]

Reporting the termination of hostilities on April 18, 1895, the

[33] Plesur, "Looking Outward," 180–181; Bald, "Expansionist Sentiment," 95–99; Isaac Taylor Headland, *Some By-Products of Missions* (Cincinnati, 1921), 33–34.

[34] Tyler Dennett, "American 'Good Offices' in Asia," *American Journal of International Law*, XVI (1922), 19–20; Gresham, *Life of Gresham*, II, 788–789; Gresham to Denby, Nov. 24, 1894, China, Instructions, Conversation between Pauncefote and Gresham, July 9, 1894, Memoranda of Conversations, and Dun to Gresham, April 25, 1895, Japan Despatches, NA, RG 59.

American Minister to Japan wrote: "Thus has ended one of the most remarkable wars of the nineteenth century. . . . The changed conditions to ensue will be far reaching, not only upon China and Japan, but upon the entire world as well." The Cleveland administration moved rapidly to adjust to these "changed conditions." The Navy Department doubled the size of the American fleet in Chinese waters, and Gresham pleaded with Herbert for more ships. In spite of this increase, however, "as a military force the Navy is not counted," wrote one young American naval officer from China. "I make numerous reports on vessels of the *Charleston*'s tonnage that could 'lick' us while we were spitting on our hands." [35]

Olney's action to protect American missionaries in the interior was more forceful. When bloody massacres erupted in Szechuan in 1895, the Secretary of State agreed with Denby's decision not to evacuate the missionaries, but to protect them with all possible American authority. When Chinese officials refused to allow a United States investigating commission to travel to the scene of the riots, the Secretary of State warned the Chinese to reverse their decision or the United States would correct the wrongs to their citizens "by such means as it may find most expeditious and effective." To emphasize his concern, Olney attempted to impress the Chinese by refusing to allow the American commission to travel by water; he forced the commission to make a laborious overland journey. He did, however, allow the commission to return by water. Olney was determined to "get" the former Viceroy of Szechuan, who had permitted the outbreaks, and the Secretary of State succeeded. The State Department, Olney believed, had convincingly paraded before the European powers the two dominant American policies in China: first, by refusing to cooperate with the British in the investigating commission the United States had demonstrated its basic disagreement

[35] Herbert to C. C. Carpenter, Sept. 24, 1894, Area 10 file, Box 10, NA, RG 45; Morison, *Sims*, 42; Herbert to Cleveland, Oct. 7, 1894, Cleveland MSS.

with European policies; second, the State Department could move quickly (and ostentatiously) to protect American interests.[36]

The State Department hoped to exact a price for its efforts in helping China through mediation and for refusing to cooperate with European claims after the war. The State Department notified Denby on June 8, 1895, "This country will expect equal and liberal trading advantages—certainly in Korea and presumably in China—as the result of the war, and all your efforts, so far as they may be properly put forth, should be exerted to secure expanded privileges of intercourse, trade and residence in which our citizens may share." Two weeks later Olney demonstrated that this instruction was not mere rhetoric, for he changed long-standing policy in order to strengthen the position of American concession seekers in China. No longer would Denby have to report each concessionaire's plan to the State Department before supporting the plan. Now Denby could save valuable time by formally introducing any American, "of whose character and responsibility you are satisfied," to the Chinese government without clearance from Washington. Olney also took advantage of a Chinese-French agreement to help American missionaries enlarge their property holdings in the Chinese interior.[37]

These two State Department actions, especially the granting of enlarged powers to Denby, dramatized the growing realization in Washington that in order to preserve present holdings and to encourage new interests to move into Asia, the growing aggressiveness of the European powers would have to be countered with stronger policies by the United States. During the depression years of 1895 and 1896, the apparently bottomless China market seemed well worth the effort. When the State Depart-

[36] Dun to Gresham, April 18, 1895, Japan, Despatches, and Olney to Denby, Sept. 20, 1895, Adee to Denby, Aug. 12, 1895, Olney to Denby, Nov. 21, 1895, Olney to Denby, Sept. 19, 1895, China, Instructions, NA, RG 59.

[37] Uhl to Denby, June 8, 1895, Olney to Denby, July 18, 1895, Olney to Denby, June 22, 1895, China, Instructions, NA, RG 59.

ment's Bureau of Foreign Commerce spoke hopefully of "what may be termed an American invasion of the markets of the world" in 1896, it noted that China was "one of the most promising." The State Department attempted to make the promise come true by working for peace in 1894–1895, by refusing to cooperate with the aggressive forces of the European powers who wanted to make territorial demands, and by moving quickly to preserve and enlarge American interests in the area. "Under these circumstances," a State Department official wrote of America's Far Eastern policy in May, 1895, "The opening up of China to the commerce of the world, which was one of the conditions of peace, cannot fail to be of special value to the United States." [38] But in the Far East, the fruits of the new empire refused to fall so easily.

New Friends

Since the late 1870's when William Evarts occupied the top State Department post, the United States had attempted to keep the open door in Asia ajar through unilateral dealings with China, Japan, and Korea. Seward's approach, which posited cooperation with the European powers, especially England, was replaced by policies attempting to preserve American freedom of action. Until 1895 American policy makers operated from a double assumption: first, that they had or would soon have adequate economic power to win the battle for Far Eastern markets; second, that the maintenance of the open door would allow the strongest economic power to be the first to cross the threshold into the dreamland of the vast Asian market.

But by late 1895 these assumptions were crumbling. Japan first attempted to combine military and political force to win economic and territorial concessions which would cancel out

[38] A. Whitney Griswold, *The Far Eastern Policy of the United States* (New York, 1938), 56–57, quotes the Bureau of Foreign Commerce statement. The clipping from Baltimore *Sun*, May 27, 1895, is enclosed in Frederic Emory to Bayard, May 28, 1895, Bayard MSS.

superior American industrial mechanization and the open-door policy. Then Russia, France, and Germany exerted strong political pressure on China and Japan to expand their economic and territorial control in South China, North China, Manchuria, and Korea. By 1896 and 1897 American policy makers began to realize that unilateral action in Asia, unsupported by adequate military force (which the United States lacked), would not maintain the open door. Friends were sought who shared American objectives and who occupied a more advantageous power position to defend the goals. These friends were found in Japan and Great Britain.

It was ironic to befriend Japan so soon after she had attempted to win exclusive favors from China. But the sweeping action of the continental powers, which forced Japan to surrender her hard-won gains of the 1894–1895 war, also forced Nippon's leaders to realize that they needed time and friends if they hoped to oppose successfully the grasping hands of Russia, France, and Germany. The United States offered one possibility. Astounded by Japan's naval successes, American military men sang the praises and publicized the power of the Island Kingdom's newly found might. In a series of lectures delivered at the Naval War College in 1895, Captain Richard Wallach declared that Japan "must no longer be regarded only in the light of tea-houses, quaint art and gentle manners. . . . Japan is at once the England and the Germany of the Far East." [39]

Japan promised to be a welcome ally. Militarily strong and inclined, after her 1895 experiences with the European powers, to favor an open-door approach, she did not seem to many Americans to offer an industrial challenge to the United States. The Baltimore *Sun* believed that it would be "some years yet" before Japan could compete with the American cotton industry. John Barrett, United States Minister to Siam, wrote in the *North*

[39] Richard Wallach, "The War in the East," *Proceedings of the United States Naval Institute*, XXI (1895), 734–736; Frank Marble, "The Battle of Yalu," *Proceedings of the United States Naval Institute*, XXI, 479–522.

American Review that the American exporter would always find large markets in Japan. The *Overland Monthly* declared flatly that the Japanese had "no decided manufacturing taste or aptitude." Japan indeed promised to be a perfect partner in the Far East.[40]

Japan responded by sending one of its most distinguished diplomats, Shinichiro Kurino, as Minister to Washington. The State Department meanwhile negotiated a new commercial treaty which restored some of the rights extracted from Japan in 1866. More important, Olney severely reprimanded Horace Allen and John M. B. Sill, the American Minister to Korea, for opposing Japanese attempts to control the Hermit Kingdom in 1895. In view of the continental powers' shabby treatment of Japan after the war, Olney apparently believed that the Japanese would better cooperate with American interests in Korea than would the aggressive Russians.[41]

But the developing Japanese friendship was distinctly less important and less dramatic than the historic realignment of American and British interests. The settlement of the "Alabama" claims in 1871 probably marked the beginning of the end for the century-old enmity between the two nations. During the following three decades intermarriage and cultural exchange on the Newport-Brighton level increased. Americans learned the stories of Disraeli and Kipling and admired the tortured logic of Herbert Spencer. The difficult problem of pelagic sealing in the Bering Sea, which had severely strained Anglo-American relations in 1890–1892, had so receded in importance by 1897 that Sir Charles Dilke could write that only one member of the House of Commons, "who is not myself," even bothered to try to understand the issue. By the mid-1890's the importance of the divisive Irish

---

[40] *Public Opinion*, April 2, 1896, 427–428, and June 11, 1896, 763–764.
[41] There is a good sketch of Kurino in the Washington *Post*, Aug. 7, 1894. See also Kurino to Gresham, Nov. 18, 1894, Gresham MSS. Allen's reprimand is in Olney to Allen, Nov. 20, 1895, Area 10 file, Box 14, NA, RG 45.

question in American politics had also considerably dwindled. The British thoroughly disliked the American high tariff policy, and this dislike tainted their opinion of William McKinley in 1896. But a mounting fear of Bryan and free silver soon overcame their qualms on the tariff, and McKinley entered the White House in 1897 with the best wishes of most of the British people. The last gasp of the silver advocates in 1896 removed one of the gravest threats to Anglo-American relations. The silverites had long railed against Anglo-American cooperation, since, according to the 1896 Democratic platform, the gold standard had "brought other nations into financial servitude to London." Finally, the growth of Canadian-American trade and the settlement of several outstanding questions had lessened animosities between the two great nations of North America. This change was a prerequisite for a meaningful *rapprochement* between London and Washington.[42]

These were important contributions, but the key reasons for the *rapprochement* lay in three other areas. First, Americans began to appreciate their historic economic ties with Great Britain. When the Venezuelan crisis flared on December 18, 1895, the New York *World* struck its blow for peace by detailing the amount of American goods the British consumed and the $3,193,-500,000 the English had invested in United States corporations. In numerous popular articles during the mid-1890's, Edward Atkinson emphasized the economic links that stretched across the Atlantic. British and American businessmen kept a wary eye on each other's moves in Latin America (the British especially feared the National Association of Manufacturers), but after the settlement of the Venezuelan problem in 1896, this commercial expansion did not threaten to precipitate armed conflict. In March,

[42] The Dilke quote is in the New York *World*, Dec. 12, 1897, 35:1; for Canadian relations see Pauncefote to Salisbury, May 15, 1896, F.O. 5/2290; also *Journal of Commerce*, Nov. 10, 1897, 4:2, for a good analysis of trade relations with Canada; and also despatches in F.O. 5/2423 in April, 1898; Charles S. Campbell, Jr., *Anglo-American Understanding, 1898–1903* (Baltimore, 1957), 3, 4, 7.

1896, one American writer could even advocate an Anglo-American alliance (with the superior American economic power serving as senior partner) for the development of the "swiftly expanding commerce" to the south. A State Department official could justifiably conclude in mid-1895, "For 'business reasons' alone, we ought to cultivate friendly relations with Great Britain." [43]

British recognition of the State Department's claims in the Venezuelan episode decreased American apprehension of England's commercial expansion into Latin America; the results of the Venezuelan crisis provided a second major reason for Anglo-American friendship. When Salisbury informed the United States on January 9 that he was "prepared to 'trim' his views to meet the requests of the United States Government," the Cleveland administration had scored a signal victory in assuring a dominant American position in hemispheric affairs. Ambassador Bayard, pro-British as he was, could nevertheless brag that the Venezuelan crisis had made the "doctrine of European abstention" from colonialism in Latin America "a fixed fact." Henry White, who knew British society and politics as well as any American of his day, concurred with Bayard's assessment. The prime example of this change of British attitude toward Latin-American affairs was Whitehall's evolving policies toward the Cuban revolution. In August, 1895, the London *Times* threatened that Spain should maintain control over Cuba: "For obvious political reasons, the annexation of Cuba to the United States would be regarded with little favour by British statesmen." Within two years her new

[43] New York *World*, Dec. 21, 1895, 3:3–4; Edward Atkinson to Rev. Josiah Strong, May 19, 1896, Box 147, J. B. Moore MSS. The British analysis of the N.A.M. is proudly printed in an N.A.M. circular of May 12, 1897, "An English View of the National Association of Manufacturers," which contains a long editorial from the London *Financial News*, March 23, 1897; the alliance idea is in Sidney Sherwood, "An Alliance with England the Basis of a Rational Foreign Policy," *Forum*, XXI (March, 1896), 89–99; the same idea is in Emory's anonymous article in the Baltimore *Sun*, May 27, 1895, sent to Bayard, May 28, 1895, Bayard MSS.

evaluation of American power, her loathing of Spain's *reconcentrado* policies, and her own growing isolation in world affairs would force Great Britain to assume a position directly contrary to the tone of this editorial.[44]

This attitude toward American rights in the Western Hemisphere was also influenced by events in a third area, Asia. Here Great Britain found her strong position undermined by aggressive Russian-German policies. England had an immense stake in maintaining the open door, for she controlled 70 per cent of China's trade, and this in turn accounted for one-sixth of total British commerce. British officials and publicists had often hinted that they would appreciate open American support in the Far East. Sometimes the United States responded. In 1894 China attempted to restrict imports of foreign machinery. England protested strongly and then asked the State Department to support the protest. Gresham assured Pauncefote that United States views "were quite in accord" with those of the Foreign Office. Usually the United States was reluctant to cooperate, however, since it believed its traditional policies were working properly. The Sino-Japanese War and its aftermath destroyed most of this illusion. Then State Department concern about British incursions in Hawaii hindered the development of a common policy in the Pacific. By 1897 British reassurances had removed this obstacle. Finally, when conditions worsened in Cuba, Americans were forced to solve this more immediate problem before becoming deeply involved elsewhere. But they did not exclude all interest in the Far East. The growing activity of the State Department

[44] Salisbury's sentiment is in David Dwight Wells to Bayard, Jan. 9, 1896, Bayard MSS; Bayard's comment is in letter to Moore, Feb. 25, 1896, Box 5, Gen. Correspondence, J. B. Moore MSS; see also Allan Nevins, *Henry White* . . . (New York and London, 1930), 110, and Bemis, *Latin American Policy of the United States*, 122; on England aiding the U.S. in Latin America, see Boston *Herald*, Jan. 2, 1898, 12:5; on British attitude on Cuba in 1895, Bayard to Olney, Aug. 23, 1895, Great Britain, Despatches, NA, RG 59; a good analysis of Britain's 1897 attitude is in Woodford to McKinley, Aug. 10, 1897, McKinley MSS.

and American business interests in Asia, and the development of the Anglo-American friendship during the 1895–1897 period, laid the basis for deep American involvement in the Orient after 1898.[45]

Manifestations of this friendship appeared before 1898, however. As a result of the Venezuelan crisis, Pauncefote and Olney had negotiated a general arbitration treaty. Salisbury apparently had little interest in the treaty, but he hoped that it would help smooth over the differences which had arisen from the boundary dispute. The overwhelming majority of vocal American opinion strongly supported the pact. But the Senate weakened the treaty with amendments and then killed it outright by voice vote in the spring of 1897. The Senators expressed concern that the pact would make the Monroe Doctrine and the Clayton-Bulwer Treaty liable to arbitration. They also feared that the Senate might lose some of its precious control over foreign relations. The virulently anti-British silver bloc found that mutilating the treaty was a happy release for their postelection frustrations.[46]

The defeat of the treaty was misleading as an indication of Anglo-American relations. As Richard Olney wrote Joseph Chamberlain in September, 1896, since England had recognized United States rights in the Western Hemisphere, Americans wanted "to stand side by side and shoulder to shoulder with England." Alfred Thayer Mahan, Henry Cabot Lodge, and Theodore Roosevelt, who had opposed the arbitration treaty, could nevertheless agree with Olney's statement. Mahan, constantly warning his British friends against the German threat, pleaded for an informal Anglo-American alliance to solve common problems in the Far East and Latin America. The war in 1898 would, as

---

[45] Pauncefote to Kimberley, July 3, 1894, F.O. 5/2234; Campbell, *Anglo-American Understanding*, 12; Lionel Gelber, *The Rise of Anglo-American Friendship* . . . (London, 1938), 5; Marder, *Anatomy of British Sea Power*, 252.

[46] The best analysis is Nelson M. Blake, "The Olney-Pauncefote Treaty of 1897," *American Historical Review*, L (January, 1945), 228–243; Olney's analysis is in a letter to Henry White, May 14, 1897, Olney MSS.

Henry Adams bragged, bring "England into an American system." But events in the international exchanges, Latin America, and the Far East had momentously changed relations between the two nations from distrust to warm friendship in the several years before that war.[47]

New Foes

Like the balancing pans of a scale, as the hopes for Anglo-American relations rose, Russo-American relations began to sink. It was not coincidental that a century of friendship between the United States and Russia cooled at the moment the century of distrust between Americans and British began to disappear. The cordial relations which Washington enjoyed with St. Petersburg had depended upon the absence of conflicting interests and a common anti-British attitude.[48]

For more than half a century Russia had bowed to the demands of American expansion. The Czar's government had placated John Quincy Adams in 1824 by abandoning its claim to the Pacific coastline south of 54° 40′. Forty-three years later Russia sold Alaska, her last stronghold on the North American continent, to the United States. Throughout the last half of the nineteenth century, Russian foreign ministers gladly recognized American predominance in Hawaii. Americans misinterpreted the visit of the Russian navy to New York City in 1863 as a demonstration of the Czar's support for the North. The fleet was actually searching for a suitable refuge in case war broke out between England and Russia.

During the fur seal dispute in the early 1890's, the Russians, who possessed material interests in the matter, had been con-

[47] Garvin, *Chamberlain,* III, 300; Mahan to J. R. Thursfield, Dec. 1, 1897, Mahan MSS. See also *Letters of Cecil Spring-Rice,* I, 248–249.

[48] Pauline Tompkins comments: "Thus the decade of the nineties was an auspicious one. . . . The conditions for friendship existing between 1800 and 1870 had vanished, and without them the tradition of friendship was meaningless" (*American-Russian Relations in the Far East* [New York, 1949], 14–15).

spicuously friendly to the American arguments. As the 1890's
dawned, there were few indications that this would be the transition decade in relations between the two nations. Americans
raised $77,000,000 to help famine victims in Russia in 1891; the
Czar offered a large gold loan (which the United States refused)
to help the stricken American Treasury in 1893; and the Carnegie
steel works and the Cramp Shipbuilding Company were busy
filling large Russian orders.[49]

But these events were misleading. A growing American ab-
horrence of Russian autocratic methods, especially its anti-Jewish
pogroms, had begun to undermine the century-old friendship. A
review in 1889 of W. T. Stead's *Truth about Russia* had noted
that "except in time of war, there never was, perhaps, a greater
interest taken in the Russian Empire"; then the reviewer described Russia as "that distant and darkly mysterious hot-bed at
once of despotic inhumanity, indescribable horrors, Nihilism, and
disturbance to the peace of Europe." In more moderate terms,
Andrew Dickson White, United States Minister to Russia in the
early 1890's and a respected and widely read author, could agree.
Believing that "Russia's strong point is not adherence to her treaty
promises," White severely criticized her statesmen and concluded,
"The atmosphere of Russian autocracy is fatal to greatness in any
form." George Kennan's *Siberia and the Exile System* became the
most popular presentation of this viewpoint. With strong support from Mark Twain, James Russell Lowell, and Julia Ward
Howe, Kennan traveled throughout the United States to publicize his book and to tell of the horrors of Russian oppression.
The Philadelphia *Ledger* responded by proclaiming that "civilized nations" could have nothing to do with such "cannibals."
But the anti-Czarist forces in Russia found little American sympathy either. This opposition was becoming too radical for

[49] Russian assurances on Hawaii are found in Memorandum on Diplo-
matic Day, Feb. 2, 1893, Harrison MSS; gold loan in Gresham to White,
May 3, 1893, Cleveland MSS; business relations in Carnegie to Blaine,
May 9, 1891, and Schwab to Carnegie, March 7, 1898, Carnegie MSS.

middle-class taste in the United States. Many anti-Russian spokesmen in the 1890's, including Kennan, would fight for the Keren-
sky government of 1917, but bitterly oppose the Bolsheviks.[50]

"But the circumstance that presented the greatest danger,"
Walter Quintin Gresham told John Bassett Moore in 1894, "was
the Jewish question." Russia had begun an anti-Jewish campaign in the 1870's; by the 1890's American Jews who were in
Russia for family visits or business were also being persecuted.
Harrison and Blaine bent to the political uproar in the United
States and sent strong protests to St. Petersburg. Harold Frederic,
a New York *Times* reporter, added to the bitterness with a vivid
description of the pogroms in his *New Exodus*, published in
1892. These feelings reached a climax in 1892–1893 when the
Cleveland administration attempted to pass a new Russian extra-
dition treaty through the Senate. Such influential journals as the
New York *Times*, New York *World*, Louisville *Courier-Journal*,
Philadelphia *Record*, Chicago *Herald*, and Washington *Star* condemned the treaty and freely used the terms "despotic" and
"despotism" in discussing the Czar's regime.[51]

These bitter feelings promised trouble if American and Russian
claims ever conflicted in any area of the international arena. And
in the mid-1890's the conflict appeared to be taking shape in the
Far East. Determined to exert "control over the entire movement
of international commerce in Pacific waters," as Count Witte,

[50] Andrew Dickson White, *Autobiography* . . . (New York, 1905),
II, 27, 51. Max M. Laserson notes that White's acquaintances were largely
limited to the pro-American groups in Russia; see *The American Impact
on Russia—Diplomatic and Ideological, 1784–1917* (New York, 1950),
298–299, 302–303; there is a good discussion of Kennan, 304–319. The
Stead review is in *Public Opinion*, March 2, 1889, 475; see also Feb. 22,
1890, 468.

[51] The Gresham statement is in Diary, May, 1894, J. B. Moore MSS;
Messages and Papers of the Presidents, IX, 188. For the political importance see J. S. Clarkson, chairman of the Republican National Committee
to Halford, Feb. 23, 1892, Harrison MSS. See also *Public Opinion*, June
17, 1893, 263–264; Feb. 11, 1893, 441; March 25, 1893, 593; April 29, 1893,
93–94; July 8, 1893, 330–331.

the Russian Finance Minister, declared in 1892, the Russians had surrendered their claims in North America in the middle of the nineteenth century in order to concentrate on affairs in the Far East. They had taken their major step in 1895 by forcing Japan to leave the Liaotung Peninsula and then establishing new levers of power in Korea, China, and especially Manchuria. With staunch support from the German Emperor, the Czar moved steadily toward his goal of replacing British dominance in the Far East with Russian power.[52]

But as the State Department recognized, a threat to the British position was also a threat to American interests. Only Great Britain, and possibly Japan, shared the American enthusiasm for the open door. This common Anglo-American stake in the area, combined with the implicit new agreement on Latin America, removed at a stroke the traditional grounds of Russian-American friendship. Now Russian and American interests threatened to conflict, and unlike 1824 or 1867 neither side entertained thoughts of retreating. As for the once-shared anti-British feelings, the Russians held on grimly—and alone.

When American financiers failed to win the Chinese indemnity loan in 1895, and when the American China Development Company lost a prize railroad concession in 1897, United States officials were quick to place the blame on the Russian-Chinese Bank. This bank, controlled by Russian and French capital, was fully backed, in fact manipulated, by the Czar's government. Denby abhorred such governmental intervention, especially since he could not convince the American government to use such methods. A similar rivalry developed in Korea. Here Horace Allen had worked with the Russians in opposing Japanese influence in 1895 and 1896. By early 1897, however, Allen was convinced that Russia was attempting to drive out the Americans and con-

---

[52] B. A. Romanov, *Russia in Manchuria, 1892–1906* . . . , translated by Susan Wilbur Jones (Leningrad, 1928), 2, 50–61; Breckinridge to Gresham, Feb. 18, 1894, Russia, Despatches, NA, RG 59; Zabriskie, *American-Russian Relations*, 27–29, 30–31.

trol the Hermit Kingdom. Allen fought the Russians with all the considerable intrigue and power at his command. By November he thought "the jig is up," and when the Russians suddenly and wonderfully left Korea in April, 1898, Allen warned that they would be back soon and "then come for good and all." He believed that only a Japanese-British alliance or "an alliance between the U.S. and England" could preserve American interests.[53]

If Russia consolidated her power in the Far East, and her power would be immense after the completion of her Trans-Siberian Railroad, she could close the open door at will. Faced with this dilemma, Americans differed on the proper solution. For a short time Denby apparently wanted to cooperate with the Russians, confident that the Russian-Chinese banking group would allow Americans to help in the division of the Chinese melon. He was partially disabused of this hope when his fellow countrymen lost the indemnity and the railroad concessions. Ethan A. Hitchcock, McKinley's Ambassador to the Czar's government, nursed similar hopes of working with the Russians; he especially wanted American firms to fulfill the Trans-Siberian's demand for steel rails.[54]

Others were not so sanguine. An American naval official published an essay which predicted a gigantic war between the Slavs and the Aryan race. Theodore Roosevelt confided to a close friend that "indeed Russia is a problem very appalling." Henry Adams worried: "Russia is omnipotence. . . . I fear Russia much!" John R. Proctor, an official in the Cleveland administration and a close friend of Roosevelt's, wrote in the *Forum* in September, 1897, that "the cotton-growers of the South, the wheat-growers of the West, the meat-producers on our plains, and

[53] Zabriskie, *American-Russian Relations*, 34–37; John Foster to Wilson, Aug. 16, 1895, James Harrison Wilson papers, Library of Congress, Washington, D.C.; Denby to Olney, July 8, 1895, Olney MSS; Harrington, *God, Mammon, and the Japanese*, 296–301.

[54] Zabriskie, *American-Russian Relations*, 34, 41–42.

manufacturers and wage-earners all over our land" must realize "that exclusion from Asian markets will be disastrous to their best interests," and "the expansion of Russia in Asia . . . will extend the Russian system of exclusion." Another article in the same issue of that magazine predicted that perhaps a "sudden revolution" would overthrow the Czar; if this failed to occur, "great evil" would engulf the world.[55]

Clifton R. Breckinridge, Cleveland's Minister to Russia, summarized the change in Russian-American relations in November, 1896. Noting that Russians had lost almost all interest in American friendship, he blamed this loss on inadequate trade relations and especially on the new Anglo-American alliance. He promised to maintain polite relations during his remaining months in St. Petersburg, but he would "predicate nothing more upon traditional friendship or any other matters of that kind." [56]

German-American relations paralleled the course of Russian-American affairs. The United States had warmly supported the German cause in the Franco-Prussian War of 1870, but by the 1890's this support had turned to disdain. The clash of the new empire with German ambitions in Samoa had set off a chain reaction of bad feelings. Justifiably, Americans began to fear German penetration into Latin America in the 1890's. When in 1897 Germany gave Haiti eight hours to pay an indemnity for the arrest of a German citizen, the State Department did nothing, but the Kaiser's ultimatum did little to increase his popularity in the United States. The New York *World* attacked the action as "a first step toward aggression and the acquisition of territory on

[55] R. P. Hobson, "A Summary of the Situation and Outlook in Europe," *Proceedings of the United States Naval Institute*, XXI (1895), 350–351; *Letters of Theodore Roosevelt*, I, 555; *Letters of Henry Adams*, II, 70; John R. Proctor, "Hawaii and the Changing Front of the World," *Forum*, XXIV (September, 1897), 34–45; Thomas Davidson, "The Supremacy of Russia," *Forum*, XXIV, 67–68; Thomas R. Jernigan, U.S. Consul General to China, "Commercial Trend of China," *North American Review*, CLXV (July, 1897), 63–69.
[56] Breckinridge to Olney, Nov. 11, 1896, Cleveland MSS; quoted in part in Zabriskie, *American-Russian Relations*, 37.

this side of the ocean." German discriminations against American meat products and fruit were returned with interest by the passage of the Dingley tariff of 1897, which discriminated against German sugar producers.[57]

The two greatest points of friction were American attacks on German militarism and "aristocratic classes," and the growing conflicts in the Far East and Latin America. Articles in the *Forum* and the *North American Review* blistered the German Emperor for his alleged attempt to restore the Holy Roman Empire in order "to govern his subjects as absolute sovereign—their bodies through the army, their souls through the Church." Murat Halstead, a leading Republican and an adviser to both Harrison and McKinley, predicted a war pitting the democratic powers (England and the United States) against the despotic nations (Germany and Russia). Halstead also warned his fellow countrymen against German ambitions in Latin America. The Kaiser, many Americans felt, apparently had not learned the lesson of the Venezuelan incident and so had to be closely watched. Surveying affairs in the Far East, these Americans tended to add "and Germany" where they read "Russia." The two powers, in American eyes, were working together in order to abolish the open door and weaken the British. German actions in Samoa, her hesitancy over recognizing American ascendancy in Hawaii, and her anti-British policy elsewhere in the world strongly substantiated these fears.[58]

---

[57] Clara Eve Schieber, *The Transformation of American Sentiment toward Germany, 1870–1914* (Boston, 1923), 86–88. German complaints about American commercial aggressiveness in Samoa are in *Public Opinion*, Oct. 8, 1896, 461; New York *World*, Nov. 30, 1897, 6:2. See also *Journal of Commerce*, Jan. 26, 1898, 16:1; and Vagts, *Deutschland und die Vereinigten Staaten*, I, 618–621, 780–797.

[58] William L. Langer, *The Diplomacy of Imperialism, 1890–1902* (New York and London, 1935), 447; Vagts, *Deutschland und die Vereinigten Staaten*, I, 608–617, 964–968; Mahan to J. R. Thursfield, Jan. 25, 1898, Mahan MSS; Thomas Davidson, "The Imperialization of Germany," *Forum*, XXIII (April, 1897), 246–256; Poultney Bigelow, "The German Press and the United States," *North American Review*, CLXIV (January,

Arriving as American Ambassador to Germany in 1897, Andrew Dickson White could remark that the "changes in public sentiment since my former stay as minister, eighteen years before, were great indeed." The press, the intellectuals, the agrarians had become strongly anti-American. The intellectuals, White recalled in 1904, spoke so strongly that "some of their expressions seemed to point to eventual war." White had noted a similar break in the traditional friendly relations between America and Russia in 1894.[59]

The United States was realigning its traditional friends and foes in the course of its expansion into Latin America and Asia. Some of this reordering of friendships had been caused by matters extraneous to the new empire, such as the Jewish pogroms and the disdain for Russian and German autocracy. But the dynamics of the new empire in Latin America, Samoa, and especially in the Far East played a crucial role in this realignment, a realignment that had begun to be evident in the 1890's and became increasingly important in the early years of the twentieth century.

1897), 12–23; Murat Halstead, "American Annexation and Armament," *Forum*, XXIV (September, 1897), 56–66.

[59] White, *Autobiography*, II, 144–148, 168–170. White notes that officially Germany treated the United States fairly during the war with Spain.

VIII

Reaction: Approach to War

IN the eight years between Benjamin Harrison's ascendancy to power in 1888 and the success of the next Republican presidential nominee in 1896, the United States transformed its foreign relations. The speed and intensity with which this transformation reached its climax in the 1890's is, from the vantage point of sixty years, quite amazing. Gently urged by Harrison, Blaine, and the McKinley tariff and then frightened by the economic and social maladjustments of the 1893–1897 depression, many of the most powerful American industries began to believe that their survival depended upon the markets of the world. Walter Quintin Gresham, Richard Olney, and Grover Cleveland had used the nation's foreign policy to aid the aspirations of the business community. Renewed commercial and investment interests in the Far East, plus the flouting of open-door principles by the continental European powers, forced the United States to change long-standing Asiatic policies, increase State Department support of these interests, and reorder the list of the nation's traditional friends and enemies. Little wonder that Josiah Strong and Henry and Brooks Adams looked about them and concluded that history was stepping up its pace to the uppermost tempo of human endurance.

These far-reaching changes had only been initiated when William McKinley entered office in March, 1897. "Business conditions," the new Chief Executive reported in his Inaugural Address, "are not the most promising." These conditions were not improved by a bloody Cuban revolution which consumed investments and trade and touched the tender hearts of American politicians. McKinley assumed power with the promise of restoring prosperity and the hope of ending the Cuban struggle. The President would find that the two issues were not disconnected. In the realm of foreign affairs, he would also have to deal with new events which intensified the previous threats to the open door.

Fortunately, however, the administration would not fight these battles alone. An American business community that had learned to think in world-wide terms during the 1890's would also devote its attention to restoring good times, stifling the Cuban disturbance, and maintaining the open door. These three problems could not be separated, although the administration could, and did, assign priorities to them. McKinley and the business community would work in tandem. The President would emphasize this point many times. Business, reorganizing itself after a half century of industrial revolution and a quarter century of depression, would provide the dynamic. A friendly government would provide the leadership. And inside that government the center of power would be found at the White House.

McKinley

William McKinley came into the White House equipped with the two qualities all presidents need for political survival: an understanding of the social and economic realities of his time and the political talents needed to cope with these realities. His political abilities were particularly noticeable. Always adequate in the political arena, he could at times be superb. Anyone who could survive the tough school of Ohio politics in the last quarter of the nineteenth century was indeed an uncommon political animal. As a congressman in the 1880's, McKinley worked closely with the John Sherman faction, but he shrewdly broke away long enough in 1884 to back Blaine in the Republican Convention. By 1889 the Sherman forces had been splintered by Harrison's nomination the year before; "Fire Alarm Joe" Foraker, the leader of the other Republican faction in Ohio, had been well smeared in the gubernatorial campaign; and McKinley, moving nimbly from one to the other, walked unscathed out of the wreckage of both factions. He had also found a new friend, Marcus Hanna, Cleveland industrialist and political operator extraordinary.

The elections of 1890 appeared to mark the end of the Mc-Kinley luck. With his district gerrymandered by a Democratic legislature for the third time in his career, McKinley suffered defeat by the thin margin of 300 votes. The Democrats swore that he should have lost by 3,000 votes. But this told the lesser part of the story, for Ohio Republicans and independents proclaimed the defeated congressman as a martyr sacrificed to the foul gods of the Democracy and promptly elected McKinley as Governor of Ohio in 1891. Frank Carpenter, the acute observer of the Washington scene, could conclude a detailed description of the Ohioan's nose by remarking, "It is a watchful nose, and it is a nose that watches out for McKinley." And Henry Adams, who said few nice things about anybody who held power after 1828, nevertheless believed McKinley's "judgment of men was finer than common in Presidents," and even described him as a "marvellous manager of men." McKinley also, Adams observed, chose several manipulators to help him (such as John Hay). McKinley, however, was always equal to manipulating the manipulators.[1]

Major McKinley (a rank received for bravery in the Civil War) had early accepted Rutherford B. Hayes's advice that a thorough knowledge of the tariff was the key to a successful political career. In the 1880's he became a leading spokesman on this issue, showing unshakable devotion to high tariff principles.

---

[1] Morgan, "Congressional Career of McKinley," ch. iii, 80–81, 189–192; Adams, *Education*, 373–374.

The McKinley tariff was the culmination of his work. But he had just begun to grasp the prodigious meaning of the industrial revolution.

The post-1893 depression gave him a thorough education on the nature of the American economy and society. He had always been a close friend of the working man. Samuel Gompers fondly recalled that he and the Major had been friends "for many years" before 1897. As Governor, McKinley had begun to comprehend some of the same labor-management problems which troubled Walter Quintin Gresham. The Ohioan responded by encouraging the formation of unions and whipping through the state legislature an industrial arbitration bill. This measure proved somewhat effective in the strike-ridden years of 1894–1895. But when the threat of violent strikes began to spread across the state, McKinley did not hesitate to order out in force the state militia, believing, as he remarked later, that when a brigade met a division there would be no battle. His prompt action avoided the bloodshed and the bitter feelings which wracked Illinois and Pennsylvania that year. As was usual with most of his policies, his action did not tarnish his reputation with either labor or management.[2]

When he entered the White House in 1897, the depression surged on "entailing idleness upon willing labor and loss to useful enterprises," as the new President phrased the problem in an early speech. McKinley had no intention of allowing the business cycle to take its course. One of the more striking themes which emerged from his post-1896 speeches was his emphasis on the necessity for an active national government to cooperate in friendly fashion with the businessman. McKinley's first Inaugural Address outlined this position. If the nation could not promptly restore "the prosperity of former years," McKinley declared, "we can resolutely turn our faces in that direction and aid its return by friendly legislation. However troublesome the situation may appear, Congress will not, I am sure, be found lacking

[2] Margaret Leech, *In the Days of McKinley* (New York, 1959), 53–55; Gompers, *Seventy Years of Life and Labor*, I, 522–523.

in disposition or ability to relieve it as far as legislation can do so."
In fact, the new President proclaimed, "the restoration of confidence and the revival of business . . . depend more largely
upon the prompt, energetic, and intelligent action of Congress
than upon any other single agency affecting the situation." On
several later occasions, McKinley severely deprecated the idea
that Congress could best serve the people by packing as rapidly
as possible and leaving Washington. He stressed these beliefs in
his several appearances before the National Association of Manufacturers, especially in his speech to the N.A.M. convention in
January, 1898.[3]

Perhaps the controlling words of the passage quoted above
from the Inaugural were "friendly legislation." McKinley condemned bad corporations, those "organized in trusts or otherwise,
to control arbitrarily the condition of trade among our citizens."
But very few Republicans—or Democrats—seriously contem-
plated a rigid enforcement of the antitrust legislation in the 1890's.
The President wanted to stimulate, not regulate. Production had
to climb, financial stability had to be ensured, and markets had to
be found. Government could become a partner with business in
achieving these objectives.

Government could help considerably, for example, by settling
the question of the monetary standard. The Republicans had won
on a strong gold platform in 1896, but their presidential nominee
did not belong in the extreme monometallist camp. Throughout
his congressional career McKinley had advocated bimetallism.
Enticed by the vision of an enlarged foreign trade with Latin-
American and Asian nations on the silver standard, he had helped
Blaine secure a silver trade dollar at the 1889 Inter-American
Conference and had promised in 1896 to send a bimetallist delegation to Europe if he was elected. True to his word, he sent a
commission, but it promptly ran into a stone wall of British and
French opposition. Fortunately, a rising export trade and dis-

[3] William McKinley, *Speeches and Addresses of William McKinley,
from March 1, 1897, to May 30, 1900* (New York, 1900), 23, 62, 8.

coveries of gold in Alaska had eased the monetary situation. Mc-Kinley, however, in the hope of allaying political discontent and finding foreign markets for American products, had considered the alternative.[4]

Conditions in the 1890's changed his mind about the tariff as well as the monetary standard. "My fellow-citizens," McKinley told a joint meeting of the Philadelphia Museums and the Manufacturers' Club in June, 1897, "there is no use in making a product if you cannot find somebody to take it. The maker must find a taker. You will not employ labor to make a product unless you can find a buyer for that product after you have made it." The President thought he had found the key to the doors of foreign markets in the formula of reciprocity. As the handmaiden to protection, reciprocity did not disturb McKinley's devotion to his traditional high tariff views. But his stress on the law of supply and demand in the 1896 campaign, and his belief that the workings of reciprocity would ferret out crucial foreign demand needed to balance the two points of this law, indicated that a significant change of emphasis had occurred in his thinking during the 1890's. McKinley had worked for Blaine's ideas in 1890, but the Ohioan became a fervent disciple of reciprocity only after the economic crisis of 1893.[5]

At the first N.A.M. convention in 1895, McKinley outlined the perfect trade program: "our own markets for our manufactures and agricultural products" and "a reciprocity which will give us foreign markets for our surplus products." In his Inaugural, the new President boasted of the aid given American foreign trade by the 1890 provision and declared, "The end in view always [should] be the opening up of new markets for the products of our country." After three months in office he could remark

[4] Morgan, "Congressional Career of McKinley," 166; Chandler to William R. Day, Oct. 6, 1897, Aldrich MSS; Hay to McKinley, Oct. 11, 1897, McKinley MSS; Gage to Winfield N. Burdick, Aug. 20, 1897, Letterbook, Lyman Gage papers, Library of Congress, Washington, D.C.

[5] McKinley, *Speeches, 1897–1900*, 28; Leech, *Days of McKinley*, 142.

that "no worthier cause can engage our energies at this hour" than the enlargement of foreign markets; these markets allow "better fields for employment, and easier conditions for the masses." Seven months after entering the White House, McKinley told the Commercial Club of Cincinnati: "No subject can better engage our attention than the promotion of trade and commerce at home and abroad. Domestic conditions are sure to be improved by larger exchanges with the nations of the world." He noted hopefully, "We are already reaching out with good results." Nearly a year after assuming the presidential powers, McKinley warned the N.A.M. that the depression had not yet fully lifted because "of their present insufficient facilities for reaching desirable markets." These remarks substantiate Robert LaFollette's recollection that McKinley told him in 1897 that he (McKinley) hoped to crown his presidency with American control of the markets of the world.[6]

The President's abilities were fully appreciated by close associates and observers of the passing scene. John Hay visited McKinley during the 1896 campaign after "dreading" the visit for a month, since "it would be like talking in a boiler factory." But McKinley had taken Hay into a quiet upstairs room and "calmly and serenely" discussed political matters for two hours while the howling mob trampled the lawn below. Hay, a full-fledged McKinley admirer now, told Henry Adams of his marvelous experience at Canton and ended, "And there are idiots who think Mark Hanna will run him." After the election, Mayo Hazeltine wrote in the *North American Review* that political observers agreed that "one thing . . . is certain and obvious," namely, that McKinley would control foreign affairs with an iron hand. Theodore Roosevelt, after discussing foreign and naval policies with the President, remarked with wonderment, "He shows an astonishing grasp of the situation." Roosevelt would not always

[6] Steigerwalt, "N.A.M.," 32; McKinley to Curtis, Dec. 2, 1895, Letterbooks, McKinley MSS; *Congressional Record*, 55th Cong., 1st Sess., 3; McKinley, *Speeches, 1897–1900*, 54; Leech, *Days of McKinley*, 62, 142.

admire McKinley, but it should be noted that Roosevelt's later pique was chiefly due to McKinley's control over a situation which Roosevelt found unendurable—not because the President had lost control. Senator Shelby Cullom's assessment of McKinley agrees with these observations and has particular relevance to an interpretation of the causes of the Spanish-American War. "We have never had a President," the Illinois Senator recalled, "who had more influence with Congress than Mr. McKinley." In fact, Cullom continued, "I have never heard of even the slightest friction between Mr. McKinley and the party leaders in Senate and House." [7]

McKinley's contemporaries recognized his talent as a politician. His analysis of the depression problems of the mid-1890's may not have satisfied an erudite classical economist, but the President's views put him in the mainstream of American economic expansion. These abilities were the tools he used in chipping away the three obstacles to American economic prosperity—the Cuban revolution, the threatening situation in the Far East, and the lack of adequate demand for the glut of American goods.

Cuba, 1897 to March 17, 1898

Much evidence supported the views of those pundits who forecast that the new administration would employ a more aggressive policy toward Cuba than had the Cleveland cabinet. Republicans had led the *Cuba Libre* cries in Congress since 1895; and the party's 1896 foreign policy plank, although denying intentions of military intervention, had asked that the United States "actively use its influence and good offices" in obtaining independence for the Cubans. Without Spanish assent any such action, of course, would have ended in war with Spain. The Democratic plank,

[7] Hay to Henry Adams, Oct. 20, 1896, John Hay papers, Library of Congress, Washington, D.C.; Mayo W. Hazeltine, "The Foreign Policy of the New Administration," *North American Review*, CLXIV (April, 1897), 479–486; Roosevelt to Long, June 18, 1897, Letterbooks, Roosevelt MSS; Shelby M. Cullom, *Fifty Years of Public Service* . . . (Chicago, 1911), 275–276.

on the other hand, merely extended "sympathy" to the Cubans. The election was not waged on this issue and the results of the campaign were certainly not a mandate for a more vigorous foreign policy, but the difference between the two planks signaled a basic difference in attitude.[8]

There were other indications that McKinley would pursue a militant foreign policy. Each new day of the warfare devastated more American investments and trade. These investments had mushroomed to more than $33,000,000 since the conclusion of the Ten Years' War in 1878. United States trade had soared to new heights after the 1890 tariff had opened Cuban markets to American flour and industrial goods and had made mainland consumers dependent upon the Cuban sugar grower. These economic links, along with the inhumanities of the *reconcentrado* policies, added to the rising cry that the revolution had to end quickly. If Spain could not terminate the warfare, the United States would have to intervene.[9]

McKinley's Secretary of State had taken precisely this view as a member of the Senate. Once in the State Department, however, John Sherman began to waver. Rapidly becoming senile, his forgetfulness, indecisiveness, and growing distrust of associates were, as John Foster noted, "pitiable in the extreme." One of McKinley's close friends from Ohio, Judge William R. Day, became Assistant Secretary of State and assumed the most important responsibilities of the department. Day did not share Sherman's earlier tendencies toward a belligerent Cuban policy.[10]

Day's moderate opinions, however, did not typify the first months of the administration's actions. After proclaiming in his Inaugural that "peace is preferable to war in almost every con-

[8] *Proceedings of the Republican Convention* (1896), 84; Pratt, *Expansionists of 1898*, 212. McKinley fully backed Cleveland's stand on the Venezuelan controversy; see New York *World*, Dec. 18, 1895, 2:1.

[9] For the causes of the increased American investments in Cuba after 1878, see page 38, above.

[10] Foster to Porter, Aug. 11, 1897, and Sherman to McKinley, Feb. 15, 1897, McKinley MSS.

tingency," McKinley adopted a policy toward Spain which ended in a virtual ultimatum in early autumn, 1897. The administration thus moved to the edge of conflict half a year before actually declaring war on Spain. Only the promise of Spanish reforms in October and November brought McKinley back from the precipice. It should be especially noted that neither the yellow journals nor a towering wave of public opinion, so often viewed as the sole causes of the ultimate war, significantly influenced the administration's policies during these months. As defined by the State Department in 1897, America's interest in the revolution was derived from more than humanitarian sentiment. The development of, and the reasons for, this policy deserve emphasis.

In the late spring of 1897, Cánovas resigned as Spanish Prime Minister. The State Department hoped that a more liberal ministry would assume power, but these hopes were dashed in June when the Queen renamed Cánovas after expressing, as Hannis Taylor noted in a dispatch from Madrid, "unqualified approval of present Cuban policy." Shortly afterward Spain answered Sherman's protest of the *reconcentrado* policy by denying that brutal methods were used; the reply then awkwardly compared Spain's campaign in Cuba with General W. T. Sherman's march to the sea during the American Civil War. The comparison did not exactly appease the Secretary of State, who happened to be the brother of the famous general.[11]

In the face of this Spanish intransigence, Sherman and McKinley approved the basic instructions of July 16, which were to be sent to Stewart L. Woodford, the new Minister to Spain. After stating bluntly that Spain could never again subdue the island, the State Department demanded that somehow the revolution must be immediately halted. The serious danger posed to American material interests (interests which were "not merely theoretical or sentimental") necessitated the immediate cessation

[11] Taylor to Sherman, June 3 and 7, 1897, Spain, Despatches, "Memorandum" of Day's, June 8, 1897, and de Lôme to Sherman, Aug. 26, 1897, Notes from Spain, NA, RG 59.

of warfare. These material interests were more than direct investments in, and trade with, Cuba. The "chronic condition of trouble and violent derangement" on the island, the State Department warned, "keeps up a continuous irritation within our borders, injuriously effects the normal functions of business, and tends to delay the condition of prosperity to which this country is entitled." Spain would have to end the disturbance immediately, perhaps through the good offices of the United States, or the President would have to take a "course of action which the time and the transcendent emergency may demand." The note may be summarized, then, as, first, a notice to Spain that the State Department had no confidence that Spanish officials could regain control of the island; second, a definition of American involvement in the conflict on the grounds of economic interests and the threat the struggle posed to the social, economic, and political tranquillity of the United States; and third, a notice to Spain that she must accept American good offices, immediately terminate the revolution by other means, or face the intervention of the United States.[12]

As Woodford traveled to Madrid with this note, relations further deteriorated. Spain again refused to discuss the *reconcentrado* orders. The State Department failed in efforts to release American citizens held in Cuban jails. Spanish authorities on the island were slow in protecting American property from rebel depredations. After surveying the situation, the Department advised Tasker H. Bliss, Woodford's military attaché, not to take his family to Spain because of the possibility of war. The President, about to replace the energetic Fitzhugh Lee with a more pacific Consul General, changed his mind. In spite of a warning from former President Cleveland that Lee's presence in the Cuban capital was a threat to any moderate approach, McKinley retained the Virginian in Havana. It remains an interesting enigma why the President, who sincerely wanted to avoid a conflict, retained such a militant-minded representative (and lifelong Dem-

[12] Sherman to Woodford, July 16, 1897, Spain, Instructions, NA, RG 59.

ocrat) in one of the most sensitive overseas posts. McKinley probably did so in 1897 because he wanted an experienced man at the key Cuban position in the event that war broke out.[13]

Then, on August 8, the situation dramatically changed. Woodford sent a hurried cable that Cánovas had been assassinated by an anarchist. The State Department, however, did not immediately discern the full significance of the event. An interim conservative ministry assumed the reins. The Liberal party, which had urged far-reaching Cuban reforms in June, remained out of the policy-making circles. Adee, discounting the change, wrote a long memorandum which extensively discussed the possibility of intervention. Day called in John Bassett Moore on September 11 to discuss the legal niceties of whether Congress or the Executive had the power of intervening in Cuba, "should such intervention be undertaken, on the ground of protecting American property in the island." Moore recorded in his diary that "it occurred to me that the President probably was thinking" of this alternative.[14]

But in the first week of October, Práxedes Mateo Sagasta led a Liberal party cabinet into power. In June, Sagasta had promised far-reaching reforms in Cuba should his party assume leadership. Within two months after becoming Premier he fulfilled his promises. By March, 1898, the McKinley administration would be bitterly disappointed because of the moderate nature of these reforms. In view of the complex problems confronting Sagasta in late 1897, however, it is amazing that he satisfied American demands as fully as he did.

Two factors worked in Sagasta's favor. The Conservative party had been disrupted by Cánovas' murder and so presented less opposition than it might have. Also, wealthy Spaniards who held property in Cuba had concluded that their holdings could be

[13] Offner, "McKinley and Origins of Spanish-American War," 96–97, 149–151; Lee to Lamont, Feb. 3, 1897, Lamont MSS; New York *World*, Nov. 6, 1897, 1:8.

[14] Adee to Sherman, Aug. 19, 1897, McKinley MSS; Diary-Memoranda, 1897, Moore MSS.

preserved only if the United States aided Spain in pacifying the island. But the obstacles to the success of Sagasta's program were immense. The rebels displayed little inclination to compromise after two years of hard fighting, especially when the McKinley administration evinced some interest in the objectives for which they were fighting. Factions of Sagasta's own party disagreed on the extensiveness of his reforms, and he was forced to name a weak cabinet for the sake of political expediency. Nor could the new Prime Minister look for help from friendly European powers. Sagasta, apparently more frightened by the tone of the American requests than the Duke of Tetuán had been, attempted to outflank the Americans by asking the powers to form a coalition in support of Spain. Weakened by lack of preparation in Madrid and indecision in the European capitals, especially London, the Spanish venture was not fruitful. State Department emissaries on the continent, constantly keeping their fingers on the pulses of the European foreign offices during the autumn, returned reassuring reports that the major powers had concluded they would do nothing unless the United States approved or invited outside aid. Rumors even began to spread in Madrid that the United States and Great Britain were closely cooperating on the Cuban problem. The British Ambassador angrily reported to London that Woodford was encouraging this falsehood at every opportunity.[15]

The American Minister in Madrid had "serious apprehension," as he reported to McKinley, "that my efforts will fail" in maintaining peace. Hannis Taylor did not encourage Woodford by predicting that "the outside limit" of the new Minister's stay in Spain would be one hundred days. Woodford was doubtlessly burdened by these feelings when he faced the Duke of Tetuán,

15 Wolff to Salisbury, Aug. 12 and 18, 1897, Nov. 12, 1897, F.O. 72/2035; New York *World*, Oct. 5, 1897, 7:1; Oct. 23, 1897, 7:3; Woodford to Sherman, Aug. 30, 1897 (from Paris), Spain, Despatches, and Porter to Sherman, July 13, 1897, France, Despatches, NA, RG 59; Dugdale, *German Documents*, II, 496; Wolff to Salisbury, Jan. 12, 1897, From Spain, 1897, Salisbury MSS; Ferrara, *Last Spanish War*, 82.

Foreign Minister of the interim Conservative Government, in their first formal meeting on September 18. Woodford first read most of Sherman's July instructions. In the conversation which followed he emphasized that the American people could no longer tolerate the continuance of the revolution. "I therefore suggested, in bringing our interview to an end, but without pointing out any formula, that the Spanish Government should give to me before the first of November next such assurance as would satisfy the United States that early and certain peace can be promptly secured"; otherwise the United States would take its own steps to restore "the general tranquility." Two weeks later Woodford rather proudly wired the State Department that *that interview probably changed the Ministry*." [16] Considering the pressures of the Spanish political situation, Woodford claimed too much credit. Sagasta, nevertheless, now worked under the shadow of an ultimatum.

During the first three weeks of October, as Sagasta organized his cabinet, American patience wore thin. On October 1, Day renewed American offers of good offices. Five days later Woodford wrote Day that although Sagasta was planning reforms, "this Ministry . . . may have come in too late." Only "complete independence will induce the insurgents to lay down their arms." Sir Henry Drummond Wolff, the knowledgeable British Ambassador in Madrid, reported to Salisbury late in October that Woodford had been talking about the " 'richest slice of earth,' " which the United States was determined to have. "As things appear drifting much more rapidly than I anticipated," Sir Henry wrote, "the time for palliatives seems passed." [17]

Wolff had underestimated Sagasta's ability. In mid-October, Spain sent General Ramón Blanco y Arenas to replace Weyler.

[16] Woodford to McKinley, Sept. 6 and 3, 1897, Woodford to Sherman, Sept. 20, 1897, Woodford to Day, Oct. 6, 1897, Spain, Despatches, NA, RG 59.

[17] Wolff to Salisbury, Oct. 25 and 26, 1897, From Spain, 1897, Salisbury MSS; Day to Woodford, Oct. 1, 1897, Spain, Instructions, and Woodford to Day, Oct. 6, 1897, Spain, Despatches, NA, RG 59.

Blanco had gained an excellent reputation as an efficient but humane soldier while quieting the revolution in the Philippines the year before. Sagasta followed the dispatch of Blanco with promises that the *reconcentrado* orders would be moderated. On November 17 Spain began releasing American prisoners held in Cuba; eleven days later Spanish officials informed Woodford that no American subject remained imprisoned on the island. A month later Spain revoked an order which had discriminated against tobacco exported to the United States. But most important, on October 26, five days before the November 1 deadline, Spain handed Woodford a program designed to bring into effect the reforms promised by Sagasta in June. Military operations would not be interrupted, but the Cubans would be granted self-government in all areas except foreign relations, the army, the navy, and the administration of justice, "which involve national requirements or needs." This notice occupied only half the message. The last eight pages of the fifteen-page memorandum expressed the sincere wish that the United States would cut off aid to the Junta and to the numerous Cuban filibustering expeditions which used American ports. Only then, the message said, would this grant of autonomy be effective. After a bitter debate in the Cortes, the Queen Regent signed the reforms into law on November 25.[18]

Sherman replied to the Spanish announcement of the reforms with a long note which praised the changes, although he observed that Spain "is silent as to the manner and form in which the . . . United States might exert good offices." He fervently denied that the administration was shirking its responsibility under the neutrality acts. The tension was broken. Spain had acceded to, and would now be allowed to carry out, the American demands of reform. But Spain would have only seven weeks for

[18] New York *World*, Oct. 3, 1897, 9:4; Woodford to Sherman, Nov. 13, 28, and 15, Dec. 31, Oct. 30, 1897, Spain, Despatches, and Sherman to Woodford, Nov. 6, 1897, Spain, Instructions, NA, RG 59.

this immense project before the tension would mount again. Even those seven weeks between November 25 and January 12 would be weeks of only relative calm. Former Minister Hannis Taylor set off an intense debate in newspaper columns and lecture platforms by publishing a long article in the *North American Review* asking for intervention. American financial pages printed the news that some large property holders in Cuba had little faith in the new reforms and had decided to work for American annexation. The question of war or peace indeed revolved around the success of the Spanish reforms. Few responsible persons in the McKinley administration evinced any optimism. By late December the President had become so concerned that he refused to allow Woodford to return to the United States for urgent private business. The Navy Department, meanwhile, had quietly sent out orders instructing Squadron commanders to retain all men whose enlistments were to expire shortly.[19]

Rumors even began to spread that in his annual message of 1897 McKinley would give Spain a time limit for the successful application of the reforms. The President stopped short of that extreme, but two passages presaged later events. McKinley rejected the possibilities of recognizing insurgent belligerency, Cuban independence, or intervention, and refused to consider annexation, which "by our code of morality would be criminal aggression." He rejected recognition of belligerent rights, however, on other grounds. Spain would gain all the advantages, the President warned, since she would be able to keep Americans away from Cuban waters. The creation of similar advantage to the Cubans, however, "through aid or sympathy from within our domain would be even more impossible than now." Interpreted literally, McKinley's words were encouragement to those Americans aiding the revolutionary cause. The other notable passage,

[19] Sherman to Woodford, Nov. 20, 1897, Spain, Instructions, NA, RG 59; Taylor, "Review of the Cuban Question," 610–635; Offner, "McKinley and the Origins of the Spanish-American War," 181–182.

reminiscent of Cleveland's words of December, 1896, began with McKinley's assurances that he wished to give the reforms adequate time, but if they appeared not to be successful in the near future, the United States would take action "without misgiving or hesitancy in the light of the obligation this Government owes to itself, to the people who have confided to it the protection of their interests and honor and to humanity." Woodford reported that the Spanish response to the message was "simply acquiescent and not cordial." [20]

The reforms never had a chance of demonstrating their effectiveness. Two of the three most important groups in Cuba, the insurgents and the conservative landholding and capitalist interests, had by the end of 1897 refused to accept the reforms. Upon first hearing of the Sagasta program, Lee had warned Day that "the Insurgents will accept nothing but independence." Equally important, the conservative interests were beginning to fear that the reforms might breed a radical, wholly Cuban government. Lee wrote Day, "It is known that all classes of the Spanish citizens are violently opposed to a real or genuine autonomy because it would throw the island into the hands of the Cubans —and rather than that they prefer annexation to the United States or some form of an American protectorate." The American Consul at Santiago also noted an important reason for this growing tide of opinion. He reported that although the *reconcentrado* prisoners had been freed to work in American- and Spanish-owned sugar, coffee, and manganese ore industries, they could accomplish nothing, since the insurgents would not allow any production. As for the over-all effect of the revocation of the *reconcentrado* orders, Lee commented in early December that since in some places cats "are used for food purposes, selling at 30 cents a piece," he believed it "a fair inference" to conclude that Spanish officials would be able to do little to relieve the

[20] New York *World*, Nov, 23, Dec. 8, 1897; *Congressional Record*, 55th Cong., 2nd Sess., 3–5; Woodford to McKinley, Dec. 18, 1897, Spain, Despatches, NA, RG 59.

critical situation. "It certainly cannot be done by proclamations," Lee remarked.[21]

In mid-January the third group, the Spanish army, joined the other two key groups in reacting against autonomy, and by so doing set off a chain reaction of events which within three months climaxed in war. On the morning of January 12 a group of Spanish army officers destroyed the presses of a new Havana newspaper which had been attacking Weyler. Havana authorities carefully pointed out that, since the Constitutional Unionists, the foremost autonomist party, had helped suppress the riots which followed, the incident could not be construed as the collapse of the reform program. American officials did not so interpret the incident. Lee reported that the riots proved the ineffectiveness of autonomy and added that he had heard from a credible source that Blanco considered the carrying out of the reform program impossible. De Lôme was quite shaken by the administration's reaction. He informed Madrid that McKinley had noticeably cooled toward the reforms after hearing of the riots. The Spanish Minister warned that the outbreak had "produced deep disgust among the moderate and those disposed to accommodate differences." [22]

For several reasons these riots marked the beginning of the end of any chances for peace. They demonstrated to McKinley's satisfaction that the autonomy scheme was crumbling. They also indicated that Spanish officials could not have complete confidence in their army. The New York *Tribune* commented, "The army is hereafter a dominant political force in Cuba," and believed that the army's opposition stifled any chances the autonomy program might have had. Finally, the riots spread the fear in the United States that Havana was in such a combustible condition

---

[21] Lee to Day, Nov. 17, Dec. 7, 1897, Consular, Havana, and P. F. Hyatt to Day, Jan. 12, 1898, Consular, Santiago, NA, RG 59.

[22] Barclay to Salisbury, Jan. 14, 1898, F.O. 72/2062; Lee to Day, Jan. 12, 13, 14, 15, 1898, Consular, Havana, NA, RG 59; *Spanish Diplomatic Correspondence and Documents*, 63–67.

that American life and property were not safe. After consulting McKinley the day before, Representative Robert Hitt of Illinois rose in the House on January 18 and expressed concern that, since the reform program had not worked, the United States would have to intervene to protect American citizens and property. The same day that Hitt spoke with McKinley, Secretary Long began reordering the fleet in the South Atlantic, since, as he wrote in secret orders, "Affairs are very disturbed at Cuba." The administration decided on the twenty-fourth to send the armored cruiser "Maine" to Havana. The Spanish Minister fully supported the decision to send the vessel. The ostensible purpose of the sailing of the "Maine" was to resume friendly visits of American ships to Spanish ports.[23] In the context of McKinley's reaction to the Havana riots and Long's maneuvering of the fleet, however, the sending of the "Maine" was an attempt to discourage future outbreaks on the island and to provide notice of the administration's concern over the inadequacy of the Spanish reforms.

The Pittsburgh *Press* observed that the sailing of the "Maine" had led to "a strong popular suspicion that the administration is preparing for intervention," a rumor which Day promptly denied. But the *Journal of Commerce* noted "as a matter of interest that the United States now has assembled near Key West the most formidable fleet of warships that has gotten together in our home waters for many years." The most discouraged—and frightened —reaction occurred in Madrid. There, the British Chargé reported, the decision to send the "Maine" was believed to be "inopportune and dangerous." The Chargé noted that the decision was especially inopportune since the Philippine situation had recently quieted, the new Cuban reforms had just begun, the United States and Spain had after a long delay initiated friendly negotiations on a commercial treaty, and, finally, General Juan

[23] New York *Tribune*, Jan. 17, 1898, 1:4; Long to Chester, Jan. 17, 1898, Ciphers Sent, 1888–1898, NA, RG 45; Lee to Day, Feb. 12, 1898, Consular, Havana, NA, RG 59.

Massó and 110 of his men had voluntarily deserted the revolutionary cause. Massó had been especially close to Máximo Gómez, and the desertion buckled rebel spirits. In Spanish minds, the sailing of the "Maine" threatened to cancel out these vestiges of progress.[24]

The Spanish regime expressed its concern at the American reaction when Woodford met with the Queen and then with Segismundo Moret, Spanish Minister for Colonies, on January 15 and 16, respectively. Repeating the Queen's assurances, Moret said that Blanco had the situation in Cuba well in hand and that Weyler would never return to the island. The Spanish Minister then added that, since "we have done all that you asked or suggested," would Woodford "urge the President to do something that shall show the Cuban rebels that they had better accept autonomy and give up their struggle? I feel that we are entitled to this after what we have done." He then recalled that the Cleveland administration had offered to do this if Spain granted autonomy. Woodford's reply was significant in revealing the American position. Since "our American idea is that Governments derive their just authority from the consent of the governed," the American Minister retorted, the United States could not interfere "to keep a people under monarchical rule, who are seeking to establish a republic." In reporting this to McKinley, Woodford made explicit the assumption of such an American position: "When it becomes clear that [Blanco] cannot succeed or that the United States must intervene, the Queen will have to choose between losing her throne or losing Cuba at the risk of war with us." Woodford believed Spain would try to save the dynasty.[25]

The American Minister was apparently attempting to undermine Spanish influence in Cuba in every possible way. One of his

[24] Pittsburgh *Press*, Jan. 25, 1898, 1:1; *Journal of Commerce*, Jan. 25, 1898, 1:3; Barclay to Salisbury, Jan. 26, 1898, F.O. 72/2062. Woodford to Sherman, Jan. 24, 1898, Spain, Despatches, NA, RG 59, contains information on the commercial treaty.

[25] Woodford to McKinley, Jan. 17, 1898, Spain, Despatches, NA, RG 59.

best opportunities for doing this was through a new commercial treaty which he was negotiating with Spain. In late January he commented: "I regard the successful and early consummation of this treaty as very important. It seems to me vital. Unless some accident shall occur, such a treaty should obtain for us the practical control of the Cuban market." On February 4, however, Woodford notified Sherman that the discussions had revealed that the commercial privileges given to Cuba in the reform program were not as extensive as the American Minister had first thought. Cubans could only offer suggestions, "while the actual making of the treaty is to be under the control of Spain." This interpretation of the reform program not only detracted from Cuba's autonomy, but it allowed merchants in Spain, who were bitterly anti-American, to influence the final terms of the pact.[26]

Five days after Woodford's report, another episode profoundly weakened not only American hopes for a favorable commercial treaty, but the administration's confidence in Spain's good faith in all realms of diplomacy. John J. McCook, a dapper, handsome, and wealthy New York lawyer of the venerable firm of Alexander & Green, had often called in 1897–1898 on his good friends from Ohio, McKinley and Day. The President had considered McCook as a possibility for Secretary of the Interior, a post which McCook rejected because it did not give full rein to his interest in foreign affairs. McKinley refused to offer the New Yorker the Attorney General's post because, as the President remarked to a caller, "I do not understand Col. McCook's interest in Cuban affairs." McCook had become deeply involved in the New York Junta, so much so, in fact, that he had created an international syndicate to purchase Cuba from Spain and present it to the Junta. His ties with McKinley and with American businessmen in Cuba had proved invaluable in this venture, but the

[26] Woodford to McKinley, Jan. 28, 1898, and Woodford to Sherman, Feb. 3 and 4, 1898, Spain, Despatches, NA, RG 59; Barclay to Salisbury, Feb. 8, 1898, F.O. 72/2062.

plan foundered on Spain's unwillingness to discuss the matter.[27]

On the morning of February 9, McCook walked into Day's office and handed to the Assistant Secretary the original of a letter which Dupuy de Lôme had written. The Spanish Minister, who had gained an apparently unwarranted reputation as the "Spanish Fox," had in a few brief moments in December delivered himself of his opinion that McKinley was a weak, vacillating, and venal politician. McCook's associates in the Cuban Junta had discovered the letter, and now the New Yorker "had the satisfaction," as he wrote James Harrison Wilson the following day, of putting the damning note "in the hands of the President and . . . Day." Wilson, another businessman closely tied with the Junta and the cause of intervention in Cuba, called it "a master stroke." That it certainly was from McCook's and Wilson's point of view. De Lôme was immediately replaced by a new minister, but the damage had been done. Any faith the moderate American press and the administration had invested in Spanish goodwill was now badly shaken.[28]

Sherman revealed the full significance of the de Lôme letter in a message to Woodford on February 23. The Spanish Minister's usefulness was "utterly destroyed," Sherman wrote, not only because of his statements about the President, "but more gravely still by reason of the want of candor which appeared to underly the proposition for a reciprocity arrangement with the autonomous government of Cuba" and the disparaging and sarcastic references to the entire reform program which the letter contained. The administration's fears about the limitations of the

[27] Wilson to McCook, Dec. 5, 1897, Wilson MSS, contains McKinley's statement; see Reid to McKinley, March 8, 1898, McKinley MSS.

[28] McCook to Wilson, Feb. 10, 1898, Wilson MSS; Sherman to Woodford, Feb. 23, 1898, Spain, Instructions, NA, RG 59; Wilson to McCook, Feb. 11, 1898, Letterbook, Wilson MSS. It is noteworthy that there is no significant material on the incident in *Correspondencia diplomática de la delegación cubana en Nueva York durante la guerra de independencia de 1895 a 1898* (Publicaciones del Archivo Nacional de Cuba; 5 vols., Havana, 1943–1946).

reforms were apparently justified, at least they were justified if de Lôme was representative of his nation's statesmen.[29]

Seven days after McCook delivered the de Lôme letter, word flashed from Havana that the night before, the fifteenth, the "Maine" had been shaken by a terrific explosion and then had settled at the bottom of Havana harbor. More than two hundred fifty men had been trapped in the flaming wreckage. Jingo papers and militant congressmen now screamed for war, convinced that the explosion had been caused by an outside, that is, Spanish, source. But war did not come for more than two months. The fact remained that neither the yellow journals nor the United States Senate controlled American foreign policy. That control rested in the hands of McKinley and Day, and it would be another five weeks before they would decide to use American military force to stop the bloodshed in Cuba.

During the next four weeks McKinley carefully prepared his course of action. He would demand an indemnity from Spain if the Navy Department's investigation concluded that the explosion had occurred outside the "Maine." Meanwhile, with the unlikely assistance of such interventionists as Henry Cabot Lodge, the President prevented the Senate from taking precipitate action. He considered, then rejected, a proposal to send a special mission to Spain. The President was serious when he told Senator Charles W. Fairbanks of Indiana, "I don't propose to be swept off my feet by the catastrophe." [30]

McKinley's thinking was perhaps closely approximated by the views of Woodford. At the close of February the American Minister continued to hope that something might be salvaged from autonomy, although he was no doubt more optimistic on this score than McKinley or Day. But Woodford had become

[29] Sherman to Woodford, Feb. 23, 1898, Spain, Instructions, NA, RG 59.
[30] Reid to McKinley, March 14, 1898, McKinley MSS; Olcott, *McKinley*, II, 12–13; Garraty, *Lodge*, 188.

concerned about a remark which Moret had dropped in a conversation on March 1. The Spanish Minister had given notice that the Sagasta government would convene the new Cortes and the Cuban Parliament on April 25 instead of earlier, as Sagasta had previously planned. Moret explained that the Cuban Autonomist party needed more time. Woodford noted in his despatch to McKinley that perhaps Spain was setting a trap, for the rainy season would begin before the twenty-fifth, and this would make operations during the summer impossible. Spain consequently must "so far crush the rebellion by the 1st of May" as to satisfy "the common sense of our people" in the United States. "If the United States must," Woodford continued, "for the protection of the health of our coast next summer and for the protection of our great financial interests, practically intervene about the 1st of April," is the American position "sufficiently clear and definite as to justify effective action" before the rainy season begins? [31]

That the President's thinking was moving along the same lines was indicated by several administration moves during the first week of March. McKinley called Joe Cannon, chairman of the House Committee on Appropriations, to the White House on Sunday night, March 6. Cannon later recalled the President's saying: "I must have money to get ready for war. I am doing everything possible to prevent war but it must come, and we are not prepared for war. Who knows where this war will lead us; it may be more than war with Spain." Cannon agreed to propose a $50,000,000 emergency military appropriation in Congress. The measure went through more easily than expected. McKinley had tightened his control of Congress, but the effects of the measure did not stop there. Woodford reported that the appropriation "has not excited the Spaniards—it has simply stunned them. To appropriate fifty millions out of money in the treasury, without

[31] Woodford to McKinley, March 2, 1898, Spain, Despatches, NA, RG 59.

borrowing a cent, demonstrates wealth and power. Even Spain can see this." [32]

But Woodford's comment was misleading in the light of another repercussion of the appropriation measure. Secretary of the Navy Long began hurriedly building an American military power by buying vessels abroad, and he ordered the battleship "Oregon" to leave her dock at Bremerton, Washington, to sail around the tip of South America, and to move into the Caribbean as soon as possible. If the administration hoped that these actions would deter further warlike moves by the Spanish, it was badly mistaken. Woodford reported on the same day the commander of the "Oregon" received his orders, March 12, that Spain was intensifying its preparations to send a fleet of torpedo boats to bolster naval units in Cuban waters. This news, combined with Spain's refusal to rescind its announcement that the Cortes would not bother meeting to discuss the worsening situation until April 25, indicated that the intensified American preparations for war had not intimidated Spain.[33]

Finally, there was another result of the appropriation measure which was of special importance. The congressional action had killed all lingering hopes that the autonomist forces in Cuba might resolve the situation. The rebels had now received too much encouragement to settle for any compromise.[34]

Sherman and Day vividly described the situation in messages to Woodford on March 1 and 3. The key to Sherman's long instruction of the first was the acid comment, "So far as my opportunities

---

[32] L. White Busbey, *Uncle Joe Cannon: The Story of a Pioneer American* (New York, 1927), 187. See also the remarks on McKinley's leadership in New York *Tribune*, March 8, 1898, 1:6; Woodford to McKinley, March 9, 1898, Spain, Despatches, NA, RG 59.

[33] Long to "Oregon" and to "Brooklyn," March 7, 1898, Ciphers Sent, 1888–1898, NA, RG 45; Day to Woodford, March 12, 1898, Spain, Instructions, NA, RG 59.

[34] See Woodford to McKinley, March 9, 1898, Spain, Despatches, NA, RG 59; for the Junta's reaction to the appropriation (that the action indicated either war or preparation for war) see *Correspondencia diplomática*, V, 124–126.

of observation and knowledge go I am as yet unable to discern the favorable advances which were gladly anticipated from [the Sagasta reforms]." The Secretary of State noted that two months had elapsed since the reforms had been instituted; Sherman evidently believed that period had given the reforms ample time to demonstrate their effectiveness. He then made four observations. First, he admitted that Spanish troops had committed "fewer regrettable excesses," but Sherman then promptly turned this on the debit side of the Spanish ledger: "Indeed, their operations have not appeared, during the past three months, to have been as energetic as before." Second, Sherman observed that the grant of autonomy was "circumscribed in its operations" and hamstrung by a lack of finances. Third, autonomy had been opposed not only by insurgents but by the "Spanish element" in Cuba as well. "Fourthly, the condition of the island in its financial and productive aspects" had worsened.

This message marked a toughening of American policy. Before March 1 the United States had emphasized the necessity of reforms which would lead to autonomy. It had condemned harsh military action and demanded social and political remedies. Now Sherman decided "that autonomy is of itself, and unaided by military success, capable of winning over the insurgent element remains a doubtful proposition." The State Department had lost faith in the reform program, refused to allow the continuance of harsh military measures (many of which the rebels used with effectiveness), and asked Spain to pacify the island immediately by fighting guerrilla bands with orthodox military methods. A month later, the United States would add the demand of an immediate armistice. In the face of these American demands, the wonder is not that war finally began in mid-April, but that hostilities did not begin at least six weeks earlier.[35]

[35] Sherman to Woodford, March 1, 1898, and Day to Woodford, March 3, 1898, Spain, Instructions, NA, RG 59; also Ernest R. May, *Imperial Democracy: The Emergence of America as a Great Power* (New York, 1961), 149.

The Far East, 1897 to March, 1898

The growing involvement of the United States in the Cuban struggle was matched, although in a less intensive manner, by American concern with events in the Far East. The United States did not suddenly realize the value of the far Pacific area after Dewey's victory at Manila on May 1. Until the de Lôme letter incident and the "Maine" sinking in mid-February, events in Cuba shared prime newspaper space with stories relating Russian and German threats to the open door in China and Manchuria. This interest in the Far East trailed off only in a relative fashion after March 1.

The McKinley administration continued Olney's attempts to open new areas of China for American merchants and missionaries. An important result of this policy was the first movement of American missionaries into the rich Hunan province in 1897. In a long report to Washington, Denby reiterated his belief that the trader would follow the missionary into Hunan, listed the limitless economic possibilities of the province, but strangely neglected the religious significance of the event. After State Department prodding, Hangchow was also opened to American merchants for the first time.[36]

Such State Department action, along with the opening of new concession and trading areas by the major European powers, encouraged American concessionaires and exporters to pay close attention to the Far Eastern scene. Two of the more prominent and colorful promoters were Wharton Barker and James Harrison Wilson. Barker, a Philadelphia banker and publisher, had been an agent of the House of Baring until the 1890 crash. He had worked closely with the Russians since 1878, when he had been knighted by Alexander II, and he never tired of quoting Tocqueville's phrase regarding "the two great nations in the world which seem to tend toward the same end." With Russian cooperation he had nearly succeeded in selling the Chinese a $20,000,000 tele-

[36] McCormick, " 'Fair Field and No Favor,' " 130–132.

graph, telephone, and banking project in 1887. Ten years later Barker was passionately advocating bimetallism and working with Chinese and Russian agents to obtain railroad concessions in the Orient.[37]

Wilson agreed with Barker that China was a "Russian protectorate." With assistance from John J. McCook and Jacob Schiff of Kuhn, Loeb, and Company, Wilson attempted to work through St. Petersburg to obtain rail and mining rights in Manchuria and China. But Wilson concerned himself more with the fundamentals of the situation than did Barker. Wilson, McCook, Schiff, Theodore Search of the N.A.M., Theodore Roosevelt, and Lodge, among others, visited the White House to urge McKinley to place McCook in the cabinet, Roosevelt in the Navy Department, Wilson in St. Petersburg as American Minister, and to appoint William W. Rockhill, an expert on Asiatic affairs and an intimate of Wilson's schemes, as Minister to China. Only Roosevelt received the desired position; the others fell before the President's distrust of McCook's and Wilson's Cuban schemes and McKinley's desire for an even geographical distribution of patronage. The President's decision marked the last opportunity for pro-Russian sentiment to appear in policy-making circles.[38]

Other promoters enjoyed more success than did Barker or Wilson. The American China Development Company had lost a rich railroad concession to a Belgian group in 1896, but within four years after its founding in 1895, the American company boasted a $1,000,000 war chest and listed Rockefeller representatives, Schiff, E. H. Harriman, the American Sugar Refineries

[37] Memorandum, Box 7, and Li Wing to Barker, Feb. 25, 28, March 3, 4, 16, 23, 1898, in Wharton Barker papers, Library of Congress, Washington, D.C.

[38] Wilson to McCook, Oct. 28 and 6, 1896, Wilson to McKinley, Feb. 22, 1897, Wilson to John Hay, Nov. 14, 1896, Wilson to McCook, May 26, 1897, Wilson to Roosevelt, Aug. 5, 1897, Wilson to McCook, Aug. 10, 1897, Letterbooks, Wilson MSS; Roosevelt to D. C. Gilman, June 17, 1897, and Roosevelt to Othniel C. March, June 17, 1897, Letterbooks, Roosevelt MSS.

Company, Carnegie Steel Company, and several American railway companies as active members. On April 14, 1898, it received its first concession, the right to build a railway between Hankow and Canton.[39]

American exporters had a far larger stake in oriental markets than did the concession hunters. The exporters also had more to fear from European threats to the open door. Cotton goods industries had especially become dependent on Asian consumers; exporting $1,741,942 worth of goods to China in 1895, by 1897 they had increased their exports to $7,489,141. One Alabama plant, built with half a million dollars of Boston capital, sold its entire product to China in 1897. The oriental consumer of cotton goods became especially important, when, as one commercial journal noted, over-all business failures increased in early 1897, and "the whole increase in failures [occurred] in the cotton industry." Other products, especially kerosene, wheat flour, and iron and steel, were increasingly dependent on Asian markets. The New York *Commercial Advertiser* noted in January, 1898, that since "civilized markets are developed," it has become "supremely important that we should retain the free entry into the Chinese market which we enjoy to-day. . . . We cannot submit to being excluded from trade in that territory."[40]

But American trade faced just such a threat. On November 18, 1897, Germany seized the key port of Kiaochow on the Shantung Peninsula. The seizure menaced the large American exports flowing into Manchuria and North China through Shantung and threatened to set off a series of European attempts to carve China into exclusive spheres of interest. Denby became apoplectic, insisting in cables to the State Department that "partition would tend to destroy our markets," and hinting that outright American intervention would be the only remedy. Sherman,

---

[39] Charles S. Campbell, Jr., *Special Business Interests and the Open Door Policy* (New Haven, 1951), 21–22.

[40] *Ibid.*, 19–24; Chattanooga *Tradesman*, Dec. 15, 1897, 59; *Public Opinion*, May 13, 1897, 602: *Commercial Advertiser*, Jan. 26, 1898, 6:5.

at first unconcerned about the turn of events, assured Denby and troubled businessmen that the German Ambassador had guaranteed free and equal access through Kiaochow to all nations.[41]

Businessmen who had cherished the hope of a great Asian market had long feared that European powers might partition the area. Sherman's assurances now did little to quiet these fears. James Harrison Wilson sadly reported to friends that he had spoken with Charles Denby, Jr., who had "expressed the greatest discouragement as to the future of China and as to the possibility of exploiting American business in that part of the world." [42]

Ambitious Americans such as Wilson, however, refused to give up the battle. Throughout the first three months of 1898 they emphasized that American surplus goods were becoming increasingly dependent on Asian markets and then urged that, if necessary, the United States should cooperate with England in order to counterbalance the German and Russian threat to the open door.

The Kiaochow incident and Sherman's mild reaction to that event led commercial journals and business groups to explain forcefully and fully to both the State Department and the public the dangers which American interests faced in the Far East. Some journals compared the situation with that in Madagascar three years before. Americans had held large interests on that island until France had moved in and abolished equal trading rights with effective political discriminations. As the Committee on American Interests in China informed the State Department, "we certainly do not wish to have our experience of exclusion from Madagascar practised in a greatly enlarged scale in the case of China." [43]

The committee which authored this petition had been organ-

[41] Dugdale, *German Documents*, III, 4; Denby to Sherman, Jan. 31, 1898, China, Despatches, and Day to Adee in note appended to Hitchcock to Sherman, Jan. 19, 1898, Russia, Despatches, NA, RG 59; McCormick, "'Fair Field and No Favor,'" 141–143.

[42] Wilson to Rethick, Dec. 23, 1897, Letterbooks, Wilson MSS.

[43] Boston *Herald*, Feb. 12, 1898, 6:3.

ized on January 6, 1898, when Clarence Cary and John Foord of the *Journal of Commerce* met with representatives of the Standard Oil Company, Frazer and Company (a large American trading house in China), Deering, Milliken and Company (cotton exporters), and the Bethlehem Iron Company. The meeting was a direct response to the Kiaochow incident. It was also a manifestation of the increasing fear that the McKinley administration did not comprehend the meaning of events in China. "It is felt," the *Journal of Commerce* explained, "that we stand at the dividing of the ways between gaining or losing the greatest market which awaits exploitation." The State Department simply was not moving rapidly enough to suit the more ambitious members of the American business community.[44]

These businessmen made their voices heard in several ways. On February 2 the New York City Chamber of Commerce sent a petition to the State Department demanding immediate action in China. A second petition from this group explained in detail the extent of American trade and investment in China. One incident in the Chamber's meeting strikingly revealed the realignment of allies and enemies. A member arose and asked that the Chamber move slowly. After all, he reminded his fellows, such action as the petitions demanded goes "against our old friends, Russia, Germany and France." England, on the other hand, had been the "persistent and vigilant foe of this country. She tried to enslave us in '76." At this point the speaker was interrupted by an aroused membership, and the chair promptly ruled his remarks out of order. Chambers of Commerce in Boston and San Francisco and the Philadelphia Board of Trade followed the example of the New York petitions. The China and Japan Trading Company, large cotton exporters, sent a note demanding "immediate action" to the Secretary of the Interior, Cornelius N. Bliss, a partner in Bliss, Fabyan and Company, which also exported cotton to China. John Foord later declared that shortly after these

[44] Campbell, *Special Business Interests*, 30–31; *Journal of Commerce*, Dec. 31, 1897, 1:1.

petitions were sent "the whole subject of American interests in the Far East began to assume a position of national prominence." [45]

Commercial journals printed numerous articles and editorials asking for a stronger American stand in Asia, cooperation with England, and the containment of Russia and Germany. In early January the New York *Commercial Advertiser* had been unable to see any threat of discriminations, but at the end of that month the journal wrote an editorial which included all the themes— the threat of the surplus, pro-British views, and the desire for the open door:

The time is not far distant when probably all of the principal industries of the Republic will be either compelled or in a position . . . to seek outlets for their products abroad, and Great Britain, by her resolute stand for free and equal opportunity in the markets of the Orient, is paving the way for their easy and rapid conquest by the United States.

The Philadelphia *Manufacturer* urged a triple alliance of the United States, England, and Japan to offset Germany and Russia. The Cincinnati *Commercial Tribune* noted that, since the British were fighting American battles in China, the United States should assist England, "not because we love that nation for we do not, but because our material and selfish interests coincide with hers." As could be expected, John Foord's *Journal of Commerce* led all other periodicals in pointing to the multifold dangers which threatened the open door. This periodical believed that the Russian policy of sealing off territory (which the Russians were forced to do, the *Journal* explained, since they were incapable of competing with the United States on equal terms) "is the greatest danger which our expanding commerce has to fear." [46]

[45] *Journal of Commerce*, Feb. 3, 1898, 1:7; Campbell, *Special Business Interests*, 24–31; New York *Tribune*, Feb. 4, 1898, 2:5.

[46] *Commercial Advertiser*, Jan. 26, 1898, 6:4; Jan. 5, 1898, 6:1; Jan 10, 1898, 6:2; Baltimore *Sun*, Jan. 19, 1898, 4:2; Cincinnati *Commercial*

Pro-British views could also be found in circles close to the administration. In early January, Charles Emory Smith's Philadelphia *Press,* one of the leading administration mouthpieces, had been cool to cooperation with England in Asia. By the last week of that month, however, this journal noted that Germany, France, and Russia had apparently decided on strong colonial policies; the *Press* then warned, "Where the United States and Great Britain are publicly agreed the rest of the world will hesitate to oppose their policy." Cushman Davis, chairman of the Foreign Relations Committee, told a reporter that a coalition with England would be possible since "it is not to be expected that if our commercial interests were threatened abroad that we would sit with folded hands and make no sign." Henry Cabot Lodge told British friends that he would welcome an Anglo-American alliance in Chinese affairs. Ambassador John Hay made his own and Lodge's views, which coincided, known to British officials.[47]

In early February, Joseph Chamberlain, British Colonial Secretary, instigated a formal request that the United States cooperate with England in preserving the open door in Asia. Whitehall had approached Russia with a similar offer the previous month and had been met with a flat refusal. The British gambit might have been a spur-of-the-moment idea, a desperate reaction after the Russian refusal. But Americans could not deny that several of their officials had been encouraging just such an approach throughout January. The State Department, however, could not afford to be so encouraging. Day informed Pauncefote that the United States would have to refuse the offer, but the Assistant Secretary added that the President thoroughly sympathized with the British position in China. The war in Cuba simply made it impossible for the administration to devote such attention to the

Tribune, Jan. 20, 1898, 6:1; Feb. 7, 1898, 6:1; *Journal of Commerce,* Feb. 7, 1898, 6:1–2; Boston *Herald,* Feb. 8, 1898, 6:3; *Public Opinion,* Jan. 6, 1898, 4–6; New York *Tribune,* Jan. 23, 1898, 6:1.

[47] Philadelphia *Press,* Jan. 7, 1898, 6:4; Jan. 23, 1898, 8:4 and 6:2; Campbell, *Anglo-American Understanding,* 15–16, 18; Garraty, *Lodge,* 204–205.

Far East. The British then turned to Germany. The Kaiser, trusting neither British motives nor dependability, refused the advances.[48]

Day's refusal did not mean that the State Department had deserted the Far East. It could hardly have done so in view of the business clamor for action and in view of the rumor, assiduously circulated by the *Journal of Commerce*, that the world money markets were sinking not only because of the Cuban crisis but also because of the dangers in China. The McKinley administration first demonstrated its interest in the Far East when it changed its ministerial appointment for the Chinese post. The appointment of Charles Page Bryan, an inexperienced diplomat (the *Journal of Commerce* always condescendingly referred to him as "the young Mr. Bryan") had aroused little opposition until the Kiaochow incident. But in December, the editors of those commercial journals that had apotheosized the China market attacked the nomination. McKinley, working rapidly, withdrew Bryan's name from the Senate. Senator Frye later recalled that James Harrison Wilson appeared to have the President's approval, then Bryan's backers changed to Edwin Conger, Minister to Brazil, in order to block Wilson. Bryan went to Brazil. Conger, an experienced and older diplomat, was welcomed by the special China interests. The *Journal of Commerce* viewed the appointment as an indication that McKinley had gained "a growing perception . . . of the gravity of the situation in the Far East in respect to its bearing on the future of American trade." Meeting in March with the Committee on American Interests in China, Conger "decidedly impressed" his listeners with the statement that he "regarded commerce and not politics as the best guide in diplomacy." The committee departed "with the idea that the care of American interests in China had been committed to eminently safe and capable hands." [49]

[48] Pauncefote to Salisbury, March 17, 1898, F.O. 5/2361; Dugdale, *German Documents*, III, 21-24.
[49] *Journal of Commerce*, March 14, 1898, 1:1 and 6:3; Jan. 12, 1898,

McKinley also began fortifying American naval power in the Pacific. In mid-December, 1897, the cruiser "Raleigh" moved from the Mediterranean to the Asiatic Squadron, a change which "has excited much comment here," as the New York *World* reported, since it seemed to indicate a stronger American approach to the Far East crisis. But the Navy Department focused its attention on another Pacific area besides the Asian mainland. When the Philippine insurrection erupted in 1896 (with, it seems, much Japanese help and encouragement), the United States displayed more than passing interest in the affair. The commander of the Asiatic Squadron told Secretary Herbert that "the most credible reports of the situation that I have seen are those taken from the American newspapers." The general public was evidently better informed than the commander of the American Asiatic fleet. The Navy Department quickly remedied this lack of information. In late 1896 Lieutenant William W. Kimball, an officer in Naval Intelligence who was a vigorous proponent of Mahan's ideas, formulated a battle plan for offensive warfare against the Philippines. Working through the Naval Attaché in Madrid, the Department also kept close watch on Spanish naval strength in the South Pacific.[50]

Secretary Long, aided and abetted by his overenergetic assistant, Theodore Roosevelt, intensified Herbert's vigil and preparations in the Philippine area. Roosevelt had cooperated with Wilson's pro-Russian schemes earlier in the year, but by August, 1897 (doubtless after long conversations with Brooks Adams and Mahan), the Assistant Secretary concluded that "Russians and Americans, in their individual capacity, have nothing whatever in common"; Russia, in fact, would offer "a very much more serious problem than the Germans" to later generations of Anglo-

1:3; March 7, 1898, 1:3; New York *World*, Dec. 23, 1897, 7:1; Frye to Wilson, March 5 and Jan. 13, 1898, Wilson MSS.
     [50] New York *World*, Dec. 19, 1897, 8:1; Wolff to Salisbury, Jan. 4, 1897, F.O. 72/2033; NcNair to Herbert, Area 10 file, Box 15, Oct.-Dec., 1896, folder, NA, RG 45; Long, *New American Navy*, 168–169.

Saxons. Roosevelt watched Far Eastern events closely. He told the War College in June, 1897: "The enemies we may have to face will come from Asia. . . . Our interests are as great in the Pacific as in the Atlantic." Roosevelt also communicated such thoughts, no doubt with characteristic vigor, to President McKinley when the two men enjoyed long rides through Washington parks on warm autumn afternoons. The President and the Assistant Secretary became close friends in late 1897. In a conversation in 1898 McKinley, as hoary legend relates, could not estimate within a couple thousand miles where those "darn" islands were. He nevertheless could, after his long conversations with Roosevelt, judge their location closely enough to agree to Navy Department orders of December, 1897, which instructed Commodore George Dewey to strike the Philippines should war occur between the United States and Spain.[51]

Papers in the McKinley manuscripts indicate that the White House followed the course of the Philippine insurrection in early 1898. Thus when Roosevelt, taking advantage of Long's absence on the afternoon of February 25, ordered Dewey to prepare for war, it is not strange that McKinley and Long did not bother to countermand the orders. Historians have too long overlooked this crucial aspect of Roosevelt's order-sending spree. Although the President and the Secretary of the Navy rescinded more than half of Roosevelt's other plans, they allowed Dewey to prepare to strike Manila. The Assistant Secretary's actions, moreover, did not result from a sudden inspiration; Roosevelt acted after months of conversations with Mahan, Adams, Lodge, and, be it not forgotten, McKinley.[52]

Two weeks later Long received a letter from a Boston lawyer who urged seizure of the Philippines, noted rumors of "a good

[51] Theodore Roosevelt, "Washington's Forgotten Maxim," *Proceedings of the United States Naval Institute*, XXIII (1897), 447–456; *Letters of Spring-Rice*, I, 231; Leech, *Days of McKinley*, 161–162.
[52] Otis to Adjutant General, Dec. 31, McKinley MSS; Roosevelt to Dewey, Feb. 25, 1898, Ciphers Sent, 1888–1898, NA, RG 45.

understanding" between England and the United States in the Far East, and concluded, "I do not think we can too carefully provide for the great future of those Pacific interests of ours." The administration had already arrived at much the same conclusion. Naval Intelligence maintained a close surveillance on Spanish fleet movements in the Pacific. The American Asiatic Squadron was hurriedly strengthened with the giant "Baltimore" in mid-March. With these events in mind the result of the Battle of Manila Bay can hardly be termed a lucky accident. The threat of war with Spain in Cuba, combined with the dangerous threat to the open door in Asia, had constrained the administration to make thorough preparations for offensive operations in the Pacific.[53]

Hawaii

In the context of this intensified attention on the Far East, McKinley submitted a treaty to annex the Hawaiian Islands in 1897. Congress later passed a joint resolution, but the Hawaiian debate, which raged for a year following the President's request for ratification, offers several insights into the policies which shaped the new empire during the months preceding the war with Spain. First, strong Japanese protests destroyed key assumptions of the Cleveland-Gresham argument against annexation and forced new empire expansionists to change their Hawaiian policies. Second, the annexation treaty nearly passed Congress in the early months of 1898, *before* the war with Spain, because expansionists had begun to emphasize the relationship between formal control of Hawaii and maintenance of the American commercial rights in the Far East.

As early as 1891 McKinley had fought for the retention of Pearl Harbor and had worried about the encroachment of foreign

---

[53] John Davis Long, *Papers of John Davis Long, 1897–1904*, selected and edited by Gardner Weld Allen (Boston, 1939), 69–70; memorandum by Crowninshield for Office of Naval Intelligence, March 10, 1898, Area 10 file, Box 16, NA, RG 45; Long, *New American Navy*, I, 172–173.

powers in Hawaii. Political observers had predicted in 1897 that the new administration would attempt to annex the islands. But when the President submitted the treaty in June, 1897, many of these observers were surprised at the amount of opposition which suddenly appeared. Of twenty newspapers polled by *Public Opinion*, more than half condemned the treaty; most of the opponents raised the old cry of "no colonialism." The American Federation of Labor, little concerned with foreign expansion until now, split on the Hawaiian issue, but for the most part opposed annexation. The railroad brotherhoods and the iron workers saw the islands as a virgin frontier for their trades, but most members of the labor federation feared Hawaii's unskilled labor, contract labor, and especially the large number of Orientals. Senator Stephen M. White of California summarized the opposition arguments in an article published in August, 1897. He stressed that annexation would require a large military establishment, raise new racial problems, and propel the republic to a suicidal colonial policy. White emphasized that Americans already controlled the trade of the islands. Moreover, he insisted, "There is no danger of foreign interference." [54]

But such danger did exist, and this threat severely shook the antiannexationist argument. Germany wanted to protest, but she was forced to drop the project when Great Britain stalled and then refused to cooperate in a joint note. Japan, however, presented a strong protest, probably the strongest protest Japan had ever issued to another power up to that time. Tokyo disclaimed designs on the islands, but warned that the rights of Japanese citizens in Hawaii must be protected. The State Department could not brush off this protest. Japanese accounted for one-quarter of the total Hawaiian population. Tokyo demonstrated

---

[54] Stevens, *American Expansion in Hawaii*, 284–286; *Public Opinion*, June 24, 1897, 771–773; John C. Appel, "American Labor and the Annexation of Hawaii: A Study in Logic and Economic Interest," *Pacific Historical Review*, XXIII (February, 1954), 5; White, "The Proposed Annexation of Hawaii," *Forum*, XXIII (August, 1897), 723–736.

that it meant to protect the rights of these citizens when it dispatched a cruiser to Honolulu in July. Japanese newspapers bitterly attacked the annexationist pact.[55]

The State Department flatly rejected the Japanese protest, but the administration did not let the matter rest at that point. Both Long and Roosevelt were, in Roosevelt's words, "strong" believers "in our taking possession of Hawaii in some shape or other." On July 10 the Navy Department ordered American sailors to prepare to land and take Hawaii by force if the Japanese made threatening moves. Three days later, Long sent the "Oregon," perhaps the strongest ship in the fleet, to Hawaii. The American press, rather unconcerned about Hawaii in early June, suddenly came alive with strong anti-Japanese editorials. The Democratic Baltimore *Sun* summarized many of these editorials in a phrase: "It is Japan that will seize the islands if we do not." Cushman Davis and Roosevelt criticized the Japanese in public statements during late summer. Roosevelt gave the Naval War College a special war problem: "Japan makes demands on Hawaiian Islands. This country intervenes. What force will be necessary to uphold the intervention. . . . Keeping in mind possible complications with another power on the Atlantic Coast [Cuba]." Assistant Secretary of State Day had attempted to placate the Japanese from the beginning of the crisis, however, and the Kiaochow incident in November, which presented a much more immediate threat to her interests, finally forced Japan to accept assurances. These six months had been a hiatus in Japanese-American friendship, but by December, 1897, good relations had been restored.[56]

[55] Dugdale, *German Documents*, II, 483–493; Dun to Sherman, April 12, June 21, 1897, Japan, Despatches, NA; RG 59; Stevens, *Expansion in Hawaii*, 282–284. Dennett, *Americans in Eastern Asia*, 613, remarks about the lack of precedence for the Japanese protest. The best analysis is in William Adam Russ, Jr., *The Hawaiian Republic, 1894–1898 . . .* (Selinsgrove, Pa., 1961), ch. iv.

[56] Roosevelt to Hartwell, June 7, 1897, Letterbooks, Roosevelt MSS;

The Kiaochow incident had also affected American interests in the far Pacific. In early 1898 a rash of articles and editorials appeared linking the Hawaiian and Chinese problems. The islands, as James Harrison Wilson wrote in the *North American Review*, would serve as a "naval station and a halfway house" to the "commerce of the Pacific islands and of the countries beyond." The Philadelphia *Press*, a journal close to the administration, agreed with Wilson: the annexation question "presents the broad issue of entering into the world's competition for enlarged commerce, or of renouncing all serious effort for commercial expansion." The Louisville *Commercial* tied the opportunity in Hawaii with markets in the Far East, as did the Cincinnati *Commercial Tribune* and the Pittsburgh *Press*. Senator Frye announced that annexation should be quickly accomplished so "the whole world will accept that as the first step in the direction of exercising our moral influence to preserve the integrity of China." The New York *Tribune* argued, "Recent events in China have put a new face" on the annexation issue. A day later this journal noted that the United States "by nature and by situation [is] fitted to enjoy the major share of all Pacific commerce," but then warned that "Hawaii is the commercial key to the whole Pacific." [57]

Important spokesmen for the business community agreed with these assessments. *Bradstreet's*, the New York *Commercial*, and the San Francisco Chamber of Commerce wanted annexation of

---

Sherman to Dun, June 25, 1897, Japan, Instructions, NA, RG 59; Long to "Oregon," July 13, 1897, Confidential Correspondence, NA, RG 45; *Public Opinion*, July 1, 1897, 6; Garraty, *Lodge*, 199; Roosevelt to Goodrich, May 28, 1897, Letterbooks, Roosevelt MSS.

[57] Wilson, "America's Interests in China," *North American Review*, CLXVI (February, 1898), 128–141; Philadelphia *Press*, Jan. 8, 1898, 6:2; Feb. 7, 1898, 6:2; Louisville *Commercial*, Jan. 3, 1898, 4:2; Cincinnati *Commercial Tribune*, Nov. 30, 1897, 6:2; Pittsburgh *Press*, Jan. 10, 1898, 1:1; New York *Tribune*, Jan. 6, 1898, 7:5; Jan. 7, 1898, 6:2; Campbell, *Special Business Interests*, 17.

the islands, and the *Journal of Commerce* became a strong advocate after the turmoil began in China in late 1897. In a speech frequently punctuated by applause, Senator Frye told the National Association of Manufacturers' annual convention on January 28, 1898, that, although the home market was a great one, "four years ago we had a new teacher," the depression, which taught Americans to undertake "a determined advance and march upon the foreign market." "The first market you are trying to reach," Frye continued, "is the market of the Orient. You don't propose to leave that to be closed against you." In this context the Nicaragua canal project and the annexation of Hawaii were crucial policy steps. Drawing a horrible picture of what would result if Great Britain controlled Hawaii, Frye cried to his audience, "Now, will you help us in the Senate? [Cries of 'Yes, yes: we will!'] We only lack two or three votes, and if you will help us we will get them." [58]

McKinley had preceded Frye on the rostrum and had seen the response to the Maine Senator's enthusiasm for annexation, but the President needed no urging on the issue. While conversing with senators earlier in January about matters of patronage, McKinley had used the opportunity to sound them out on their position on Hawaii. One White House reporter who knew much about these conversations commented: "The Administration is beginning to view the growing power of Japan with keen interest. . . . [Annexation] would also, [the President] thinks, do wonders in increasing the trade of the United States with the east." Another friend quoted the President as saying: "We need Hawaii just as much and a good deal more than we did California. It is Manifest Destiny." When the beet sugar lobby appeared to be making headway against the treaty, the Secretary of Agriculture, James Wilson, who had previously opposed annexation, sent a thick pile of papers to the Senate, proving with statistics that Hawaii could not injure the American beet sugar interests.

[58] The best survey is in Pratt, *Expansionists of 1898*, 254–263; the Frye speech, and the reaction, is in New York *Tribune*, Jan. 28, 1898, 2:2–4.

The administration was obviously intent on obtaining annexation.[59]

The treaty had been signed with Hawaiian representatives on June 17, 1897, but debate in the Senate did not begin until mid-January, 1898. Perhaps the primary theme of the debates appeared in the opening argument over whether the bill should be considered in executive session or not. The annexationists urged that a closed session was necessary, since many remarks would have to be made about other foreign powers now involved in China, remarks which would not win friends for the United States if they appeared in the *Congressional Record*. The annexationists carried their point. Initiating the debate in executive session, Cushman Davis, chairman of the Foreign Relations Committee, emphasized two aspects of the issue, both related to the Orient. First, he referred to the commercial utility of the islands. Second, he mentioned Hawaii's "military importance," which had been made manifest by "the opening of a new condition of affairs in the Far East." The islands would be of special strategic importance also in safeguarding "that great gateway of commerce," the proposed Isthmian canal.[60]

Other senators amplified these themes to such an extent that George F. Hoar became worried. The Massachusetts Senator wanted Hawaii, but he did not want this action to initiate a widespread American colonial policy in the western Pacific. He recalled in his memoirs that so many of his colleagues were tying Hawaii in with the Far Eastern situation that he became concerned that the Hawaiian question "could not be separated, at least in debate, from the question of entering upon a career of conquest in the Far East." Hoar went to McKinley for assurances. The President told him that the administration had no ideas about getting "our share of China," and then McKinley emphasized the

[59] Washington *Evening Star*, Jan. 12, 1898, 4:2; Jan. 19, 1898, 14:1; Russ, *The Hawaiian Republic*, 240.

[60] New York *Tribune*, Jan. 11, 1898, 1:1; Jan. 13, 1898, 4:4; Feb. 2, 1898, 1:1; Washington *Evening Star*, Jan. 13, 1898, 14:1.

Japanese danger. The Chief Executive no doubt was talking about territorial, not commercial, shares. Hoar went away satisfied and provided influential support for the treaty, but a year later he exhibited more than a little bitterness when McKinley forced him to take a stand on the annexation of the Philippines.[61]

Many other points of the Hawaiian discussion, both inside and outside of Congress, presaged the Philippine debate of 1899. Few of the antiannexationists spoke about commercial benefits; they tended instead to emphasize the constitutional and racial arguments. When they did mention commercial advantages, they believed that control of Pearl Harbor and the present trading arrangements would suffice to keep the trade in American hands. The annexationists polished off that argument by noting that Pearl Harbor was useless against an enemy unless the United States controlled the hinterland of the naval base as well. As for the trading arrangements, any foreign power which gained influence over the island government could abrogate the commercial treaties at will. When the antiannexationists urged the continuation of a *de facto* protectorate instead of assuming new and unknown political responsibilities, the Washington *Evening Star* printed the rebuttal: "A protectorate is a half and half measure, involving endless complications with the other strong powers which are soon to develop active competition for the possession and control of the Pacific ocean." All these questions would arise in the Philippine discussion, and the answers would be nearly the same.[62]

The Japanese threat and the renewed concern over Far Eastern events nearly provided enough impetus to drive the annexation treaty through the Senate in February and March, 1898. The de Lôme letter and the "Maine" catastrophe focused primary

[61] George F. Hoar, *Autobiography of Seventy Years* (New York, 1903), II, 306–308.
[62] Washington *Evening Star*, Jan. 24, 1898, 9:6. For a similar argument on the weaknesses of protectorates, see the Senate Foreign Relations Committee's majority report on Hawaiian annexation, *Senate Report No. 681*, 55th Cong., 2nd Sess. (serial 3267), 1–119.

attention on Cuba, and the beet sugar lobby exerted much influence on wavering senators, but at one point in late February, Cushman Davis believed that he had all but four of the sixty votes necessary for ratification. The administration forces then suddenly switched tactics. On March 16 the Foreign Relations Committee reported a joint resolution for annexation, which required only a majority of both houses. The resolution appeared to be so certain of quick passage that the next day, the seventeenth, sugar prices broke sharply downward on the New York Stock Exchange. Again, affairs in Cuba prevented debate. But in June the House passed the resolution 290-91 amidst arguments eulogizing the bottomless Asian markets and the necessity of preserving American interests in the far Pacific. On July 6 the Senate passed the measure 42-21 and McKinley made annexation official the following day.[63]

The President proclaimed that the annexing of Hawaii marked the "inevitable consequence" of three-quarters of a century of American interest in those islands. Few if any events in history are inevitable. Certainly the Cleveland administration had proven that the issue of Hawaiian annexation was not blessed with kismet in 1893. But during the next five years American policy makers began to view the matter in a new light. Both Cleveland, during his later years in office, and McKinley accepted the Dole regime as a stable government; the United States forgot about the methods which that government had employed to assume power. Second, Americans lost much of their fear of bringing new races into the Union, especially when a third factor became evident— a Japanese threat posing a danger with which Cleveland and Gresham had not been forced to deal. Finally, and most important, the United States had decided that its interests in the far Pacific could be preserved only if the Hawaiian Islands were politically stabilized and if American naval and commercial holdings were freed from all foreign threats. The Battle of Manila

[63] Stevens, *American Expansion in Hawaii*, 290–293; Washington *Evening Star*, March 17, 1898, 2:7.

Bay raised this last argument into full prominence, but the argument had been popularized many months before Dewey conjured up new visions of the Asian market during the dawn of that May morning.

The American Business Community before the War with Spain, 1897 to February, 1898

During the eighteen months before the United States went to war with Spain, American businessmen began their most intensive search for foreign markets. A Mexico City newspaper marveled, in fact, that "enterprising manufacturers" in the United States "are able, by unremitting effort, to overcome the obstacles raised by the legislators at Washington." To outdistance the McKinley administration in the quest for foreign markets required some hard running. At approximately the same time the Mexico City journal printed its comment, McKinley was declaring that he wanted to climax his career by making the United States supreme in the markets of the world. These two factors—the intensive search by American producers for foreign markets, and the McKinley administration's urgent desire to aid the business community in this venture—are the two clues to understanding the economic aspects of the new empire in 1897 and 1898.[64]

The annual convention of the National Association of Manufacturers in January, 1898, offered a case study of these factors. The N.A.M. had grown from three hundred members in 1895 to over nine hundred, and, as its President boasted, "in capital invested, in value of products and in number of hands employed the membership . . . probably represents a larger aggregate than any other business organization in the world." Certainly no other group of businessmen could have matched the association's drive for foreign markets during the 1895–1898 period. On January 27 the convention welcomed back the man who had been the featured speaker at the first convention, William McKinley.

[64] *Public Opinion*, July 8, 1897, 37; Leech, *Days of McKinley*, 142.

The President recalled those depression days of three years before:

It was a cold day. You had lost everything but your pluck, or thought you had. . . . Your speeches and resolutions at that first convention were directed mainly to the question of . . . how to stop further loss. But your object now, as I gather it, is to go out and possess what you have never had before. You want to extend, not your notes, but your business. I sympathized with your purposes then; I am in full accord with your intentions now.[65]

As McKinley spoke, statisticians were calculating that 1897 had been the greatest year in history for American exports. An enormous amount of agricultural goods had entered foreign markets as a substitute for ruined European crops. But business journals slighted these agrarian exports and emphasized the industrial sector. They could do so with good reason. Industrial exports had soared from $258,000,000 in 1896 to $311,000,000 in 1897. They would rise another $23,000,000 in 1898 and, as in 1897, approximate one-third of all exports. The most notable upsurge had occurred in iron and steel. Pig iron manufacturers, happily driving British producers out of some new area of the globe virtually every month, increased their exports from $471,-803 in 1896 to $2,331,771 in 1897. Steel ingots, bars, rods, and especially rails followed suit. Oil, copper, and cotton manufactures surged ahead. Railroad equipment and electrical goods began to control European markets. Although this export drive was occurring in industries throughout the nation, some of the most rabid economic expansionists could be found in the South. Textile and iron and steel industries in this section threatened to outstrip their older northern competitors in the quest for foreign markets. In the 1889 to 1891 issues of the Chattanooga *Tradesman*, few articles referred to foreign markets. In 1898 a single

[65] *Annual Report of the President of the National Association of Manufacturers, Feb. 1, 1897* (Philadelphia, 1897); McKinley, *Speeches, 1897–1900,* 61. For the opening in Caracas of the N.A.M. warehouse for industrial goods, see Chattanooga *Tradesman*, May 1, 1898, 48.

issue of this journal included articles entitled, "American Iron in Europe," "Our Foreign Trade," "The Development of Southern Seaports," "American Trade in the Baltic," "Expansion of Southern Export Trade." [66]

But the *Tradesman* provided only one example of the interest of commercial periodicals in foreign markets. The topic was so common that business journals soon reached an agreement on the bases and objectives of this commercial expansion. The first assumption was pulled innocently out of Brooks Adams' theories. Businessmen had replaced soldiers and priests as the dominant forces in the world; "the world belongs to the producers and distributers." The "spirit of trade" and "not religious feeling . . . is the ruling force of national and social action." "The chief object of domestic government is to encourage production and facilitate exchange. . . . The chief object of diplomacy is to extend profitable markets for home industry." [67]

If commercial expansion was the dominant fact in the world of the 1890's, then, as *Commercial America* commented, in this "international strife of today that simmers below the surface," the United States must take "a pronounced pre-eminence because of her vast supremacy as a manufacturer among nations." Centuries of world history had been a mere preparation for this American supremacy. "All former centuries had outlets for discontent," the New York *Commercial Advertiser*, explained. Now all these frontiers had been "exhausted" and the "safety valve" for "every discontented and restless fellow" had closed. This point had been rammed into the American consciousness by the depression of the 1890's. The *Journal of Commerce* and the Boston *Herald* (the spokesman for the Boston Chamber of Com-

[66] *Ibid.*, Jan. 1, 1898; Bullock, Williams, Tuckner, "Balance of Trade," 228–229; *Journal of Commerce*, Dec. 14, 1897, 6:4; Oct. 8, 1897, 1:1. For the growing power of American finance capital in international centers, see White to Sherman, Jan. 21, 1898, Great Britain, Despatches, NA, RG 59.

[67] *Journal of Commerce*, Nov. 12, 1897, 4:2; *Commercial Advertiser*, Jan. 27, 1898, 6:2.

merce) agreed with the President of the N.A.M. The depression, insisted Theodore Search, had been a "valuable experience" in teaching Americans the value of foreign markets.[68]

But fate could not receive all the credit. American producers had prepared for their conquest of world markets, according to the New York *Commercial Advertiser,* by learning to produce goods so cheaply "that we can undersell Europe and still enjoy a profit." Labor-saving machines developed by the United States had doomed British exporters, as one American manufacturer of machinery explained happily to the London *Times.* With growing agreement on this point, fewer cries arose for a subsidized merchant marine. "Cheap transportation" would always be a "dominating factor," noted one commercial journal, but of much more significance would be technological advances and proximity of raw materials to mills. "This is our new status; this is our manifest destiny," proclaimed the *Journal of Commerce,* "and it means a cheapness that will open to us the markets of the world." [69]

Echoing the arguments of Grover Cleveland and William Wilson in 1894, business spokesmen prophesied that expanded foreign trade would be the balm for both international and domestic ills. But in 1897 domestic problems were still uppermost. The shock waves of the depression were still rattling through American society in the form of low prices and labor discontent. In September, 1897, one of the worst strikes of the decade ended with twenty-one Hazleton, Pennsylvania, coal miners gunned down by a sheriff's posse. Throughout the summer McKinley had issued warnings that the economy still had to make a long upward

[68] *Commercial America* quoted in Boston *Herald,* Feb. 25, 1898, 5:3; *Commercial Advertiser,* Feb. 27, 1898, 6:1–2; Chattanooga *Tradesman,* Jan. 1, 1898, 99; *Journal of Commerce,* Sept. 22, 1897, 4:2; Dec. 11, 1897, 6:2.

[69] *Commercial Advertiser,* Jan. 13, 1898, 6:1; Chattanooga *Tradesman,* Oct. 15, 1897, 78; Boston *Herald,* Feb. 27, 1898, 12:5; N.A.M. circular, "Foreign Trade of Argentine, Uruguay and Brazil," [n.d.], vi–vii; *Journal of Commerce,* Feb. 15, 1898, 6:1–2; Nov. 24, 1897, 6:2.

climb before prosperous conditions returned. But the tremendous wheat exports in late 1896 and 1897 had quieted the Populist complaints in the West and South, and when industrial employment began to rise in late 1897, observers quickly gave the enlarged foreign markets much of the credit. "Most significant of all the favorable conditions," the Louisville *Commercial* declared on the last day of 1897, is that "the United States is to be the supply depot for increasing territory on both continents. . . . There is no room in America for the pessimist at the beginning of 1898." [70]

Thus the business community shaped its outlook at the close of 1897. The destinies of commerce swayed the destinies of the world. The closing of the frontier, cheap depression prices, and increased use of laborsaving machinery had given American businessmen the golden opportunity to control this commerce. With this control, markets could be found for the industrial and agricultural surpluses. The resulting impetus to employment would end labor discontent and restore prosperous conditions.

The control of foreign markets provided the key link in the philosophy. The export tables proved that American producers were most ambitious to conquer these markets. Other incidents pointed to the same conclusion. McKinley called a special session of Congress to consider the tariff in 1897. Nelson Dingley of Maine and Albert J. Hopkins of Illinois had been holding hearings throughout 1896 in preparation for the next tariff bill. When Hopkins held a special hearing for business opinion on a possible reciprocity clause, the session turned into a prolonged chant on the benefits of foreign trade. The National Board of Trade, New York Board of Trade and Transportation, New York State Chamber of Commerce, and Pittsburgh Chamber of Commerce

[70] Higham, *Strangers in the Land*, 89–90; Curtis to Charles W. Dabney, Jr., W. E. Curtis papers, Library of Congress, Washington, D.C.; Gage to Robert Benson, Nov. 2, 1897, Gage MSS; Louisville *Commercial*, Dec. 31, 1897, 4:1.

first appeared before the committee to proclaim: "At no time in the history of our country has a commercial question of equal importance presented itself. . . . The necessity of finding new markets is an imperative one." [71]

These groups were followed by particular business interests. The Illinois Steel Company, which had discounted the need for foreign markets in 1894, now declared that increased foreign trade through reciprocity was absolutely necessary if the company was to maintain full employment. The Baldwin Locomotive Works reported that if the entire nation was prosperous all locomotives made in the country could find markets at home. "Such a condition, however, never has existed for more than a year or two at a time. Only once in the last twenty-five years, viz., about fifteen years ago, have all the locomotive builders been fully employed." The Farquhar Farm Implement Company and Moline Plow Company emphasized that the key to full employment and high wages was the exporting of "half of our product." The American milling industry, still staggering under the impact of the repeal of the reciprocity provision in 1894, noted that most of the 18,470 mills in the United States were either idle or running half time. This industry insisted: "We do not believe that over 50 percent of the wheat produced in this country can be absorbed in our domestic markets." J. C. Ayer Company, speaking for some drug, medicine, and chemical firms, commented, "Our observation leads us to believe that were it not for the outlet given by exportation to foreign countries the competition for the United States market would be disastrously felt by manufacturers." A leading manufacturer of freight and street-railway cars asked for "a dumping ground for the excess of our manufacture beyond our needs." Representatives from the wire and steel industry, buggy companies, the American Paper Makers' Association, the National Cash Register Company, and the National

[71] *House Report No. 2263*, 54th Cong., 1st Sess. (serial 3466), 312, 147–148, 176, 178.

Live-Stock Exchange repeated these statements. The one group which denied the benefits of reciprocity and expanded foreign trade was the Board of Trade of Tupelo, Mississippi.[72]

The tariff debates of the next spring revealed that a striking change had occurred since the days of James G. Blaine. Now the businessman blazed trails to new foreign markets; the politician dragged his feet. Although the Republicans had written a strong reciprocity plank in the 1896 platform, although McKinley had emphasized reciprocity at every opportunity, and although Dingley and Hopkins stressed the necessity of increased foreign trade in their introductory statements to the special session, the reciprocity amendments of 1897 were a weakened version of the 1890 clause. Sugar and hides—the key to the success of the 1890 provision—went off the free list in order to placate western, prosilver interests and to bring more revenue into the Treasury. Coffee, tea, tonka beans, and vanilla beans now comprised the free items. No agreements could be made with Latin-American countries on the basis of these offerings. A second clause was aimed at western Europe. The United States offered to set lower rates on argols, tartar, wine, brandies, champagne, paintings, and statuary in order to open France, Germany, Italy, and Spain to American exports. A third type of reciprocity most excited trade expansionists. The bill authorized the President to conclude treaties with any nation for general reductions on any duty up to 20 per cent. But there was a joker; the entire Congress had to approve such pacts. No treaties of this sort became law.[73]

Disappointed in their hopes for an effective reciprocity treaty, the business community was similarly disappointed when it began a drive for consular reform in 1897. Cleveland had taken a step forward when he had issued an executive order in 1895 which provided that consular candidates would be required to take ex-

---

[72] *Ibid.*, 20, 265–267, 384–385, 382–383, 428–429, 430–431, 27–28, 442, 471–472, 20, 474–478, 180–181, 488–490, 162, 52.

[73] *Congressional Record*, 55th Cong., 1st Sess., 133–136; Laughlin and Willis, *Reciprocity*, 278–281; Taussig, *Tariff History*, 332–333, 352–354.

aminations. But in spite of an intensive drive by leading business spokesmen, including the New York Board of Trade (Oscar Straus was particularly active here), the New York *Journal of Commerce*, the Baltimore *Journal of Commerce* (which noted that "the merchants and manufacturers of the country are pleading for a reorganization of the consular service"), the National Business Men's League, the N.A.M., and numerous chambers of commerce, the federal government refused to move. New York *Business* noted the reason for this upsurge of business interest: competition abroad "is continually increasing" and consular reform must be obtained "if the United States is to extend its commerce so as to finally hold the commercial supremacy of the world." [74]

Even without governmental assistance the American businessman was conquering world markets. Search boasted in February, 1898, that the $1,032,998,880 export trade of fiscal 1897 had been "without an equal in the annals" of the country. No one realized the significance of these figures any more than the European businessmen and statesmen who watched the lengthening shadow which the American entrepreneur was throwing over world markets. European journals and politicians had seethed over this competition throughout the 1890's, but the combination of the Dingley tariff, which excluded many European goods, and the continuing success of cheap American products in international trade finally caused an anti-American explosion in late 1897. [75]

On November 20, 1897, Count Agenor Goluchowski, Minister

[74] *Public Opinion*, July 15, 1897, 91; Nov. 18, 1897, 666–667; William Barnes and John Heath Morgan, *The Foreign Service of the United States: Origins, Development, and Functions* (Washington, 1961), 149–150; *Journal of Commerce*, Jan. 26, 1898, 8:2; *Commercial Advertiser*, Jan. 27, 1898, 6:3.

[75] Quotation of *Iron Trades Review* of London in *Journal of Commerce*, Oct. 7, 1897, 4:4; Vagts, *Deutschland und die Vereinigten Staaten*, 346; Sherman to Tower, Dec. 14, 1897, Austria, Instructions, NA, RG 59.

of Foreign Affairs of the Austro-Hungarian Empire, declared in a formal address that Europe was engaged in a life-and-death commercial struggle with "countries beyond the seas." He urged all European nations to "fight shoulder to shoulder against this common danger" and to "go into this contest armed with every weapon of defense that their resources can afford." The State Department interpreted this speech as more than a declaration of commercial war. In the summer of 1896 Olney had believed that Goluchowski had inspired Spain's attempts to line up a common European front against the United States. Perhaps Goluchowski was now making another such attempt. The *Journal of Commerce* interpreted the Minister's speech as another indication of the growing Russian menace. Austria, the *Journal* premised, was only "third-rate" commercially; thus Goluchowski must be acting as front man for the grasping Czar. But although Americans worried about the political meaning of Goluchowski's speech, few were concerned about the throwing down of the gauntlet if this meant commercial warfare. As the Cincinnati *Commercial Tribune* commented in a direct reply to Goluchowski, "A power higher than that of thrones and ministries has decreed that Europe shall play second fiddle to Uncle Sam in the commerce of the world, and you fight against fate when you try to prevent it." [76]

As the United States entered the new year of 1898, new syndicates and lobbying groups were organizing to advance American economic interests in the Orient. The Bureau of American Republics was having difficulty in meeting the mounting demand from businessmen who sought information and aid in finding new Latin-American markets. In March, 1898, the New York *Commercial Advertiser* could justifiably brag of the existence of "a new Monroe doctrine, not of political principles, but of com-

[76] Tower to Sherman, Nov. 24, 1897, Austria, Despatches, and Taylor to Olney, Aug. 13, 1896, Spain, Despatches, NA, RG 59; *Journal of Commerce*, Nov. 30, 1897, 6:1–2; Cincinnati *Commercial Tribune*, Nov. 24, 1897, 6:1.

mercial policy. . . . Instead of laying down dogmas, it figures up profits." [77] The Chattanooga *Tradesman* lost all restraint in proclaiming, "The Baltic trade properly belongs to the Americans, especially to those in the South." [78] In summary, the American business community would not suddenly discover the advantage of and need for foreign markets during and after the Spanish-American War. Indeed, the American businessman's quest for these markets was one of the most striking characteristics of the national scene in the months immediately preceding the war with Spain. The results of this war provided these businessmen with new opportunities for further economic expansion. But the war did not provide the impetus for this expansion. The impetus had been provided by the impact of the industrial revolution, especially the depression that followed the panic of 1893.

The Decision for War

The long-range importance of the multiplying American interests in the Far East and the expansive tendencies of the business community would only become apparent after the summer of 1898. Throughout the first six months of that year Americans would consider the Cuban revolution as the paramount problem of their foreign policy. Before the turn of the next century, developments in these three areas would blend into a single, concerted, expansionist movement, but in February and March, 1898, the de Lôme letter, the destruction of the "Maine," and the growing preparations for war in both Spain and the United States turned all eyes to the Caribbean theater. Actually, the McKinley administration had not diverted its attention from Cuba since Sherman had sent the somber instructions to Woodford in July, 1897. The promise of Spanish reforms in November and December did little to allay McKinley's apprehension, an apprehension which mounted rapidly after the Havana riots of January 12. In

[77] Joseph P. Smith to McKinley, July 31, 1897, and Smith to Porter, Dec. 1, 1897, McKinley MSS; *Commercial Advertiser*, March 7, 1898, 6:2.
[78] Chattanooga *Tradesman*, Jan. 1, 1898, 102.

the immediate aftermath of these riots, the administration decided to send the "Maine" to Havana harbor. From that time, Spain and the United States marched toward war with the regularity of drum taps.

The President and State Department officials could not, however, devote exclusive attention to the devastated island. At the very time the administration debated the desirability of toughening its demands, Russia and Germany gravely challenged the open-door principles. During the last week of February, Germany refused to allow an Anglo-American syndicate to build a railway from Tientsin to Tsingkiang on the grounds that the track would pass through Shantung, a German sphere of influence. This was certainly not the way the United States interpreted the open door. But even more disheartening events were in the offing.[79]

On March 6 Germany received a formal ninety-nine year lease on the strategic tip of Shantung. France and Japan used the German move as an opportunity to advance their own interests in South China and in Fukien respectively. But affairs at Port Arthur and Talienwan most concerned the State Department. These ports provided the main channel for the mushrooming number of American exports to reach North China and Manchurian markets. On March 8 both cities fell under the control of the Czar. In a cable to Sherman, Denby called the Russian move "tortuous treachery. . . . International intercourse does not contain an episode of greater moral baseness than this." John Hay wrote from England that British officials smelled "an understanding between Russia, France and Germany to exclude, as far as possible, the trade of England and America from the Far East, and to divide and reduce China to a system of tributary provinces." Sherman asked desperately for German and Russian assurances that the open door would be preserved. The Wilhelmstrasse blandly gave such a promise, but the Russians proved extremely reluctant to

[79] White to Sherman, Feb. 23, 1898, Great Britain, Despatches, NA, RG 59.

do so. When the Czar at last complied, the State Department had been rocked by the news that the British, having failed in their search for assistance in maintaining the open door, had entered the scramble for territory by seizing Wei-Hai-Wei. The United States, apparently, was now isolated in the Far East.[80]

Spokesmen for American commercial groups interested in China and Manchuria reacted swiftly. The New York City Chamber of Commerce signed a common petition with American merchants in Shanghai and rushed the document to Washington. The week before McKinley sent in his Cuban war message, Day had to reply to a letter of the Boston Chamber of Commerce which demanded that, since Boston and New England interests in the China trade were so large, "fullest protection" was required from the State Department. Day assured the Chamber that his department was giving the subject "the most careful consideration." The Boston *Herald*, strongly against intervention in Cuba, commented, "It is easy to conceive of conditions under which it would be both our right as well as interest" to offer "physical aid" to England "in preventing the closing of those far-away markets." The Pittsburgh *Press*, spokesman for the area's steel interests, doubted whether the "Muscovite is much better than the Mongolian," asked "how much of the Chinese trade will [we] get under European auspices," and concluded, "What the United States should do is to arm itself as soon as possible against European aggression." The Philadelphia *Press*, a journal close to the administration, worried in February that England would be unable to handle the Russian-German threat. The *Press* then declared that this observation should influence American actions, since "the future must not be put in peril. . . . China holds one-fourth the human race. Its free access to

---

[80] Denby to Sherman, March 19, 1898, China, Despatches, Hay to Sherman, March 25, 1898, Great Britain, Despatches, Sherman to White, March 16, 1898, Great Britain, Instructions, and Sherman to Hitchcock, March 16, 1898, Russia, Instructions, NA, RG 59; McCormick, "'Fair Field and No Favor,'" 145–146, 153–154.

our trade and manufactures is vital to our future." The New
York correspondent of the *Economist* reported "much talk" in
business circles about an alliance with England to maintain "open
ports in China against the combined influence of Russia and
Germany." On April 4 Whitelaw Reid ordered the New York
Tribune's editor to watch the Orient closely; "as soon as Cuba is
out of the way the present Chinese complications are likely to
develope a great deal of interest for us, particularly if England
should get involved in war over the conflicting claims." Clarence
Cary wrote optimistically from Washington on March 18 that
the capital was "beginning" to understand how British friendship
provided the key to both American freedom of action in Cuba
and the preservation of United States interests in the Far East.[81]

In commenting upon this crisis, journals provided evidence of
how these new involvements were realigning the nation's friends
and enemies. The Cincinnati *Commercial Tribune* and Foord's
Journal of Commerce warned that Russia had "goaded" England
into the territorial scramble. England's power still represented the
last, best hope for the open door. The New York *Tribune* spoke
more passionately: "As between Russian rule and Japanese rule,
a large share of the civilized world would choose the latter every
time. Slav-Tartar-Cossack rule means tyranny, ignorance, reaction. Japanese rule means freedom, enlightenment, progress.
If in a contest between the two opposite principles the latter does
not win the human race will suffer a dire catastrophe." [82]

In dealing with these complex problems in the Orient, the State
and Navy Departments had to concern themselves first with the
Spanish force in the Philippines. As early as December, 1897,
McKinley had agreed to attack these islands if war was declared

---

[81] *Journal of Commerce*, March 19, 1898, 1:1; Boston *Herald*, March
8, 1898, 6:4; Pittsburgh *Press*, April 11, 1898, 4:1; Reid to Nicholson,
April 4, 1898, Letterbooks, Reid MSS; *Congressional Record*, 55th Cong.,
2nd Sess., 3204–3205, also 3222.

[82] *Commercial Tribune*, April 9, 1898, 6:3; *Journal of Commerce*,
March 7, 1898, 6:1; March 19, 1898, 1:1; New York *Tribune*, March 18,
1898, 6:4.

against Spain. But there are indications—no more than that—that some members of the administration were thinking of America's Far Eastern interests in larger terms. Alfred Thayer Mahan dominated the three-man Naval War Board, which formulated the general blueprint for operations in the Pacific. Mahan had long coveted the China market, and his recent writings had revealed a rapidly increasing interest in the far Pacific. Albert Shaw could correctly observe in mid-1897 that Mahan "is as much in evidence these days, through his discussion of naval matters, as was ever Perry or John Paul Jones through naval victories." And Theodore Roosevelt, who had explained the Far Eastern situation to McKinley during the autumn and winter of 1897, had in turn been schooled on the importance of the Orient by Mahan. There were other signs of a larger American interest. On May 5 the London *Times* reported that the United States had searched for naval bases north of Shanghai *before* the war with Spain. Commodore G. W. Melville, Chief Engineer of the United States Navy, published an article in the *North American Review* in March, 1898, which quoted Seward on American destiny in the Pacific and noted that an increasing amount of the "swelling tide" of United States exports would have to find markets in the Orient.[83]

This interest in the Far East was in the background—but the immediate background—when, in late March, McKinley decided to make ultimate demands of Spain. Sometime between March 18 and 27 the President decided that war was inevitable unless Spain was prepared to surrender Cuba, an action which the Sagasta ministry could not take without threatening its own political life and that of the Spanish monarchy. Several developments forced McKinley to make this decision at this time. The adminis-

---

[83] *Review of Reviews*, XV (March, 1897), 331; Leech, *Days of McKinley*, 161–162; Seward W. Livermore, "American Naval-Base Policy in the Far East, 1850–1914," *Pacific Historical Review*, XIII (June, 1944), 113–135, contains the *Times* comment; G. W. Melville, Chief Engineer, U.S. Navy, "Our Future on the Pacific—What We Have There to Hold and Win," *North American Review*, CLXVI (March, 1898), 281–296.

tration had concluded that the Sagasta reform program, hardly three months old, was a failure. Another reason was the President's fear that after the publication of the report of the "Maine" investigating commission Congress would be uncontrollable. This factor, however, probably played only a minor role when McKinley formulated his final policy. Two other factors were of greater importance: the fear of political repercussions on the Republican party, and, perhaps most important, the growing belief of many sections of the business community that somehow the disturbances on the island would have to be terminated before the United States could enjoy full prosperity.

Elections in 1897 had not gone well for McKinley's party, nor had more recent elections in New York and Kentucky. During the first three months of 1898 the President and other Republican leaders received many letters which drew bleak pictures of the party's future if the administration failed to deal with Cuba immediately. McKinley's letters on this point were capped with a long message from Henry Cabot Lodge on March 21. Lodge had recently returned from taking a private poll of Massachusetts opinion. The Senator first assured McKinley that the masses were firmly behind the administration. But, Lodge continued, "if the war in Cuba drags on through the summer with nothing done we should go down in the greatest defeat ever known before the cry 'Why have you not settled the Cuban question.' " Clarence Cary, who opposed a strong Cuban policy, wrote in the *Journal of Commerce* in late March that mail was pouring in "even from conservative city districts" warning of the Republican losses which would inevitably result if the Democrats could "proclaim from every stump that it was they who forced the hand of the Republican President and with the aid of a few Republicans secured the liberty of Cuba." These letters, Cary concluded, were having a "potent effect." [84]

Most of the "conservative city districts" which Cary men-

[84] Lodge to McKinley, March 21, 1898, McKinley MSS; *Journal of Commerce*, March 30, 1898, 1:5.

tioned had long opposed war with Spain.[85] There were exceptions, however. The American business community was by no means monolithic in its opposition to war. To say as a generalization that businessmen opposed war is as erroneous as saying that businessmen wanted war. It is possible to suggest, however, that by the middle of March important businessmen and spokesmen for the business community were advocating war. It is also possible to suggest that at the same time, a shift seemed to be occurring in the general business community regarding its over-all views on the desirability of war.

Financial journals which advocated bimetallism had long urged a stronger attitude toward Spain in the hope that the resulting conflict would force the Treasury to pay expenses in silver. More important, business spokesmen in such midwestern and western cities as Cincinnati, Louisville, St. Louis, Chicago, San Francisco, and especially Pittsburgh were not reluctant to admit that they would welcome war. The Louisville *Commercial* believed, "Only a few of the eastern newspapers are pessimistic as to the business outlook at the beginning of war. . . . Everywhere in the west and south there is a disposition among businessmen . . . to keep their feet, and their heads, too." This journal was not reticent in providing its own viewpoint: if war occurred, transportation lines would prosper, "other enterprises would find more profit and securities would go up all along the line. Nor would the credit of the United States be in the least impaired." The Pittsburgh *Press*, mouthpiece for that area's booming steel interests, strongly supported the Cincinnati businessmen's resolutions that asked for war. The *Press* added, "It is not to be doubted that this expresses the feeling of the real business interests of the country. . . . The mistake made in some quarters is supposing that the stock jobbers are the business interests." [86]

[85] Julius Pratt discusses this opposition in detail in ch. vii of his *Expansionists of 1898;* see also Boston *Herald*, March 6, 1898, 12:13; and *Journal of Commerce*, April 1, 1898, 6:2–3.

[86] Louisville *Commercial*, April 14, 1898, 4:1; March 5, 1898, 4:2;

The Pittsburgh *Press* represented one of the special interests that would benefit from war. The Pittsburgh Chamber of Commerce also advocated the use of force, and the Chattanooga *Tradesman* suggested one reason why: the "small prospect" of conflict, the *Tradesman* noted on March 1, "has decidedly stimulated the iron trade." This journal, which did not want war, also commented, "Actual war would very decidedly enlarge the business of transportation," especially railroads. William E. Curtis wrote from Washington that the "belligerent spirit" which had infected everyone in the Navy Department, with the possible exception of Secretary Long, had been encouraged "by the contractors for projectiles, ordnance, ammunition and other supplies, who have thronged the department since the destruction of the *Maine*." These contractors, Curtis charged, had also assisted "correspondents of sensational newspapers in manufacturing canards and scare news." [87]

A strong possibility exists that the antiwar commercial journals in New York spoke for the less important members of that financial community. Russell Sage, claiming that he spoke "not only my own views on this point, but those of other moneyed men with whom I have talked," demanded that if the "Maine" was blown up by an outside force "the time for action has come. There should be no wavering." If war did occur, "There is no question as to where the rich men stand"; they would buy government bonds as they had during the Civil War and do all in their power to bolster the nation's war resources. W. C. Beer, who attempted to make a thorough survey of leading businessmen's opinion, concluded that "the steady opponents of the war among financiers were simply the life insurance men and small bankers." Beer found such giants as John Jacob Astor, John Gates, Thomas Fortune Ryan, William Rockefeller, and Stuy-

Cincinnati *Commercial Tribune*, March 30, 1898, 10:1; Pittsburgh *Press*, March 30, 1898, 4:1; Pratt, *Expansionists of 1898*, 243–244.

[87] *Tradesman*, March 1, 1898, 58; *Journal of Commerce*, April 7, 1898, 6:3. Curtis' statement is in the Pittsburgh *Press*, March 16, 1898, 1:1.

vesant Fish "feeling militant." On March 28 J. Pierpont Morgan declared that further talk of arbitration would accomplish nothing.[88]

Beer's findings can be supplemented with an analysis of the membership of the Cuban League of the United States. This organization began advertising in early 1897 that it would gladly receive donations to finance its efforts to free Cuba from Spanish control. As a part of these efforts, the league sold bonds for the Cuban Junta. This organization included such militants as Theodore Roosevelt, Colonel Ethan Allen, and Charles A. Dana. But the following conservative businessmen were among the Vice-Presidents: J. Edward Simmons, former President of the New York Stock Exchange, President of the Fourth National Bank of New York; Thomas F. Gilroy, builder and real estate operator in New York City; Chauncey M. Depew, railroad president and director of numerous railway and banking corporations; Thomas L. James, Chairman of the Board of Lincoln National Bank in New York City, President of the Lincoln Safe Deposit Company; John R. Dos Passos, New York lawyer who engaged in banking, corporate, and financial law and who had been active in the formation of large business amalgamations, including the sugar trust. Seated on the Board of Directors were General Daniel Butterfield, Civil War hero, bank president, and Executive Officer of the Steam Boat and Ferry Company; and Colonel John Jacob Astor.[89]

A group of interests that depended upon Cuban trade formed another category of business support which demanded that the revolution be terminated. A group of importers, exporters, bankers, manufacturers, and steamship and vessel owners sent McKinley a petition in February, 1898, which noted that the fighting had created a loss of one hundred million dollars a year in business

[88] New York *Tribune*, Feb. 27, 1898, 5:1; Thomas Beer, *Hanna* (New York, 1929), 199–200.
[89] *Review of Reviews*, XV (February, 1897), 137; *Who Was Who in America*, I (1897–1942) (Chicago, 1943).

conducted directly with the island, not to mention the destruction of American properties on the island. The petition demanded peace before the rainy season in May; otherwise, the sugar crop of 1898 and 1899 would be ruined. Those who signed this petition included "a large number of well-known and influential firms" in New York City, the New York *Tribune* noted, and also the names of businessmen in Philadelphia and Mobile.[90]

The petition noted the immense losses suffered by property owners and merchants who had invested in the island itself. By early 1898 these persons were becoming alarmed about something other than the day-to-day destruction of property, although this was certainly troublesome. The State Department began receiving reports that, as Fitzhugh Lee phrased the problem, "there may be a revolution within a revolution." Conservative interests feared that continued Spanish rule or autonomy, no matter how developed, would result in Cuban radical forces gaining control of the government. A strong feeling was growing which demanded American intervention to end this threat. The American Consul in Santiago summarized this feeling on March 23, 1898: "Property holders without distinction of nationality, and with but few exceptions, strongly desire annexation, having but little hope of a stable government under either of the contending forces. . . . [B]ut such a move would not be popular among the masses." These interests, the Consul reported, regretted that Americans did not favor outright, immediate annexation. McKinley learned of this sentiment from a letter written by "a gentleman of high standing, who has close personal relations with influential Cubans who have favored the rebellion," as Levi P. Morton, former Vice-President under Harrison and a wheelhorse of the Republican party, described the author. This letter warned that the rebellion had to end quickly or the radical classes would come to power. The writer believed that educated and wealthy backers of the rebellion now wanted either annexation or autonomy under American control. "They are most pro-

[90] New York *Tribune*, Feb. 10, 1898, 2:3.

nounced in their fears," he continued, "that independence, if obtained, would result in the troublesome, adventurous and nonresponsible class" seizing power.[91]

Many of these businessmen in Cuba hoped that annexation could be accomplished through peaceful means, but they found themselves trapped when they realized that Spain would not surrender her sovereignty on American terms without war. Among those who were so trapped was Edwin F. Atkins, one of the largest American investors in Cuban plantations. He deprecated the possibility of war on behalf of the insurgents, especially since the protection provided by Spanish troops enabled his plantations to continue their harvests throughout the revolution. But as early as January, 1897, Atkins had written Lodge that the best thing that could happen would be the annexation of Cuba by the United States. Other investors, however, evaded this trap by hoping for, or openly advocating, forceful American intervention. Fitzhugh Lee wrote Day in January, 1898, "The Spanish merchants and property holders generally favor some form of intervention on the part of the United States, but are prevented from an open expression on the subject lest they be disturbed by the soldier element." The New York *Tribune* noted in a front-page story on March 14, 1898, that European, especially British, capital had been flowing into Cuba in the belief that the United States would shortly replace Spain as the sovereign power. "Large enterprises welcome peace or forcible intervention as the means of freeing them from burdens," the article continued. "The Government [of Cuba] owes everybody," the *Tribune* observed, especially the large utility and railroad companies.[92]

[91] Lee to Day, Nov. 27, 1897, Consular, Havana, and Hyatt to Day, March 23, 1898, Consular, Santiago, NA, RG 59; enclosure in Levi P. Morton to McKinley, March 20, 1898, McKinley MSS.

[92] Atkins' views are in Lodge to Charles Francis Adams, Jan. 22, 1897, Letterbooks, Lodge MSS; Lee to Day, Jan. 18, 1898, Consular, Havana, NA, RG 59; New York *Tribune*, March 14, 1898, 1:6; Barrington to Salisbury, Nov. 11, 1897, Salisbury MSS.

Perhaps the American business community exerted the most influence on the administration during the last two weeks in March when influential business spokesmen began to welcome the possibility of war in order to end the suspense which shrouded the commercial exchanges. Although other historians have touched briefly on this important change,[93] it should be noted that some important business spokesmen and President McKinley apparently arrived at this decision at approximately the same time.

During the first two months of 1898 the United States began to enjoy prosperous conditions for the first time in five years. The de Lôme and "Maine" incidents affected business conditions only in the stock exchanges, and even there the impact was slight. Business improved, especially in the West and Northwest. In early March very few business journals feared a return of depression conditions, and with the gold influx resulting from discoveries in Alaska and from the export surplus, even fewer business observers displayed anxiety over the silver threat.[94]

But in mid-March financial reporters noted that business in commodities as well as stocks had suddenly slowed. Henry Clay Frick had been optimistic in his business reports to Andrew Carnegie, who was vacationing in Scotland. But on March 24, Frick reported that "owing to uncertainty . . . of the Cuban trouble, business is rather stagnant." A Wall Street correspondent wrote on March 22 that "the last two days have been the dullest for many a month." On March 26 the *Commercial and Financial Chronicle* summarized the situation. No "sudden and violent drop in prices" had occurred. But the rapid progress in trade had stopped and now "frequent complaints are heard. The

[93] See especially Pratt, *Expansionists of 1898*, 246–247.
[94] *Bradstreet's*, March 12, 1898, 161, 170; March 19, 1898, 186; March 26, 1898, 202; *Economist*, March 5, 1898, 356; *Journal of Commerce*, March 26, 1898, 6:5.

volume of trade undoubtedly remains large, but the reports speak of new enterprises being held in check." [95]

Businessmen had been particularly influenced by the speech of Senator Redfield Proctor of Vermont on March 17. Proctor was known for his conservative, antiwar disposition, an attitude he shared with his intimate friend, William McKinley. But the Senator had just returned from a visit to Cuba, a visit that had profoundly shocked him. Proctor discounted Spanish reforms as "too late," but he advised against going to war over the "Maine." The United States should use force, Proctor intimated, only to deliver the Cuban people from "the worst misgovernment of which I ever had knowledge." Conversations with businessmen in Cuba had provided him with most of his information; these men had declared "without exception" that it was too late for any more schemes of autonomy. They wanted an American protectorate, annexation, or a free Cuba. Although Proctor did not say so explicitly, none of these solutions was immediately possible without war with Spain. This speech deeply impressed almost all of the conservative and business journals which had opposed war. Many of these journals did not overlook Proctor's role as one of McKinley's "most trusted advisors and friends." Two weeks later the New York *Commercial Advertiser* looked back and marked this speech as the turning point in the road to war. [96]

This journal had steadily attacked the jingoes throughout January and February. But on March 10 it began to rationalize intervention not for "conquest," but for "humanity and love of freedom, and, above all, [the] desire that the commerce and industry of every part of the world shall have full freedom of development in the whole world's interest," especially "in that

[95] Frick to Carnegie, March 24, 1898, Carnegie MSS; *Economist*, April 5, 1898, 356; *Commercial and Financial Chronicle*, March 26, 1898, 590.
[96] The speech is in *Congressional Record*, 55th Cong., 2nd Sess., 2916–2919; *Public Opinion*, March 24, 1898, 358–360; *Commercial Advertiser*, April 2, 1898.

of nations in position to trade with it." In the week following Proctor's speech, important business opinion, tired of what the *Economist's* correspondent termed "the sudden revolutions of sentiment," began to fall into line back of the *Commercial Advertiser*. The *Wall Street Journal* noted that Proctor's speech had "converted a great many people in Wall Street" who had formerly opposed war. The *Journal of Commerce* asked for "one result or the other" to end the "present uncertainty," and wanted to present Spain with an ultimatum. The Pittsburgh *Press* noted business indecision on March 19, then remarked, "The sooner the administration executes its Cuban program the better." The Philadelphia *Press*, which was quite close to the administration, reported on March 21 that McKinley would make his final decision during the next few days. On the same day as this *Press* report, Lodge wrote McKinley a long letter assuring the President: "I talked with bankers, brokers, businessmen, editors, clergymen and others in Boston," Lynn, and Nahant, and "everybody" including "the most conservative classes" wanted the Cuban question "solved." "They said," Lodge reported, "for business one shock and then an end was better than a succession of spasms such as we must have if this war in Cuba went on." [97]

Perhaps the most influential note the President received that week was a telegram from W. C. Reick, a trusted political adviser in New York City and city editor of the New York *Herald*. This message arrived at the White House on March 25: "Big corporations here now believe we will have war. Believe all would welcome it as relief to suspense." On March 27, the New York *Tribune* ran a front-page article which indicated that Reick's evaluation also applied to the London Stock Exchange, a financial institution which some American investors considered of more importance than the New York Exchange. "What is

[97] *Ibid.*, March 10, 1898; *Economist*, April 9, 1898, 556; Pratt, *Expansionists of 1898*, 246; *Journal of Commerce*, March 14, 1898, 6:2–3; March 23, 1898, 6:1; Pittsburgh *Press*, March 19, 1898, 1:1; Philadelphia *Press*, March 21, 1898, 6:2; Lodge to McKinley, March 21, 1898, McKinley MSS.

wanted first of all is relief from the suspense. . . . Even a declaration of war would be preferred by bankers and stockbrokers
to the continuance of a stagnant market, with hourly flurries,
caused by sensational journalism and the rumors of impending
hostilities," the *Tribune* reported. If war occurred, a "speculators' movement" might result in a "temporary flurry in American stocks." But other investors would hold their securities "in
confident expectation that these will rise with the increased
movement of railway traffic caused by war." [98]

Two days after the receipt of Reick's telegram, McKinley
and Day presented an ultimatum to Spain. This move climaxed
a week of hurried consultations and policy changes. Before
March 20 the President had considered purchasing the island
or attempting to work out a plan which would ensure American
control while maintaining the trappings of Spanish sovereignty.
Spain refused to sell the island, however, and the Junta and the
rebels on the island would not listen to the second proposal. Now
in the new climate created by Proctor's speech and the changing
ideas of the business community, McKinley prepared to take
more forceful steps. For the first time in the crisis the President
called in a number of Democratic senators for consultations on
March 22. Doubtlessly reflecting the changed attitudes of both
McKinley and some business spokesmen, the war party in the
Senate now claimed for the first time a majority of the forty-
three Republicans, including representatives of the large corporations. These changes threatened to provoke Congress into
its most belligerent outbursts on March 29 and 30. [99]

[98] Reick to John Russell Young, March 25, 1898, McKinley MSS; New
York *Tribune*, March 27, 1898, 1:6. The *Tribune* reported on March 25,
1898, 1:1, that a movement had begun on Lombard Street to stop the
war by helping Spain pay an indemnity to the United States. American
bankers were reported to be organizing the drive, supposedly with help
from the Rothschilds. Diplomats doubted whether the bankers would
achieve any success.

[99] Leech, *Days of McKinley*, 183, 184; *Journal of Commerce*, March 30,
1898, 1:5; Washington *Evening Star*, March 23, 1898, 1:1

The President, however, was a week ahead of the war party on Capitol Hill. On March 20 Day instructed Woodford to ask Spain to restore peace in Cuba promptly and make a "full reparation" for the "Maine." Noting that "feeling in the United States very acute," Day declared that "April 15th is none too early date for accomplishment of these purposes" and threatened to lay the question before Congress if Spain did not respond properly. The Spanish government asked that these demands be delayed until the Cuban parliament met, that is, until the rainy season began. Woodford replied that such a delay was not possible. When the Spanish Foreign Minister, Pio Gullón, expressed surprise "at the apparent change in the attitude of the United States," Woodford said that there had been no change; the American government had always wanted peace. The American Minister then outlined four reasons why this peace had to come immediately: first, the terrible suffering in Cuba in which "during little more than three years" the deaths "had exceeded the births by nearly four hundred thousand"; the danger of sanitary conditions breaking down and plagues and diseases threatening the United States; the American dependence upon Cuban sugar and commerce; and, finally, "the large amounts of American capital invested in Cuba." "I emphasized," Woodford reported to McKinley, "the tremendous pecuniary loss which the people of the United States suffer and must suffer until peace is restored." [100]

Despite Spain's reluctance to meet Day's demands, Woodford cabled Washington on March 25 that he believed that Spain would grant a truce which would lead to negotiations with the rebels. If these negotiations did not result in peace by mid-September, Spain and the United States would "in such event jointly compel both parties in Cuba to accept such settlement as the two Governments should then jointly advise." Woodford's comments on this offer

[100] Day to Woodford, March 20, 1898, Spain, Instructions, NA, RG 59; Barclay to Salisbury, March 28, 1898, F.O. 72/2068; Woodford to McKinley, March 22 and 24, 1898, Spain, Despatches, NA, RG 59.

are especially crucial in view of what was to occur on April 9 and 10. The proposition, the American Minister told McKinley, "has the advantage of immediate truce and of practical recognition by Spain of an insurgent government with which the insular congress can deal. It also admits and even invites possible intervention by the United States. It may lead to the recognition of Cuban independence during the summer." On the same day, Woodford wrote the President: "A truce once established and negotiations begun, I see but two possible results. The one will be the independence of Cuba. The other may be annexation to the United States. Truce and negotiations in Cuba mean, in my respectful judgment, that the Spanish flag is to quit Cuba." [101] At this point the Spanish government refused to put forward such an offer formally. Two weeks later, however, Spain would take the initiative in offering such an armistice, and Woodford's comments on the meaning of a truce would again be relevant.

On March 26 Day attempted to prod the Sagasta regime by demanding that Cuban independence be worked out with American mediation during an armistice period. The following day the Assistant Secretary of State issued the first points of an ultimatum: first, an armistice until October 1 during which time the President would use his friendly offices to bring permanent peace to Cuba; second, "immediate revocation of reconcentrado order." The next day, Woodford reminded Day that under the Spanish Constitution the Ministry was powerless to recognize Cuban independence or nominal sovereignty. Only the Cortes could act on these issues, and this body would not meet until April 25. Day replied that the United States demanded the immediate promise of Cuban independence. On the 29th Day cabled that negotiations for an armistice must be concluded by March 31.[102]

<hr>

[101] Woodford to McKinley, March 24, March 25, Spain, Despatches, NA, RG 59.

[102] Day to Woodford, March 26, 27, 28, 1898, Spain, Instructions, and Woodford to Day, March 28, 1898, Spain, Despatches, NA, RG 59.

The Spanish reply of March 31 renounced the *reconcentrado* orders (the Spanish further modified their position on this aspect of the negotiations on April 4 and 5), but would not promise an armistice at Spain's initiative. Woodford grieved over this last point as "a question of punctilio," forced upon the Spanish government by "Spanish pride" and the threat of revolution inside the nation. The Ministry realized, the American Minister reported, "that armistice now means certain peace next autumn." Woodford continued his efforts and on April 4 Day received a copy of the latest Spanish plan for Cuban autonomy. The Assistant Secretary tersely informed Woodford, "It is not armistice," but a Spanish appeal "urging the insurgents to lay down their arms and to join with the autonomy party. . . . The President's Message," Day concluded, "will go in Wednesday afternoon." McKinley did not send in his war message for another six days, however. He granted Fitzhugh Lee's request for time in order to remove American citizens from Havana.[103]

On April 9 Spain granted a suspension of hostilities "in order to arrange and facilitate peace on the island." Woodford cabled immediately that this move would mean "immediate and permanent peace in Cuba by negotiations" if Congress gave the President authority to conduct such discussions and full power to use the army and navy to enforce the results of the negotiations. The American Minister told McKinley that the talks would result in autonomy which the insurgents could accept, or complete independence, or cession of the islands to the United States. "I hope," Woodford asked, "that nothing will now be done to humiliate Spain as I am satisfied that the present Government is going and is loyally ready to go as fast and as far as it can." Day replied that the President "must decline to make

---

[103] Woodford to McKinley, March 31 and April 1, 1898, Spain, Despatches, Day to Woodford, April 4, 1898, Spain, Instructions, and Woodford to Day, April 4, 1898, Spain, Despatches, NA, RG 59. See also comment of Leech, *Days of McKinley*, 180; and Barclay to Salisbury, March 30, 31, April 1, 1898, F.O. 72/2068.

further suggestions" to Spain, but "that in sending in his Message tomorrow the President will acquaint Congress with this latest communication." McKinley did append the Spanish offer to the end of his war message. Both the administration and Congress then proceeded to overlook the significance that Woodford attached to the offer. During the next nine days Congress debated the means, not the question, of intervention.[104]

McKinley had had the choice of three policies which would have terminated the Cuban revolution. First, he could have left the Spanish forces and the insurgents fight until one or the other fell exhausted from the bloodshed and financial strain. During the struggle the United States could have administered food and medicine to the civilian population, a privilege which the Spanish agreed to allow in March, 1898. Second, the President could have demanded an armistice and Spanish assurances that negotiations over the summer would result in some solution which would pacify American feelings. That is to say, he could have followed Woodford's ideas. Third, McKinley could have demanded both an armistice and Spanish assurances that Cuba would become independent immediately. If Spain would not grant both of these conditions, American military intervention would result. The last was the course the President followed.

Each of these policy alternatives deserves a short analysis. For American policy makers, the first choice was the least acceptable of the three, but the United States did have to deal, nevertheless, with certain aspects of this policy. If Spain hoped to win such a conflict, she had to use both the carrot of an improved and attractive autonomy scheme and the stick of an increased and effective military force. Spain could have granted no amount of autonomy, short of complete independence, which would have satisfied the rebels, and whether Americans cared to admit

[104] Woodford to Day, April 9, 1898, Spain, Despatches, Day to Woodford, April 10, 1898, Spain, Instructions, "Memorandum" handed to Day from Spanish Minister on April 10, 1898, Notes from Spain, and Woodford to McKinley, April 10, 1898, Spain, Despatches, NA, RG 59.

it or not, they were at least partially responsible for this ob-
stinacy on the part of the insurgents. The United States did
attempt to stop filibustering expeditions, but a large number
nevertheless reached Cuban shores. More important, when the
Spanish Minister asked Day to disband the New York Junta,
the financial taproot of the insurgent organization, the Assistant
Secretary replied that "this was not possible under American
law and in the present state of public feeling." Woodford had
given the Spanish Queen the same reply in mid-January. It was
perhaps at this point that Spain saw the last hopes for a negotiated
peace begin to flicker away.[105]

Seemingly unrelated actions by the United States gave boosts
to the rebel cause. The sending of the "Maine," for instance,
considerably heartened the rebels; they believed that the warship
diverted Spanish attention and military power from insurgent
forces. When the vessel exploded, the New York Junta released
a statement which did not mourn the dead sailors as much as it
mourned the sudden disappearance of American power in Havana harbor.[106] The Junta interpreted the passage of the $50,-
000,000 war appropriation measure during the first week of
March as meaning either immediate war or the preparation for
war. Under such conditions, it was not odd that the rebels were
reluctant to compromise their objective of complete independence.

If the insurgents would not have accepted autonomy, no matter how liberal or attractive, then Spain might have hoped to
suppress the rebels with outright force. To have done so, however, the Spanish government would have had to bring its army
through the rainy season with few impairments, resume to a
large extent the *reconcentrado* policies, and prevent all United

[105] *Spanish Correspondence and Documents,* 91–92; Ernest May comments, "When even this personal appeal to McKinley produced no results, the Queen and her ministers had to face the fact that the United
States would not help to bring about a negotiated peace" (*Imperial
Democracy,* 162–163).

[106] New York *Tribune,* Feb. 17, 1898, 10:1.

States aid from reaching the rebels. The first objective would have been difficult, but the last two, if carried out, would have meant war with the United States. The State Department could not allow Spain to reimpose methods even faintly resembling Weyler's techniques, nor could the Department have allowed the searching of American vessels. McKinley and the American people hoped that Spain would stop the revolution, but they also insisted on taking from Spain the only tools with which that nation could deal with the Cubans.[107]

Having found this first alternative impossible to accept, McKinley might have chosen a second approach: demand an armistice and ultimate pacification of the island, but attempt to achieve this peacefully over several months and with due respect for the sovereignty of Spain. This was the alternative Woodford hoped the administration would choose. He had reported during the two weeks before McKinley's message that the Spanish had given in time and time again on points which he had believed they could not afford to grant. In spite of the threat of revolution from the army, the Queen had granted a temporary truce. The American Minister continued to ask for more time to find a peaceful settlement. On April 11, the day the war message went to Congress, Woodford wrote the President, "To-day it is just possible that Moret and I have been right [in our pursuit of peace], but it is too soon to be jubilant." [108] The American Minister sincerely believed that the negotiations during the period of truce could, with good faith on both the American and Spanish sides, result in Spain evacuating the island. This would have to be done slowly, however.

---

[107] Chadwick denies "that the desolation of Cuba was wholly or even mainly the work of the Spanish administration" and justifies "the right under international law" of Spain to use the *reconcentrado* policies to stop the revolution. On the other hand, Chadwick believes American feeling correct in protesting the Spanish carelessness in feeding and caring for the *reconcentrados* (*United States and Spain*, 486–503).

[108] Woodford to McKinley, April 11, 1898, Spain, Despatches, NA, RG 59.

No sovereign nation could be threatened with a time limit and uncompromising demands without fighting back. The fact that Spain would not grant McKinley's demand for immediate Cuban independence makes the Spanish-American War which began in April, 1898, by no means an inevitable conflict. Any conflict is inevitable once one proud and sovereign power, dealing with a similar power, decides to abandon the conference table and issue an ultimatum. The historical problem remains: which power took the initiative in setting the conditions that resulted in armed conflict, and were those conditions justified?

By April 10 McKinley had assumed an inflexible position. The President abjured this second alternative and demanded not only a truce, but a truce which would lead to a guarantee of immediate Cuban independence obtained with the aid of American mediation. He moreover demanded such a guarantee of independence before the Cortes or the Cuban parliament, the two groups which had the constitutional power to grant such independence, were to gather for their formal sessions.[109]

The central question is, of course, why McKinley found himself in such a position on April 10 that only the third alternative was open to him. The President did not want war; he had been sincere and tireless in his efforts to maintain the peace. By mid-March, however, he was beginning to discover that, although he did not want war, he did want what only a war could provide: the disappearance of the terrible uncertainty in American political and economic life, and a solid basis from which to resume the building of the new American commercial empire. When the President made his demands, therefore, he made the ultimate demands; as far as he was concerned, a six-month period of negotiations would not serve to temper the political and economic problems in the United States, but only exacerbate them.

To say this is to raise another question: why did McKinley

---

[109] Washington *Evening Star*, April 11, 1898, 2:3, has an interesting comment from an unidentified cabinet member on the meaninglessness of the Spanish truce offer.

arrive at this position during mid-March? What were the factors which limited the President's freedom of choice and policies at this particular time? The standard interpretations of the war's causes emphasize the yellow journals and a belligerent Congress. These were doubtlessly crucial factors in shaping the course of American entry into the conflict, but they must be used carefully. A first observation should be that Congress and the yellow press, which had been loudly urging intervention ever since 1895, did not make a maiden appearance in March, 1898; new elements had to enter the scene at that time to act as the catalysts for McKinley's policy. Other facts should be noted regarding the yellow press specifically. In areas where this press supposedly was most important, such as New York City, no more than one-third of the press could be considered sensational. The strongest and most widespread prowar journalism apparently occurred in the Midwest. But there were few yellow journals there. The papers that advocated war in this section did so for reasons other than sensationalism; among these reasons were the influence of the Cuban Junta and, perhaps most important, the belief that the United States possessed important interests in the Caribbean area which had to be protected. Finally, the yellow press obviously did not control the levers of American foreign policy. McKinley held these, and he bitterly attacked the owners of the sensational journals as "evil disposed . . . people." An interpretation stressing rabid journalism as a major cause of the war should draw some link to illustrate how these journals reached the White House or the State Department. To say that this influence was exerted through public opinion proves nothing; the next problem is to demonstrate how much public opinion was governed by the yellow press, how much of this opinion was influenced by more sober factors, and which of these two branches of opinion most influenced McKinley.[110]

---

[110] There is an excellent discussion of this point in Offner, "McKinley and the Origins of the Spanish-American War," 69–74; see also George W. Auxier, "Middle Western Newspapers and the Spanish-American

Congress was a hotbed of interventionist sentiment, but then it had been so since 1895. The fact was that Congress had more trouble handling McKinley than the President had handling Congress. The President had no fear of that body. He told Charles Dawes during the critical days of February and March that if Congress tried to adjourn he would call it back into session. McKinley held Congress under control until the last two days of March, when the publication of the "Maine" investigation forced Thomas B. Reed, the passionately antiwar Speaker of the House, to surrender to the onslaughts of the rapidly increasing interventionist forces. As militants in Congress forced the moderates into full retreat, McKinley and Day were waiting in the White House for Spain's reply to the American ultimatum. And after the outbreak on March 31 McKinley reassumed control. On April 5 the Secretary of War, R. A. Alger, assured the President that several important senators had just informed him that "there will be no trouble about holding the Senate." When the President postponed his war message on April 5 in order to grant Fitzhugh Lee's request for more time, prowar congressmen went into a frenzy. During the weekend of April 8 and 9, they condemned the President, ridiculed Reed's impotence to hold back war, and threatened to declare war themselves. In fact, they did nearly everything except disobey McKinley's wishes that nothing be done until the following week. Nothing was done.[111]

When the Senate threatened to overrule the President's orders that the war declaration exclude recognition of the Cuban insurgent government, McKinley whipped the doubters into line and forced the Senate to recede from its position. This was an all-out battle between the White House and a strong Senate faction. McKinley triumphed despite extremely strong pressure exerted by sincere American sentiment on behalf of immediate

---

War, 1895–1898," *Mississippi Valley Historical Review*, XXVI (March, 1940), 524, 532.

[111] Alger to McKinley, April 5, 1898, McKinley MSS; Offner, "McKinley and the Origins of the Spanish-American War," 289–300.

Cuban independence and despite the more crass material interests of the Junta's financial supporters and spokesmen. The President wanted to have a free hand in dealing with Cuba after the war, and Congress granted his wishes. Events on Capitol Hill may have been more colorful than those at the White House, but the latter, not the former, was the center of power in March and April, 1898.

Influences other than the yellow press or congressional belligerence were more important in shaping McKinley's position of April 11. Perhaps most important was the transformation of the opinion of many spokesmen for the business community who had formerly opposed war. If, as one journal declared, the McKinley administration, "more than any that have preceded it, sustains . . . close relations to the business interests of the country," then this change of business sentiment should not be discounted.[112] This transformation brought important financial spokesmen, especially from the Northeast, into much the same position that had long been occupied by prointerventionist business groups and journals in the trans-Appalachian area. McKinley's decision to intervene placated many of the same business spokesmen whom he had satisfied throughout 1897 and January and February of 1898 by his refusal to declare war.

Five factors may be delineated which shaped this interventionist sentiment of the business community. First, some business journals emphasized the material advantages to be gained should Cuba become a part of the world in which the United States would enjoy, in the words of the New York *Commercial Advertiser*, "full freedom of development in the whole world's

[112] Chicago *Times-Herald* quoted in Cincinnati *Commercial Tribune*, Dec. 28, 1897, 6:2. The Chicago paper was particularly close to the administration through its publisher's friendship with McKinley. The publisher was H. H. Kohlsaat. Ernest May remarks, regarding McKinley's antiwar position in 1897 and early 1898, "It was simply out of the question for him [McKinley] to embark on a policy unless virtually certain that Republican businessmen would back him" (*Imperial Democracy*, 118). The same comment doubtlessly applies also to McKinley's actions in March and April.

interest." The *Banker's Magazine* noted that "so many of our citizens are so involved in the commerce and productions of the island, that to protect these interests . . . the United States will have eventually to force the establishment of fair and reasonable government." The material damage suffered by investors in Cuba and by many merchants, manufacturers, exporters, and importers, as, for example, the groups which presented the February 10 petition to McKinley, forced these interests to advocate a solution which could be obtained only through force.[113]

A second reason was the uncertainty that plagued the business community in mid-March. This uncertainty was increased by Proctor's powerful and influential speech and by the news that a Spanish torpedo-boat flotilla was sailing from Cadiz to Cuba. The uncertainty was exemplified by the sudden stagnation of trade on the New York Stock Exchange after March 17. Such an unpredictable economic basis could not provide the springboard for the type of overseas commercial empire that McKinley and numerous business spokesmen envisioned.

Third, by March many businessmen who had deprecated war on the ground that the United States Treasury did not possess adequate gold reserves began to realize that they had been arguing from false assumptions. The heavy exports of 1897 and the discoveries of gold in Alaska and Australia brought the yellow metal into the country in an ever widening stream. Private bankers had been preparing for war since 1897. *Banker's Magazine* summarized these developments: "Therefore, while not desiring war, it is apparent that the country now has an ample coin basis for sustaining the credit operations which a conflict would probably make necessary. In such a crisis the gold standard will prove a bulwark of confidence." [114]

[113] *Commercial Advertiser*, March 10, 1898, 6:3; *Bankers' Magazine*, LVI (April, 1898), 519–520.

[114] *Bankers' Magazine*, LVI (March, 1898), 347–348; LVI (April, 1898), 520; Pittsburgh *Press*, April 8, 1898, 4:1; *Commercial and Financial Chronicle*, April 23, 1898, 786.

Fourth, antiwar sentiment lost much strength when the nation realized that it had nothing to fear from European intervention on the side of Spain. France and Russia, who were most sympathetic to the Spanish monarchy, were forced to devote their attention to the Far East. Neither of these nations wished to alienate the United States on the Cuban issue. More important, Americans happily realized that they had the support of Great Britain. The *rapprochement* which had occurred since the Venezuelan incident now paid dividends. On an official level, the British Foreign Office assured the State Department that nothing would be accomplished in the way of European intervention unless the United States requested such intervention. The British attitude made it easy for McKinley to deal with a joint European note of April 6 which asked for American moderation toward Spain. The President brushed off the request firmly but politely. On an unofficial level, American periodicals expressed appreciation of the British policy on Cuba, and some of the journals noted that a common Anglo-American approach was also desirable in Asia.[115] The European reaction is interesting insofar as it evinces the continental powers' growing realization that the United States was rapidly becoming a major force in the world. But the European governments set no limits on American dealings with Spain. McKinley could take the initiative and make his demands with little concern for European reactions.

Finally, opposition to war melted away in some degree when the administration began to emphasize that the United States enjoyed military power much superior to that of Spain. One possible reason for McKinley's policies during the first two months of 1898 might have been his fear that the nation was not adequately prepared. As late as the weekend of March 25 the President worried over this inadequacy. But in late February and

[115] Dugdale, *German Documents*, II, 500–502; Porter to Sherman, April 8, 1898, France, Despatches, and Hay to Sherman, March 26, 28, 29, April 1, Great Britain, Despatches, NA, RG 59; *Public Opinion*, March 24, 1898, 360–361.

early March, especially after the $50,000,000 appropriation by Congress, the country's military strength developed rapidly. On March 13 the Philadelphia *Press* proclaimed that American naval power greatly exceeded that of the Spanish forces. By early April those who feared a Spanish bombardment of New York City were in the small minority. More representative were the views of Winthrop Chanler who wrote Lodge that if Spanish troops invaded New York "they would all be absorbed in the population . . . and engaged in selling oranges before they got as far as 14th Street." [116]

As the words of McKinley's war message flew across the wires to Madrid, many business spokesmen who had opposed war had recently changed their minds, American military forces were rapidly growing more powerful, banks and the United States Treasury had secured themselves against the initial shocks of war, and the European powers were divided among themselves and preoccupied in the Far East. Business boomed after McKinley signed the declaration of war. "With a hesitation so slight as to amount almost to indifference," *Bradstreet's* reported on April 30, "the business community, relieved from the tension caused by the incubus of doubt and uncertainty which so long controlled it, has stepped confidently forward to accept the situation confronting it oweing to the changed conditions." "Unfavorable circumstances . . . have hardly excited remark, while the stimulating effects have been so numerous and important as to surprise all but the most optimistic," this journal concluded.[117] A new type of American empire, temporarily clothed in armor, stepped out on the international stage after a half century of preparation to make its claim as one of the great world powers.

[116] Leech, *Days of McKinley*, 176; Philadelphia *Press*, March 13, 1898, 8:3; Garraty, *Lodge*, 191.

[117] *Bradstreet's*, April 9, 1898, 234, also April 30, 1898, 272, 282.

Epilogue

IN his classic autobiography, Henry Adams recalls sitting at John Hay's table and discussing "the Philippines as a question of balance of power in the East" with members of the British cabinet. Adams suddenly realized "that the family work of a hundred and fifty years fell at once into the grand perspective of true empire-building, which Hay's work [in the Far East] set off with artistic skill." In less than a century and a quarter the United States had developed from thirteen states strung along a narrow Atlantic coastline into a great world power with possessions in the far Pacific.

Until the middle of the nineteenth century this had been, for the most part, a form of landed expansion which had moved over a large area of the North American continent. The Louisiana Purchase in 1803 had been followed by further important acquisitions in 1819, 1848, 1853, and 1867. But when William H. Seward entered the State Department in 1861, the nature of American expansion had begun to change. Under the impact of the industrial revolution Americans began to search for markets, not land. Sometimes the State Department seized the initiative in making the search, as in the Harrison administration. Frequently the business community pioneered in extending the interests of the United States into foreign areas, as in Mexico in the 1870's and in China in the 1890's. Regardless of which body led the expansionist movement, the result was the same: the growth of economic interests led to political entanglements and to increased military responsibilities.

Americans attempted to build a new empire, an empire which differed fundamentally from the colonial holdings of European powers. Until 1898 the United States believed that its political insitutions were suitable only for the North American continent. Many policy makers and important journalists warned that extra-continental holdings would wreck the American republic just as they had ruined the Roman republic. Such sentiment helped to prevent the acquisition of Hawaii in 1893.

In 1898, however, the United States annexed Hawaii and demanded the Philippines from Spain. These acquisitions were not unheralded. Seward had pushed his nation's claims far out into the Pacific with the purchase of Alaska and the Midway islands. Fish, Evarts, Bayard, Blaine, and Cleveland had maintained a tight hold on Pago Pago in Samoa, although they strongly disliked the political entanglements with England and Germany which were necessarily part of the bargain.

One striking characteristic tied these acquisitions to the new territory brought under American control in 1898 and 1899, immediately after the war with Spain. The United States obtained these areas not to fulfill a colonial policy, but to use these holdings as a means to acquire markets for the glut of goods pouring out of highly mechanized factories and farms.

The two acquisitions which might be considered exceptions to this statement are Alaska and Hawaii. It is most difficult, however, to understand the purchase of "Seward's Icebox" without comprehending the Secretary of State's magnificent view of the future American commercial empire. This view did not premise a colonial policy, but assumed the necessity of controlling the Asian markets for commercial, not political, expansion. As the chairman of the House Foreign Affairs Committee commented in 1867, Alaska was the "drawbridge" between the North American continent and Asia.

Hawaii had become an integral part of the American economy long before Harrison attempted to annex it in 1893. Missionaries had forged strong religious and secular links between the islands and the mainland, but of much more importance were the commercial ties. After the reciprocity treaty of 1875 the United States possessed a virtual veto power over Hawaii's relations with foreign powers. American capital, especially attracted by the islands' fertility during the depression years that plagued the mainland in the 1870's and 1880's, developed sugar plantations whose prosperity depended upon the American consumer. Exports of finished industrial goods left United States ports in increasing amounts for Hawaiian consumers. When the 1890 tariff severely retarded the export of Hawaiian sugar, American exports moved without abatement into the islands. The economic expansion of the United States, in terms of both capital and goods, had tied Hawaii irrevocably to the mainland.

By 1893 only the political tie remained to be consummated. The United States enjoyed the benefits of Hawaiian trade without the burdens of governmental responsibilities. But in five years the situation changed. Regaining confidence in American political institutions as the depression lessened in severity, and fearful of Japanese control, the McKinley administration attempted to annex the islands in 1897–1898. But one other factor was also of prime importance. American interests in Asia suddenly assumed much significance. And in this new framework, the Isthmian canal project gained added importance and support, for many expansionists believed the canal to be absolutely necessary if the eastern and Gulf states hoped to compete in Asian markets. As Senator John T. Morgan, Alfred Thayer Mahan, and Senator Cushman Davis noted, Hawaii was essential if the United States was to safeguard the Pacific approaches to the canal. When the Senate Foreign Relations Committee issued its majority report in March, 1898, which advocated annexation by joint resolution, the committee argued that the strategic position of Hawaii was "the main argument in favor of the annexation" plan. This, the report explained, meant not only the shielding of the western coast of the United States, but the "efficient protection" of American commerce as well. This report also noted the irrelevance of one of the antiannexationist arguments, then combined the strategic factor with the fear of Japanese encroachment as reasons for annexation: "The issue in Hawaii is not between monarchy and the Republic. That issue has been settled. . . . The issue is whether, in that inevitable struggle, Asia or America shall have the vantage ground of the control of the naval 'Key of the Pacific,' the commercial 'Cross-roads of the Pacific.'"[1]

The administration forces finally won their objective during the summer of 1898. By July both the business community and policy makers had fully realized the value of Asia as a potential area for American financial and commercial expansion. The operations of Admiral George Dewey in the Philippines had, moreover, taught Americans that Hawaii was absolutely essential as a coaling station and naval base if the United States hoped to become a dominant force in the Far East.

The Philippines marked the next step westward. In 1899 the Secretary of the American Asiatic Association analyzed the reason for the annexation of these islands in a single sentence: "Had we no interests in China, the possession of the Philippines would be meaningless." Mark Hanna, a somewhat more objective observer of the Far East than the gentleman just quoted, also desired "a strong foothold in the Philippine Islands," for then "we can and will take a large slice of the commerce of Asia. That is what we want. We are bound to share in the commerce of the

---

[1] *Senate Report No. 681*, 55th Cong., 2nd Sess. (serial 3627), 1–119, especially 31; Stevens, *American Expansion in Hawaii*, 297–299; James Harrison Wilson, "America's Interests in China," *North American Review*, CLXVI (February, 1898), 140; *Commercial Advertiser*, Feb. 8, 1898, 6:3; clipping of London *Times*, June 17, 1897, enclosed in Hay to Sherman, June 17, 1897, Great Britain, Despatches, NA, RG 59.

Far East, and it is better to strike for it while the iron is hot." The interests of missionaries and of investors who believed the islands had great natural wealth no doubt encouraged McKinley to demand the Philippines. But it should be noted that, when the President first formulated his peace terms, he wanted the islands to "remain with Spain, except a port and necessary appurtenances to be selected by the United States." He changed this view only when convinced that Manila would be insecure and indefensible unless the United States annexed the remainder of the islands. Mahan had followed similar reasoning to reach the same conclusion. The key to the Philippine policy of both men was their view of Manila as a way station to the Orient.[2]

Throughout the 1890's, debate had raged around the desirability of annexing yet another outlying possession. The growing desire for an American-controlled Isthmian canal partially explains the interest Hawaii held for some Americans. But it should be emphasized that in the 1890's, at least, Americans did not define their interests in a future canal as military; they termed these interests as economic. Policy makers viewed the control of strategic areas such as Hawaii or Guantánamo Bay in the same light as they viewed the Philippines, that is, as strategic means to obtaining and protecting objectives which they defined as economic. Few persons discussed the military aspects of the canal, and to interpret American expansion into the Pacific and the Caribbean as expansion for *merely* strategic objectives distorts the true picture. Most of those who were concerned with a canal agreed with McKinley's statement in his annual message of 1897: the Nicaragua canal would be of "utility and value to

---

[2] Campbell, *Special Business Interests,* 16; memorandum of McKinley's terms, Day to Hay, June 4, 1898, copy in Box 185, and Hay to Day, May 18, 1898, Box 185, J. B. Moore MSS; *Economist,* June 11, 1898, 877; F. F. Hilder, "The Philippine Islands," *Forum,* XXV (July, 1898), 534–545; Truxtun Beale, "Strategical Value of the Philippines," *North American Review,* CLXVI (June, 1898), 759–760; Livermore, "American Naval-Base Policy in the Far East, 1850–1914," 116–117; Philadelphia *Press,* June 29, 1898, 6:3.

American commerce." The foremost advocate of a Central American passageway, Senator Morgan, constantly discussed the canal's value in economic terms.[3]

American control of these areas followed logically if two assumptions were granted: first, the general consensus reached by the American business community and policy makers in the mid-1890's that additional foreign markets would solve the economic, social, and political problems created by the industrial revolution; and, second, the growing belief that, however great its industrial prowess, the United States needed strategic bases if it hoped to compete successfully with government-supported European enterprises in Asia and Latin America. The *Journal of Commerce* summarized opinion on the first point when it remarked in early 1895 that "within the last half century" the industrial and transportation revolutions had made it a fact that "we are a part of 'abroad.'" Commenting upon one aspect of the frontier thesis, this journal warned that the nation was no longer "a vast public domain awaiting agriculture"; as a result of this transformation, Americans could not afford "to imagine that we can maintain ourselves in isolation from the rest of the commercial world." [4]

Almost all Americans agreed on this first assumption. It was only on the second (how the United States could best protect its commercial interests abroad), that important disagreement flared. Walter Quintin Gresham, Edward Atkinson, and Carl Schurz were three of the leaders of the antiannexationist cause, but they were also strong advocates of increased commercial expansion. This point became evident when Atkinson and Schurz had to defend their ideals after the Spanish-American War. Atkinson presented his case through the pages of his periodical, *The Anti-*

[3] *Public Opinion*, May 26, 1898, 646; *Congressional Record*, 55th Cong., 2nd Sess., 6 and 3222; Melville, "Our Future on the Pacific," 293–294. There is a good discussion of the canal issue in Campbell, *Special Business Interests*, 14–15.

[4] *Journal of Commerce*, Jan. 22, 1895, 4:2–3; also Chapter IV, above.

Imperialist. He admitted at the outset that "the export demand is the balance-wheel of the whole traffic of this country," but he believed that the largest demand would be found in Europe, not in the Pacific area. He had to face the fact, however, that many Americans did believe the Far East to be of great importance, and he attempted to destroy their premises by pointing out that the Philippines bought only $100,000 worth of goods from the United States each year. This was quite beside the point as far as the new empire expansionists were concerned. Atkinson began to see the weakness of his argument and countered with an attack which struck closer to the annexationists' theme: the Philippines, Atkinson remarked, could be maintained as a "sanctuary of commerce" without American involvement. Once he had gone this far, however, he had granted the McKinley forces their major assumption.[5]

Schurz developed his case in more detail. In a speech of August 19, 1898, he noted a report from the Foreign Commerce desk of the State Department which demanded more foreign markets. "I fully agree," Schurz said. "We cannot have too many. But can such markets be opened only by annexing to the United States the countries in which they are situated?" This was his first mistake. Few people, other than some missionaries, viewed the Philippines as a great market. Certainly the McKinley administration did not. Schurz then made his second mistake when he repeated his staple argument that if the Philippines remained neutral, "we shall not only be able to get coaling-stations and naval depots wherever we may want them, but we shall qualify ourselves for that position which is most congenial to our democratic institutions." Other Americans were not as certain that such naval bases could be protected in the face of European encroachment, and this doubt had become stronger since the continental powers had shown their hands in China in late 1897 and early 1898. Annexationists could legitimately ask Schurz

[5] *The Anti-Imperialist*, I, 16, 26–32, 45–46.

what power the United States could use if other nations used force or disciminatory methods to exclude Americans from Asian markets. Schurz replied in a letter to McKinley on June 1, 1898, that the nation could use the immense moral power inherent in posing as "the *great neutral Power of the world.*" He could find no better answer, and to these policy makers, schooled in the theories of Mahan, the answer was insufficient. In their eyes Schurz had granted the common premise of the necessity for commercial expansion, and then had made the two crucial errors of, first, utterly confusing the strategic, new empire policies of McKinley with the colonial policies of European powers; and, second, believing that such commercial expansion could be continued without defensible strategic bases.[6]

Thus when the debates began on the annexation of Hawaii and the Philippines, the antiannexationists had ironically undercut their own argument. When the minority of the House Foreign Affairs Committee declared that "political dominion" over Hawaii "is not commercially necessary," the majority report replied that a continuation of a protectorate meant responsibility without control, but by annexation the United States "would assume no more responsibilities, and would acquire absolute control." Under a protectorate, Hawaii would still remain an incubator of international friction. And when Senator Vest introduced a resolution condemning the annexation of the Philippines, probably the most important of the antiannexationist moves in the Senate, he made the mistake of saying that the federal government could not annex a whole area as a colony, "except such small amount as may be necessary for coaling stations." The McKinley administration could accept this argument and then ask how the coaling station of Manila, for example, could be useful without Luzon, and how Luzon could be de-

[6] *Speeches, Correspondence and Political Papers of Carl Schurz,* edited by Frederic Bancroft (New York, 1913), V, 489–490, 473, 476. The same anti-imperialist approach may be found in Oscar Straus to A. D. White, Aug. 1, 1898, papers of Andrew Dickson White, Ithaca, New York.

fended or maintained without the remainder of the Philippines.

The principal antiannexationist argument, that the Constitution and traditional American society would be ruined by expanding to noncontiguous areas, was, in fact, quite irrelevant granted the common assumption of the need for commercial expansion. By agreeing that a constantly expanding trade was also vital to the economic and political well-being of the nation, the antiannexationists had opened themselves to the devastating counterargument that this trade could not find the crucial markets in Asia and Latin America without the security which the Philippines and Hawaii would provide.[7]

As for the annexationist forces, Lodge could espouse "large policies," but correctly argue, "I do not mean that we should enter on a widely extended system of colonization." When Alfred Thayer Mahan urged the State Department to demand only Manila in the summer of 1898, he differed little from many antiannexationists. His studies had convinced him, however, that a naval base could be strong and secure only when the hinterland of the base was strong and secure. He would accept the political burdens of the hinterland if this was necessary in order to safeguard the naval base and the trade which depended upon that base. McKinley apparently arrived at the same conclusion in much the same way. The President actually occupied a middle-of-the-road position on the issue, for by the early summer of 1898 some business periodicals, military experts, and such politicians as "Fire Alarm Joe" Foraker of Ohio urged the annexation of other Pacific islands and wanted to renege on the Teller Amendment in order to annex Cuba.[8] The administration's Cuban

[7] Fred Harvey Harrington, "The Anti-Imperialist Movement in the United States, 1898–1900," *Mississippi Valley Historical Review*, XXII (September, 1935), 211–212; *House Report No. 1355*, part 2, 55th Cong., 2nd Sess. (serial 3721), 1–2; *Senate Report No. 681*, 55th Cong., 2nd Sess. (serial 3627), 1–119. *Congressional Record*, 55th Cong., 3rd Sess., 20, contains Vest's resolution.

[8] Lodge's statement is given in Stevens, *American Expansion in Hawaii*, 279; on Mahan, see Chapter II, above; on the business views, see Pratt, *Expansionists of 1898*, 274–275.

policy is one of the best examples of the new empire approach. Not wanting the political burdens or the economic competition inherent in annexation, the problem was neatly solved by the Platt Amendment, which gave the Cubans their independence; but the measure also gave to the United States the Guantánamo Naval Base as a safeguard for American interests in the Caribbean, created a Cuban tariff which opened the island to American agricultural and industrial products, and recognized the right of American military intervention in the event that Cuban political life became too chaotic.

It may be suggested that one fruitful way to approach the "imperialist versus anti-imperialist" clash in the 1890's is to view the struggle in terms of a narrow and limited debate on the question of which tactical means the nation should use to obtain commonly desired objectives. Schurz's view of overseas empire differed from that of Mahan's in degree, not in kind. Few Americans believed that the Latin-American and Asian markets were of little importance to the expansive American industrial complex. On the other hand, few agreed with Foraker's intimation that the United States should claim and occupy every piece of available land in the Pacific. The mass opinion fell between these two views, and within that consensus the debate was waged. The fundamental assumptions of the consensus were never fought out. The grace note to this was appropriately supplied by William Jennings Bryan, who first successfully urged that the Philippine annexation measure be passed by Congress, and then tried to use the Philippine issue in the 1900 presidential campaign. He discovered on election night that, whatever the effect of other issues in the campaign, the issue of "imperialism" was apparently of little importance to the voters. McKinley, having solved this problem during the two previous years, had moved so far ahead of Bryan that the distance could be measured in political light years.

By 1899 the United States had forged a new empire. American policy makers and businessmen had created it amid much debate and with conscious purpose. The empire progressed from a continental base in 1861 to assured pre-eminence in the Western Hemisphere in 1895. Three years later it was rescued from a growing economic and political dilemma by the declaration of war against Spain. During and after this conflict the empire moved past Hawaii into the Philippines, and, with the issuance of the Open-Door Notes, enunciated its principles in Asia. The movement of this empire could not be hurried. Harrison discovered this to his regret in 1893. But under the impetus of the effects of the industrial revolution and, most important, *because of the implications for foreign policy which policy makers and businessmen believed to be logical corollaries of this economic change*, the new empire reached its climax in the 1890's. At this point those who possessed a sense of historical perspective could pause with Henry Adams and observe that one hundred and fifty years of American history had suddenly fallen into place. Those who preferred to peer into the dim future of the twentieth century could be certain only that the United States now dominated its own hemisphere and, as Seward had so passionately hoped, was entering as a major power into Asia, "the chief theatre of events in the world's great hereafter."

Selected Bibliography

THE following is by no means an inclusive bibliography. Here are listed all manuscript and archival sources used, the most frequently cited unpublished dissertations, articles and books frequently cited, and those works which have been most valuable in the research.

PERSONAL PAPERS AND MANUSCRIPTS

(Unless otherwise noted, the personal papers and manuscripts of the following men may be found in the Library of Congress, Washington, D.C.)

Nelson Aldrich, Wharton Barker, Thomas F. Bayard, James G. Blaine, Andrew Carnegie, William E. Chandler, Grover Cleveland, William Augustus Croffut, William E. Curtis, Cushman Davis (St. Paul, Minnesota), Donald M. Dickinson, John W. Foster, Lyman Gage, Robert Arthur Talbot Gascoyne-Cecil (Third Marquis of Salisbury) (Christ Church College, Oxford, England), Walter Quintin Gresham, Benjamin Harrison, John Hay, Hilary Herbert (Chapel Hill, North Carolina), Daniel Lamont, Henry Cabot Lodge (Boston, Massachusetts), Robert M. McElroy, William McKinley, Alfred Thayer Mahan (Library of Congress and Flowers Collection, Durham, North Carolina), Louis Michener, John Bassett Moore, John T. Morgan, Richard Olney, Joseph Pulitzer, Whitelaw Reid, Theodore Roosevelt, George Washburne Smalley, John Coit

Spooner, Oscar Straus, William Sulzer (Ithaca, New York), Benjamin Tracy, Andrew Dickson White (Ithaca, New York), James Harrison Wilson.

ARCHIVES (UNPUBLISHED)

Great Britain, Records of the Foreign Office, Public Records Office. London.
United States, Records of the Department of State and Department of the Navy, National Archives. Washington, D.C.

PUBLISHED ARCHIVAL AND OTHER GOVERNMENTAL RECORDS

A Compilation of the Messages and Papers of the Presidents, 1789–1897. By James D. Richardson. 10 vols. Washington, D.C., 1900.
Congressional Record. Washington, D.C.
Correspondencia diplomática de la delegación cubana en Nueva York durante la guerra de independencia de 1895 a 1898. (Publicaciones del Archivo Nacional de Cuba.) 5 vols. Havana, 1943–1946.
German Diplomatic Documents, 1871–1914. Selected and translated by E. T. S. Dugdale. 4 vols. London, 1928–1931.
International American Conference, Reports of Committees and Discussions Thereon. 4 vols. Washington, D.C., 1890.
Papers Relating to the Foreign Relations of the United States. . . . Washington, D.C.
Spanish Diplomatic Correspondence and Documents, 1896–1900: Presented to the Cortes by the Minister of State. Translation. Washington, D.C., 1905.

UNPUBLISHED DISSERTATIONS AND THESES

Bald, Ralph Dewar, Jr. "The Development of Expansionist Sentiment in the United States, 1885–1895, as Reflected in Periodical Literature." Ph.D. dissertation, University of Pittsburgh, 1953.
Dozer, Donald Marquand. "Anti-Imperialism in the United States, 1865–1895: Opposition to Annexation of Overseas Territories." Ph.D. dissertation, Harvard University, 1936.
McCormick, Thomas Joseph. " 'A Fair Field and No Favor,' Amer-

ican China Policy during the McKinley Administration, 1897–1901." Ph.D. dissertation, University of Wisconsin, 1960.

Morgan, H. Wayne. "The Congressional Career of William McKinley." Ph.D. dissertation, University of California, Los Angeles, 1960.

Offner, John L. "President McKinley and the Origins of the Spanish-American War." Ph.D. dissertation, Pennsylvania State University, 1957.

Plesur, Milton. "Looking Outward: American Attitudes toward Foreign Affairs in the Years from Hayes to Harrison." Ph.D. dissertation, University of Rochester, 1954.

Smith, Joe Patterson. "The Republican Expansionists of the Early Reconstruction Era." Ph.D. dissertation, University of Chicago, 1930.

Steigerwalt, Albert Kleckner. "The National Association of Manufacturers: Organization and Policies, 1895–1914." Ph.D. dissertation, University of Michigan, 1952.

Stutz, Frederick H. "William Henry Seward, Expansionist." Master's thesis, Cornell University, 1937.

White, Gerald Taylor. "The United States and the Problem of Recovery after 1893." Ph.D. dissertation, University of California, Berkeley, 1938.

ARTICLES

Auxier, George W. "Middle Western Newspapers and the Spanish-American War, 1895–1898," *Mississippi Valley Historical Review*, XXVI (March, 1940), 523–534.

——. "The Propaganda Activities of the Cuban *Junta* in Precipitating the Spanish-American War, 1895–1898," *Hispanic American Historical Review*, XIX (August, 1939), 286–305.

Benson, Lee. "The Historical Background of Turner's Frontier Essay," *Agricultural History*, XXV (April, 1951), 59–82.

Blake, Nelson M. "Background of Cleveland's Venezuelan Policy," *American Historical Review*, XLVII (January, 1942), 259–277.

Brown, E. H. Phels, with S. J. Handfield-Jones. "The Climacteric of the 1890's," *Oxford Economic Papers*, n.s., IV (October, 1952), 266–307.

Bullock, C. J., J. H. Williams, and R. S. Tuckner. "The Balance of

Trade of the United States," *Review of Economics and Statistics*, I (July, 1919), 215–266.

Cochran, Thomas C. "Did the Civil War Retard Industrialization?" *Mississippi Valley Historical Review*, XLVIII (September, 1961), 197–210.

Ford, Worthington C. "Commerce and Industry under Depression," *The Bankers' Magazine and Statistical Register*, L (March, 1895), 480–486.

——. "Foreign Exchanges and the Movement of Gold, 1894–1895," *Yale Review*, IV (August, 1895), 128–146.

——. "Memoir of Brooks Adams," *Proceedings, Massachusetts Historical Society*, LX (May, 1927), 345–348.

——. "The Turning of the Tide," *North American Review*, CLXI (August, 1895), 187–195.

Hoffmann, Charles. "The Depression of the Nineties," *Journal of Economic History*, XVI (June, 1956), 137–164.

Morrow, Rising Lake. "A Conflict between the Commercial Interests of the United States and Its Foreign Policy," *Hispanic American Historical Review*, X (February, 1930), 2–13.

Rothstein, Morton. "America in the International Rivalry for the British Wheat Market, 1860–1914," *Mississippi Valley Historical Review*, XLVII (December, 1960), 401–418.

Schurz, Carl. "Manifest Destiny," *Harper's New Monthly Magazine*, LXXXVII (October, 1893), 737–746.

Seager, Robert, II. "Ten Years before Mahan: The Unofficial Case for the New Navy, 1880–1890," *Mississippi Valley Historical Review*, XL (December, 1953), 491–518.

Taylor, Hannis. "A Review of the Cuban Question in Its Economic, Political and Diplomatic Aspects," *North American Review*, CLXV (November, 1897), 610–635.

Vevier, Charles. "Brooks Adams and the Ambivalence of American Foreign Policy," *World Affairs Quarterly*, XXX (April, 1959), 3–18.

Volwiler, Albert T. "Harrison, Blaine, and American Foreign Policy, 1889–1893," *Proceedings of the American Philosophical Society*, LXXXIX (November, 1938), 637–648.

Williams, William A. "Brooks Adams and American Expansion," *New England Quarterly*, XXV (June, 1952), 217–232.

——. "The Frontier Thesis and American Foreign Policy," *Pacific Historical Review*, XXIV (November, 1955), 379–395.

Young, George B. "Intervention under the Monroe Doctrine: The Olney Corollary," *Political Science Quarterly*, LVII (June, 1942), 247–280.

BOOKS

. Adams, Brooks. *The Law of Civilization and Decay: An Essay on History*. London and New York, 1895.

Adams, Henry. *The Education of Henry Adams: An Autobiography*. Boston and New York, 1930.

——. *Letters of Henry Adams*. 2 vols. Edited by Worthington Chauncey Ford. Boston and New York, 1930–1938.

Anderson, Thornton. *Brooks Adams, Constructive Conservative*. Ithaca, N.Y., 1951.

Bancroft, Frederic. *The Life of William H. Seward*. 2 vols. New York, 1900.

Barnes, James A. *John G. Carlisle: Financial Statesman*. New York, 1931.

Barrows, Chester Leonard. *William M. Evarts, Lawyer, Diplomat, Statesman*. Chapel Hill, N.C., 1941.

Beringause, Arthur F. *Brooks Adams: A Biography*. New York, 1955.

Blaine, James G. *Political Discussions, Legislative, Diplomatic, and Popular, 1856–1886*. Norwich, Conn., 1887.

Bruce, Robert V. *1877: Year of Violence*. Indianapolis, 1959.

Callahan, James Morton. *American Foreign Policy in Mexican Relations*. New York, 1932.

Campbell, Charles S., Jr. *Anglo-American Understanding, 1898–1903*. Baltimore, 1957.

——. *Special Business Interests and the Open Door Policy*. New Haven, Conn., 1951.

Chadwick, French Ensor. *The Relations of the United States and Spain: Diplomacy*. New York, 1909.

Cleveland, Grover. *Letters of Grover Cleveland, 1850–1908*. Selected and edited by Allan Nevins. New York and Boston, 1933.

——. *Presidential Problems*. New York, 1904.

Curti, Merle. *The Growth of American Thought.* 2nd ed. New York, 1951.

Dennett, Tyler. *Americans in Eastern Asia: A Critical Study of the Policy of the United States with Reference to China, Japan, and Korea in the Nineteenth Century.* New York, 1922.

Donovan, Timothy Paul. *Henry Adams and Brooks Adams: The Education of Two American Historians.* Norman, Okla., 1961.

Dyer, Brainerd. *Public Career of William M. Evarts.* Berkeley, Calif., 1933.

Foster, John W. *Diplomatic Memoirs.* 2 vols. Boston and New York, 1909.

Hamilton, Gail [Mary Abigail Dodge]. *Biography of James G. Blaine.* Norwich, Conn., 1895.

Harrington, Fred Harvey. *God, Mammon, and the Japanese: Dr. Horace Allen and Korean-American Relations, 1884–1905.* Madison, Wisc., 1944.

Harrison, Benjamin. *Speeches of Benjamin Harrison . . . : A Complete Collection of His Public Addresses from February, 1888, to February, 1892. . . .* Compiled by Charles Hedges. New York, 1892.

Higham, John. *Strangers in the Land: Patterns of American Nativism, 1860–1925.* New Brunswick, N.J., 1955.

Hofstadter, Richard. *Social Darwinism in American Thought.* Boston, 1955.

Hutchins, John, G. B. *The American Maritime Industries and Public Policy, 1789–1914: An Economic History.* Cambridge, Mass., 1941.

James, Henry. *Richard Olney and His Public Service.* Boston, 1923.

Kirkland, Edward C. *Industry Comes of Age: Business, Labor, and Public Policy, 1860–1897.* New York, 1961.

Lambert, John R. *Arthur Pue Gorman.* Baton Rouge, La., 1953.

Langer, William L. *The Diplomacy of Imperialism, 1890–1902.* 2 vols. New York and London, 1935.

Latourette, Kenneth Scott. *A History of Christian Missions in China.* New York, 1929.

Laughlin, James Laurence, and H. Parker Willis. *Reciprocity.* New York, 1903.

Leech, Margaret. *In the Days of McKinley.* New York, 1959.

Livezey, William E. *Mahan on Sea Power.* Norman, Okla., 1947.

Logan, Rayford W. *The Diplomatic Relations of the United States with Haiti, 1776–1891.* Chapel Hill, N.C., 1941.

Long, John D. *The New American Navy.* 2 vols. New York, 1903.

——. *Papers of John Davis Long, 1897–1904.* Selected and edited by Gardner Weld Allen. Boston, 1939.

McKinley, William. *Speeches and Addresses of William McKinley, from March 1, 1897 to May 30, 1900.* New York, 1900.

Mahan, Alfred Thayer. *The Influence of Sea Power upon History, 1660–1783.* Boston, 1890.

——. *The Interest of America in Sea Power, Present and Future.* Boston, 1897.

——. *Retrospect and Prospect: Studies in International Relations Naval and Political.* Boston, 1902.

May, Ernest R. *Imperial Democracy: The Emergence of America as a Great Power.* New York, 1961.

Muzzey, David Saville. *James G. Blaine: A Political Idol of Other Days.* New York, 1935.

Nevins, Allan. *Grover Cleveland: A Study in Courage.* New York, 1933.

——. *Hamilton Fish: The Inner History of the Grant Administration.* New York, 1936.

Noyes, Alexander Dana. *Thirty Years of American Finance: A Short Financial History of the Government and People of the United States since the Civil War, 1865–1896.* New York, 1898.

Perkins, Dexter. *The Monroe Doctrine, 1867–1907.* Baltimore, 1937.

Pletcher, David. *The Awkward Years: American Foreign Relations under Garfield and Arthur.* Columbia, Mo., 1963.

Pratt, Julius W. *Expansionists of 1898: The Acquisition of Hawaii and the Spanish Islands.* Baltimore, 1936.

Rippy, J. Fred. *The United States and Mexico.* Rev. ed. New York, 1931.

Romanov, B. A. *Russia in Manchuria, 1892–1906: Essays on the History of the Foreign Policy of Tsarist Russia in the Epoch of Imperialism.* Translated by Susan Wilbur Jones. Leningrad, 1928.

Roosevelt, Theodore. *The Letters of Theodore Roosevelt.* 8 vols. Selected and edited by Elting E. Morison *et al.* Cambridge, Mass., 1951–1954.

Russ, William Adam, Jr. *The Hawaiian Republic, 1894–1898.* Selinsgrove, Pa., 1961.

——. *The Hawaiian Revolution, 1893–1894.* Selinsgrove, Pa., 1959.

Ryden, George Herbert. *The Foreign Policy of the United States in Relation to Samoa.* New Haven, Conn., 1933.

Seward, William H. *The Works of William H. Seward.* 5 vols. Edited by George E. Baker. Boston, 1853–1883.

Smith, Henry Nash. *Virgin Land: The American West as Symbol and Myth.* New York, 1959.

Sprout, Harold, and Margaret Sprout. *The Rise of American Naval Power: 1776–1918.* Princeton, N.J., 1946.

Stevens, Sylvester K. *American Expansion in Hawaii, 1852–1898.* Harrisburg, Pa., 1945.

Stolberg-Wernigerode, Otto zu. *Germany and the United States during the Era of Bismarck.* Reading, Pa., 1937.

Strong, Josiah. *Our Country: Its Possible Future and Its Present Crisis.* New York, 1885.

Summers, Festus P. *William L. Wilson and Tariff Reform.* New Brunswick, N.J., 1953.

Tansill, Charles Callan. *The Foreign Policy of Thomas F. Bayard, 1885–1897.* New York, 1940.

Taussig, F. W. *The Tariff History of the United States.* 7th ed. New York, 1923.

Treat, Payson. *Diplomatic Relations between the United States and Japan, 1853–1895.* 2 vols. Stanford, 1932.

Turner, Frederick Jackson. *The Early Writings of Frederick Jackson Turner.* With a list of all his works compiled by Everett E. Edwards and an introduction by Fulmer Mood. Madison, Wisc., 1938.

——. *The Frontier in American History.* New York, 1947.

Tyler, Alice. *The Foreign Policy of James G. Blaine.* Minneapolis, 1927.

Vagts, Alfred. *Deutschland und die Vereinigten Staaten in der Weltpolitik.* 2 vols. New York, 1935.

Volwiler, Albert T. *The Correspondence between Benjamin Harrison and James G. Blaine, 1882–1893.* Collected and edited by Albert T. Volwiler. Philadelphia, 1940.

White, Andrew Dickson. *Autobiography of Andrew Dickson White*. 2 vols. New York, 1905.

Wisan, Joseph E. *The Cuban Crisis as Reflected in the New York Press, 1895–1898*. New York, 1934.

Younger, Edward. *John A. Kasson: Politics and Diplomacy from Lincoln to McKinley*. Iowa City, 1955.

Zabriskie, Edward H. *American-Russian Relations in the Far East: A Study in Diplomacy and Power Politics, 1895–1914*. Philadelphia, 1946.

Acknowledgments

THE following provided the financial help which enabled me to complete the manuscript: a research fellowship from the University of Wisconsin Graduate School, a faculty research grant from Cornell University, and a grant for summer research from the American Philosophical Society. In a book which emphasizes the importance of economic factors, it is perhaps unnecessary for me to elaborate upon my debt to these institutions. Thanks are due to the American Historical Association for assistance in publishing this book and to the Committee on the Albert J. Beveridge Award for 1962 and its chairman, Professor Charles Gibson of the State University of Iowa, for the constructive criticism the committee offered.

J. F. A. Mason of Christ Church, Oxford, graciously permitted me to use the Marquess of Salisbury manuscripts. The Henry Cabot Lodge papers were opened to me through the kindness of George Cabot Lodge, Jr. Research was made easier because of the helpfulness of the staffs of the Cornell University Libraries, the Wisconsin State Historical Society, the Library of Congress Manuscript Division, the Foreign Affairs and Naval Affairs branches of the National Archives, the British Public Record Office, the University of North Carolina Library, and Duke

University Library. I want to extend special thanks to Ron Heise of the Foreign Affairs branch of the National Archives, Kate Maclean Stewart and David C. Mearns of the Library of Congress Manuscript Division, and Evelyn Greenberg of Cornell University Libraries. I appreciate the care with which Mrs. John Quincy Adams (*sic*) typed the manuscript. I wish to thank the editors of the *American Historical Review, Mississippi Valley Historical Review, Hispanic American Historical Review,* and *Business History Review* for allowing me to use material from articles which I have published in their journals.

I owe personal and professional debts to the following men for encouragement and for constructive criticism: Knight Biggerstaff, David B. Davis, Paul W. Gates, and Curtis P. Nettels, all of Cornell; Thomas A. Bailey, of Stanford University; Robert E. Bowers, of Hanover College; and Cushing Strout, of California Institute of Technology. David Pletcher of Hamline University was very kind in allowing me to examine his important research on the foreign policies of the Garfield and Arthur administrations when his work was still in manuscript form.

I owe my largest debts to Fred Harvey Harrington, now the President of the University of Wisconsin, who read about half of this book when it was a thesis, and whose tolerance and kindness as a supervisor of doctoral dissertations must be unequaled; William Appleman Williams of the University of Wisconsin; Thomas McCormick of Ohio University; and Lloyd Gardner of Rutgers University. I would not care to acknowledge publicly all the ideas which I have stolen from them. I can only plead that the extenuating circumstances are friendships which have been for me the nicest result of my professional life. The fifth person to whom I owe a special debt is my wife Sandra, who somehow found time from her full-time duties as wife, mother, and student to spend nearly as many hours as I did on the manuscript, and who endured both of us—the book and me—with awesome patience.

Index